F. R Grahame

Life and Times of Alexander I., Emperor of all the Russias

Vol. III

F. R Grahame

Life and Times of Alexander I., Emperor of all the Russias
Vol. III

ISBN/EAN: 9783337165130

Printed in Europe, USA, Canada, Australia, Japan

Cover: Foto ©ninafisch / pixelio.de

More available books at **www.hansebooks.com**

LIFE AND TIMES

OF

ALEXANDER I.

EMPEROR OF ALL THE RUSSIAS.

LIFE AND TIMES

OF

ALEXANDER I.

EMPEROR OF ALL THE RUSSIAS.

BY

C. JOYNEVILLE.

"My rival in glory and power."—Napoleon, *loq.*

IN THREE VOLUMES.

VOL. III.

LONDON:
TINSLEY BROTHERS, 8, CATHERINE STREET STRAND.
1875.

[All rights of Translation and Reproduction are reserved.]

LONDON:
SAVILL, EDWARDS AND CO., PRINTERS, CHANDOS STREET,
COVENT GARDEN.

CONTENTS

OF

THE THIRD VOLUME.

CHAPTER I.

THE CAMPAIGN IN FRANCE, AND CAPTURE OF PARIS.

Napoleon and his Allies, 1. Alexander's Address to his Army, 4. Wellington, 4. Peace Negotiations, 6. Alexander Imparts his Polish Scheme to Sir C. Stewart, 7. Battle of La Rothière, 9. Schwartzenberg's Inactivity, 9. Battle of Champaubert, 11. Alexander's Memoir, 15. Treaty of Chaumont, 19. Battle of Craonne, 20. Battle of Arcis, 23. Battle of Fère-Champènoise, 25 Alexander's Cavalry Charge, 26. March on Paris, 27. Its Defence, 28. Napoleon at Fontainebleau, 35. Alexander's Popularity, 38. His Conference with the French Ministers, 39. Caulaincourt and Alexander, 46. Napoleon is Deposed, 53. His Journey to Elba, 58.

CHAPTER II.

ALEXANDER IN PARIS AND LONDON.

Flight of the Bonapartes, 63. Alexander and Bernadotte, 64. Maria Louisa, 65. Josephine, 66. A Dinner Party at Malmaison, 68. The Queen of Westphalia, 69. Madame Junot, 70. The Bourbons return, 73. Alexander visits Louis, 74. Presses a Charter upon him, 76. The Treaty of Peace, 81. Kosciusko, 83. Hortense, 84. The Empress Elizabeth at Baden, 85. Lafayette, 89. Alexander's Reception at the Institute, 91. Invited to England, 93. The

Princess Charlotte, 93. The Grand Duchess Catherine, 94. Nicholas, 95. Alexander lands at Dover, 96. Arrives in London, 97. Goes to Oxford, &c., 99. His Reflections on his Visit, 102. His Portraits, 103. The Hague, 104. Zaandam, 104. Meets the Empress at Bruchsal, 104. He refuses the Honours offered to him at St. Petersburg, 108. His Levée, 109. Rostopchine and Romanzov retire, 112. Humboldt, 112. Correspondence, 114. Alexander visits Moscow, Vilna, &c., 118. America, 120.

CHAPTER III.

THE CONGRESS OF VIENNA.

Assembly of Sovereigns and Statesmen, 121. The Empress Elizabeth, &c., 122. Conference, 123. Alexander's Irritation, 123. His Accident, 126. He visits Pesth, 128. Sees Talleyrand, Castlereagh, and Metternich, 128. His Correspondence about Poland, 132. Excessive Warmth, 136. Alexander's Illness, 137. Hardenberg's Disclosures, 150. Alexander challenges Metternich, 150. Explanation, 151. The Secret Alliance, 153. Napoleon's return from Elba, 161. Preparations for another War, 167.

CHAPTER IV.

ALEXANDER'S SECOND CAMPAIGN IN FRANCE.

Madame de Krudener, 171. She reproves Alexander, 177. The Battle of Waterloo, 178. The Allies march on Paris, 181. Napoleon's Exile, 182. Louis visits Alexander, 186. English Correspondence, 187. Alexander prevents the Dismemberment of France, 188. The Grand Duchess Anna, 189. Madame de Krudener comes to Paris, 197. A Great Review, 201. The Holy Alliance, 203. La Harpe and Napoleon's opinion of it, 208. Alexander leaves France, 210. Anxiety in Russia for his return, 212.

CHAPTER V.

RUSSIA AT PEACE.

Poland, 217. Alexander's return to Russia, 219. The Jesuits, 223. The Russian Dissenters, 225. The Persian Ambassador, 227. Marriages of Alexander's Sisters, 228. Finances, 229. The Military Colonies, 233. The Press, 237. Alexander goes to Moscow and Warsaw, 239. De Maistre, 242. The new Bank, 245. Nicholas's Marriage, 246. The Court winters at Moscow, 247. Alexander's journey to the Crimea, 251. Birth of his Nephew (Alexander II.), 252. King of Prussia's visit, 253. Austrian Memoir on the state of Russia, 255.

CHAPTER VI.

CONSPIRACIES AND REVOLUTIONS.

Congress of Aix-la Chapelle, 266. Conspiracy to Assassinate Alexander, 267. Wellington's Precautions, 268. The Allies evacuate France, 270. Alexander visits Louis XVIII., 275. Secret Societies in Russia, 278. Illness of the Empress, 279. Alexander visits Archangel, 281. His conversation with Constantine, 281. And with Nicholas, 282. Pushkin's Poem, 285. Speranski, 287. Poland, 288. Insurrections in Spain and Italy, 292. Disturbances in Poland, 293. Jesuits banished, 294. Stormy Session of the Warsaw Diet, 296. Congress of Troppau, 298. Revolt, 299. Napoleon's Death, 301. The Greek Revolution, 302.

CHAPTER VII.

THE LAST YEARS OF ALEXANDER'S REIGN.

The Greeks, 310. Madame de Krudener, 311. Photi, 312. Russian Conspirators, 314. Alexander's Solitary Life, 315. The Freemasons, 326. Spanish Revolution, 327. Congress of Verona, 327. Wellington and Chateaubriand, 330. The Turkish Question, 331.

Speech in the House of Commons, 337. Rostopchine on France, 340. Alexander's Illness and Troubles, 341. Inundation of the Neva, 345. Ultimatum to Turkey, 346. Alexander's care for Education, 349. Visits Warsaw, 349. Talks of Abdicating, 350. Leaves St. Petersburg for Taganrog, 351. Tour in the Crimea, 353. Illness, 356. Death, 361. Funeral, 366. Death of the Empress, 369.

LIFE AND TIMES

OF

ALEXANDER I.,

EMPEROR OF ALL THE RUSSIAS.

CHAPTER I.

1814.

THE CAMPAIGN IN FRANCE AND CAPTURE OF PARIS.

ÆTAT. 36.

THE battle of Leipsic caused a great sensation throughout every part of Europe still in any way connected with France; and Napoleon's flight across the Rhine convinced his partisans that, although he still declared he had gained a succession of victories, their result bore all the consequences of a decisive defeat. The appearance of an Austrian army in the north of Italy increased the agitation in that country, and Murat perceived that to keep his throne he must make peace with the Allies. He had been very favourably impressed by the Russians, and on his return to Naples appeared more than once at a fête with all his courtiers dressed as Cossacks. Added to this growing predilection, he smarted under the insults heaped on him by Napoleon, who had no right to complain of ingratitude from those Sovereigns who turned against him; for, in the first place, they had fully earned the honours he had bestowed, not as gifts, but as recompenses, and often bribes; and, in the second, he had already repaid himself by the enjoyment of humiliating these new-made kings, and constantly reminding them that their power and dignities were only derived from his. The insolence which even the Kings of Bavaria and Würtemberg supported must have made them often writhe in their chains; and petty slights, such as dining with his hat on in their presence, while they were of course uncovered, or keeping them waiting an hour in a carriage in the midst of a drive, while he transacted some trivial business that just occurred to him, were not at all unfrequent. He certainly understood coarse human nature as represented in the lower ranks, but not human nature when it has acquired any real refinement. His injustice towards his officers—picking out some innocent but uninfluential man for especial reprobation, when it was necessary, as he said, to find a scapegoat; or marking out another for especial honours, or favour, merely because he was wealthy; and he was resolved (he said) to have only rich and magnificent persons about his Court—was fast raising up enemies, even among the military. The title he bestowed on Ney of the "bravest of the brave," excited jealousy. "We are all brave," said a French officer; "the quality has no degree of comparison; a man may be foolhardy, but he cannot be more than brave."

In December Murat returned to Italy, and there wrote urging Napoleon to make peace, or to proclaim the unity and independence of Italy, as the only means of preserving her as an ally to France. "If you put at my disposal," he wrote, "the provinces beyond the Po, I will engage that the Austrians shall never cross the Adige." He added, that without those provinces he dare not bring an army to assist France, leaving between himself and his own kingdom a district ready to rise for Austria and Sardinia. Napoleon sent him no answer, but permitted the Pope to return, whereupon Murat took possession of Rome; the French garrison retiring into St. Angelo. He proclaimed to his soldiers it was "no longer possible to give credit to the illusion that Napoleon fought for the peace and happiness of France. There are but two banners in Europe—Religion, Morality, Justice, Law, Peace, and Happiness on one side; on the other, Persecution, Artifice, Violence, Tyranny, War, and mourning to all nations." He ended by signing a treaty of peace with the Allies, January 10th, 1813.

The Grand Army crossed the Rhine in nine columns; the Austrian contingent under Schwartzenberg on December 20th, at Schaffhausen, whence it wended its way through Switzerland; and Alexander, with the last of the Russian reserves, at Basle, on January 13th, 1814. It is very difficult to arrive at an exact estimate of their forces, because each division tried to swell its numbers, to increase its own importance.* Napoleon understated his own army as much after his abdication as he overstated it when preparing for the defence of France; but, including the garrisons, the best authorities count his forces on the French side of the Rhine as amounting to 305,700 men. In Holland and the Netherlands he had still 70,000 in garrison, 50,000 under Beauharnais in the north of Italy, and 70,500 in the German fortresses of Hamburg, Magdeburg, and Erfurt.

The Allied Army of the North did not at this period enter France. The Silesian army consisted of 54,460 Russian troops, 38,931 Prussian, and 20,000 German, on paper; but some deduction must be allowed for exaggeration; though all accounts agree that the Russians formed the largest proportion of this zealous force. Of the Grand Army, the Austrians were set down on *paper* as 130,000, but were very much below that standard; and, in fact, where in winter could such enormous forces have been fed so far from their own countries, and after a year and a half of war? The Russians in this army were said to number 51,550, which, from the losses they sustained, and the imposing force with which they still entered Paris, must have been nearer the truth. The Prussians, Germans, and Cossacks were rated at about 60,000 more; but the contingent of the Elector of Hesse, 24,000 strong, was not ready till the end of March,† and a strong reserve remained in Germany. Altogether, the Russian forces engaged in garrison duty in Germany and Holland as partisan corps, and in France, are said to have numbered 278,000.

The plan now proposed in the invasion was the same Alexander pressed on his allies after Leipsic, and the armies entering France from the north-east and south were intended to close on Paris. As he crossed the French boundary, he addressed his soldiers, and probably for the first time in the course of history, a Sovereign leading an army against an

---

* Wilson says one division of only 9000 drew rations and counted its strength at 36,000.

† It was promised contingents like this which swelled the amount on paper so far above the real truth.

enemy reminded them of their duties as Christians, and exhorted them to remember mercy. " Warriors ! your valour and perseverance have brought you from the Oka to the Rhine. We are about to enter the country with which we are waging a sanguinary and obstinate war. We have saved and glorified our native land, and restored freedom and independence to Europe. It remains but to crown this great achievement with the long desired peace, to restore to every State its own independent laws and government, and religion, arts, science, and commerce, for the general welfare of the people. This is our object, and not the continuance of war and destruction. The enemy, entering our empire, brought on us great evils, but suffered for it an awful punishment. Let us not take example from them; inhumanity and ferocity cannot be pleasing in the eyes of a merciful God. Let us forget their deeds, and render them, not vengeance and hatred, but friendship, and a hand stretched out for peace. Such is the lesson taught by our holy faith. Divine lips have pronounced the command, ' Love your enemies; do good to them that hate you.' Warriors! I trust that by your moderation in the enemy's country, you will conquer as much by generosity as by arms; and uniting the valour of the soldier against the armed with the charity of the Christian towards the unarmed, you will crown your exploits by keeping stainless your well-earned reputation of a brave and moral people."

When Napoleon heard of the invasion, he said if he could have gained two months the enemy should not have crossed the Rhine. On January 23rd, being Sunday, he heard mass, and held a levée to receive the principal officers of the national guards. He then went through a scene he had previously rehearsed with a professional actor; standing in an attitude, and holding his wife and child by the hand, solemnly commended them to their care. On the 25th he parted from the Empress and her son for ever, leaving his brother Joseph to act as Lieutenant of the Empire, and set out to join the head-quarters of his army at Châlons-sur-Marne.

In the mean time Wellington's advance from Spain seemed slow in comparison with the rapid movements of the Allies. He put his army into winter quarters at Oleron and San Juan de Luz, a small seaport town on the frontier; and, as a French commissaire from Bayonne admitted, his policy and the good discipline he maintained did the Imperial cause more honour than ten battles. "Every peasant wishes to be under his protection." The Duke wrote, January 14th, from San Juan de Luz: "We have found the French people exactly what we might expect (not from the lying accounts in the French newspapers, copied into all others of the world, and believed by everybody, notwithstanding the internal sense of every man of their falsehood, but) from what we know of the government of Napoleon, and the oppression of all descriptions under which his subjects have laboured. It is not easy to describe the detestation of this man. What do you think of the French people running into our posts for protection from the French troops, with their bundles on their heads, and their beds, as you recollect to have seen the people of Portugal and of Spain?" Even Count Beugnot owns that the French army of the north pillaged the neighbourhood of Lille as if it had been a conquered country.*

"There was a peace party," says Muffling, "always working in the camp of the Allies," and the English Government, who refused to accept the terms of peace offered in 1806, or to treat with Napoleon after Tilsit and Erfurt, preferring to continue a war productive of the greatest misery to the Continent and of great loss to the British trade, was now induced, by Metternich's representations, to take alarm when they saw the French Empire almost prostrate at the feet of Russia, and wished to avert the catastrophe which for years it was the chief aim of the British policy to effect. Russia, led on by an able and energetic Sovereign, seemed more formidable in the eyes of Austria, Sweden, and England than France under the rule of even Napoleon. Without reflecting that Napoleon would infallibly, and perhaps in self-defence, break any treaty limiting his power, as soon as he was in a position to do so, and that France possessed greater capabilities of repairing her losses than perhaps any country in Europe, they now tried to preserve the ancient boundaries of France, and proposed an

* It is a strong proof of the comparatively small damage which the Allies perpetrated in France, that the French loudly complained that some Prussians, for mischief, cut down a crocodile in the museum at Brienne, and it broke some glass cases in its fall; yet forty years later we see the French crushing every curiosity in the museum of Kertch.

offer of the same terms of peace refused by the Allies before Leipsic. In the course of European history no army had ever marched so far in one year as the victorious Russian legions which now crossed the borders of the Rhine, for the homes of many of them lay on the Ural and the Caspian. Their empire had certainly made unprecedented efforts to carry on the campaign; but still the success of those efforts, and the victories achieved one thousand miles from its own frontiers, was a proof that it was not the cold alone which expelled Napoleon's armies from Russia. Her allies reflected that a Power so difficult to assail, and so rapidly gaining strength in offensive warfare, would be left unbalanced in Europe. But their policy, swayed alternately by the fear of France and Russia, underwent several oscillations before it finally agreed to the general peace.

The conference was transferred from Frankfort to Châtillon as the Allies continued their march,* and was opened February 3rd; Razoumovski acting for Russia, Count Stadion for Austria, Baron Humboldt for Prussia, and Lord Aberdeen, Lord Cathcart, and Sir Charles Stewart for England; Lord Aberdeen being unable to speak French, and guided entirely by Metternich. Eugene Beauharnais also sent a representative to support his interests in Italy.

Castlereagh first repaired to Basle to meet the Sovereigns, but found only Francis and the King of Prussia, Alexander having left with the armies, of whose rapid march and bold entrance into France in the depths of winter he writes in great praise. The Austrian Emperor's conversation showed him his fear of Russia; and Lord Bathurst afterwards said he had prevented a quarrel between Francis and the Czar.

Louis XVIII. wrote to Alexander in 1813, as if to remind him of his own claim to the throne of France, and the Comte d'Artois landed at Rotterdam February 2nd, and followed the Czar through Basle, Vesoul,† and Langres to Troyes. The Duc d'Angoulême joined Wellington in Spain, and the Duc de Berri sailed for Jersey, in case of a rising in Brittany.

---

* Sir C. Stewart, writing January, 1814, says that Alexander wishes to march direct on Paris, and to dethrone Napoleon, before he makes peace.
† Alexander slept in his mother's old home at Montbéliard on January 17th, and at Vesoul on the 18th.

Schwartzenberg was proceeding by slow marches through Switzerland, wishing to remain within reach of Lombardy, and to preserve the Austrian armies entire, to give them more influence over the terms of peace. But Russia had already done far more than her share in the war. Blucher's vanguard was entirely composed of her troops, led by Sacken, Sherbatov, and Pahlen, who captured Ligny, St. Diziers, Nancy, and Brienne as early as January 29th, and Napoleon's attention was first directed to this division when he took the field January 27th.

The English and Austrian statesmen seem to have thought Alexander would be sufficiently repaid for his sacrifices by the mere fame of a conqueror, and would not even fulfil the imperative duty of securing his frontiers from a possible repetition of the invasion of 1812. That invasion showed him that so long as Poland either enjoyed independence under her old republican government, or under the protection of Saxony, France, Austria, or Prussia, she might at any moment be made the head-quarters of a war against Russia, who had often felt the need of a natural frontier between Poland and Moscow. England had furnished large sums of money during the war, but what were her losses, either in men or material, compared with those of Russia? And she had rewarded herself by an immense booty on the sea, and rich colonies, which she had no idea of restoring entire to either France, Holland, Denmark, Portugal, or the knights of St. John. Her lands had not been pillaged by an invading hand; and her people had enjoyed as much tranquillity in their island home during the long war as if in the midst of the most profound peace. The destinies of Antwerp and Belgium were to be made subordinate to her safety; but the bravery of her sons was to be enough to protect Russia against the obvious ill-will of all Europe. Alexander had to wage nearly as hard a warfare with the diplomatists as with the French. He had mentioned the subject to Metternich, who, as usual, acquiesced, and then urged the English to oppose it. Frederick and Hardenberg were also acquainted with it, when he held an unofficial conversation with Sir Charles Stewart (February, 1814), who reported that he "dwelt at great length on the immense sacrifices of Russia," and how necessary it was for him on the eve of a settlement of Europe to look to the permanent interests of his own empire. "Every principle of justice and right called upon him to restore such a constitution to Poland as would secure the happiness of so fine and so great a people;" but if he gave up seven million of his subjects in the Polish provinces without a sufficient guarantee to Russia for the advantage of the measure, it would be more than his crown was worth. The union of these provinces with the Duchy of Warsaw, under such a constitutional administration as Russia would name, might produce the happiest effects. He thought Europe ought to depend on his character. "I remarked, that Europe could not always ensure an Alexander on the throne." He answered that Constantine shared his sentiments entirely, as well as his two youngest brothers. He believed the proposal he had started, and the mode in which he viewed it, was seen by Austria in the same light; as he had a very long conversation with Metternich a day or two since, in which he opened the whole of his plan, and the prince 'n'avait rien contre,' or words to this purpose." Sir Charles expressed surprise, and assured him Metternich held a very different language to the English. "I never could suppose he would leave to us the task of opposing his Imperial Majesty's views alone, in case they did not meet with general concurrence, when they were of so much more vital interest to Austria and Prussia. His Imperial Majesty next alluded, rather in a menacing manner, to his power of taking military occupation of Poland, and seemed to be certain of obtaining his end; and I doubted much, from the firm and positive manner in which he expressed himself, whether he would ever be diverted from the purpose."

Alexander marched with his guards to Trannes, according to the plan by which he was to join Sacken's division, while Schwartzenberg loitered along;* though a rapid movement of the Grand Army might have completed the war in a fortnight. He seemed anxious to give Napoleon the time required to bring up his recruits. Alexander intended to march direct on Fontainebleau, but Napoleon was at the head of 70,000 men,

* Montenegro had just caused some discord. Her chief had appealed to Russia to garrison Cattaro, and refused it to Austria, to both Austria and England's discontent.

threatening Blucher, who required his support as the Austrians remained inert. "I tremble," wrote Napoleon to Joseph, February 13th, 1814, "lest those rascally Russians should retaliate by setting fire to Fontainebleau." The Allies quitted Brienne on Napoleon's advance, but defeated him at La Rothière, where eighty pieces of cannon and 4000 French prisoners were captured, and 5000 killed and wounded. The Russians and Prussians lost nearly 6000 in killed and wounded; "the Emperor of Russia and King of Prussia were present," writes Sir Charles Stewart, "and by their heroic conduct infused life and vigour into all the operations." The French peasants were not left passive by their own Government, and measures being taken to arm them, Schwartzenberg issued a general order to treat all natives found with arms as prisoners.

Schwartzenberg's arrangements during this battle were, as General Mitchell says, "the most extraordinary we have yet found recorded in military history. He had an army of at least 130,000 men (on paper), perfectly disposable and ready in hand; but instead of using them to crush an adversary close in his front, he deputes a subordinate to attack the enemy with half that number, and gratifies the other half of the army with the display of a brilliant military spectacle! But if the orders were extraordinary they were at least boldly executed." Alexander ordered the allied troops to wear a white band on their left arms, to distinguish them from the enemy; as the uniforms of the various contingents were not yet familiar to each other, and the Germans wore clothes closely resembling the French. He decided the fate of the battle by bringing up the grenadiers of Little Russia and Astrakhan to support Blucher at a moment when the Field-Marshal was hard pressed by Napoleon in person; and the French had driven the Allies from La Rothière, which the Russians, unsupported by artillery, carried once more at the point of the bayonet.

The defeated army retreated in great confusion upon Troyes, a town on the left bank of the Seine, eighty-eight miles from Paris, and Napoleon at St. Helena said he had then serious thoughts of resigning his crown. It is certain this victory might have brought the Allies on to Paris at once if they had followed it up with rapidity; but Schwartzenberg had secret orders on no account to cross the Seine. As King Leopold writes: "Political difficulties prevented its going to Paris, which might easily have been done;"* and though Alexander tried to conciliate him, he could not be induced to proceed. The Czar followed the retiring enemy with the Bavarian corps, and attacked the rear-guard under Marmont, left to cover Napoleon's retreat. He was exposed as at La Rothière in the thickest of the fight; but a heavy snow-storm suspending it, Marmont knowing the ground, contrived to cross the Seine. "I wished," wrote Napoleon to Joseph, February 6th, from Troyes, "to attack Bar-sur-Seine to-morrow, in order to beat the Emperor Alexander, who seems to have made false dispositions, but I sacrificed everything to the necessity of covering Paris." Joseph writing, February 11th, to his brother, complained of the disorderly conduct of the French troops, and said it was not uncommon to hear it publicly asserted, "The enemy could not do worse."† Writing again on the 15th, he urges Napoleon to come to Paris, but the latter was bent on saving Fontainebleau before everything else. On the 19th he says, "The Austrians were protecting Fontainebleau, and Schwartzenberg's retreat from Bray prevented an attack on that town. On the 23rd he writes again, "The enemy appears to have given up all thought of Paris." On the 25th, "The Crown Prince of Sweden is at Cologne; send some one to make him sensible of his folly, and persuade him to alter his conduct." Joseph replied, "The Prince of Sweden says he is temporizing, to give you an opportunity of making peace." As the Princess of Sweden was living in Paris, unable to tear herself away, there was every opportunity for carrying on a negotiation with him. On March 11th Joseph writes to Napoleon, "I was with the Empress when she received a letter from her father. From what she said, he appears well disposed. It seems he has answered your letter." It was announced

---

* Recollections of King Leopold.
† In addition to other evidence, Napoleon's own proclamation to his soldiers, dated February 8th, 1814, shows the excesses to which the French were addicted, even in France; though he refused to check them till they pillaged a castle near Nogent, the property of his mother. "The inhabitants," he says, "are flying on every side, and the troops, instead of being their country's defenders, are becoming its scourge."

in the *Moniteur*, February 21st, that the Austrians had saved Fontainebleau from being captured by the Allies.

Alexander was aware there was some understanding between the Austrians and French, as well as between Bernadotte and the French;* but he could not openly quarrel with his allies on French territory; and if he showed them he knew it, a quarrel was inevitable. He tried to guard against the consequences, and positively refused to grant peace on the conditions he offered at Frankfort, which allowed the Rhine from Rotterdam to Basle to constitute the frontier of France. Napoleon had delayed the negotiations beyond the stipulated time; and as it had cost the Allies an extra amount of bloodshed he would not now make peace unless the French territory was reduced to its dimensions before 1792.

When the Czar entered Troyes a royalist deputation waited on him, headed by the Marquis Widranges and M. Gonalt, wearing the cross of St. Louis and the white cockade, forbidden in the empire under pain of death. They requested him to re-establish the Bourbons. "Gentlemen," he replied, "I receive you with pleasure. I wish well to your cause; but your proceedings are rather premature. The chances of war are uncertain, and I should be grieved to see brave men like you compromised or sacrificed. We do not come ourselves to give a king to France; we desire to know its wishes, and to leave it to declare itself." "But it will never declare itself as long as it is under the knife," replied the Marquis; "never so long as Bonaparte rules in France will Europe be tranquil." "It is for that reason," replied Alexander, "the first thing we must think of is to beat him." The same day, owing to Schwartzenberg's inertness, Blucher's force was surrounded at Champanbert. "You see," he exclaimed in the midst of the battle, "how my brave Russians fight." While retreating they formed squares as coolly as if at a review, and resisted every effort of the French cuirassiers, animated by Napoleon's presence, to penetrate their ranks. Their loss was great, but not a Russian was taken prisoner,

---

* Sir Charles Stewart writes on the 28th to Sir G. Jackson, with regard to a proclamation Bernadotte had addressed to the French: "What a weak wretch Charles John must be not to see that this very declaration on his part lets the cat all out of the bag!"

though 2500 Prussians were captured. Altogether Blucher missed 6000, in killed, wounded, and prisoners, out of his force, consisting of 20,000 men; but he reached Châlons in safety, while Napoleon sent a magnified account of this victory to Paris, and diffused fresh hopes of triumph throughout the country, which was much depressed.

Schwartzenberg remained resting his army at Troyes, till prevailed on by Alexander to put his columns in motion; and satisfied that Napoleon with his main army was following Blucher, and only a small portion of the enemy remained in front, he raised his camp February 11th, and advanced to Nogent, while the Russians, the Prince of Würtemberg, and Bianchi crossed the Seine, and the Cossacks and Russian irregulars made themselves masters of the palace and forest of Fontainebleau and Montargis; Nemours was occupied by Platof, and the Russian general, Seslavin, pushed his outposts to the gates of Orleans. "The Emperor of Russia," writes Muffling, "had done his utmost to infuse activity into the Grand Army, and to undertake offensive operations on Bonaparte's rear, foreseeing the consequences of the enemy's march. But the Grand Army lost time behind the Seine, being too much scattered. In addition to this, the Austrian army in the neighbourhood of Lyons desired reinforcements, and it was resolved to send Colloredo's corps there." True to the system he had hitherto pursued, Schwartzenberg contented himself with his forward march, and withholding all the troops under his immediate control, left the Bavarians under Wrede, and the Russians under Pahlen and Wittgenstein, to bear the whole weight of the enemy; when, on hearing the Grand Army was in movement, it retraced its steps to cover Paris. In this arrangement the effect of Metternich's tortuous diplomacy was easily discerned; the Russians and the Bavarians were the two sovereignties he regarded as Austria's greatest enemies; for the Bavarians held a portion of the Austrian territory, which in the event of a general peace he meant to be restored. It was essential her army should be weakened or annihilated, in which case she would carry no weight in the councils of Europe. According to the French accounts, not a Bavarian would have escaped if the French general, Héritier, had done his duty; and Pahlen and Wittgenstein, commanding 3000 infantry and 1800 horse, were left to maintain the left bank of the Seine against the newly arrived army from Spain, and after a heroic resistance lost 1359 men.* Pahlen was so cast down by this defeat, although he had only carried out Schwartzenberg's orders in remaining on the spot where he was attacked, that he kept carefully out of Alexander's way. The Czar met him in one of the combats before Paris, and said to him, "You think I am angry with you, but I know you were not in fault." The Austrian commander gave this defeat as a reason for ordering an immediate retreat; and at a council of war held on the 17th, Alexander alone of all the generals urged a rapid advance. He was so greatly annoyed by Schwartzenberg's conduct, and was becoming so convinced that if he was permitted to retain the command the campaign could never end favourably, that he raised no further objection to the acceptance of Napoleon's terms. At four A.M. he visited Schwartzenberg in his bed, and telling him an open enemy was better than a half-hearted ally, he said he saw the Austrian Government were resolved, cost what it might, to support Napoleon. He was therefore willing to accept the basis of a peace, which might at least free him from an alliance worse than useless to the cause of Europe; without doubt the war would be renewed; for though Napoleon might agree to their terms for the sake of freeing his country from invaders, he would never adhere to them as soon as the danger was past; but Russia and Prussia would enter on a new campaign in a better position, knowing clearly who were their friends and who their enemies. The half of the Austrian army, separated from the main body to march on Lyons, under pretence of keeping open the communications with Italy, had allowed the French to intercept these communications and renew their

* A Russian general, named Polteratsky, was taken prisoner and brought before Napoleon, who said to him, "I now tell you, that as I have routed you to-day I shall annihilate Sacken to-morrow; on Thursday the whole of Wittgenstein's advanced guard will be disposed of. On Friday I shall give Blucher a blow from which he will never recover, and I then hope to dictate peace to Alexander on the Vistula. Your old fox Kutuzov deceived me by his march on our flank; the burning of Moscow was a barbarous act—it was the work of the Russians. I took Berlin, Madrid, and Vienna, and no such thing happened." "The Russians," replied Polteratsky, "do not repent of that sacrifice, and are delighted with its results." "Leave the room, sir," replied the Emperor, stamping with his foot.—Alison's History of Europe, chap. lxxxv.

own with Beauharnais; and now, with a force which, if concentrated, far exceeded the French, Schwartzenberg demanded an armistice from Napoleon, who refused it, sending word to his plenipotentiary at the Congress of Châtillon that he withdrew his powers, which had only been granted to gain time and avoid a battle, for he hoped to annihilate the allied army before it recrossed the Rhine, and that he was to sign no peace.

Blucher sent an aide-de-camp to Schwartzenberg, asking to give battle alone, the Grand Army merely forming his reserve rather than retreat; but he was answered that a retreat was already prepared. The officer asked if the Sovereigns whose armies Blucher commanded had expressly ordered his division to retreat, and whether they had sent orders to this effect, and he heard that such was not the case. "Many of his suite," says Muffling, "believed Blucher was intentionally left in the lurch, to weaken him, so that he should not be able to form any opposition against peace."

In the mean while Bernadotte, at the Czar's demand, left the Danish frontier and proceeded as far as Cologne; but the Russian and Prussian contingents of the Army of the North obeyed more resolute orders than those of the Crown Prince, and leaving a blockade round Antwerp, proceeded by Avesnes to Laon. Avesnes surrendered to Czernichef, who also attacked and captured the important town of Soissons; but being too weak to spare a garrison to hold it, was obliged to quit it the next day, and join his countrymen at Rheims, whence a detached portion of Blucher's army proceeded to reinforce their commander at Châlons.

The retreat was decided in a second council of war at Troyes on the 23rd, though Alexander protested against it till peace was actually declared, and even advocated another battle at once. But Schwartzenberg was resolved to show Napoleon by deed as well as word that he was his friend; and Prince Lichtenstein, the bearer of his proposal for an armistice, carried to Napoleon a letter from Francis in answer to one received six days before. This letter contained the most conciliatory expressions, saying that the plans of the Allies were seriously deranged, and that in the rapidity and force of his strokes the Emperor recognized the great character of his son-in-law. Napoleon asked Lichtenstein if the report were true, that the Sovereigns meant to dethrone him and place the Bourbons on the throne, and Lichtenstein warmly contradicted it. As Napoleon declined an armistice, and Schwartzenberg was still resolved to retreat, Alexander directed the Russian division under Vinzingerode to pay no attention to any intimation he might receive of a suspension of hostilities unless it came from himself; and desired Blucher to give him the details of his plan, in case Schwartzenberg separated from him, and he marched alone with the Russians and Prussians on Paris. The old man wrote out on a torn piece of paper his reasons for objecting to the retreat. "Most heartily," he continued, "do I thank your Majesty for your permission to resume the offensive; I flatter myself with hopes of success, if your Majesty will give positive orders to Generals Vinzingerode and Bulow to place themselves under my command. Joined by them I shall march on Paris, fearing neither Napoleon nor his marshals should they come to meet me."

"Alexander," writes Muffling, "had formed a sagacious judgment of Napoleon's situation and that of the Allies, and he was the rock round which all gathered, to which every one clung who comprehended the necessity of continuing the war and dethroning Bonaparte. To him we owe much, perhaps all. Without his firm will his armies would not have borne what they did, and acted with readiness; for there were many superior and inferior officers belonging to them who longed for peace." On February 15th the Czar presented a memoir of his opinions to the Allied Sovereigns, and the strong view expressed in it on the dethronement of Napoleon is believed to have determined the Austrians to proceed no further in the invasion of France. "Victory," he said, "having brought us to Frankfort, the Allies offered to France conditions of peace proportionate to the successes then obtained; at that period these conditions might have been called the object of the war. I strongly opposed the proposal to negotiate then; not because I did not desire peace, but because I thought time would offer us more favourable opportunities when we had proved our superiority to the enemy. All are now convinced of the truth of my arguments, for to it we are indebted for the vast difference between the terms offered at Frankfort and at Châtillon—that is, the restoration by France of territories without which Germany and Italy would be lost on the first offensive movement. The destruction of the enemy's political power is not the grand aim of the efforts left to make; but it may become so, if the fortune of war, the example of Paris, and the plain inclination of the provinces give the Allies the possibility of proclaiming it. I do not share the opinion of the Allies on the greater or less degree of importance attached by them to the dethronement of Napoleon, if that measure can be justified on grounds of wisdom. On the contrary, I should consider it as the completion of the deliverance of Europe; as the brightest possible example of justice and morality, and the happiest event for France herself, whose internal condition must always influence the peace of her neighbours. Nobody is more convinced than I am of the inconstancy of fortune in war; yet I do not consider a partial failure, or even the loss of a battle, as a misfortune which should in one day deprive us of the fruit of our victories; and I feel sure that the skill of our generals, the valour of our troops, our superiority in cavalry, the reinforcements following us, and public opinion would never allow us to fall so low as some seem to apprehend. I am not averse to continuing the negotiations at Châtillon, or giving Caulaincourt the explanations he desires regarding the future of Europe, provided France returned to her old frontiers. As to the armistice requested in the letter to Prince Metternich," (this was written before Schwartzenberg asked for one himself,) " it is contrary to the existing usages of negotiations, and only advantageous to the enemy. I am as much convinced as ever of the probability of success if the Allies keep to the views and obligations which have guided them so far with reference to their grand object, the destruction of the enemy's armies. With a good understanding among themselves their success will be complete, and checks will be easily borne. I do not think the time has arrived for us to stop short; and I trust that, as in former conjunctures, new events will show us when it is come."*

On February 25th the Allies held another stormy council-of-war, at Bar-sur-Aube, in the house of General Knesebeck. It was attended by the three Sovereigns, Volkonski, Diebitch,

* Danilevski.

Nesselrode, Schwartzenberg, Metternich, Hardenberg, Castlereagh, and Radetzky. Alexander was the first to speak. He advocated more vigour in the movements of the army, and said he should authorize Blucher to recommence the offensive in spite of the armistice Schwartzenberg had thought fit to conclude, and which did not extend beyond the Grand Army; but that Blucher must be reinforced by the Russian and Prussian divisions under Vinzingerode, Voronzov, and Bulow— the first being still in Flanders, but close to the French frontier, and the two last in the neighbourhood of Laon. Schwartzenberg said it was impossible to withdraw them from the Army of the North without Bernadotte's consent; and that consent would never be given if they were placed under the command of Blucher, who was known to be the inveterate enemy of France. Most of the council agreed with Schwartzenberg; but Castlereagh, having inquired of the most experienced officers present whether this transfer was necessary to the success of Blucher's advance, and heard that it was, declared that the motives urged against it were insufficient to satisfy England, who had a right to expect Sweden to do her best to further the interests of the alliance; and if necessary he would withhold her monthly subsidies till the arrangement was made. This was enough to silence Austria, who felt her own payments in peril; and her sovereign, minister, and general allowed the order to be issued that Blucher should be forthwith recruited by the corps of Bulow, Vinzingerode, and Voronzov. Still they maintained it would be most advantageous for both the armies to retreat. Alexander decidedly opposed it; rather than consent he would separate from the Grand Army, with the guards, grenadiers, and Wittgenstein's corps, and march with Blucher on Paris. "I hope," he said to the King, "that your Majesty, like a faithful ally, will not refuse to accompany me?" "I will do so with pleasure," said Frederick William. "I have long ago placed my troops at your Majesty's disposal." Yet this separation would have enabled Austria to make her own peace with France; and her army, with those of the German States, would have retreated at once across the Jura, never to return. Alexander wrote a pencil note to Blucher, informing him the three corps were placed under his orders, to act with according to his discretion, on condition of observing certain rules of military prudence; and a compromise was made with the Grand Army, which was to retire only as far as Langres, to join some Austrian reserves during the term of the armistice, and then to resume operations, Alexander and the King marching with it as before.

Blucher was rejoiced to be relieved from Schwartzenberg,[*] and lost not a day before he crossed the Aube, and drove Marmont in front of him as far as La Ferté-sous-Jouarre, where the French marshal joined Mortier, pursued by the Russians under Vinzingerode. Sacken occupied half of the town of Meaux, on the left bank of the Marne, and the roar of his guns was distinctly heard in Paris; where, to stimulate the people to active resistance, it was announced that Constantine had sworn not a house should be left standing in the French capital, to revenge Moscow; and pictures of gigantic Cossacks devouring little children were posted on the walls all over the town. On the 27th Napoleon left Troyes to pursue Blucher. He had signalized his entrance into Troyes by causing the royalist deputy, M. Gonalt, to be shot, disregarding the tears and petitions of his family, and the most influential people in the town. A placard declaring him to be a traitor to his country was affixed to his back when he was brought out for execution, and the Marquis de Widranges only escaped by a timely flight to Basle.

As soon as Blucher heard of Napoleon's advance he sent a messenger to Schwartzenberg and the allied Sovereigns; but it was only on the pressing demand of Alexander, and the King alarmed for his general, that he made a retrograde movement, and resumed the offensive; though it was again not an Austrian but the Russian and Bavarian corps of Wittgenstein and Wrede which were put forward to oppose the enemy. After a sanguinary battle, where Wittgenstein was severely wounded and disabled, the Allies drove the French out of Bar-sur-Aube, and captured 500 prisoners. On the 1st of March, the Russian cavalry under Pahlen and Eugene repulsed the French at Bar-sur-Seine without any support; for Schwartzenberg refused to move forward, either in this or the previous battle, to com-

---

[*] Schwartzenborg's instruction to the Prussian generals was, "Above all, not too much zeal."

plete the enemy's defeat, on the plea that he must first be informed of the exact position of Macdonald's division. However, by the time Oudinot's defeated columns had rallied, and united with Macdonald in a strong post at La Ferté-sur-Aube, he ventured to bring forward his head-quarters to Bar-sur-Aube; and after a battle at Laubressel, in which the Allies captured nine cannon and 1500 men, he entered Troyes on the 5th, but stoutly refused to advance another step during the next fortnight. Metternich correspondence with Caulaincourt, still secret but very friendly accompanied him, and carried on a hoping to avert the capture of Paris, which now lay at the mercy of the Allies, and to preserve the throne for Maria Louisa and her son, if Napoleon could not be induced to recognize his position and accept his enemies' terms. The victorious corps of Wrede and Racffskoi (who replaced Wittgenstein) were sent at his instigation to Sens and Pont-sur-Yonne, a forward post, indeed, but quite out of reach of the enemy; Alexander's letters to Schwartzenberg, both through Volkonski and in his own hand, show his impatience at this delay. "The Emperor," he writes, 1st March, 1814, "considers the advance of the Grand Army to Sens is drawing us away from the enemy, and it is therefore indispensable to direct all our forces to the right towards Arcis, between that town and Vitry, and at all events to reinforce them with the reserves which should be moved forward." Again on the 11th: "In consequence of intelligence received from Marshal Blucher, the Emperor considers it indispensable to move by the right between Arcis-sur-Aube and Vitry." On the 12th, Volkonski writes: "I hasten to communicate to your highness the reports received from Count St. Priest. His Majesty charges me to inform you that, according to his opinion, it is now more necessary than ever to act on the offensive. Henceforth your hands will be completely unbound, and you may act according to military calculation."

The last referred to the final termination of the Châtillon negotiations, only resulting in a renewed bond between the Allies, called the treaty of Chaumont; which, in addition to the public articles relating to the number of men to be maintained in the field by the three great Powers, and the English subsidies, contained several secret engagements as to the smaller States. Holland and Belgium were to be united under the Prince of Orange; and Spain restored to Ferdinand VII. Nothing was said about Poland and Saxony. Alexander had stated his intentions on these points; and his allies were prepared to oppose him eventually, but now thought it better to let him exhaust his armies in doing their work. Well might the young Englishmen who accompanied the allied head-quarters write, " they were playing Bonaparte's game ever since they crossed the Rhine."*

Napoleon could not be convinced that he had better avail himself of the proffered modes of escape, and only dreamed of revenge. While the French army committed every excess, the Bavarian and Rhenish troops were the most marauding division of the Allies, having learned the system when serving under Napoleon. He proclaimed, March 5th, that the peasants were required to take up arms, " to scour the woods, break down the bridges, and fall on the enemy. Every French citizen taken by the enemy who shall be put to death shall be forthwith avenged by the shooting of a prisoner from the enemy." " All mayors or other public functionaries who, instead of stimulating, strove to cool patriotic ardour, to be put to death." An insurrection was raised in the Ardennes, but in the provinces occupied by the Allies there was a difficulty in providing the people with arms. This proclamation contrasts curiously with Napoleon's denunciation of the patriotic peasantry in Spain. But the Allies continued to gain ground; the Russians retook Soissons, and re-occupied Rheims. Commanded by Voronzov, and supported by the corps of Yorck and Sacken, they defeated the French at Craonne; and again at Laon, under Blucher, when opposed by Napoleon, the Russian corps of General Vassilchikov leading the attack. Fifty guns and the baggage, besides 2500 prisoners, were taken by the Allies; and Napoleon probably owed the escape of any of his army to a mistake of Vinzingerode, who was unacquainted with the road, and followed one rendered impassable by the heavy rains; and

---

* " I do not by any means think this event," writes Sir Robert Wilson of the capture of Paris, " will ultimately prove beneficial to Europe. I fear the great A. of the future as much as the bouncing B." This feeling was so widely prevalent, and so much influenced the military movements of the Allies, that the length of time is not surprising which elapsed before they entered Paris after crossing the Rhine.

the illness of Blucher, who on the day of the battle suffered too much from headache and inflamed eyes to order a pursuit, and on the 10th was obliged to keep his bed. But the honour of Napoleon was more tarnished by his order to shoot some Russian prisoners than by his disorderly flight. He justified it by no complaint of ill-treatment of the peasantry on the part of the Russians, or any breach of the rules of war. It was merely puerile spite, to avenge his own defeat.

Napoleon afterwards said the reason he refused peace at Châtillon was, because the British Government insisted on the separation of Antwerp from France. Antwerp being opposite to London, entailed a heavy cost in British coast defences and guardships while it was owned by a strong Power. However, when the Allies, at Caulaincourt's request, added six days to the term originally fixed as the limit within which Napoleon was to send in his reply, and no answer was publicly returned, they announced the negotiations at an end; but Caulaincourt then came forward with a counter-proposition from Napoleon, demanding Piedmont, Belgium, and the left bank of the Rhine for France, Westphalia for Jerome, Italy for Beauharnais, and various dukedoms and principalities for other members of his family, which had no reference whatever to the real interests of the French Empire. He could not therefore claim the credit of sacrificing himself to the cause of France. Of course these demands were rejected. Their very extravagance showed that either he depended on the support of his friends among the Allies, or had no intention of making peace.

Blucher is accused of separating his army too much, and enabling Napoleon to seek out a weak detached corps and overwhelm it; but his activity at an important moment was checked both by his illness and want of provisions and forage. For nine days after Laon he kept his bed, while his generals, longing for repose, thought it was time the Grand Army relieved them. "The true object of our stay here," he wrote on the 14th, "is not a military one: my only design is to give repose to a harassed army, and as far as possible to provide it with bread." "I am struggling," he wrote to Schwartzenberg on the 17th, "with the greatest want of provisions; the soldiers have been for days without bread, and I am cut off from Nancy, so have no means of procuring it." Napoleon having been forced to retreat from Laon, received information that Rheims was retaken and held by an isolated corps of Russians under St. Priest. Hoping to raise the spirits of his soldiers by a victory, he marched on the city. The Russians were surprised, but still prepared for defence against a vigorous assault; till greatly overmatched, and their commander mortally wounded, they left the town in perfect order, and retreated safely under cover of the darkness. The French took three Prussian battalions in the neighbourhood, but very few Russians, and those all wounded; and Napoleon, with his fondness for inventing coincidences to work on the superstition of his people, stated in his exaggerated account of the action that St. Priest fell by a shot fired from the same gun which killed Moreau.[*]

As if Fortune was still resolved to remain faithful to the French, Schwartzenberg's natural slowness was increased by an attack of the gout. His army was spread over eighty miles, and Napoleon was marching with his forces concentrated to cut off the weakest portion of it, when Alexander received news of the loss of Rheims. He rode from Troyes to Arcis, where Schwartzenberg, like Blucher, was confined to his bed; and entering the antechamber with Volkonski, on the evening of the 18th, found Toll, the quartermaster-general, and asked him "What they were all about?—There was no doubt Napoleon was marching towards them; did they wish to lose the whole army?" "It is a great blessing," replied Toll, "your Majesty has come; we could not persuade the generals of that, but now you will set all to rights." The Emperor at once gave his orders, and a notice was despatched in all directions for the various corps of the Grand Army to concentrate between Pogny and Troyes.

Napoleon was easy about Blucher, as Bernadotte, who had arrived at Liége, was trying to keep him quiet and prevent his emissaries from obtaining supplies in Belgium; but the sudden concentration of the Grand Army completely disconcerted him. He neglected an opportunity of falling upon Wrede, and

---

[*] Even after the battle of Rothière, when it was evident that Caulaincourt must sooner or later learn the truth, Napoleon wrote to him at Châtillon, "Schwartzenberg's report is a piece of folly. There was no battle. The Old Guard was not there," &c., February 14th.

marched straight to Arcis with 60,000 men, being attacked the next day by about 70,000 of the Allies. Alexander posted himself, with the King and the Russian reserves, on the heights of Ménil-la-Comtesse, above the battlefield. He had some fear " lest Napoleon should be only feigning a defence, and in the mean time move the main body of his forces on to Brienne, and interrupt their communications," and he disposed the Russian army to anticipate such a manœuvre. His anxiety till this movement was accomplished, and during the last two days, had been excessive. " Those gentlemen," he said of the Austrian generals, " have turned half my head grey." The French position was so strong as to counterbalance their inferiority in numbers, and they contested it for nearly two days, during the whole of which time Alexander and Frederick were personally engaged, and Napoleon was also exposed like a common soldier. Schwartzenberg tried to spare his old ally as much as possible in this last hour of his political existence, by opposing the battle being renewed on the second day till three P.M., leaving Macdonald the time and opportunity to cross the river and unite with Napoleon, whom he intended to make use of the delay to effect a clear retreat. However, towards night the French retired, but instead of taking the road to Châlons, along which he had come, or to Paris, Napoleon withdrew his army to Vitry, on the direct course towards the Rhine.

A Cossack was the first who brought the news to Alexander. " The enemy is retreating," said the messenger, " not on Paris, but on Moscow." The reason was explained when he read some intercepted despatches forwarded straight to him by one of his generals, containing a report from Savary to Napoleon, of the exhausted resources in Paris, and the excited state of the people; and a private letter from Napoleon to Maria Louisa, which called the late battle a *victory*, and told her the enemy had posted himself to protect the march of his columns on Brienne and Bar-sur-Aube, so he had resolved to approach the Marne, to drive him further from Paris, and be near his own fortified posts. " This evening," he said, " I shall be at St. Dizier." These despatches reached Alexander at Dampierre at one A.M., and as he read them Count Pahlen sent to announce the arrival of Blucher's advanced guard at Châlons, and its junction with the outposts of the Grand Army, which placed the whole allied force between Napoleon and Paris.

"I marched on St. Dizier," said Napoleon at Elba, to the Austrian General Kohler, "because twenty experiments convinced me I had only to send a few hussars on your line of communication to spread dismay. Now I stood on it with my whole army, but you never troubled your heads about me. The devil had possession of you." Alexander had proceeded after the battle towards the outposts, and at Dampierre, being the anniversary of his accession, he was assisting at a mass for the repose of Paul's soul.* He set off to Sommepuis, where he summoned Volkonski, Barclay, Diebitch, and Toll, and asked their opinion on the two plans now open to them—to unite with Blucher at Vitry, and pursue Napoleon, to attack him wherever they could find him, or to cover their march direct on Paris. Volkonski alone spoke in favour of the last, which Alexander said he approved, and should carry out. He rode at once towards Vitry, but met Schwartzenberg and the King within six miles, on their road to congratulate him. He never cared to be reminded of his accession, and cut short their gracious speeches by telling them he had an important plan to lay before them; and desiring Toll to unroll a map on the grass, they all got off their horses, while he pointed out the route by which he proposed the two armies should march on Paris. The King agreed at once; Schwartzenberg consented, but expressed regret at the probable loss of his magazines at Chaumont, as well as of the allied sick and wounded, and Alexander's personal baggage. The head-quarters were removed to Vitry, and couriers sent out with orders to the various chiefs.† The messenger to Blucher crossed a letter from him to Alexander, strongly pointing out the necessity of an advance at once on Paris, which caused some of his biographers to give the idea as originating with him, though it was adopted by all the commanders at least half an hour before his message arrived. A friend of Talleyrand also tried to obtain credit for the renegade diplomatist, by saying it was proposed on the receipt of a letter from him to Alexander, written when he discovered

---

* As Paul died in the night of the 23rd or 24th of March, the mass for his soul was celebrated at night every year in presence of his family.

† On these two days, March 23rd and 24th, Alexander marched thirty-five and thirty miles on horseback.

the Austrian correspondence with Napoleon. But even if such a letter arrived the plan was already formed, and the measures really suggested by Schwartzenberg are a sufficient refutation of any such step having occurred to the Commander-in-Chief, though one Austrian writer has given him the honour of it. "It is but just to say," writes Sir C. Stewart, speaking of Alexander, "that the determination and boldness of the enterprise of the march on Paris was mainly his own."

By the prompt exertions of the Russian General Ertel and General Kohler, the magazines at Chaumont and the sick and wounded in the rear were saved. Blucher having obtained supplies, had advanced towards Châlons as soon as he heard the Grand Army was threatened; and on the other side Marmont and Mortier received orders from Napoleon to join him in the vicinity of Vitry. While proceeding to obey they were obliged to cross the communications of the Grand Army, and at Fère-Champenoise engaged with its advanced guard, headed by Constantine, General Nostitz, Pahlen, and Prince Eugene. The French were driven back in utter confusion into the town, and lost many of their guns. Alexander, the King, and Schwartzenberg left Vitry the same morning at nine for Fère-Champenoise, and hearing distant firing hurried towards the front. They reached the town, which was in possession of the Allies, as the sun was setting; but the Emperor, instead of halting, rode with Schwartzenberg and a small escort to the outposts, where shots were still being exchanged. On their way they perceived a considerable body of troops, with sixteen guns, at first supposed to be a part of Blucher's army, but in reality the French General Pacthod, on his road to join Napoleon with a reinforcement. They had resisted a charge from General Korff and Vassilchikof, and abandoning a store of provisions they were convoying, and some artillery waggons, formed themselves into a compact mass, and were effecting their retreat. The resistance they had opposed to the allied cavalry gave the two French marshals time to re-form their scattered ranks; and Pacthod, perceiving that, late as it was, a considerable force was collecting again at Alexander's command, ordered his troops to stand to their arms, and prepare for battle. Alexander, hoping to avoid useless bloodshed, sent Moreau's old aide-de-camp, Rapatel, with a flag of truce, to summon them to surrender; but a flag of truce was frequently disregarded by Napoleon, and his subordinates, acting on the same principle, fired on it, and Rapatel fell dead. Though naturally incensed at this breach of the rules of war, which cost him a faithful adherent, who had followed him more from gratitude for his kindness to Moreau and his wife than from any attachment to the Allies, Alexander was still too chivalrous to order the 13,000 now with him to fall upon a body of 6000 infantry, and turn the battle into little better than a massacre. He put himself at the head of his chevalier guards, and with these only dashed into the centre of the compact mass, which was soon penetrated on all sides, without a musket being fired by the Russian troops; and Pacthod, in the middle of the square, surrendered his sword to Alexander in person, and was afterwards greatly astonished when he found that the officer who led on the cavalry, and at great personal risk prevented a massacre, was the Emperor himself. A second French general was also captured; and the trophies of the day amounted to 7000 prisoners, two generals of division, four of brigade, 80 guns, 200 ammunition waggons, and the whole of the convoy and baggage. During this cavalry action the fugitive French marshals escaped through the over-caution of the Prince of Würtemberg, who, afraid of losing his artillery in the cross-roads, recalled Pahlen, much against his will, from continuing the pursuit. Some Cossacks penetrated as far as Provins, and the marshals, believing them to precede a larger force, abandoned the town and fled to Nangis, whence, without further loss, they reached Paris.

The next day the Allies resumed their march, the Russians of Raeffskoi's corps heading the van to their national airs and the rolling of the drums. Alexander rode along by the side of his columns, and frequently conversed with the commanders. "My children," he said to his guards, "it is but a step further to Paris." "We will take it, father," they answered; "we remember Moscow." The morning before, Volkonski expressed some fear as to the number of their opponents, and Alexander hastily replied, "You always see the enemy double." He now called him forward, and, in the hearing of the King and several of his suite, told his aide-de-camp he had wronged him, and asked his pardon. That night Alexander passed in despatching orders in all directions to Vinzingerode, Czernichef, and the other partisans, enjoining them to preserve the communications, to keep a vigilant watch, and to forward the earliest news to head-quarters of any French movements. If Vinzingerode had been Barclay, and skilled in retreat, he might have avoided a battle; but his zeal to cover the march on Paris engaged him with the whole French army under Napoleon at St. Dizier, where the inhabitants furnished the French with information of the Russian approach; and the prisoners taken in this disastrous combat gave them the first intelligence of the march of the Allies on Paris.

Napoleon had amused his people with glowing accounts of his success during this campaign, always concealing his defeats. He wrote to Caulaincourt that he had captured 30,000 or 40,000 prisoners at Champaubert, when he had taken not more than 3000; and that he had deprived the enemy of 200 pieces of artillery when he had only obtained 24. He said he had destroyed *several armies* when he had not annihilated one; and tried to justify his refusal of the terms offered at Châtillon by saying the Allies were not sincere. His bulletins stated the three Sovereigns "very narrowly escaped being shut up in Troyes, where they had retired precipitately to Bar-sur-Aube;" whereas Alexander and the King did not quit the head-quarters from March 16th* till the entry into Paris. But his letter to Joseph from Rheims on the 16th shows he was not blind to his own situation. "You are in no event to permit the Empress and the King of Rome to fall into the hands of the enemy. I am about to manœuvre in such a manner that you may possibly be several days without hearing from me. Should the enemy advance upon Paris with such forces as to render all resistance impossible, send off in the direction of the Loire the Empress, the King of Rome, the great dignitaries, the ministers, the officers of the Senate, the President of the Council of State, the great officers of the crown, and the treasure, &c." When convinced at St. Dizier that the Allies had actually marched on Paris, and were three days in advance of him, he drew off his troops and guns from an attack on the Russians at Vitry, and spent the night in poring over maps and plans. He was not a man who came to rapid decisions, if not previously

* Unless Alexander's night at Dampierre may be thought to form an exception.

revolved in his own mind, and in a great emergency was often hesitating and slow. But on the 28th he resolved to make a retrograde movement, and, avoiding the allied army, to reach Paris with forced marches, by Vassy, Troyes, Sens, and Fontainebleau. His victory over Vinzingerode had spread such terror in the rear that Francis, Metternich, Lord Aberdeen, Razoumovski, Stadion, and the other diplomatists employed in the negotiations at Châtillon, set off at once by cross-roads to Dijon, where one division of the Austrians was encamped; and they did not halt till they had completed a journey of at least thirty-three miles.

The same day Maria Louisa and her son left Paris; though Talleyrand* and more than one of her advisers opposed it, as depriving the Imperial dynasty of its last hope of the throne. But Joseph showed Napoleon's letter, which he said left him no choice. On March 29th an official proclamation was affixed to the walls of Paris, calling on the people to barricade their streets and resist the Allies, who, it informed the Parisians, regarded the pillage and destruction of their capital as the reward and end of the invasion. It stated that Alexander proposed to send off the élite of its artistes and workmen to people Russian deserts, and would then set fire to all the quarters of the town. "No!" it ended, "the Allies shall never approach Paris." Joseph assured the inhabitants that Napoleon was close at hand with all his army for their support. A day's delay on the part of the allied forces might indeed have turned the scale of victory; but they had got the start of their adversary, and kept it.

Alexander issued an order to all the commanders in the Russian army, March 26th: "Let the troops under your command observe the strictest discipline, and on no account whatever leave their bivouacs to go into the villages. Their requirements, such as firewood, straw, &c., must only be supplied through the intervention of the mayor. You know how much the good conduct of our troops may influence the common success, and therefore his Majesty will hold you

---

* Napoleon ordered Talleyrand to accompany Maria Louisa, but he contrived to be stopped at the barrier, and Capefigue states he saw Alexander at Château de Bondy on the morning of the 31st; but Capefigue is very inaccurate, and this is denied by more competent authorities.

personally responsible for the execution of this order." He also wrote to the commander of the Bavarians: "At the moment we are approaching Paris it is only by the strictest subordination among the troops that we can hope to obtain our objects. You were one of the first to be convinced of the necessity of gaining over the affections of the Parisians to our cause; but shall we be acting on this conviction if the villages round Paris are left a prey to plunderers instead of finding protection from our armies? I entreat you to use every possible means to prevent acts of violence. Every commander of a corps or detachment should be made personally responsible for every disorder. Your active exertions on this occasion will secure you the general gratitude and double the high respect I feel for you." The difference between these orders, the admirable manner in which they were carried out, and the conduct of Napoleon's armies both in foreign countries and in France, where he promised his soldiers four hours' pillage of Paris if they recaptured it from the Allies, even suggested itself to his people. When all was over they felt ashamed of the Napoleonic system, which had drawn on them such a reproach, and to Alexander is chiefly due the inauguration of a more civilized mode of war.

The country through which the Allies marched to Paris from Fère-Champenoise was rich in villas, orchards, and vineyards, not yet presenting much token of spring. The Russian vanguard of Blucher's army was reduced by numerous battles from 20,000 to 6000, and bore traces of their exertions in their haggard faces and worn-out clothes. The Emperor publicly thanked them, and distributed rewards both in money and decorations. The Imperial Guard still preserved its accoutrements and bright cuirasses, as if it had spent the last year in barracks in St. Petersburg. The three Grand Dukes of Russia marched with their various regiments, the two youngest— Nicholas and Michael—having only recently arrived. In the Prussian army many a youthful warrior has since had another opportunity of entering Paris in triumph. Prince William, the King's second son, and now Emperor of Germany, received the cross of St. George from Alexander after Bar-sur-Aube; he was the same age as the late Emperor Nicholas, and the intimacy between them, which continued through life, began on the fields of France. The Prince of Prussia and Prince Charles also accompanied their father; but chance or design kept the Austrian princes from sharing in the last struggle with the French.

The Parisians were not wanting in the hour of danger, and the military and National Guards prepared for an energetic defence. The civilians are described by an English prisoner as lounging outside the cafés and restaurants, apparently uninterested spectators of the wounded French who were brought into the city and laid down to die on the pavement. The garrison consisted of 35,000 men, and 150 guns were quickly posted on the heights of Belleville and Montmartre, which had been fortified, and the country round flooded, to impede the march of the Allies. From Mont Valérien on the west to the fortress of Vincennes on the east, a line of hills offers a natural protection to Paris, and the pupils of the Polytechnic School and other public institutions came forward as volunteers to work the artillery.* Marmont and Mortier took the chief command: and at 2 A.M., March 30th, the drums called all to arms. At five they could discern the Allies in full march towards the city, on the road from Meaux. Raeffskoi's Russian corps was charged with the attack on the French centre between Pantin and Vincennes, and especially on Belleville; on the right the Silesian army, which, Blucher being still unable to command, was led by Barclay, was to advance on Montmartre on two sides, but it did not arrive till eleven o'clock, three hours after the attack had commenced; Langeron from Clichy and St. Denis; Kleist, Yorck, and Voronzov on the allied left, from the villages of La Villette and La Chapelle. In the absence of Metternich to support him, and still suffering from gout, Schwartzenberg left Alexander to take the undisputed direction of the assault; and, owing to the lateness of the Silesian army, the Russian troops bore the chief weight of the battle; for while their loss in killed and wounded was not less than 7100, the army of Würtemberg counted 153 as missing,

---

* The heroic defence of Paris has occasionally been attributed mainly to the Polytechnic School and the National Guard, and great injustice done to the brave soldiers of the corps of Marmont and Mortier. There were only three wounded and none killed among the pupils of the Polytechnic. Five of the National Guard were placed *hors de combat*, and nearly 5000 of the regular army.

and the Prussians 1840. "Father Paris, you shall now pay for Mother Moscow!" was the exclamation of a Russian artilleryman as he loaded his gun; and as soon as the heights of Clichy, Chaumont, Belleville, and Montmartre were carried by assault, there were many in the Russian army who longed to wreak their revenge, and waited with impatience for the signal to fire into Paris.

Napoleon was struck with the effect of the gilded domes and cupolas in Moscow, and on his return to Paris gilded the dome of the Hôtel des Invalides (the hospital built by Louis XIV. for old soldiers), and it now flashed a conspicuous object in the sun. At 5 A.M. of the 30th, Joseph destroyed all the foreign standards hung round its chapel, and the sword of Frederick suspended in the middle was broken, so that Blucher might not be able to keep his oath, that he would not lay down arms till he had wrested it from the enemy. At twelve on the following day, Joseph quietly left the city, giving directions to the National Guard to protect the palaces, and authority to the marshals to enter into terms with the enemy as soon as resistance proved useless. The ministers followed his example, with as much of the public treasure as they could secure. In the mean time, the marshals kept their men to their posts with the most loyal valour. Mortier's troops resisted the Prussian and Russian army for four hours, till Voronzov brought up his Russian corps to support them. The Russian and Prussian guards of the reserve were at Alexander's order called forward to assist Raeffskoi in the centre; and the heavy loss that the assailants sustained showed the force of the resistance. A Prussian colonel ordered up to reinforce Barclay, rushed forward at the head of his regiment with such impetuosity that Alexander took the Cross of St. George from his brother's coat and sent it to him on the field. The Prince of Würtemberg arrived at his post at the extreme left of the Allies about one o'clock, and the Austrians were never under fire throughout the day. The advance of the Russian centre so early as eight has been blamed as the cause of a heavier loss than if they had allowed more time for the Prussians and Austrians to join them. A rapid movement was important when so skilful an enemy as Napoleon was arriving with the utmost speed; and a delay might have given the citizens time to fortify their streets, and encouraged them with the hope of a prolonged defence. So far Napoleon had done nothing towards assisting the Parisians, as even Marmont and Mortier were present contrary to his orders, from having been unable to carry them out, or their armies would have been at least fifty miles distant. On March 30th, 1813, he declared to his senate that he would not resign a German village if the enemy was encamped at Montmartre. But exactly a year later, he sent Caulaincourt twice to make any terms of peace with Alexander, and even offered to curtail the territory of France to save his throne. When, after a march of forty miles in one day, he arrived at Troyes, and found it was impossible to overtake the Allies, he despatched an aide-de-camp to the marshals to say he was coming at once to Paris, and that negotiations were renewed with the allied Powers, through the medium of Metternich and Francis, who were disposed to make peace.* Mortier received this information at 3 P.M., and at once forwarded it with a flag of truce to Schwartzenberg, who showed it to Alexander, by whose desire this answer was returned: "The intimate and indissoluble union subsisting between the sovereign powers affords a guarantee that the negotiations you suppose are on foot separately between Austria and France have no foundation; and that the reports which you have received on that head are entirely groundless."

Throughout the morning the assailants and the defenders of Paris were very equally matched, and Alexander had remained on horseback on the field of battle since eight A.M., ordering up reinforcements where required, and marking out his most distinguished officers for promotion and reward. But as the afternoon wore on the Allies greatly outnumbered the French troops, almost to the extent of three to one; the Cossacks penetrated on the side of Vincennes as far as the suburb of St. Antoine; 1000 prisoners, 86 guns, and two standards were captured by the Russians, and the heights carried to the sound of mingled huzzas, and vivas, and cries of "Fire upon Paris." A battery of light artillery under Miloradovitz sent a few shots into the Boulevards, and nearly 300 cannon were being planted at an elevation from which they

* This was asserted to be true by Talleyrand at the Congress of Vienna. (See Munster's Political Sketches.)

could have completely swept the streets. The marshals perceived that in another half-hour the French must inevitably be chased within the gates of Paris, and the conquerors would enter after them, subjecting the city to all the chances of a capture by assault. They sent an officer to Alexander, who was on the projecting part of the hill of Belleville, immediately overlooking the Faubourg St. Martin, and requested an armistice. The Emperor answered, he could only grant one on condition that Paris surrendered, and as the officer was not empowered to accept such terms, he sent his aide-de-camp, Colonel Orlof,* with him to Marmont, whom he found in the first line encouraging his men. The Russian bombs were at this moment bursting in the Chaussée d'Antin, and one or two fell close to the church of St. Eustache: thirty howitzers carrying bomb-shells commanded the entire city, and Paris lay at the Czar's mercy. The marshals had therefore no alternative but to trust to his generosity or to watch its destruction, and they were not deceived in their estimate of Alexander when they gave it unconditionally into his hands. The capitulation was signed by Orlof and Schwartzenberg's aide-de-camp, Count Paar, as well as by two of Marmont's officers, and orders were sent round to stop the firing, and obeyed by 100,000 men. No army Napoleon ever commanded would have listened to his voice in a moment of such excitement, if he had given an order as much opposed to their natural instinct of revenge. He led them, but it was through pandering to their human weaknesses, and he was known to envy the Russian discipline. The wind was in a quarter most favourable to the Allies, and it was allowed on all sides that nothing but the Czar's personal influence over his soldiers could at that moment have saved Paris and her 600,000 inhabitants. The terms of the capitulation were signed at two A.M. of March 31st, though the armies, extinguishing their burning matches, had piled their muskets and rested for several hours. The town of St. Denis surrendered to the Silesian army the same day. A suspension of arms once obtained, and the threatened danger averted for the moment, the marshals were inclined to haggle over the terms, hoping that Napoleon's arrival would turn the tide of the war.

* He signed the treaty of Paris in 1856.

They wished to be allowed to leave the city with their troops in any direction they might choose. Alexander was not inclined to be hard with them, and rightly judging that with Paris in their power the Allies would be virtually masters of France, and a dispirited army of 20,000 men would be no great obstacle in the settlement of peace, he granted this condition, but gave them notice they must leave Paris before seven A.M., for he should enter it with his army in the course of the day. The arsenals and magazines were to be surrendered, the National Guard either disbanded or employed by the Allies, and the wounded or stragglers found after ten A.M. would be prisoners of war. Schwartzenberg and the King retired to their night quarters, while messages were still being exchanged by Alexander and Nesselrode with Mortier and Marmont. At last, when the signatures were affixed, the Czar went to the Château de Bondy, where he had rested the previous night, and at half-past two lay down to sleep. But he rose an hour later to receive a deputation from the Municipality of Paris, to offer him the keys of the city, and to implore his protection. They had left it at two o'clock, and lighted by the numerous watch-fires on their road, drove rapidly through their sleeping enemies. While the Emperor was dressing they talked to Nesselrode, who questioned them as to the state of public feeling in Paris. They answered by describing the three political parties, Bonapartists, Legitimists, and Republicans; and said the best French statesmen habitually resorted to Talleyrand's house, where the real feeling of the educated men of France could be most fully ascertained. These observations induced Alexander to resort to M. Talleyrand's house before he established himself in the Palace of the Elysée in the course of the same day.

The deputation delivered an address to the Emperor as soon as he admitted them. He answered, "Your Emperor, who was my ally, came into the heart of my empire, carrying there a destruction which years will not efface. I am far from wishing to return to France the calamities I have received from her. Napoleon is my sole enemy. I promise my special protection to the town of Paris. I will guard and preserve all the public establishments. It is for yourselves to secure your own future happiness. I must give you a government which will insure your own repose and that of Europe." Caulaincourt arrived an hour or two later from Napoleon, with full powers to accept not only the terms offered at Châtillon, but to promise the payment of a war contribution or the surrender of fortresses; in short, any concession which would permit him to keep his throne. Alexander saw the deputy for a few moments, but only to tell him he could no longer treat with Napoleon, who reached Fontainebleau the previous day, and taking Caulaincourt, proceeded in a carriage to within a few miles of Paris. There, as he was changing horses, some stragglers informed his escort of the capitulation of the city, confirmed by the arrival of a column of cavalry under General Belliard, whom Alexander had permitted to retire, and was on his way to join his master. Napoleon laid the blame on all his faithful servants, and accused them of not executing orders which he had never given. He said his horses had been as swift as the wind; he only asked them to hold out twenty-four hours: "miserable wretches, they had my orders, and knew that I should be here with 70,000 men. I see every one has lost his senses. This comes of employing fools and cowards." He talked of going on to Paris at the head of this cavalry corps, but was easily deterred. "When I am not there they do nothing but heap blunder on blunder. Entered into the capital of 800,000 souls! It is too dreadful." He ordered Caulaincourt to fly to the allied head-quarters, and arrange something with Alexander in person; and then returned to Fontainebleau. His envoy following him to report the failure of his mission, was so touched by his disappointment that he declared he would try once more and penetrate, dead or alive, into Alexander's room, to appeal to him for his rival in the name of their former friendship. Napoleon must certainly have reached an astonishing depth of humiliation before he could try and work on the feelings of a man whom he had injured and endeavoured to deceive as he had injured Alexander; but he despatched Caulaincourt with renewed hope, telling him he depended entirely on his efforts. It has been stated that he sent orders to one of the marshals to destroy Paris if the Allies entered it, and he certainly seemed to regret at St. Helena that such a plan was not carried out. A story to this effect was circulated in Paris, and Colonel

Le Comte Lescours received the decoration of St. Anne from Alexander for having given up to him the order intrusted to him (Lescours) by the marshal when he quitted Paris, on the colonel promising faithfully to ignite the magazines* and blow up the public establishments; a promise he considered himself justified in giving, though he did not mean to keep it, lest the order should be transferred to a less scrupulous agent.

Upon the departure of the deputation from the municipality, others arrived from the various Parisian corporations to wait on Alexander, and one from the National Guard, requesting him to maintain them to keep order in the city. The Emperor asked the chief of the staff if he could rely upon them, and on being informed they would discharge their duties as honourable men, he said he could expect nothing more, and directed them to refer to General Sacken, whom he had appointed Governor of Paris, adding that they would find him in every respect a man of delicacy and honour.

It was necessary to have been educated in the system of the first Empire, and accustomed to scenes which surpassed Ismail in horror when the French entered a conquered town, to appreciate the relief the Parisians felt when they saw the manner in which Alexander used his influence over the assembled armies, and that from the moment the capitulation was signed not a drop of blood was shed or a loaf stolen by the wild-looking hosts who poured through their gates. They were even protected from an outbreak of the ragged mob of Jacobins and Communists, long a terror to the wealthier classes in the towns of France whenever there has been a change of government. The Cossacks, whom Napoleon depicted as indulging in draughts of human blood, and wearing necklaces of noses and ears, strolled leisurely about, looking quietly into the shop windows, and, like English sailors, submitting to all kinds of imposition, such as paying thirty francs for an article which pleased their fancy, when the real price was not more than five. The Russian officers were more courteous in their behaviour, and more considerate to the feelings of the inhabitants, than the Swedes on the staff of Bernadotte, a Frenchman by birth !† It was not surprising if their grati-

---

* Memoirs of Patrick Fraser Tytler.
† The Duchesse d'Abrantès and others.

tude assumed a joyful aspect when the Allied Sovereigns made their public entry. The gala reception which fear and his express orders had extracted for Napoleon from many of the vanquished towns on the Continent was the due of his more merciful conquerors, who left them at liberty to put on mourning if they preferred it, and only wished to secure their future repose. They were in no humour to scoff at those principles of religion which actuated Alexander in refusing to avail himself of the opportunity for avenging Moscow; for they were too much indebted to them, and there is little doubt that they had some effect in a nation so much influenced by fashion and the example of those above them as the French, and procured at least a more tolerant reception for the Bourbons, who were associated in the minds of their subjects with the *régime* of the priests and convents. The liberty for which they cast off their old monarchs reappeared under the auspices of the autocrat of the north, and the press threw off its fetters to indulge in controversies as to the respective merits of the claimants to their government. Alexander saw the Bourbons could not keep the throne for a month, if permitted to follow out their scheme of restoring everything as it stood before the constitution granted by Louis XVI. "Alexander," says Châteaubriand, "before he quitted Paris, left us a free charter, a liberty that we owe as much to his lights as to his influence. Chief of two supreme authorities, doubly autocrat by the sword and by religion, he alone of all the sovereigns of Europe understood that at the age of civilization to which France had arrived she could only be governed in virtue of a free constitution." A young Frenchman admiring the ease with which he allowed petitioners to approach him, Alexander replied, "What else are sovereigns made for?" His delicacy in not taking up his quarters at the Tuileries deeply impressed the French as so unlike the vulgar pride which made Napoleon hasten to occupy the Imperial rooms in the Kremlin and the Royal chamber at Potsdam. The popularity he acquired among all classes of politicians did more to banish the fallen Emperor from their hearts than any material victory. Symptoms of a peasant warfare had shown themselves on the route of the Allies, by the murder of isolated detachments; but now they would have gained nothing and lost much by such a course. "You should be our Emperor, and give us a prince like yourself," were cries not seldom heard from the Parisians when Alexander appeared in sight.

The Czar was on horseback at eight A.M. on March 31st, and rode with his staff to the King's head-quarters at Pantin, to arrange the entrance of the troops into Paris. The streets swarmed with the lowest of the populace, hoping for a riot and opportunity to plunder, and one of Alexander's aides-de-camp, attended by a few Cossacks and Bashkirs, on his way to prepare the Emperor's abode, was attacked, but the National Guard interposed. The mob shouted, "Napoleon is arriving to us, Frenchmen. Let us annihilate the enemy." But the appearance of Constantine at the head of the cavalry soon checked demonstrations. Lamartine was a spectator of the procession. The Grand Duke he describes as riding "a wild horse of the steppes, representing barbarous war evoked from the deserts of the north to spread over the south; but submissive, and a tame and attached slave to his brother, he imposed on his squadron the discipline and bearing of a peace festival."* Another spectator† observes, the physiognomy of the Russian troops indicated strongly the different nations to which they belonged. Constantine seemed much liked by the common soldiers, to whom he often nodded and smiled. M. de la Rochefoucauld came up to ask him to allow troops to surround the column in the Place Vendôme, and protect it while the statue of Napoleon was taken down. He coldly answered it was no concern of his.

Alexander, the King, and Schwartzenberg, riding together, accompanied by the brothers and sons of the two Sovereigns, entered the Porte St. Martin, followed and preceded by the Cossacks of the Guard, between ten and eleven A.M., for it was a work of time to march the long columns through the crowded streets. Their most distinguished generals rode with them, as well as several British officers. Every window and roof was crammed with spectators, and the chief object of interest with all was to see the Czar. "Vive Alexandre! Vive le Roi des Prusses! Vivent les Alliés!" was heard on all sides. The

---

* Histoire de la Restauration.
† Mémoires d'un Page de la Cour Impériale.

crowd struggled with each other to shake hands with the Emperor, so that he often was obliged to check his horse to avoid treading on them. "We have been long waiting for you," said a Royalist. "We should have arrived sooner but for the bravery of your troops," answered the Czar; a reply which elicited much applause. The procession paused a moment before the gate of St. Denis, to read the inscription to "Louis the Great," and Alexander remained in the Champs Elysées directing his troops and appointing their place of rendezvous till five P.M., when the last soldier had passed. Then he left his horse at the Elysée Palace, where rooms were prepared for him, and inquiring the road to M. de Talleyrand, went there on foot. He was accosted by La Rochefoucauld, who asked him to restore her legitimate princes to France. He answered, that he must know the spirit of the army and the national voice before he took an irrevocable step. He knew the constitution of the French Government as well as a Frenchman, and his first direction to Talleyrand was to convoke the Senate and establish a provisional government.*

* Sir C. Stewart, in his report to the Marquis of Wellesley, says:— "It is impossible to convey an idea of the scene yesterday, when the Emperor of Russia, the King of Prussia, and Prince Schwartzenberg made their entry at the head of the allied troops. The cavalry under the Grand Duke Constantine, and the Guards of all the different allied forces, were formed in columns early in the morning on the road from Bondy to Paris. . . . . All Paris seemed to be assembled and concentred on one spot. They thronged in such masses round the Emperor and the King that with all their condescension and gracious familiarity, extending their hands on all sides, in was in vain to attempt to satisfy the populace. The air resounded with cries of Vive l'Empereur! Vive le Roi de Prusse! Vive nos libérateurs. . . . . The Sovereigns halted on the Champs Elysées, when the troops defiled before them in the most admirable order, and the head-quarters were established at Paris. . . . . The allied armies march to-morrow, with the exception of the Guards and reserves who remain here, towards Fontainebleau, and take up a post to be regulated by the movements of Bonaparte. Castlereagh is with the Emperor of Austria. When our communications were broken in upon he went to Dijon with all the ministers, &c., except Nesselrode, who is here." "It would be unjust," says the same writer on a subsequent occasion, "not to declare, that if the Continent had so long borne the scourge of usurpation under the iron sway of Bonaparte, it was also crowned with the blessing of possessing amongst its legitimate sovereigns one who by a firm and glorious conduct richly deserved the name of the liberator of mankind. This Sovereign, I have no hesitation in saying, is Alexander, for it is impossible to estimate too highly his energy and noble conduct in the short campaign from the Rhine to Paris. The management of every measure undoubtedly lay with the Emperor of Russia and the confidential cabinet which he had formed. Count Nesselrode, at no time very independent, fell somewhat into the

"To dictate laws at the gates of Paris to the people who burned his own capital," says Lamartine;* "to hold in his hand the crown or the abdication of Napoleon, was enough to intoxicate an ordinary soul; but Alexander was a great soul, and put his glory not in vengeance, but in generosity. Reprisals against a people or against a conquered man appeared to him what they are—a perversion of success. He had the grand magnanimity of the heroic races of the East. He respected humanity, he adored Providence. Young, handsome, the admired of all eyes, bearing a melancholy reflection on his features, he conducted himself with a majestic simplicity before the world." "Alexander was truly great," writes the Duchesse d'Abrantès; "the man who could avenge himself, and pushed that delicious beverage from his lips, was a being above others."† "He had something calm and sad in his

hands of M. de Talleyrand, as well as General Pozzo di Borgo, a man of consummate ability, but not yet of sufficient weight in Paris to afford any check to the mode of proceeding of the new French ministry (to which he was accredited after the Restoration as Russian ambassador). The Emperor of Russia's conduct since his arrival in Paris was carried on with so much address that it was incalculable what influence he had obtained over the Parisian character." Sir George Jackson corroborates these statements in his diary, and adds, "he is most popular with the Parisians of all grades. When he shows himself in public he is most gracious in his condescension towards the populace, who throng about him and shout till they are hoarse to do him honour. In society he is, as indeed he has always been, exceedingly affable, desiring the observance of as little form and ceremony as possible. The ladies say he is adorable. . . . He is also very popular with the army."
* Histoire de la Restauration.
† "We were struck," writes an English visitor to Paris in April, 1814, "with the simplicity of the style in which Alexander lived. He inhabited only one or two apartments in a wing of the splendid Elysée, rose at four A.M. to transact business, and was very regular in his attendance at a small chapel where the service of the Greek Church was performed. We had access to very good information concerning him, and the account we received of his character even exceeded our anticipations. His well-known humanity was described as having undergone no change from the scenes of misery inseparable from extended warfare to which his duties rather than his inclinations had so long accustomed him. He repeatedly left behind him, in marching with the army, some of the medical staff to dress the wounds of French soldiers whom he passed on his way. He was described by everybody as a man not merely of the most amiable disposition, but of superior understanding, uncommon activity, and a firm decided turn of mind. He was certainly looked on by officers who had long served under him as one of the ablest commanders in the allied armies. As a specimen of the general feeling in the Russian army at the time it invaded France, we may mention a conversation an officer of the Russian staff (Dr. Crichton) told us he held with a private of the guard

appearance," says Châteaubriand; "he traversed Paris on foot and on horseback without attendants and without affectation. . . . He was a king who had learned humanity. It was proposed that the name of the bridge of Austerlitz should be changed. 'It is enough,' said he, 'that I have passed over it with my army.'" He also preserved the Vendôme column from destruction, and when visiting the Hôtel des Invalides felt a soldier's sympathy for the disabled old men, deprived first by Joseph and then by the allied generals of all the cannon and other trophies of the battles where they had left their limbs. Several had been wounded at Austerlitz, many at Pultusk and Friedland. He ordered twelve useless Russian cannon to be restored to them, and left them brightened up, and again ready to boast of their deeds of valour.

The English tourists detained in France since the peace of Amiens was broken were now free to return to their native country; and a host of British visitors, many of rank and importance, took the earliest opportunity to cross the Channel and visit Paris after its occupation by the Allies. Their astonishment at the loose morality of the fair Parisiennes is vividly described in their letters. Paris, so long known to them only

on the march. The soldier complained of the Emperor's proclamation desiring them to consider as enemies only those whom they met in the field. 'The French,' said he, 'came into our country bringing hosts of Germans and Poles along with them; they plundered our properties, burned our houses, and murdered our families; every Russian was their enemy. We have driven them out of Russia, we have followed them to France, but wherever we go we are allowed to find none but friends. This,' he added, 'is very well for us guards who know pillage is unworthy of us, but the common soldiers and Cossacks do not understand it; they remember how their friends and relations have been treated by the French, and that remembrance lies at their hearts.' The recollection of Moscow was strong in the Russian army, and the desire of revenge so general, even amongst the superior officers, that they said nothing could have restrained them but the presence and positive commands of their Czar, nor could any other influence have maintained that admirable discipline in the Russian army during its stay in France which we have so often heard the theme of panegyric even among their most inveterate enemies. Blucher was ill, it was reported, with *delirium tremens* all the time the armies remained in Paris, and never showed himself publicly there in 1814. His army consisted at first of four Russians to one Prussian. Indeed, it was the intention of the Emperor to put himself at its head, but he afterwards gave up that idea, thinking he was more needed by the Grand Army. The arrangements of the Russian hospital staff under Wylie have attained in a few years a surprising degree of excellence. The state of the Russian hospitals at Paris, under the direction of Dr. Crichton, was universally admired."

through her newspapers issued from an enslaved press, was displayed in reality before their eyes; and her churches all falling to ruins, her manufactories converted into barracks, "the streets more dirty than Edinburgh in its worst days," and French regiments in arrear of their pay for sixteen months, showed the results of the Imperial despotism, which, after drawing from France an annual revenue of 1,500,000,000 francs, and 1,080,000,000*l*. in money and requisitions from foreign countries since Napoleon's Consulate, had left her a debt of 83,000,000*l*., which was enormously increased after Waterloo, when the French were called upon to pay the expenses of the war. Paris now resembled Moscow or Nijni Novgorod more than a European city, in the variety of strange uniforms and costumes, Polish Jews, Russian carters, Kirghiz Tartars, and Bashkirs, who swarmed in the streets. "To-day," writes an English diplomatist (April 1st), "the camp of the Cossacks in the Champs Élysées is the chief object of curiosity to all Paris." It was in a picturesque disorder, their worn and tattered uniforms, their wild weapons, lances, bows and arrows, sabres and pistols, hung on the trees. Hawkers strolled among them selling oranges, brandy, and beer, which last, it was observed, was not at all to their taste. All unite in praising the excellence of the Russian discipline, on the authority of the Marquis de Frondeville and other Frenchmen, both before and after their entrance into Paris. Lord Palmerston,* travelling through France, heard from the country people that "the Russians were the most gentle of the invading armies." The irregular horsemen belonging to the Prussian army were, as their own generals state, not kept in much discipline; and all the irregulars of the allied army being indiscriminately termed Cossacks by the French, the last have often been unjustly accredited with the depredations of their German comrades, and even with those of Napoleon's men. Count Beugnot,† says that the Russian governor of Paris, "showed himself kind and attentive to the inhabitants." He would have wished Alexander to prolong his sojourn in France, to consolidate the new Bourbon Government; but the Russian general begged him, as the director of the French police, to be on his guard and protect the Czar to the

* Diary in France, 1815-18. † Mémoires de Comte Beugnot.

best of his ability; for if he was assassinated, or even merely insulted in Paris, himself and his generals would not be able to prevent the soldiers, who adored him, from setting fire to the city. Under these circumstances, Beugnot felt infinitely relieved when Alexander departed, as the anti-Bourbon party were still rather active, and nightly assassinations made the streets unsafe after dark.

On the evening of March 31st a proclamation, signed by Alexander at three P.M., was posted about the walls of Paris. It announced the occupation of the city, and that the Allies would no longer treat with Napoleon or any of his family. It stated that Europe required France to be great and powerful, and the integrity of all France under its legitimate kings would be preserved. It called upon her to declare in favour of the kind of government she preferred, and invited the Senate to appoint a provisional administration. It was the first intimation the Parisians had received that the Bonaparte dynasty was dethroned. The Emperor and the King of Prussia dined that evening with Talleyrand in the Rue St. Florentin; but before they sat down a message was brought to Alexander, telling him that some of his soldiers were without provisions, after their hot and fatiguing day, for the shops were closed and the Government stores empty. He sent for the mayor and the chief of the National Guard, telling them he would not be responsible for disorders if his troops were allowed to want, and every species of food was conveyed to them at once. Talleyrand assembled a party to meet the Emperor, and after dinner they held a conference, which included the Duke de Dalberg, M. de Pradt, Bourrienne, the Senator Bournonville, Baron Louis, Nesselrode, Lichtenstein, and Pozzo di Borgo. They were seated to the right and left of the long table, except Alexander, who walked backwards and forwards while he was speaking, and only stopped for a few moments when he wanted to hear what another said. He opened the conference, but allowed free discussion; and for the first time in the course of history a sovereign was heard in Paris to advocate the rights of the people. France, he declared, was too advanced in civilization not to be permitted to govern herself. She had formerly been the pioneer in literature and science; she should now set an example of constitutional freedom to the Continent. The era of war and conquest he hoped was past; the last ten years were more worthy of the darkest ages of barbarism than of the nineteenth century. He was determined to leave France within her ancient boundaries, as he considered her strength necessary to the European equilibrium; and to crush her to the dust, or to destroy her independence, would provoke a rupture of that peace which might now be preserved for ever. He enlarged on the miseries of war, and ended by saying that Napoleon having merited the loss of a power he abused, France should be allowed to choose her new sovereign, and assisted against those persons who wished to maintain an order of things proved incompatible with the safety of other nations. Then turning towards the King of Prussia, who was nearly asleep, he said, "William, and you, Prince Schwartzenberg, as the representative of Austria, am not I speaking our common sentiments towards France?" They both merely bowed their assent. "He continued in truly fine and generous words," wrote one of the councillors. "It must be agreed he was great and admirable. It is justice to admit it."

Alexander had expressed his belief that the elder branch of the Bourbons would never maintain itself in France, and he was inclined to think a republic the form of government most suitable to her present state. Talleyrand rose as soon as he had spoken, and said the restoration of the Bourbons was the only way of escaping from the evils surrounding them. Under the mild rule of a race of princes who had learned wisdom in misfortune, all the necessary guarantees would be obtained for a durable freedom. If the statesman of sixty who had lived all his life in France was really sincere in this belief, he showed a less accurate knowledge of the subject than the foreign sovereign of thirty-six, who had never entered Paris till that morning, and whose predictions were all fulfilled when he asserted that the Orleans family would eventually replace the Bourbons on the throne, and that a constitutional charter would be necessary to secure a liberal government for France under Louis XVIII. Schwartzenberg put in a word for the Imperial dynasty, by observing that there were no indications of indifference to Napoleon in their passage through France. "Nor," said Alexander, "of a predilection among the military for Louis; and their opinion must be taken if we wish to establish a permanent settlement of France. It is but a few days ago since 6000 new troops suffered themselves to be cut to pieces when a single cry of 'Vive le Roi' would have saved them." M. de Pradt answered, " Such things will go on so long as there is a chance of negotiating with Bonaparte, even although at this moment he has a halter round his neck." Alexander did not understand this allusion till it was explained that the Parisians were already trying to drag down Napoleon's statue from the top of the Vendôme column. "Then," said Alexander to Talleyrand, "how do you propose to establish a restoration of the Bourbons?"* " By means," he replied, " of the Senate, whom he could answer for as being Royalists, and their example would be speedily followed by France." The Emperor turned to the Abbé Pradt and Baron Louis, and asked their opinion, declaring in energetic terms that he was not the original author of the war between Russia and France; it was Napoleon. He was not the enemy of France, but of all who were hostile to her liberties. The Baron and the Abbé both said they were Royalists, and that the great majority of the French nation were of the same opinion. The negotiations at Châtillon alone prevented this opinion from openly manifesting itself. "They need no longer be prevented by such fears," said Alexander; "I shall not treat any further with the Emperor Napoleon." "Nor with any member of his family?" said the Abbé. "No," replied Alexander: "I have thought of a regency for his son; but in such a case we should be forced to keep our armies in France to prevent Napoleon from putting himself at the head of it." Talleyrand said any attempt except for Napoleon or Louis would be an intrigue. Any other government was impossible. They separated without a decision; for Alexander said he must collect the votes of the chiefs of the French army before taking a last resolution. He repaired for the night to his rooms at the Elysée, and found many Royalists waiting to see him in spite of the lateness of the hour. Among others

---

* "In Talleyrand's house," says Beugnot, "a high-minded sovereign and some statesmen with him accomplished the great event of the Restoration." Beugnot felt certain that if the Senate had called a different family from the Bourbons to the throne it would have been accepted by Europe; so much prejudice was there in the minds of the Sovereigns, and so great was the influence of Alexander's prediction, &c.

the Countess de Cayla, who entreated him to restore the Bourbons. He told her the choice of a sovereign would be referred to the Senate and to the representatives of the army; and if they agreed to ask for the Bourbons they would be restored. She flew back to invite as many senators as she could to a *soirée* at her house, and repeated the Emperor's words to them, exacting a promise from each to vote for Louis. "I thought it important," she writes, "to obtain from these gentlemen their solemn oaths. Fool that I was; most of them had taken and broken at least a dozen."

But besides the Royalists anxiously waiting for Alexander, there was Caulaincourt, whom Napoleon long treated coldly, merely because, being well acquainted with Russia and the Czar, he had warned him of the consequences of breaking his alliance with them; and now when all he had foretold had come to pass, his mediation with Alexander as the personal friend of both Sovereigns was the fallen Emperor's last hope. Napoleon told him to penetrate dead or live into Alexander's room, but having arrived late at the barriers, he was refused admittance into Paris by the Russian guard. Constantine, driving up to make a last inspection, was moved by the despair of the ex-ambassador to conceal him in his carriage to the Elysée Palace; though, hearing his errand, he told him it was a great responsibility, as Alexander had given orders that no agent from Napoleon should be admitted. Caulaincourt remained for three hours in the courtyard of the Elysée, surrounded by foreign soldiers, while Constantine went in to plead his cause. "The rooms were full," he said, when he returned, "and the Emperor did not come out from the conference till midnight. I was obliged to wait till all had retired. Alexander is vexed at our escapade, but will receive you as a friend." Caulaincourt, covering himself with Constantine's cloak, followed him upstairs into the Emperor's room, where, though kindly received, he heard the Allies had resolved to dethrone the Napoleon dynasty.

"I was thunderstruck," he writes; "I had foreseen I should have to discuss hard conditions; but the Emperor deposed never occurred to me. I proposed a Regency. 'Is it just,' I said, ' to strike with the same blow the Empress and her son, who at least is not formidable to Europe?'" "We thought of it," said Alexander, " but what should we do with Napoleon? He is the obstacle to the recognition of his son." " He would make all the sacrifices his unfortunate circumstances require," said Caulaincourt. Alexander replied, " He might from necessity; but his ambition would soon return, and Europe again be convulsed." " I see," said the envoy, bitterly, " you have resolved on his fall." " Whose fault is it ?" Alexander answered, warmly ; " what have I not done to prevent this extremity? You must own I tried in every way to open his eyes to the inevitable result of his unjust policy. In my foolish credulity (sotte probité) as a young man, I believed in the sacredness of his sworn friendship, and I said to him, ' The Powers, weary of outrages and insults, must ally themselves against your insupportable rule.' His answer to my frank communication was war, and he threw away my pure attachment." " I could find no words," writes Caulaincourt, " to oppose to these recriminations, made without pride or anger." " Even now," continued the Czar, " I feel no hatred towards him." But Caulaincourt was still unable to induce him to promise any support. He was satisfied for the moment by Alexander consenting to mention the Regency at the council the following day. " Every other proposal," said the Czar, " is impossible; do not deceive yourself." " To this long discourse," writes Caulaincourt, " succeeded one of those happy conversations of other times. No one knew like Alexander how to carry into private life that gracious ease which makes distances disappear. Putting aside his official demeanour, he became the amusing and lively talker of charming frivolities." Caulaincourt asked him after " the beautiful Antoine Narishkin." He replied, " she took advantage of his weakness." He made the best resolutions against her, and then did not know how to resist her. " I have not common sense," he said. " He still loved her," says Caulaincourt, " like a madman, though she was 700 leagues away, and he had not seen her for nearly two years."

Caulaincourt had not been admitted into the palace till one A.M., and it was now four. Alexander had only rested an hour the previous night, and was to hold another council early that day. " Your Majesty," said Caulaincourt, " wants to get rid of me. I know the place well, and will go into the next room to shut myself up there." The room Alexander occupied had been Napoleon's when he inhabited the Elysée; and the boudoir into which Caulaincourt retired contained his writing table, and was still filled with plans and pamphlets on Russia, just as he had left it for the campaign. The Duke slept till nearly eight, disturbed occasionally by the sound of the officers going into the Emperor's room for orders, and saw from the windows the Russian troops bivouacking in the garden as well as in the streets. Towards eight Constantine knocked at his door and told him Alexander was obliged to go out before seeing him, but they would breakfast together in his room. "It is necessary," says Caulaincourt, "to have lived at the Court of Russia to form a true idea of the simplicity, of the familiarity with good taste of the princes of the Imperial family in the relations of private life. The distance between princes and the persons they honour with their friendship is only observed by the last."* In Napoleon's prosperous days Alexander had often laughed at the mode in which he exacted servile offices from the nobility of the French Court. "I prefer to be waited upon by an ordinary valet-de-chambre," he said; "Napoleon degrades the dignity of an ambassador when he turns Caulaincourt into a groom, and orders him to hold his horse." At breakfast Caulaincourt heard from Constantine of the havoc made by the war among those young men whom he had known so brilliant and so happy in Russia. Many also had lost an entire fortune. A serious if not melancholy tone seemed to pervade the whole Russian army, and after such great trials they felt that even now a triumphal rejoicing and self-applause would be out of place. In the campaign of 1807 an English officer writes rather sarcastically, that the Russians "have a passion for attributing all their successes to

* It has been already mentioned that Napoleon expected his own mother to stand up when he was in a room with her until he gave her permission to sit down. At the little Court of Cassel, Jerome Bonaparte and his wife followed the same system, and when they asked German nobles to dine with them it was merely to stand round the table while the King and Queen dined alone. An old German baron, sinking with fatigue and age, was asked on one of these occasions if he did not feel tired. "Yes," he answered, "having always been accustomed to sit down when I dined with Frederick the Great." The Russian nobles never submitted under Paul of Russia to the insults which the French and German courtiers sustained from Napoleon and his family.

the God of Russia." The same religious feeling when they occupied France greatly astonished the French, who never thought of attributing their victories to any agency but their own genius or glorious destiny, and their calamities to treachery, bad weather, or evil fate. "We listened," says a contemporary French journalist, "to young Russian officers on the very day of their triumphant entry into Paris, who spoke of their exploits from Moscow to the Seine as of deeds accomplished under the guidance of Divine Providence, and ascribed to themselves only the glory of having been chosen as His instruments. They spoke of their victories without exultation, and in language so simple, it seemed to us as if they did so by common consent out of politeness."* In contrast with this, an English traveller, writing in 1814, remarks on the thunders of applause every word levelled against religion or the priests received from the French audience in the Parisian theatres. The military prided themselves on not even knowing the names of the churches, saying in excuse they were soldiers. The day after the public entry the shops were reopened, and business was transacted as if nothing more than usual was going on. The allied armies made the fortunes of the Paris shopkeepers, and between March 30th and April 5th the French Funds rose from 45 to 70 per cent., a higher price than was quoted since the beginning of the Russian campaign.

At the Council held early in the morning of April 1st, Alexander told Talleyrand that, as foreigners, the Allies had no wish to dispose of the French throne, or to recall princes whom the nation might not receive from their hands. He must have the opinion of the army; the votes of at least four of the marshals were essential; for, above all things, he wished to avoid a civil war. Talleyrand at once negotiated with the army, in the hope of bringing it over to the Royalists. The sixty-four senators were already informed by Madame de Cayla and Talleyrand that their only course was to vote for Louis. At 9.30 they waited on Alexander. He received them with a short address, beginning softly, but speaking louder as he proceeded. "Gentlemen," he said, "I am delighted to find myself in the midst of you. It is neither ambition nor the love of conquest which brought me here: my armies entered

* Quoted by Alison.

France to repel an unjust oppression. Your Emperor carried war into the heart of my dominions, when I only wished for peace. I am the friend of the French people. I impute their faults to their chief alone, and I wish to protect your deliberations. You are charged with one of the most honourable missions men can fulfil, to secure the happiness of a great people, in giving France institutions at once strong and liberal, which are indispensable in her present state of civilization. I set out to-morrow to resume the command of the armies, and sustain the cause you have embraced. It is time blood should cease to flow; too much has been shed already. But yet I will not lay down my arms till I have obtained the peace which has been the object of all my efforts, and I shall be satisfied if in quitting your country I bear with me the satisfaction of having had it in my power to be useful to you, and to contribute to the repose of the world. The Provisional Government has asked me this morning for the liberation of the French prisoners of war confined in Russia. I give it to the Senate. Since they fell into my hands I have done all in my power to soften their lot. I will at once give orders for their return. May they rejoin their families in peace, and be fitted to enjoy the new order of things." One hundred and fifty thousand men were returned to France, without even the cost of their maintenance being repaid to Russia. But this generosity did not please her allies, who thought they saw a deep design for obtaining the future aid of France against the liberties and independence of other nations. They mistrusted his peaceful professions, but the result proved they were in error, for the system the Czar inaugurated, condemned as it was by the so-called Liberal party throughout the Continent, which only desired Napoleon's return, certainly secured a longer period of tranquillity than Europe had ever known. Napoleon's system fell with its author, having existed only eleven years; but Alexander's policy influenced the world till the end of his life, and for twenty-eight years after it.

As soon as he had held an interview with Schwartzenberg and various Parisian deputies, Alexander met the council on the subject of the charter of public rights to be conferred on France, whoever might be her future Sovereign, and reviewed the troops ready to proceed the next day against the remains of the army at Fontainebleau. He did not return to the Elysée Palace, where the impatient Caulaincourt awaited him, till six P.M. He was resolved on the necessity of Napoleon's abdication, but still not convinced that the Bourbons would really be acceptable to the whole nation, particularly as in such a case Austria showed symptoms of wishing to reclaim Lorraine and Alsace, when he had guaranteed the French territory as it existed before 1790. A Regency might be possible if Napoleon were exiled, but not if he was to remain in France. Such an accession to Austrian influence as their Archduchess Maria Louisa in the position of Regent would be balanced by the reconstitution of Poland under Russia, and the Prussian acquisitions in Saxony. If, therefore, a Regency seemed most popular in France, it might still be made acceptable to Europe.*

"I have been busy with your affairs," he said to Caulaincourt as he entered, "and a diplomatist for your sake, that is to say, reserved and rusé. I have avoided engaging myself in any way, so as to leave things in suspense. I closeted myself with Schwartzenberg, and returned to the question of the Regency. The discussion between us was warm. But go back *as quickly* as you can to Napoleon, give him a full account of what passed here, and without any delay return officially the bearer of his abdication in favour of his son."

"Sire," said Caulaincourt, "what will they do with the Emperor?" "I hope," said Alexander, "you know me enough to be certain that he will be properly treated. I give you my word for it."†

"When all was lost," writes the Duke, "I found this word was not given in vain. It was to Alexander Napoleon owed the sovereignty of Elba."

Constantine was obliged to conduct him as privately out of Paris as he had entered it, and he made the journey to Fontainebleau in five hours. "Well," said Napoleon, "what has

---

* This conversation is all given on Caulaincourt's authority, both repeated to others at the time, and in his memoirs written after Alexander's death.

† It would have suited Austria to have induced the Allies to make peace before entering Paris, and received the credit of it; but a peace made afterwards *with Napoleon*, in which Russia took the lead, was very different. She knew Napoleon's vindictive nature, and that she might be its first victim; and she now wished to obtain Alsace and Lorraine from the Bourbons as the price of the restoration of their dynasty.

passed? Have you seen the Emperor of Russia? What has he said to you? Tell me everything."

"Sire," said Caulaincourt, "I have seen Alexander. He is not your enemy." Napoleon made a gesture of doubt. "No, Sire, it is with him alone the Imperial cause finds any support." "What does he wish—what do they all wish?" "Sire, your Majesty is called to make great sacrifices to secure for your son the crown of France." "That is to say," replied he, in an injured tone, "they will no longer treat with me. They wish to chase me from the throne I conquered at the point of my sword; they wish to make me an object of derision and pity." He remained for three days undecided, treating as chimerical the idea of restoring the Bourbons. He refused to abdicate in favour of his son, and proclaimed to his soldiers: "Some factious men, the emigrants whom I have pardoned, have mounted the white cockade and surrounded the Emperor Alexander, and they would compel us to wear it. Since the Revolution, France has always been mistress of herself. I offered peace to the Allies, leaving France in its ancient limits, but they would not accept it. In a few days I will attack the enemy, to force him to quit our capital. I rely on you—am I right?" He was received with cheers and cries of "Yes, yes!" and on April 2nd gave orders that the head-quarters should be transferred to Essonnes, on the road to Paris. But the marshals hesitated. They heard of the establishment of the Provisional Government in Paris, and Ney in particular dwelt on the absurdity of sacrificing all their private interests for the sake of one man. Caulaincourt, as positive of the firmness of the Czar as before the Moscow campaign, maintained a Regency was all that could be hoped. Napoleon had better accept it and abdicate. On the morning of the 3rd they received the news that the Senate had formally deposed him, as he had "broken his coronation oath, by levying taxes without the sanction of the laws, and had disregarded the interests of the French nation by refusing to conclude the peace offered by the Allies." The same decree declared the right of succession in his family to be abolished, and absolved the army and the people from their oath.

Napoleon was overcome when he received this intelligence, spread far and wide with the utmost speed. His army, already disinclined to encounter the swords of 160,000 foreign troops fast accumulating in Paris and its neighbourhood, was still less anxious to engage with its own countrymen, and began to desert. Barclay published an order of the day to the Russians, giving notice that they were leaving Paris " to destroy the inconsiderable band of unfortunate men who still adhere to Napoleon, but let the agriculturists and villagers be treated as friends." This was read and commented on at Fontainebleau. At twelve o'clock, November 4th, Napoleon held a conference with Berthier, Ney, Lefebvre, Oudinot, Macdonald, Maret, Bertrand, and Caulaincourt, who all recommended abdication, though they probably saw it was too late to preserve the throne to his son. Berthier drew up a formal deed of abdication in favour of the young Napoleon, with Maria Louisa as Regent, and the Emperor signed it. He made a point of Ney and Macdonald going back with Caulaincourt to Paris. "He does not love me," he said of Macdonald, "but he is an honest man, and for that reason his voice will have more weight than any other with Alexander." The commissioners arrived in Paris on the evening of the 4th, and Caulaincourt succeeded in speaking a few moments to the Czar before the council, where he was going to present the abdication in due form. "You arrive very late," said Alexander. "Sire," said Caulaincourt, "it has not depended upon me. Surely your Majesty's disposition has not changed?" "No; but events have proceeded so quickly that what was possible yesterday is not to-day." "But, Sire," said Caulaincourt, "I return the bearer of Napoleon's abdication in favour of the King of Rome. Ney and Macdonald accompany me as his Majesty's plenipotentiaries. All formalities are filled up; nothing can now obstruct the treaty." "When I told you to make haste," said Alexander, "I had my reasons. I knew the earth shook under your feet. When you set out Napoleon's attitude was still imposing. But to-day it is no longer the same. The Senate has deposed him. The adhesion of the generals is arriving from all parts. They hide the eagerness they feel to break their connection with an unfortunate Sovereign under the appearance of a necessary submission to the orders of the chief body of the State, and contrive to join their personal interests with legality. But this displays a great accomplished fact.

Such is man." "Sire," said Caulaincourt, "those shameful exceptions find no echo in the heart of the army, which is devoted to its master." "You still deceive yourself," said Alexander; "at this very moment Fontainebleau is uncovered, and the person of the Emperor Napoleon is at our discretion." "What, Sire," cried Caulaincourt, "are there more traitors?" "People," said Alexander, "who are desirous of promoting another cause than yours have now the power to do it. The camp of Essonnes is raised; Marmont has sent in his adhesion, and that of his corps d'armée. The troops which compose it are in full march on Versailles." "I would not," writes Caulaincourt, "abuse a Frenchman to a foreigner. I replied, 'Sire, I can only hope for the magnanimity of your Majesty.'"

"The abdication waited too long," said Alexander. "In politics three days are three centuries, and I must be guided by circumstances. While Napoleon was supported by his army collected to march on Paris, powerful considerations balanced the arguments for the Imperial cause; but Fontainebleau is no longer an imposing military position, and there are now below persons of influence who have sent in their submission. During your absence discussions were raised on the subject of the Regency; something had transpired as to our interview, or Napoleon made some revelations at Fontainebleau, (that was only too true, said Caulaincourt), for they knew the whole affair and your project, and all were stirred by it. Talleyrand, D'Albert, De Jaucourt, the Abbés Louis and De Montesquieu took up the question of the Regency, and fought against it with all their might. M. de Pradt declared neither Bonaparte nor his family had any party; all France was Royalist, and demanded the Bourbons. I made some observations. Then General Desolles, addressing me personally, said solemnly, 'Sire, you promised not to treat with Bonaparte, and on the faith of that assurance we have not hesitated to declare him deposed and to recall the Bourbons. Now to proclaim the Regency is to decree the continuation of the men of the Imperial régime, and in that case the members of the Provisional Government must request the allied Powers for an asylum in their States.'"

"The Emperor," said Caulaincourt, "betrayed, abandoned to the conqueror, by those men who ought to make a rampart of their bodies and their swords for him. It is horrible, Sire!" Alexander observed it was a lesson to all Sovereigns. He pitied Caulaincourt, and forbore to remind him that a usurper, or one who owes his throne to the will of the people, has no cause to complain when those who gave it choose to take it away. Like members of the English House of Commons, they must please their constituents, and if they refuse to identify themselves with the interests of the place they have chosen to represent, they have no reason to accuse the voters of ingratitude when, as the natural consequence, they are deprived of their seats.

Shortly afterwards Caulaincourt and Macdonald entered the council-room. The Czar, with rather a careworn air, was talking to the King of Prussia in the window. A senator, Bournonville, stood a little behind them. He had persuaded the King to reject the Regency. The discussion seemed animated. On the arrival of the commissioners, the two Sovereigns seated themselves at a table in the centre of the room. "I remit to the Emperor Alexander," said Caulaincourt, "in the name of the Emperor Napoleon, the act of abdication in favour of his son, the King of Rome, and of the Empress Maria Louisa as Regent." Frederick William coldly took the initiative, and answered in measured terms, that "subsequent events did not permit the Powers to treat with Napoleon. France had manifested her wish for the return of her old Sovereigns from all parts; the first corporation of the State, supported by the assent of its fellow-citizens, had declared him to have forfeited his throne. The allied Powers did not choose to mix themselves up in the affairs of the French Government, and, contrary to the declaration of the Senate, to recognize Napoleon's right to dispose of the throne of France."*

Macdonald said Napoleon had still an army to assert the rights of his son if they chose to use it, ready to shed the last drop of their blood for him. Alexander answered, this argument came too late; and the next morning his fellow commissioner Ney sent in his allegiance to the Provisional Government. Napoleon received them with most undignified rage. He would not abdicate; he would put himself at the

* Souvenirs de Caulaincourt.

head of his armies, and would rather run the risk of any calamity than submit to it. He tore up the declaration of the Senate, trampled it under his feet, and called for maps and plans of the district of the Loire. He even promised four hours' pillage to a corps he reviewed if they would recapture Paris.* "I have 25,000 of the Guards and Cuirassiers at Fontainebleau; I will also bring 30,000 men from Lyons, 18,000 under Grenier from Italy, 15,000 under Suchet, and 40,000 with Soult. They form in all 130,000, and with them I am still erect." Oudinot reminded him he had abdicated. "Ah! but under conditions," said Napoleon. "Soldiers do not understand conditions," said Oudinot; "you cannot depend on the troops." He was at last induced to sign his name with an agitated hand to another deed, renouncing the throne "of France and Italy," for himself and his heirs, "the allied Powers having declared that the Emperor Napoleon is the sole obstacle to a general peace in Europe." "But observe," he said to his marshals, "it is with a conquering enemy I treat, and not with the Provisional Government, in whom I see nothing but a set of factious traitors."

The abdication was unconditional, and Alexander, considering that Napoleon had thrown himself on his mercy, resolved he should not be disappointed. "I have been his friend," he said, "and I will willingly be his advocate;" and the terms he exacted for him from the Provisional Government, and inserted in the treaty of peace, were more generous than the most devoted of the fallen Emperor's partisans could expect. He thought nothing would be more fatal to the future peace of France than a host of Bonapartists loose about the country, reduced from opulence to poverty, and that he had conquered a right to arrange the affairs of France as was most conducive to her peace, and consequently to that of Europe. He required no indemnity for the enormous losses Russia sustained through the war; and as his allies, except England, had all helped France to inflict these losses, and merely deserted her at last, when Russia appeared the most formidable of the two he did not see they had any right to demand a payment for their assistance in regaining their own independence. France also deserved to be taxed to support the family

* Châteaubriand.

she had chosen to maintain so long as it was crowned with success; and even if he was unwise in his liberality towards the Bonapartes, and in depending on Napoleon's word of honour, so often broken, he at least could not be accused of injustice. At the council held on the subject, he said that in the income settled on Napoleon they must enable him to remunerate his military establishment and pension his servants. When his future residence was discussed, the French councillors wished him to be sent far away to St. Helena, Corfu, or Corsica; but Alexander decided the Island of Elba should be ceded to him to enjoy during his lifetime as a sovereignty, and knowing well enough that no loss would touch him so deeply as his Imperial title, he decreed that he should be permitted to keep it.* In addition, he was to receive 2,500,000 francs, or 100,000*l.*, yearly from the revenue of the French Government; and 2,000,000 francs were settled on his mother and other members of his family, to descend to his heirs. Josephine was to have an income of 40,000*l.*, and retain her estate of Malmaison. The furniture of the various Imperial palaces and the crown jewels reverted to France, but all other movable property belonging to the Bonapartes was to remain in their hands. Napoleon was to leave for Elba on April 20th, escorted to the coast by 1500 of the Old Guard, and might keep 400 soldiers to form a body guard, and a corvette. This arrangement was made without England's agreement, or any communication with the ministers of Austria and Prussia, not yet arrived from Dijon; and when it was ascertained that Maria Louisa intended to separate from her husband, Alexander assigned her the sovereignty of Parma and Placentia, to revert to her son. She remained at Rambouillet, to Napoleon's mortification, as he expected her to join him at Fontainebleau.

"What must the allied Sovereigns think," he said, "of such an end to the glories of my reign!" He had kept poison by him during the retreat from Russia, lest he should fall into the hands of the Cossacks. On the night of April 15th, after con-

---

* At St. Helena Napoleon pretended that Elba was his own choice, and that he was allowed to select a principality. This was utterly untrue. Alexander did not give him his choice, but proposed it for him; and Lord Castlereagh strongly protested against it. Napoleon wanted Corfu.

versing upon his resolution not to survive his fall, he pretended to have taken a dose, hoping to put an end to himself, but afterwards said time had weakened its effect, and it was not the will of Providence he should die. Judging by his ordinary charlatanism, and his constant quotation of the ancient Romans, even to the extent of causing his own bust to be modelled from that of Galba, and encouraging a supposed classical style in the dress of the ladies of his Court, it seems probable that he merely made a feint of destroying himself, so that his enemies should not say, after all his boasting, he had less courage than a Roman, and preferred humiliation to death. Both his own attendants, and Colonel Campbell, Count Shuvalov, General Kohler, and Count Truchsees, the allied commissioners, bore witness that on his way to Elba he was in constant fear lest they should have received orders to rid the world of him for ever. No scene in his life was more painful than his journey to Fréjus, and the want of firmness he displayed astonished his foreign escort. He who had never been known to shed a tear for those on whom he had heaped calamities, was capable of shedding many for his own misfortunes. He made so many trivial excuses to procure a delay, that they began to fear lest he should compel them to use force. The mob, as he advanced towards the south of France, exhibited a threatening attitude. At Orange, Lyons, and Avignon he was assailed with cries of "A bas le tyran, le coquin, le mauvais gueux, Vive les Alliés, Vive le Roi!" Even the military cast invectives upon him. At Orgon a figure dressed in the French uniform was displayed covered with blood, bearing the inscription, "Such shall be sooner or later the fate of the tyrant;" and women pursued the carriage from the post-house, one screaming out that her father and her husband had been killed at Wagram, another that she had lost two sons at Mojaisk. A man with a wooden leg furiously gesticulated with his crutch, saying he had been crippled at twenty years of age. Another shouted out, "The taxes made a pot of wine cost six sous, and all to furnish the butcheries he calls his wars." They crowded round the vehicle, and Napoleon, pale and trembling, hid himself behind Bertrand. At La Calade the people surrounded the house where he was to pass the night, and with loud execrations demanded his head. He escaped them by getting out of a back window in the middle of the night when the street was clear, and driving to the next post-house, dressed in Kohler's Austrian uniform and Shuvalov's great-coat, with the white cockade in his hat. At another point in his journey he was saved by the exertions of the commissioners. Count Shuvalov rode by the side of the carriage, and asked if they were not ashamed to insult a defenceless man, now at their mercy, who had ceased to be dangerous. "It would be below the French," he said, "to take any other vengeance than contempt." The people applauded, and Napoleon afterwards thanked him. The Prussian commissioner also remonstrated with the crowd at Avignon. "Leave him," he said; "it is better the tyrant should live to be punished by his repentance and his regrets, which will give him a thousand deaths." However, when the danger* was past, Napoleon appeared cheerful again, talked of his plans for dethroning Murat and attacking the King of Sardinia, and tried to mortify Shuvalov by referring to Austerlitz. At Luc he saw his sister Pauline, and on April 28th sailed in an English vessel for Elba, begging to be conveyed by this rather than the French ship waiting to take him. He arrived at his new territory May 4th, and having carefully ascertained that the people were inclined to welcome him, he made a public entrance into the town of Porto Ferrajo on the following day. The ladies who had interfered with the domestic happiness of Maria Louisa in the Tuileries shortly joined him, and a crowd of tourists, particularly the English, favoured the new sovereignty with their visits. Always eager for notice, Napoleon welcomed them, and, though speaking of himself as one politically dead, probably to put them off their guard, he followed his old system of trying to sow seeds of dissension and mistrust between allies. To Englishmen he praised England, contradicting former assertions in every word. She was the only nation he respected; the country he should have always preferred as an ally, though foreign intrigues and untoward circumstances had made them foes. He had set the same trap with a similar bait for all the great Powers in Europe, yet there were Englishmen ready to

* Châteaubriand, Lamartine, Duchesse d'Abrantès, Count Waldburg, Truchsees, Count Munster.

fall into it once more. To Lord Ebrington he insinuated that Alexander was false and insincere, a Greek of the Lower Empire, evidently wishing to establish a want of confidence in Russia.* He meant to devote himself exclusively to literature and science, though he appears not to have paid the slightest attention to either during the ten months he lived in Elba. He had not the philosophy to resign himself to circumstances, and had led too active a life to take up a sedentary amusement when still in the prime of health and vigour. The island was only sixty miles round, and his superfluous energies expended themselves in perpetually drilling his body guard, over-legislating for his subjects, whom he soon loaded with taxes to supply his extravagance, and travelling from one of his Imperial residences to another (for he established himself in four at different points of his small dominions), and the strictest etiquette was rigidly maintained. On the Empress positively refusing to follow him, Josephine talked of removing to Elba, but she died before she had written to him on the subject.

Nothing surprised Alexander more than the flight of all Napoleon's servants, even his valet, before he left Fontainebleau, with everything valuable they could carry away; many to seek an appointment in the new Court. He said to Caulaincourt, "I believe if we had wished to establish Kutuzov on the throne of France, the people would have cried, 'Long live Kutuzov.'"

Although the Czar's allies were most anxious to make peace with Napoleon, both at Frankfort and Châtillon, on terms which would have left him on the throne and enlarged the ancient boundaries of France, they were now displeased with the

* It is evident from the line of flattery and conciliation which he pursued with regard to the English of every degree from the moment he set foot on board an English vessel to embark for Elba, and from the offers he made to England directly he landed in France after his escape, that it had throughout been his intention to detach the English from the Alliance, and not to remain in Elba longer than he could possibly help. As early as September 21st, 1814, Sir Neil Campbell writes from Elba to say that Napoleon has embarked for the Isle of Pia Nosa with several ladies of his household, and means to stay there a few days. He had annexed the island, which was three miles long and one broad, and was colonizing it. "It afforded him opportunities of receiving persons from the Continent without the means of detecting it."—Supplementary Despatches, &c., of Wellington, vol. ix.

very favourable conditions exacted from the prostrate nation, and did not see that any distinction should be made between France under Napoleon and France under a national government or Louis. Yet Alexander clearly had a right to dictate the terms, as the march on Paris was entirely due to him; particularly when those terms were what he had always held should be demanded of her to procure the peace of Europe, at a time when his colleagues thought they were unnecessarily severe. The handsome maintenance for the Bonapartes was especially censured, and Castlereagh only acceded provisionally on the part of Great Britain to the treaty signed between Napoleon and the allied Powers April 1st, by which he renounced the throne of France and Italy for ever, for himself and his heirs, and accepted Elba in its place. The treaty was signed by Caulaincourt, Macdonald, Ney, Metternich, Nesselrode, and Hardenberg. Castlereagh objected that it recognized Napoleon's title of Emperor, which England had never yet done, and gave him an independent sovereignty too close to Italy, and within a few days' sail of France. He did not consider Napoleon could be treated as a man of any feeling of honour, but merely as a condemned criminal, too debased to be controlled by anything but force, and the result unfortunately proved he was right.

Sir Charles Stewart announced the arrangement to Lord Castlereagh in a letter dated Paris, April 5th, 1814: "The conference of the marshals with the Emperor of Russia, collectively and separately, led to the determination of offering Bonaparte the Island of Elba, &c. Caulaincourt and Ney were very violent and strong in their entreaties for a Regency, Bonaparte having abdicated with that view. The Emperor of Russia was, however, firm, and gained Macdonald, Marmont having been already secured." He also says, the offer of Elba was much disapproved by Talleyrand and the French Government, and the more so the longer it was under consideration.

Count Munster, writing April 20th, from Paris to the Prince Regent, says, "I venture the belief that, if the ministers of England, Austria, and Prussia had been present at the capture of Paris, they would not have agreed to the declaration made in the name of the Allies by Alexander on March 31st (viz., to preserve old France in its integrity). We shall probably have to regret for long the consequences which it may produce." He calls it " ill-advised philanthropy which allowed the tyrant, who, possessing a very powerful party, retains ample means of injuring us, to escape." He describes the Legitimists as feeble, and the Bonapartists both strong and active, the public treasury empty, and 300,000,000 of pressing debts. The two last campaigns cost Napoleon 15,000,000,000 francs. Fifty thousand officers in France all complaining of arrears of pay due to them, and the want of present means of livelihood. " The public will complain of a deficit which, though caused by Bonaparte, will only be felt under Louis XVIII. Napoleon has carried his want of delicacy to the point of haggling over his wines and the carriages he has left. The evils inseparable from war have exasperated the people, and the Parisians, in spite of their levity, see with regret the bivouacs of the Allies, which disfigure all the avenues of the capital. The Duke of Cambridge, as Governor of Hanover, must be on his guard when the French under Davoust cross his territory from Hamburg, and the return of the Swedish troops will be a new calamity for that State." Again he writes, May 5th, " We heard yesterday of Napoleon's journey; nothing could have lowered him more than the pusillanimity he displayed. Now he speaks only of his desire to proceed to England, and he said to Colonel Campbell, that in the Island of Elba he should regard himself as an English subject."*

* Munster's Political Sketches, 1814-67.

CHAPTER II.

1814.

ALEXANDER IN PARIS AND LONDON.

ÆTAT. 36.

THE hireling flying " because he is a hireling, and careth not for the sheep," was illustrated by Napoleon's family, who obtained their immense wealth and their only claim to rank and dignities in France, yet in her hour of danger showed no sympathy for the country which had shed its blood to procure them crowns and riches. She was not their native land, but like the goldfields of Australia or California to the English labourer, who carries the treasure he has amassed in the colonies to spend where he can best display his new importance. They had no regrets for the tarnished glory of the nation when compelled, after presumptuous boasting, to yield in complete submission to its foreign foes. They merely thought of securing the fortunes their luxurious mode of living rendered indispensable to their comfort. The large sums Napoleon hoarded in the Tuileries for his personal use in case of disaster disappeared in the hands of his brothers and himself. Jerome fled from Orleans to Switzerland with a great amount of public money. Beauharnais transmitted 400,000 francs also of public money to Napoleon when at Elba, and Madame la Mère had been saving for years in case of family reverses. Joseph left Paris, though intrusted with its defence, and fled to Blois, where he tried to persuade Maria Louisa to accompany him, but on hearing she was resolved to remain till she had seen her father, he escaped to Switzerland. The ex-King of Holland had preceded him in the same track, and Madame la Mère and Cardinal Fesch went to Rome. Josephine also left Malmaison for a more distant estate at Navarre, where she was joined by her daughter Hortense. Like the rest, her chief anxiety was lest she should lose her income and private property. Yet they could accuse the brave defenders of Paris, and those who had stood out last in opposition to the Allies, of treason and corruption.

Bernadotte had advanced as far as Nancy, but retired again into Belgium before the peasants who, following Napoleon's order, were arming against the invaders. He left the Comte d'Artois protected by only a few Russian and Prussian convalescents, who might have incurred some danger if the capture of Paris had not calmed the insurrectionists. As soon as he heard of it he hastened to share in the triumph. "It is quite certain," writes Munster to George IV., April 27th, "the Prince of Sweden has not contributed, as he was bound by his engagements, to the attainment of the great end we have now attained, I venture to say, in opposition to his wishes. It is proved positively by the French officers set at liberty by him to make partisans for himself in the interior of France, as well as by intercepted letters (amongst others, by a letter from General Maison, in the possession of Marshal Wrede)." The Prince arrived in Paris at the end of the second week in April, 1814, and at an audience with Count Munster begged him "to commend his interests to the Prince Regent." Marmont told a diplomatist at Vienna, that for some time a secret correspondence was carried on between Napoleon and Bernadotte, through General Maison and others; Bernadotte having been first detached from the cause of the Allies by Napoleon's threat that he should never inherit the throne of Sweden. It was his dearest wish to establish a royal dynasty in his family, and believing Napoleon's good fortune would not finally desert him, he caught eagerly at the proposals held out as a bribe, and stipulated for further advantages if he went over to the French. The extreme watchfulness of the Allies, and their success, prevented him from declaring himself; but he abstained from aiding Napoleon's enemies, and helped him by indirect means. General Maison's baggage was intercepted by some Russian troops, and his correspondence with Bernadotte fell into the hands of the Emperor. As soon as the Prince arrived in Paris, Alexander sent for him, and taxed him with his treachery to the Allies. Bernadotte at first denied it, but when the written proofs were produced he was confounded, and owned the truth. Alexander told him he felt that even the nominal adhesion of Sweden to the common cause had been of service, so he would forget his conduct and destroy all recollection of it. He threw the papers at once into the fire, and the Prince received the promised reward, though the payment of his subsidy was opposed in England. The Emperor never referred to the subject again; but Bernadotte was less discreet, and gave an account of their interview not only to Marmont, but to several other adherents of the fallen dynasty.

Francis arrived in Paris on April 15th from Dijon, and, after an interview with Alexander, went to see his daughter at Rambouillet. Alexander had already sent his aide-de-camp, General Shuvalov, to escort her to Orleans, where she wished to go, and she was completely deserted by her own suite; but hearing all was quiet in Paris, she returned to Rambouillet, and absolutely refused to follow her husband. "History," says Lamartine,* "will blame her, but nature will pity her. She was too unaffected to feign love where she only felt obedience, terror, and resignation." Her married life had been far from happy, and though her disposition was sufficiently cold to be in some way consoled by the Imperial dignity, still the aristocratic pride of an Austrian princess felt it was the dignity of a parvenu Court which surrounded her, and not that of the descendant of St. Louis. " Her husband's evenings were passed with the young Polish countess Walewski, whom he had carried away from her husband and her country, while Maria Louisa employed her solitude in painting German views, in singing German songs, and sighing for the private life and domestic happiness of a German hearth." And the Countess Walewski was by no means her only rival. The neighbourhood of Josephine also annoyed her. Napoleon still consulted his first wife about his public affairs, and often went to see her. It was a Mahometan arrangement she had hardly contemplated, and she had never quite got over his rough greeting on their first interview. On receiving her father she gave him the warmest welcome, but possessed sufficient sense of her

---

* " Perhaps," he adds, " in becoming the wife of a soldier of fortune, she thought that she should obtain a husband far removed from the vices of the old Courts of Europe; on the contrary, Napoleon permitted himself an almost unequalled licence." No one who has read Napoleon's remarks on women, as given by Las Cases (June, 1816) and others of his biographers, could blame Maria Louisa for her want of attachment to him. He always advocated polygamy.

situation as the wife of the fallen Sovereign to object, or to feign to object, to receive Alexander, to whom she said he owed his destruction. Francis overcame her scruples, as the Czar was expected to drive over to Rambouillet early the next morning, and he accordingly arrived. She greeted him very coldly, but "he was so agreeable, and so much at his ease," writes one of her ladies, "that we were almost tempted to believe no serious event had happened in Paris. He asked to see the child, whom he kissed, and took on his knee;" while Francis, with a grandfather's pride, admired the little prince's curly hair, and during the visit talked chiefly of the boy's sharp remarks, the age at which he cut his teeth, and other interesting details of his infancy. Alexander returned to Paris the same morning, but Francis remained with his daughter for a day or two, and she soon left for Vienna, after showing very plainly, particularly to Hortense, who had joined her, that she did not wish for any more of the society of her husband's family. The ex-Queen of Holland wrote from Navarre to one of her ladies, Mdlle. Cochelet, who had remained in Paris, respecting her future prospects. "I do not doubt," she said, "that the Emperor of Russia will be generous to me. I have heard much good of him, even from the Emperor Napoleon, but if I was formerly curious to be acquainted with him, I do not wish to see him now. Is he not our conqueror?" Mdlle. Cochelet answered, that Alexander was the resource of all in trouble. "He conducts himself so well that he inspires universal esteem, and we forget the conqueror, only seeing the benefactor. His conduct is admirable. He only sees those people who require to see him on business, and for the necessary transaction of public affairs. Women cannot tax him with seeking their society." Talleyrand tried to interest Alexander for Hortense, telling him she was the only one of the Imperial family he esteemed. She was known to be an unhappy wife, and when the Bonaparte family was no longer in power many stories of the past were circulated about Queen Hortense. Prince Leopold of Saxe-Coburg, Constantine's aide-de-camp, had formerly received much kindness from her and from Josephine, who helped him to avoid entering the French service a short time before the Russian campaign. He was anxious to serve them with Alexander, who heard what he had to say, and told him he esteemed Josephine, Eugene, and Hortense because their conduct towards Napoleon was superior to that of many of his courtiers. He sent a message to Josephine, requesting her to return to Malmaison, where Madame Junot found her oppressed with fears for her fortune, and dreading lest she should be obliged to leave France; but a day or two afterwards Alexander called upon her and reassured her. Hortense hearing of this visit, requested an interview with him. He advised her to stay in France to console her mother, instead of settling in Switzerland or in Martinique. In a second visit Madame Junot found Josephine quite cheerful again, full of her interview with Alexander, and hardly able to say enough in his praise. She had been advised to write a humble letter to Louis, throwing herself at his feet, and asking his mercy, and consulted the Czar on the subject. He advised her to do nothing of the sort. "You will only lower yourself," he said. "Your maintenance will be settled by the treaty, so you have nothing further to fear;" and he composed a letter for her to write to the King, which expressed sufficient gratitude without servility. He told Constantine she reminded him very much of the Empress Catherine, both in her voice and appearance, for Josephine had become very stout in her old age, her colour was high, and she was threatened with apoplexy. The King of Prussia announced he should bring his two sons to dine with her, and she wrote to Alexander, requesting him to come and help to entertain them with his brothers Nicholas and Michael. Hortense also joined the party, and her two little sons, Napoleon Louis and Louis Napoleon, were in the drawing-room with their governess when the visitors arrived. The boys stared at the tall stature of the foreign princes as they entered the room. Alexander was fond of children, and after talking to the ex-Empress, spoke good-humouredly to the boys, who informed him when they were grown up they meant to be soldiers, and to fight against the Prussians and Cossacks. The King of Prussia was not inclined to be friendly with any one, old or young, who bore the name of Napoleon, and never very talkative, looked at them in moody silence as they chattered to the Emperor; so their governess, afraid lest they should say something more displeasing to him, drew them away. The younger one, afterwards Napoleon III., hearing that Alexander was a generous enemy, without whom they would have nothing more in the world, slipped a ring into his hand the next time he called, which the Czar promised to keep as long as he lived.

That dinner party at Malmaison included the representatives of the chief power of Europe for three-quarters of a century. Besides Alexander, and Josephine, her husband's good genius and the promoter of his early fortunes, there was Nicholas, a tall stripling, the future heir of his brother's greatness, the only Sovereign in Europe who protested in 1830 against the expulsion of Hortense and her sons from Rome, and whom Louis Napoleon himself styles the model ruler in his "Idées Napoléoniques." Little did Alexander think that the boy on his knee was destined to be the first to break the peace he had inaugurated at so much cost in Europe, that he might "repair the road to Moscow;" and as little did the Czar imagine that the first empire on which he would direct the power of the restored dynasty would be Russia. But the avenger stood by in the young Prince William of Prussia, the first Emperor of restored Germany, a stalwart youth, who, as only a younger son, was perhaps the least considered of the party present. Were the victories in the Crimea and the forts of Sebastopol, still uncaptured after a year's siege, a sufficient return to France for the calamities of Sedan, the loss of Alsace and Lorraine, the Emperor of Germany proclaimed at Versailles, the second exile of the Bonapartists, and the second capture of Paris? The policy and bloodshed of the First Empire during nearly fourteen years, only ended in leaving Russia supreme in Europe. The policy of the Second Empire, equally resulted in impoverishing France, and led to the consolidation of Germany, and the great exaltation of Prussia's political position in Europe.

It is often said that Josephine died of a broken heart,* but

---

* "The death of the Empress Josephine," says La Valette, "was the last gift of her astonishing fate. Her extravagance was such that she was always embarrassed, and if the new Government had found it difficult to pay the pension settled on her by the treaty of April 11th, it would have placed her in great difficulties. She was neither high-minded nor well-informed, but possessed sound judgment, cunning, an inimitable grace, and her Creole pronunciation added to her charms."

she had, apparently, quite recovered her cheerfulness, except now and then when some act of the new Government affronted her; for Napoleon's overthrow did not affect her so much as their divorce. Alexander saw her again on May 4th, when she gave him an antique cameo, presented to her by Pius VII. on the day of her coronation, and engraved with the heads of Philip and Alexander of Macedon. He at first refused to deprive her of it, pointing out a cup of common porcelain, painted with her portrait, which he said he should prefer. He observed she did not look well, and on his return to Paris sent Dr. Wylie to see her. The malady passed off, but ten days later she was attacked by a malignant sore throat, which caused her death on May 29th. Alexander called to inquire after her that morning, and at her request was shown up into her room, where she was attended by Eugene and Hortense; but he did not stay more than a few moments, as he saw she had not many hours to live. He sent an aide-de-camp to represent him at her funeral, and Napoleon did not conceal his annoyance, both at this attention and at the part he had taken in consoling her decline.

The army of Northern Italy yielded to the Allies, and the country was invested by the Austrian army after the fall of Paris, so Beauharnais came to France to obtain some spoil in the general settlement of Europe. The wife of Jerome, Catherine of Würtemberg, was left in Paris, where Alexander called on her, as she was his first cousin, and promised her an escort to the frontier. Her father wished to separate her from her husband; but for the first time since her marriage she had maternal hopes, and preferred to join him in Switzerland. She received a passport signed by Alexander, and Talleyrand provided her with a detachment of French cavalry. On the road their captain robbed her of her money and jewels, and she wrote in the greatest indignation to her father, intimating that it was the fault of Alexander, who was much irritated, and ordered immediate proceedings to be taken against the offender. Talleyrand protected the robber captain, on the ground that the jewels were partly public property, and were restored by him to the Crown. The affair was not concluded till 1818, when the offender, Maubreuil, was condemned to five years' imprisonment and a fine of 500 francs, but he escaped to England. In the absence of the Bourbons and the Bonapartes, Alexander was Sovereign of Paris, and petitions for situations in the new government, pensions, and even offices at the palace, flowed in from all quarters to such an extent that he inserted an advertisement in the *Moniteur*, requesting the petitioners to address themselves to the Provisional Government. Still no small part of his time was occupied in attending to complaints. He treated the French people with so much delicacy that they began to forget they were conquered, and were inclined to claim as a right the privileges conceded to them by the excessive liberality of their enemies. One of the marshals asked what rank his wife would have in the new Court, and expressed surprise that the army was not consulted as to the Constitution. Alexander said he gave orders to the military, but did not receive any from them. The widow of Junot, the Duchesse d'Abrantès, sent to request an audience with him. She was still in deep mourning for her husband, so Alexander, being aware of her case, which was a very sad one, returned for answer he would call on her. Junot had been publicly censured and disgraced for an alleged military error by Napoleon, who, when he made an unsuccessful plan, attributed it on system to some officer, and obliged him to bear the penalty. He had served in all the wars of the Republic and the Empire, and was severely wounded more than once in the head, which, added to mortified vanity, affected his brain, and he destroyed himself. Madame Junot boasted that her family, though impoverished, belonged to the race of Comneni, but her only property was an estate torn from the Crown lands of Prussia. The Emperor arrived punctually; and the Duchess, astonished at his condescension, presented herself with her children at the top of the staircase. "Sire," said she, "these children have lost their father, and in losing him they have lost all. They have no fortune if they lose their estates—the price of the blood of their unhappy father." The Emperor led her to an armchair, and seated himself on a small one opposite; but as she offered to rise, he said, "Remain where you are: I must place myself so that I can hear you well. You know I am deaf. First, what do you want with me? You must explain your business." The Duchess related it. "Write a note," he said, "detailing everything, and I will give it myself to the King of Prussia." He looked at Junot's portrait, and listened to his exploits and devotion to his master, telling her Napoleon had been ill served both by Savary and Maret. The first had tampered with his own (Alexander's) attendants, and carried on the most extraordinary proceedings. Since he came to Paris, Savary had asked for an audience twenty times, but he had refused to see him. He could not refuse one to his wife, who had also urged it, and he was to see her the next day; though if it was to ask him to excuse the Duc d'Enghien's death* to the Bourbons, that would be impossible. During the conversation Alexander rose and reseated himself continually, and walked up and down. He had only just driven from the door when Savary appeared, having concealed himself in another room during the interview. She told him what the Emperor said about the police in his palace. Savary was very curious to know how he had discovered it. "I must have been betrayed," he said. After some conversation they arranged a plan by which Napoleon, who was then still at Fontainebleau, should be brought into Paris, to her house; and, on some pretext or other, Alexander should be induced to call there again, and suddenly confronted with him, in the hope that he might yet be brought round to his cause. There was no surveillance, and passports were easy enough to obtain. Napoleon might be disguised. Alexander would refuse a formal demand for an interview, but he was so accessible that Napoleon might easily be introduced into his presence before he was aware of it. Savary said Napoleon would gladly embrace any opportunity of making an impression upon him. A letter was despatched to the ex-Emperor, proposing this scheme; but before it reached Fontainebleau he had signed the treaty of April 11th, and formally abdicated his throne.

Hardenberg called on Madame Junot to tell her that, "at the pressing solicitations of the Emperor of Russia, the King had consented to let her keep the Castle of Achen, but he had added the condition that her sons should he naturalized as Prussian subjects; and he brought papers for her to sign with that object. She was most indignant, and preferred to lose

* Savary had been principally concerned in it. See ante.

the estates; and relates it as a dishonourable act on the part of the King and Minister; though, as they were extorted from Prussia by conquest, the same law now restored them to their ancient master; and the Allies might have rewarded their own officers in a similar way, by grants of estates from the crown lands of France. Even Hardenberg's private library and family mansion had been wantonly sacked and destroyed by the French, who respected no private property in Prussia in 1806. Alexander thought the King should have given her the alternative of a pecuniary compensation; but he felt it difficult to interfere further in a matter concerning Prussia only, and contented himself with offering her a residence in Russia. "You would be well received, madame," he said; "and might convince your countrymen that we are not such barbarians as they commonly seem to suppose."

On April 3rd Alexander and the King of Prussia visited the Opera, when they were received with thunders of applause. A melodrama called the Triumph of Trajan was played in their honour, and for many subsequent nights. These verses were also sung night after night at all the theatres, and warmly cheered:—

> "Vive Alexandre,
> Vive le Roi des Rois!
> Sans nous donner des lois,
> Ce Prince auguste,
> A le triple renom,
> De héros, de juste.
> Et nous rend un Bourbon," &c.

Alexander did not take much pleasure in theatrical performances, and only went to the theatre once more while he was in Paris, and then it was on a State occasion in company with Louis; but his brothers and the King of Prussia constantly resorted to it, the last often going incognito, and indulging in most unusual peals of laughter at the broad wit often displayed on the Parisian stage. Nicholas and Michael were much admired by the Parisians, who called them "the white angels of the north," from their fair complexion and curly hair. They were lodged with their tutors in a part of the Hôtel Infantado; but their mother had permitted them to join the army with great searchings of heart, and with so many injunctions to Alexander, that he only let them visit at Prince Schwartzenberg's and Lord Castlereagh's, except when he accompanied them himself. When Louis entered the capital he had not seen since 1791, he expressed his displeasure to Madame de Cayla at the enthusiasm with which the foreigners were received in Paris. " It would be better," he said, " to observe an impassible reserve without any demonstration. A calm and dignified carriage would have inspired them with respect for the nation, and they would not quit Paris with the idea they have held for the last fifty years, that the French nation is the most frivolous and immoral in the world. You ladies, above all, have exposed yourselves to these reproaches. The Allies in a body have appeared to you so amiable, that there are many rumours not to the advantage of the French ladies." " But, Sire," she answered, " the Parisians wished to show their joy and their gratitude to the Allies for having brought back your Majesty to them. They have freely offered to the Allies what neither the tyrants of the Republic nor the heroes of the empire were able to obtain. Not one of us can regret what she has done for our good friends the Allies."

"The Princes," writes Mdlle. Cochelet, " who were at the head of the allied armies were naturally the principal objects of the Royalist ovation, though they were very indifferent to it. The Emperor of Austria was too much occupied with the future of his daughter and of his grandson; the King of Prussia too serious and too cold; all their coquetries were therefore directed on the young Emperor of Russia. But there also their enthusiasm was ill recompensed. Alexander lived in a retreat which appeared to imply an absolute want of confidence." He said the Royalist ladies " were wearying in their exasperation against the Republicans and Imperialists, and instead of enjoying their triumph, only think of annihilating their enemies. They are hardly sane on the subject."

On Easter-day, April 10th, a service was held for the troops by Alexander's order on the Place de la Concorde, the spot where Louis XVI. was beheaded. Notice was given by placards posted about the streets that salvoes of artillery would be fired when it was ended. The more serious among the French flocked to the ceremony, though it was conducted by a bishop and priests of the Greek Church. The King of Prussia, Schwartzenberg, and other foreign princes, besides the Emperor and Grand Dukes of Russia, were present. The Sovereigns remained uncovered throughout, all alike kneeling, princes and soldiers, when the benediction was pronounced, somewhat to the surprise of the Parisians, who were accustomed to see little reverence and much indifference on the part of their rulers towards religion, even during the old days of the Bourbon dynasty.

The Comte d'Artois was the first of this family to appear in Paris in the quality of Lieutenant-General of the Kingdom[*] till the arrival of the King. The Senate decreed only five days before that "Louis Stanislaus Xavier should be proclaimed King of the French, on condition that he swore to accept and enforce the new constitution." Monsieur made a triumphant entry into Paris, but Alexander, acting as he had done by the King of Prussia at Berlin, gave orders that the allied troops should not appear on his road, that it might look like a national rejoicing; and Lord Castlereagh, with the English mission, were the only foreigners who joined the train. As soon as he was installed in the Tuileries, Alexander visited him and advised him to adopt the constitution in a friendly spirit, as it alone could render the restoration popular and durable. The Royalists attracted the common people in the provinces by proclaiming no more wars, no conscription, and no taxes on the wines. But a concession was necessary to the educated classes; *that* would be found in a constitution; it would also throw the odium of measures, not always agreeable to the masses when retrenchment was necessary and there was so much to restore, upon their representatives rather than on the dynasty succeeding the empire. The country was still in a state of ferment, but the guarantee of a constitution would appease it. The Count answered by vague promises, which, by Alexander's repeated advice, were confirmed in a speech to the Senate; but he knew the disfavour with which it would be regarded by the King. Louis was now a widower, sixty years of age, and very infirm; a man of rather heavy wit, but well informed, a professed freethinker, indolent, and a bon-vivant, though less narrow-minded than many of his race. On taking leave of the Prince Regent he told him his restoration was entirely due to England, which,

[*] April 12th.

though a compliment, produced a painful impression in Russia. They arrived with the old Prince de Condé and the Duc de Bourbon at Compiègne, April 27th, and there the King remained, to avoid meeting Alexander. He was jealous of his popularity, and did not wish to be second in Paris. The Marshals and several deputations at once waited on him, enabling him to act a comedy more gratifying to them than to the attendants who surrounded him when in exile. During his first audience he appeared sinking from age and infirmity, and when his courtiers pressed forward to sustain him he repulsed them, and supported himself by the Marshals, saying, "It is on you, sirs, who have always been Frenchmen, that I shall in future look for strength." Alexander came over to see him in a plain carriage, only attended by Czernichef and one servant, leaving Paris in the middle of the night, sleeping most of the way—a confidence rarely shown by private people on the highways of France at that disturbed period. Louis received him very coldly. He often forgot benefits, but never an injury. He could forget the royal reception he received in Russia, and the princely income Paul settled on him, or that Alexander had given him a home when his life was threatened in Prussia; but he could remember when Paul, at the instigation of Napoleon, ordered him to leave his dominions in mid-winter, and that although Alexander remonstrated with his father on this particular occasion, he was the original promoter of the peace between the Czar and the First Consul of France. He pointedly walked into dinner that evening before three royal visitors, including the Emperor, who took it good-humouredly, only observing to Czernichef, "Even we northern barbarians have learned more politeness."

Before Alexander left Compiègne he tried to persuade Louis to give up his idea of counting his reign from the hour his little nephew died of neglect in the precincts of the Temple, and to recognize the reign of Napoleon. To the Bourbons he was nothing but General Bonaparte, his career was to be wiped out of history. The Czar said, public opinion no longer regarded the traditional rights of the Bourbon blood, or the mysteries of the Divine right of crowns—a doctrine now repudiated, for it had been too often broken through. He advised Louis to consent to reign in virtue of a new title by a voluntary call from the nation, expressed by the Senate, in exchange for a constitution accepted from its hands. Far from such a title being derogatory, it was glorious. Necessity and prudence must induce the King to recognize the existence of the Government which ruled France during twenty-four years. Why antedate his reign? Would not history record the Convention, the Directory, the Consulate, and the Empire? If royal families had their intrigues, nations had as many, and a liberal policy alone could silence them in France. He dwelt on the power and importance of the ambitious Republicans and Bonapartists, who would all be brought over to his cause if they were allowed some participation in the honours and government of the State.

Louis had taken an oath to the constitution granted by his brother—an oath still binding upon him if he counted his reign as unbroken since Louis XVII.; but surrounded by elderly men, he was indignant at receiving counsel from a prince no older than his nephew, the Duc de Berri, who was still sowing his wild oats, and regarded by his uncle as little more than a child. He listened impatiently, and interrupted Alexander several times. "I am astonished to have to recall to an Emperor of Russia that a crown does not belong to subjects. What right has the Senate, the instrument and accomplice of all the violence and falsehoods of a usurper, composed of his most servile and most criminal creatures, to dispose of the crown? Does it belong to the Senate? And if in fact the crown did belong to it, would it offer it freely to a Bourbon? I am too enlightened to attach to the Divine right the meaning superstition formerly attached to it; but this Divine right, only for you as for me a law of good sense, has passed into immovable policy in the hereditary transmission of the right of sovereigns. Till a few days ago I was an infirm old man, an unfortunate exile, reduced for a long time to beg a country and bread from strangers—such I was till a few days ago; but I was the King of France, and this is why your Majesty is here: this is why an entire nation, who only know me by name, has recalled me to the throne of my fathers. Yourself," he added, looking hard at Alexander, "in virtue of what title do you command those millions of men whose armies you brought to deliver my throne and my country?" Alexander refrained from a dispute, but pleaded the weight of circumstances. Yet Louis was still inexorable. "No," he said; "I will not wither the name I bear, or the few days I have to live. I will not buy a changeable opinion with the sacred right of myself and my house. I know I owe to your victorious arms the deliverance of my people; but if these important services put the honour of my crown at your disposal, I would return into exile." Then Alexander mentioned the engagements, half admitted by the Comte d'Artois. Louis did not deny them, but said he could fulfil them by his full and free authority, instead of accepting them as a condition from his subjects. The same day Francis, Frederick William, and Bernadotte arrived, but all their prejudices were in favour of an absolute monarchy. They dined with Louis, and on Francis making rather an untimely remark on the fickleness of Frenchmen, Bernadotte said: "Make yourself feared, Sire, and they will love you; only think of honour and appearances with them. Have a velvet glove on an iron hand."

Talleyrand received from the Senate the charter to present to the King, who answered, "If I accepted a constitution in the session where I swore to observe it, you would be seated, and I should remain standing."* He hoped to wear out Alexander's patience, and there was as much negotiation on the subject as had opened the gates of Paris. Talleyrand privately supported his opposition, as he hoped to be virtually supreme in the royal councils; and in spite of a promise to Alexander, day after day passed and it was still withheld. At last the Czar said he had irrevocably fixed his departure from France for the end of the month, and the charter must be accepted by the King before he left, as the Russian troops would otherwise remain. It was proclaimed the next morning, and Louis, as he signed it, observed with happy tact that it was his gift to the nation. Alexander mingled incognito with the crowd to see the procession on the King's public entry into Paris, and kept his own troops out of sight. "The National Guard," writes Count Munster, "shouted 'Vive le Roi;' the

* The very fact that Napoleon, on his return from Elba, found it necessary to promise to maintain the constitution, showed how acceptable it was to the nation at large.

troops of the line preserved a gloomy silence. In the evening (May 31st) the town was badly illuminated; however, they say it was no better in Bonaparte's time. The manner in which the King extricated himself from the constitution is generally approved."

Madame de Staël returned to Paris among a flock of royalist and republican exiles in the wake of the Allies. "As I approached it," she wrote to the Duchess of Saxe-Weimar, "Germans, Russians, Cossacks, Bashkirs were to be seen on all sides. The discipline maintained prevents them from doing any harm, except the mental oppression we could not help feeling. I entered the city as if in a painful dream. I esteemed the strangers who had given us freedom, I admired them; yet to see Paris occupied by them, the Tuileries and the Louvre guarded by troops to whom our history, our great men were less known than the last Khan of Tartary, was indeed a grief."*

* "The Czar," says her biographer, "more than either of the other Sovereigns, showed a chivalrous spirit towards France. Far from being disposed to pride himself on his success, the religious spirit of the young autocrat saw a lesson of Providence in the event which expiated our victory and inflicted humiliations upon us in our turn, and he showed a courtesy and politeness of which the extraordinary delicacy was deeply felt by the people of Paris." Madame de Staël had thought Napoleon invincible, and that the whole world must submit at last. Alexander held no such superstition. "The means he employs are most human," he often said, "but he has never been honestly opposed on land except by Russia." "Far from Alexander's merit being exaggerated by flattery," continues Madame de Staël, "I should almost say they did not render him justice, because he undergoes, like all friends of liberty, the disfavour attached to that opinion in what is called good European society. They are never weary of attributing his political views to personal calculation, as if in our days disinterested sentiments could no longer enter the human heart. It would cost me much to own that the overthrow of Bonaparte was due to Alexander, who decided contrary to advice to march on Paris, if he had not conducted himself generously towards France. I have talked several times with him at St. Petersburg and in Paris at the moment of his reverses and of his triumph. Equally simple and calm in both situations, his mind, penetrating, just, and wise, has never belied itself. His conversation was utterly unlike an ordinary official conversation—no insipid questions, no reciprocal embarrassment. His conduct in the war was as brave as it was humane, and his own was the only life he exposed without reflection.". . . . "Thanks to his enlightenment," she writes a few years later, "all possible ameliorations are being gradually accomplished in Russia. But there is nothing more absurd than the remarks we hear from those who dread his lights. This Emperor, so much praised by the friends of liberty, why does he not establish at home the constitutional régime he recommends to other countries? It is one of the thousand-and-one tricks of the enemies of human rights to try and pre-

Alexander was much struck with the contrast between the restored Bourbons, the emigrant nobility, and the people they were called upon to govern after a separation of twenty-four years: yet when the Senate and municipalities had once greeted Louis as their king, they became his obsequious slaves, too thankful that their former disloyalty should be forgotten to make any attempt to assert the popular rights; and the courtiers of Napoleon, whose birth would never have entitled them to a place in the household of Louis XVI., now felt gratified and exalted by admission to an audience with his heir. Count Beugnot, the new Minister of the Interior, owns to this sentiment, and that he felt on being introduced to the Comte d'Artois a sensation he had never known with Napoleon, " but then Napoleon was not a descendant of St. Louis." The misfortunes of the Duchesse d'Angoulême could blind no one to the fact that she was little calculated to bind the contending factions of the Bonapartists and Bourbons, or to make the restored régime acceptable to those who had presided over the Republic. Although Alexander inserted an article in the treaty confirming the titles of the nobility created by Napoleon, she openly laughed at their pretensions and disputed their claim to bear arms. At a dinner at the Tuileries, where Louis entertained the Sovereigns, she sat next to Francis, and perceiving the Duke of Baden opposite, said: " Is not that the Prince who married a relation of Bonaparte's? What weakness to ally himself with that general!" ignoring that the

vent what is possible and desirable for one nation, by asking why it is not actually so for another? There is as yet no Tiers Etat in Russia, how then could a representative government be created there? The intermediate class between the boyards and the people is almost entirely wanting. He could augment the power of the great nobles, and in this respect undo the work of Peter I.; but it would be recoiling instead of advancing, for the power of the Emperor is a social amelioration. Russia, in respect to civilization, is only at that epoch of its history where the power of the privileged classes must be limited by the Crown. Thirty-six religious communities comprehending pagans, thirty-six different nations, are not united, but spread over an immense territory. The only tie which binds them is respect for the Sovereign and national pride."—La Révolution Française.

It is a proof of the careless mode in which M. Thiers derives his information that he has quoted as genuine a letter without signature and believed only to be forged, enclosed among some communications to Castlereagh from Mr. Craufurd, repudiated by the supposed writer, Madame de Staël, in which she complains that, thanks to Alexander's vanity, France is committed to a twenty years' war with England.

Sovereign she was addressing, as well as the King of Bavaria, who sat on her left, had allied themselves with "that general." Weakness was a word very frequently in her mouth. Louis shrewdly attached himself to the cause of France directly he entered Paris, and became quite antagonistic to Alexander, as the chief representative of the Allies. "My dear friends the enemies," he styled them; and indulged in a series of sarcastic witticisms, which the Emperor quietly parried while the other guests stood by, knowing the King expected them to laugh with him, but hardly daring to join at the expense of their ruler *de facto*. Alexander could not mistake the coolness with which he was received at the Tuileries, so he kept away. He attended the weekly reception of the Duke of Orleans in the Palais Royal; but his days were spent in business: he retired early, and at four A.M., when the streets were still deserted, took his usual promenade. He would not quit Paris while 92,000 of Napoleon's soldiers were still in garrison in Germany, Flanders, Italy, and Spain; but when these had surrendered and were safely disbanded he was anxious to depart. Hamburg, Magdeburg, Wesel, Mayence, Barcelona, Antwerp, Mantua, Alessandria, and Bergen-op-Zoom yielded to the Allies during the months of April and May, and Alexander had hoped to conclude the entire settlement of Europe in Paris, but the opposition he received from Great Britain and Austria on the subject of Poland prolonged the conferences; their ministers hoping by perseverance to compel him at last to yield, till the meetings were adjourned at the special request of these two Powers to the autumn at Vienna, and the result of this delay was the campaign of Waterloo.*

Czartoriski joined Alexander in Paris in April after an absence of five years, and had frequent interviews with Baron

* "The magnanimous efforts of the Emperor of Russia," writes Sir Charles Stewart, "his unparalleled firmness and constancy, his multiplied victories, and his unrelenting perseverance, crowned with ultimate generosity and moderation towards France, turned aside gradually the current of admiration from Great Britain, and directed the gratitude of the world as due to the Russian Emperor. When the settlement of France and the treaty of Paris came under discussion it may be affirmed, without exaggeration, that the Emperor of Russia stood upon the most elevated pinnacle of human grandeur ever attained by a monarch. The glory of Great Britain was eclipsed before him; but for the sake of Poland he was ready to resign all the reputation, character, and glory he had acquired, and defy the sentiments of Europe."

Stein on the subject of the union with Poland, Prussia being willing to yield her share of the Polish territory if an equivalent was secured in Saxony, which had been considerably enlarged by Napoleon at her expense. But Austria was resolved to keep Galicia and Cracow, and demanded the circle of Tarnopol, ceded to Alexander in 1809, though she offered to give up her share of Poland entirely to Russia if allowed to recompense herself with Alsace and Lorraine. But Alexander would not hear of this. He had given his word that the ancient French territory should not be curtailed; and when Francis mentioned the subject to Louis XVIII., he told the King if he stood firm he would assist him to keep it. Another difficulty arose with England, who wished to retain some of the ancient French colonies now in her hands, so that the French must be given an exchange in Europe. The adhesion of Murat to the cause of the Allies before Napoleon's abdication was a great complication, for his kingdom had been secured to him by Austria, and this was considered most unjust by the old Royal family of Naples. Austria also claimed a portion of her old territory, ceded to Bavaria; while every prince who had gained power by allying himself with Napoleon, now expected to keep his ill-acquired possessions as a reward for joining the Allies when he had no longer a choice. The British ministers demanded that Talleyrand should be admitted to the conferences on the part of Louis XVIII., who ought not to be treated as a defeated enemy, hoping to gain a partisan in him against the views of Russia; and this added to the conflicting interests, for it was soon clearly perceived that the French Government thought it might gain prestige, if not material, by an open quarrel with the Allies and another war; and the marshals, foreseeing future disturbances if the 70,000 officers which the French army contained were disbanded without pay or employment, eagerly hailed such a prospect, and informed the King he had 450,000 men at his disposal, ready to enforce his interests. At another audience with the Austrian Emperor, Louis mentioned this fact. Francis answered, if the King wished a new war he could easily rekindle it, but he perhaps did not foresee when it would end. Louis's tone softened in consequence; nevertheless he sent the Marquis d'Osmond with a note to the Conference of May 13th, stating that he was entitled to territories containing 1,000,000 inhabitants more than were comprised in ancient France, and the new boundary marked out only gave him 212,611; rejecting a small portion of Savoy, " as he could not accept territory belonging to the King of Sardinia, who was nearly related to him." Yet this new boundary gave to France several districts lying within her provinces, formerly German, such as Montbéliard, Avignon, Sambre, and Meuse, &c., besides a department of Savoy, all of them having been annexed by the French Republic. Louis asked for a portion of Belgium (which would have left the other half at his mercy) instead of part of Savoy, and when refused gladly took Savoy. Talleyrand claimed Luxembourg, and on being thwarted tried to obtain more Savoyard territory. It was evident France would do her best to slip out of every engagement unless enforced by superior power. Prussia, Holland, and Italy claimed the pictures wrested from them, and now adorning the Louvre; but Louis said his subjects would impute to him the pillage of the museums of Paris if the Allies insisted on reclaiming their own property, and his popularity would not stand it. The Allies with great liberality agreed to forego all pecuniary State claims if some compensation was made to private individuals; and the pictures and objects of art were left. But even with this great concession France could not be honest, and declined to recompense the ruined merchants at Hamburg, whose bank Davoust had completely pillaged; and as he had paid his soldiers for three months in advance with the contents, this last payment was clearly a French debt to Hamburg. Prussia claimed 130,000,000 francs, due for contracts of merchandize of all sorts which she agreed to furnish while the two countries were allied during the war with Russia, and of which the price was to be deducted from the Prussian war contribution, which was never done. Louis consulted Alexander, who thought the war had annulled the debt, the two countries being restored to their original positions, which was entirely to the advantage of Prussia; and this decision was final: but Hardenberg and Stein were very angry about it; for, as the King was willing to adopt Alexander's views on Poland, they thought the Czar might have given an opinion contrary to strict equity for the benefit of Prussia. Austria and Prussia went so far as to admit the advantage of his frontier extending as far as Kalisch, but they had no intention of allowing Poland to be restored even in name; and hoping he might be able to confer with the Cabinet ministers during his visit to England, where he had been invited by the Prince Regent, and convince them that his plan of a restoration of Poland under the Russian Government was not entirely dictated by ambition, he agreed to let the article in the treaty of peace which concerned her be adjourned to a future day, though he fairly told the Allies he should yield nothing of his claims if it even compelled him to brave all Europe.

The prospect for his country produced a letter from the veteran Kosciusko to Alexander, who had not seen him since the time he accompanied Paul to give to him his unconditional release. He was in Paris at the time of its surrender, but remained in obscurity till warmed into enthusiasm by the unexampled moderation Alexander exhibited, and by the sight of the excellent discipline of the Russian troops. "Sire," he wrote, "if I venture from my retirement to address my urgent prayers to an exalted monarch, a great captain, and above all a protector of humanity, it is because I regard as the greatest of men him whose magnanimity equals his genius. In the confidence this conviction inspires, I supplicate that your Imperial Majesty, the benefactor of mankind, will grant an unrestricted amnesty to Poland; and that on declaring yourself King of Poland, you will give her a Constitution similar to that of Great Britain. Should my prayers be listened to, Sire, I have only one more boon to ask, that I may be permitted, though ill, to throw myself at your feet to take the first oath of fidelity to you, and to render that homage due to you as my sovereign and the benefactor of my country." Alexander's answer was dated from Paris, May 3rd, 1814 :—

"It is with great satisfaction that I reply to your letter. With the aid of the All-powerful I hope to bring about the restoration of the brave nation to which you belong: I have taken a solemn engagement to do so, and its welfare has always occupied my thoughts. Political circumstances have alone raised obstacles preventing the execution of my designs. These obstacles no longer exist. Two years of a terrible but glorious struggle have removed them. A little time, and with prudence, the Poles will recover their country and their name; and I shall have the happiness of convincing them that, forgetting the past, he whom they consider their enemy will realize all their wishes. It will be the greatest satisfaction to me to have you as my assistant in these labours. Your name, your character, your talents will be the best support I could have.

"ALEXANDER."

The Czar found more difficulty in compelling Louis and his ministers to make the provision for the Bonaparte family than with any other part of the engagement. Foreseeing this, he had caused it to be inserted in the treaty; but Louis was backed by all the rest of the Allies. Even before Alexander quitted Paris it was asked if Napoleon was really to be an independent Sovereign at Elba; and the Czar replied, he had given his word, and could not retract from it. Jerome's wife had a protector in her father, the King of Würtemberg; Eugene, in the King of Bavaria; but the ex-Queen of Holland, unconnected with any dynasty, was despised by everybody now that ancient nobility and legality was the fashion; and the Court party even affected not to recognize her marriage, as it was solemnized in the days of the Republic, and spoke of her as Mdlle. Hortense de Beauharnais. She complained of this to the Emperor, who said he would remedy it by asking Louis to create her Duchesse de St. Leu, an estate already secured to her through his good offices. The Prime Minister, Blacas, strongly objected to this title; and although Louis dared not refuse it, he delayed signing the brevet, hoping to avoid it altogether. The evening before Alexander left, he sent his aide-de-camp to the Tuileries with orders not to leave the Palace, even if he was forced to sleep there, till the brevet was given into his hands. When it came, it was made out to Mdlle. Hortense de Beauharnais, a circumstance which much annoyed her; but Alexander told her to take it, and assume the title it gave her; though he advised her strongly not to visit at the Palace, where she might only find herself subjected to similar insults. The temptation was too great for her to resist it, and following the counsel of less judicious friends, she sought an introduction at the new Court when the Allies had retired, and found herself treated most contemptuously, as Alexander anticipated. She is said to have left it in tears, and shortly afterwards went to Baden to visit her relative, the Grand Duchess.

This Princess was summoned to France by Napoleon when it was clear Baden must join the Allies. She had not been happy as a wife, but had two daughters; and, for their sake, disobeyed the command. She went to meet Alexander at Mannheim in 1813; and, with tears, threw herself down on her knees before him, appealed to their relationship, and entreated him not to enter France, and to have compassion on her adopted father. He could seldom resist a woman's grief; but he had proof that a good deal more of the affairs of Russia were transmitted to Napoleon through Stephanie and the Court of Baden than ought to have gone beyond the frontier, and in a cool but courteous tone, he desired his pretty sister-in-law to rise and wipe her eyes; and then more kindly told her his plans were irrevocably fixed; the time for altering them had passed when the French army crossed his frontier on its way to Moscow. The Duke of Baden joined the allied army in Paris; and there were many, especially at the Tuileries, who tried to induce him to annul his marriage. He was a weak man, and was almost persuaded; but Alexander told him he had no right to divorce her unless she also wished it; and the Duke, hoping for his support at the Congress, took his advice. During the spring and summer of 1814 she was in great agitation, aware this subject was discussed in the family, and distressed at the fall of the Bonapartes. The Empress Elizabeth arrived early in the year at Carlsruhe to the home she had not seen since she left it a child. She found, indeed, the mild climate and beautiful scenery of the valley of the Rhine, for which she had sighed so long in the palace at St. Petersburg; but everything else was changed: discord and anxiety distracted the once happy domestic hearth. Her mother was divided by the various sentiments of her relatives; and the Duchess went into paroxysms of grief over the allied victories in France; Elizabeth felt little sympathy for her sister-in-law, whom she treated with disdain. She had no reserve in boasting of her husband's triumphs before Stephanie; and not being eclipsed by the Empress Dowager, she enjoyed her position as the wife of the most powerful Sovereign in Europe. Her sister, once the beautiful Frederika of Sweden, now a worn invalid, was at Carlsruhe, and they were joined a little later by Hortense. These envied the Empress, not only for her husband's rank; but, in spite of their differences, he had always been her kind friend. Yet, though occupying the same palace in St. Petersburg, they had latterly only met in public; and, for the sake of keeping a rash promise, she had shut herself up and refused to see him before his departure for the army. She followed him through Germany as the war receded towards the West, and pressed to be allowed to join him in Paris. This he declined: her arrival would necessitate a Court, and he was anxious to depart as soon as the political affairs were wound up. The Empress and Hortense early conceived a mutual aversion. The tongue of scandal, once busy with the ex-Queen, had not always spared Stephanie, and the Empress showed she had heard these reports. Hortense felt isolated. She tried to make a friend of the Queen of Sweden, by observing their situation was similar; but Frederika resented such a comparison. Hortense then sought to revenge herself on the Empress by asking her one day publicly at dinner, with affected simplicity, whether she was well lodged at St. Petersburg, implying that she believed her to be in the position of the Princess of Wales, for it was well-known the sumptuous Imperial residences in Russia were second to none in Europe. As the Empress saw the purport of the question it embarrassed her, and Hortense was afterwards blamed by the rest of the family for trying to insult the wife of her benefactor. The Empress's maid of honour continued to correspond with Madame Svetchine, who wrote from Russia, "I share your admiration for our dear Emperor. No one knows what he is worth till tried by the vicissitudes of life, and perhaps happiness is more necessary than suffering to temper the soul and give it all the energy of which it is susceptible. This memorable epoch will have, I do not doubt, a marked influence on him. He is now above other men in glory; he will be raised above himself through the influence of religion. He has never wished anything but what is good, and he will now venture upon all that he has wished. Let us hope we see the dawn of the finest day for Russia. Ah! if his soul, touched by the impression of virtue, was also brought back to her who has suffered so long with such noble and resigned calmness! I cannot tell you the extent to which I have been pained by that cessation of correspondence of which you spoke to me. What it has not even been granted to her to taste in its fulness, the joy of such happy events." In another letter, written on hearing of a Russian victory, she alludes to a slight misunderstanding between Mdlle. Stourdza and the Empress. "The last news received from the army, which announced the victory gained by our dear Emperor himself, has reanimated hearts strangely cast down by the continual transitions of hope and fear. May God crown so many efforts and such devotion by a rest dearly bought. The word glory no longer moves me; the cord it touched in my heart is doubtless broken, and I would willingly beg a little peace for the world and myself, even though it should be a little dull. The death of M. de St. Priest has deeply affected me; that of Count Strogonof (one of Alexander's early friends) has been much felt. The Count de Lagarde writes from Vienna that the Austrian enthusiasm for the Russians is at its height: to the plates on the table all is à la Cosaque. In Berlin a Rostopchine bonnet was introduced." She speaks with great compassion of the Empress for the loss of all her children, " her lips having approached this cup of felicity, only to feel the bitterness of its being refused." She counsels the young maid of honour to bear the inequalities of her temper with amiability. "Think of the deep and constant wound in her heart. In such arid, bitter trials the soul of an angel would succumb. How easy it is to be gentle and good in success and happiness! Madame de R. (the Empress)* has always appeared to me a most interesting being; but she has never been so frequently in my thoughts as since the vagueness and uncertainty into which her hopes and our own have returned. I love M. de R. (the Emperor) with faithfulness and justice. I honour his fine qualities, but I own to you, I am surprised at his resisting, as he does, to the most holy and most amiable seductions of virtue. How can any other thing entangle him by its attraction, above all when that other thing is so different, so inferior to him?" . . " How many thanks to return," she writes again on the news of the capture of Paris, "and how much

---

* Madame de Svetchine sent her letters by the Court courier, so she thought it prudent to disguise the Imperial names.

our dear Emperor deserves them! How glad I feel to have always recognized in his soul what he displays now, with so much glory, and a glory so fine and so pure! He is truly the hero of humanity: he realizes in his conduct all my dreams of moral dignity; and I find at last in this union of religious feelings with liberal ideas, the resemblance so long sought to a type I have borne in my mind, and till now might have set down as a fantastic being, the creation of an exalted imagination. Alexander has delighted me. Even on the throne, in the tumult of different interests, of unchained passions, he could remain a man, a Christian, and a philosopher, pursuing the wisest and most generous plans, and putting into execution all that there is most beautiful on earth, from the noblest equity to the most touching modesty; and that young and admirable sage is our master. The Russians are too happy if they always feel his price to the same degree. The fall of Napoleon is such as we might expect from the Divine justice. His death on the field of honour would have nobly closed an unworthy career. As to the happy change worked in the mind of the French nation, it has not astonished me. With them, to change is to remain the same."

The invitation the Prince Regent sent to Alexander to visit England did not include the Empress, who was connected through her deceased sister, the Duchess of Brunswick, with the Princess of Wales; and apart from other considerations, it was difficult for any one at that time to be on friendly terms with both the Prince and Princess. Lord Castlereagh requested Lord Liverpool to represent to the Prince that it would be desirable to extend the invitation to Francis and Frederick William. The last, wrote Count Munster, on April 27th, was uneasy on the subject; the Emperor of Austria, though he wished for the compliment, had little desire to visit England. He feared he might not be well received. The invitation was sent and accepted by the King, but declined by Francis on the ground of the inconvenience of a sea voyage, and of his return to Vienna being necessary for the settlement of his affairs in Italy, where the first measure he took was to suppress the Legislative Corps and the Senate. The treaty of peace remained to be signed, and was not accomplished till May 30th, by which time Alexander saw that unless the Bourbons altered their system it could not last. Lafayette met him one evening at Madame de Staël's. "His noble and simple manners," he writes, "pleased me much when he entered this select society. He was polished, amiable, and above all, liberal. He complained of the servility of our journals. 'We can do better than that in Russia,' he said. I assured him he misjudged the nation. He complained of the wrong turn his intentions for our liberty had taken; he had found in France neither patriotism nor support; the Bourbons had only the prejudices of the ancient régime; and as I answered that misfortune must have improved them, he said, 'Improved! they are uncorrected and incorrigible. There is only one of them, the Duke of Orleans, who has liberal ideas, but for the others, never hope anything from them.' 'If that is your opinion, Sire, why have you brought them back?' 'They came in on every side,' he said; 'I wished at least to stop them till the nation could impose a constitution upon them. They gained on me like an inundation. You saw me go to the King at Compiègne? I wished to make him renounce his nineteen years of reign, and other things of that kind. The deputation of the Corps Législatif was there as soon as I was, to recognize him from all time and without conditions. The deputations and the King were agreed. It is a failure. I shall leave Paris much distressed.'"

On May 8th Alexander visited Versailles, accompanied by Nicholas and Michael. The wounded Russians had been conveyed there, and he thanked all who had charge of them, besides writing to the mayor. "I have been informed, sir, of the zealous, kind, and constant attention paid at Versailles to the wounded of my armies. I am very sensible to a zeal which does honour to humanity. I am also grateful to yourself personally, and wish to express these sentiments and my esteem.—ALEXANDER."

Two attendants had been faithful to Napoleon up to the moment of his departure for Elba, Caulaincourt and a Polish officer named Kosakoski, who, believing Napoleon would be able to restore Poland, and that his fortunes would again be in the ascendant, had not availed himself of the general amnesty of 1813, to all those who should quit Napoleon's service within two months, and his large landed estate in Poland was sequestered. Napoleon gave Caulaincourt a letter of recommendation to Louis, but for Kosakoski he could do nothing. The Pole boldly presented himself at a levée Alexander held in Paris. When his name was announced, the Emperor asked him if he had not followed Napoleon to Fontainebleau. "Yes, Sire," he replied, "I was with him till he left it, and if he had asked me to accompany him, I should not have hesitated." Alexander was pleased with his frank reply, and asked him what he desired, and hearing it was the restoration of his property, signed an order to that effect at once. Caulaincourt was not equally fortunate. Louis refused to give him any public appointment, though Talleyrand tried to include him in the list of peers, and Alexander expressed a wish to the King that he should be accredited to his Court, on Louis saying he would send any ambassador agreeable to him to St. Petersburg. In vain Caulaincourt published a denial of any share in the murder of the Duc d'Enghien in the public papers, and Alexander, at the request of Talleyrand, defended him from this charge to Louis. The King could not forgive the efforts he made to obtain the proclamation of Napoleon II., while Alexander thought that if Russia could forgive her national wrongs the Bourbons might pardon offences towards their dynasty. "Attachment and devotion to a Sovereign in misfortune is not so common that we should be otherwise than touched by it," he said. "Great good may it do him," answered Louis. "Alexander wanted to put France out of a condition to hurt, but not to crush her. He was master at home," says Caulaincourt, "and in granting satisfaction to the public spirit of Russia, very much irritated against France, he could yet consent to an honourable peace for Napoleon." His sensitive temperament had suffered so keenly in the period of Russia's calamities that he gave his victim credit for more acute feeling than after-events showed he possessed, and pitied him when he thought of his own misery after a defeat.

Talleyrand reproached the Czar with not knowing his own power, for if he made it a personal request to the King that Caulaincourt should be admitted into the House of Peers, Louis dared not refuse him. But the King, hearing the request would be made, softened Alexander by talking of the sad position of a Sovereign who, after a revolution, was free neither when he granted nor when he refused favours; and this was uttered with so much pathos, and was so true, that the Czar urged it no more, and offered Caulaincourt an establishment in Russia.

The members of the Institute of France wished to be presented to Alexander, and their senior professor, M. Suard, requested Beugnot to explain to him that the ancient French Academy, which received a visit from Paul and Peter the Great, formed the second class of that learned body. "I was invited to dine with the Emperor," writes Beugnot on the day he had appointed for his reception there. "This Sovereign of so many men and countries, who was at Paris at the head of 100,000 soldiers, was not a little embarrassed at the part he had to play before the Institute. He seriously thought his reputation in some measure depended on it. The fame of ancient French literature had long reached St. Petersburg." Although as a youth Alexander had displayed literary tastes, he had no time for their cultivation since he came to the throne, and for the last two years had lived amidst the distractions of a camp life. As he expressed it, he had been so long out of the way of anything of the kind, that he felt unfitted to address them. It was gratifying to the subdued French savants to see they were still regarded as a power by a great monarch, and especially by one who possessed more erudition than his military contemporaries; for on such an occasion Napoleon would pompously have given them a few borrowed platitudes, which would have been applauded by his illiterate courtiers as the speech of a sage. Alexander had too much respect for literature to insult it by an inferior discourse; and he disliked a public address, because he could seldom hear it. The President, M. Lacretelle, made a speech; to which he answered fluently, though briefly, in more elegant French than many of the Frenchmen present. "I have always admired the progress the French have made in literature and the sciences. I do not impute to them the misfortunes of their country, and I feel great interest in the re-establishment of their liberty. To be serviceable to mankind is my sole object, and the only motive which brings me to France." He wished also to speak a few words to each member of the Academy on his special subject, as the members were severally introduced; and he asked Beugnot to inform him of those subjects. " Unhappily," writes the Count, "my voice is not clear, and the Emperor is very hard of hearing, and the result was some embarrassment and confusion in the compliments;"* but in the eyes of the Institute the immense honour of haranguing the Autocrat of all the Russias made up for everything. During the evening, M. Suard, who was near eighty, trembled as if he had been only twenty. Besides the Institute, Alexander visited all the useful public establishments in Paris. At the Mint, a medal was struck before him, bearing on one side the head of Peter the Great, and his own on the reverse. He was shown another, engraved during Peter's visit to France in 1717, representing him and the young Louis XV. He was particularly pleased with the Asylum for the Deaf and Dumb, and invited the Abbé Sicard, who directed it, to dinner, to explain the mode employed for their education. When they separated he gave the Abbé the cross of St. Vladimir, and afterwards founded similar institutions in St. Petersburg and Warsaw.

The Polish Princess Jablonowska gave a ball a few days before Alexander left Paris, and invited her compatriots there to meet him. He recommended himself to them by taking part in the valse, which was quite the Polish national dance; and, according to Raikes, brought it fairly into fashion in England, where the elder portion of society had looked askance at such a substitute for the slow quadrille and stately minuet. The Poles were essentially a gay, dancing people; their last sovereign, Stanislaus, boasted that, if compelled to abdicate, he should gain his bread as a dancing-master; and in joining their amusements, Alexander perhaps found the surest way to the national heart. The English ministers continued to ignore the Czar's pretensions to the Crown of Poland, though it was recognized throughout the Continent.†

* Count Beugnot's Mémoirs.—*Vide* Choiseul-Gouffier, &c.
† An English diplomatist wrote from Vienna, June, 1814, " that the Russian ambassador had taken all the Poles under his protection, and his wife had presented several Polish ladies at the last Drawing-room. The Poles in general are pleased at becoming a kingdom attached to Russia for the present, in the idea that it will lead to their future independence. Some of the more reasonable look upon this as illusory; but it is remarkable among all the Poles (and I see a great many), there is not one

Lord Castlereagh wrote to Lord Liverpool from Paris, May 15th: "The Emperor wishes his means of embarkation to be at Boulogne ready the last day of May. He takes with him Count Tolstoi, Platof, and four aides-de-camp. He said nothing about the two young Grand Dukes, and I said nothing. He expressed a wish to land quietly, and not to be received with form."

Sir Charles Stewart informs Wellington, May 26th, that "letters received by the Emperor from his sister, the Duchess of Oldenburg, who has taken a very decided part in the questions agitating at Carlton House, will induce him to carry over his two younger brothers, the Grand Dukes Michael and Nicholas. The Prince of Orange has just arrived in Paris."

These letters refer to a subject then causing considerable agitation in the political circles of Europe—the marriage of the Princess Charlotte of Wales, heir-apparent to the British throne. She was engaged to the hereditary Prince of Orange, for several years an exile, who served on Wellington's staff in the Peninsula. England announced her intention of separating Belgium from France and annexing it to Holland; and this marriage, by placing both shores of the entrance into the German Ocean eventually under the same crown, and increasing her influence on the Continent, where she already possessed Hanover, was not regarded favourably by foreign statesmen. The Empress-Dowager was very anxious for the settlement of her younger children. Her daughter she had reserved for a French prince; and as soon as Louis was established on the throne, arrangements were set on foot for a marriage between the Grand Duchess and the Duc de Berri, though he was nearly eighteen years older than his proposed bride. The Empress was annoyed when she heard of the Princess Charlotte's engagement, for she had hoped her third son Nicholas might secure this prize. He was younger than the Princess; and if this were an objection there might still be a union with England through the widowed Catherine and one of the English princes, or perhaps the Prince Regent himself. It was believed an engagement of this nature, or a resolve to disturb

attached either to Russia or to any other Power, but as that Power may ultimately favour their views for the independence of Poland."—Wellington Despatches.

the one between the Prince of Orange and the Princess Charlotte, was the motive for her journey to England in the spring of 1814. She accompanied the allied armies as far as Frankfort, and then made her way to London, where she arrived the very day Paris capitulated to her brother.* Stockmar is inclined to exonerate her from the usual charge of making the Princess discontented with the Dutch prince, and says the dislike took root long before she arrived. The Princess of Wales was exerting herself to prevent the marriage; and the Prince Regent even accused his daughter of deputing a Russian lady going to Paris to negotiate a marriage between herself and one of the Grand Dukes. He could not prevent her from seeing Catherine, but seemed averse to it. When the Princess expressed her objection very strongly to the Dutch alliance, the Prince of Orange, who seems really to have been attached to her, went over to Paris and had several private interviews with Alexander. Whatever may have been the cause, Alexander apparently tried to reconcile the pair to each other (perhaps the Prince of Orange had explained that one article in the marriage contract prevented the permanent union of England and Holland); and he did not add to the complication by bringing either of his handsome brothers upon the scene, but left them in France, to pursue their travels over the most celebrated battlefields of Europe. Perhaps another reason was, that Nicholas had just confided to him the admiration he felt for the Princess Charlotte of Prussia, whom he met in Berlin on his way to France—the first time in his life

---

* "She was the lady," writes Miss Knight, "who was so much talked of for the Prince Regent if he got a divorce from the Princess. In the evening there was a large party at Carlton House and a concert, which annoyed the Grand Duchess so much that she left the room abruptly. It seems that music overcame her nerves. She was said to have frequent faintings, and to have scarcely slept at all since the death of her husband. Her figure was slight and well formed, her complexion good, her eyes fine, and her manners dignified." The Princess Charlotte, she adds, was enchanted with the Grand Duchess, whom she styles a sensible woman, and who told her young friend she thought of marrying the Archduke Charles (a proposal to that effect having been made by the Emperor of Austria to Alexander in Paris); on which the Princess replied, many people supposed she was to marry the Regent if he could have found cause for a divorce. She answered, she was so much attached to her brother the Emperor, that for his sake and the public good she would have done whatever he wished, but that now she had seen the Regent she could never think of marrying him.

that he had quitted the environs of St. Petersburg. The King was paying a short visit to his capital in the midst of the war, and had there received the younger brothers of his ally. The Princess did the honours of her father's palace with a grace and self-possession which surprised their guests, who were introduced to a happy domestic circle, where all courtly ceremonies were banished in the intercourse between children and their parent. To be fully appreciated, Frederick William required to be seen in his own home. The Imperial youths were charmed with their reception, with the Princesses, and even with the solemn King; but some time passed before Nicholas imparted his hopes to the Emperor, who felt so strongly the misery of an ill-assorted marriage, that he was resolved not to press any alliance upon his brothers, however desirable it might appear to be politically. He had known the Princess of Prussia from a child, and such an alliance would suit Russia; but it at once checked any thought of securing the English Princess for his own family, as Michael was a mere boy.

The Russian army was leaving Paris* when the Emperor quitted France. He signed the peace of Paris May 30th, in which an article, inserted expressly on the demand of England, stipulated that no member of Napoleon's family should ever be recognized again as the Sovereign of France. Russia was the only Power which remembered this article thirty-seven years later, when Napoleon III. ascended the French throne, and incurred his deadly enmity, while England eagerly embraced his offer of an offensive and defensive alliance. Such was the end of the British policy of 1798 and 1801, which had entailed years of bloodshed on Europe and increased the English National Debt by 400,000,000*l.* To acknowledge a ruler chosen by the people, instead of adhering to a legitimate dynasty, regarded as an insane freak of Paul, and a departure

---

* The Russian reviews were usually attended by crowds of Parisian ladies seated in barouches, laughing and talking with the officers. Mr. Fraser Tytler describes the last, held in 1814:—"The Emperor Alexander galloped along the line, and was received with loud and enthusiastic huzzas. He is certainly an uncommonly handsome man, and there is mildness and benignity in his expression. He is a man to be adored by his troops. Both he and his brother Constantine ride very gracefully, but Constantine is too fond of showing off his horsemanship." The Russian Guards wore moustaches, a fashion the Emperor had not adopted. The uniform of the Cossack officers was excessively rich and handsome.

from public morality on the part of Alexander, is now the recognized policy of the Continent; and Nicholas, misled by the odium they incurred for their enlightened views on that subject, and unobservant of the changes since he had shared during his boyhood in restoring Louis to the throne of France, pursued the course in 1852 which was followed by England throughout the first two decades of the present century, and he paid for the error with his life.

Alexander left Paris June 2nd, and at Boulogne found a squadron under the Duke of Clarence, ready to convoy him to England; but the King of Prussia was a day later, and he employed the interval in going on foot to various objects in the neighbourhood, while an immense crowd trailed after him. They landed at Dover at 6.30 P.M., June 6th. A volley of artillery greeted them from the castle; and besides the English noblemen sent by the Regent to meet them, the Mayor and Corporation were waiting to present Alexander with the usual address. He answered in English, " Although, gentlemen, I understand your language, I am not sufficiently acquainted with it to reply to you in English, and I must therefore request those gentlemen of the deputation who speak French to be my interpreters to those who do not." He continued in French : " I am much pleased to find, by the sentiments you express, that the services rendered by my armies in the great cause in which we have been engaged are so highly considered by the British nation. I can assure you that by no means the smallest gratification I derive from the late campaign is the opportunity it affords me of visiting England, a country for which I have long felt the highest esteem. Gentlemen, I beg you will accept my thanks for this mark of your attention, and my best wishes for the welfare of your town, and assure yourselves I shall always endeavour to preserve a cordial friendship between England and Russia."

The King of Prussia brought his two eldest sons, his nephew, and two cousins, besides Hardenberg; and Alexander was attended by Nesselrode, and preceded to England by Barclay, Prince Dolgoruki, and others. Metternich also arrived to represent Austria. The crowd remained assembled all night at Dover, under the windows of the hotel where Alexander was lodged; but he left for London very early the next morning in his ambassador's carriage, and Frederick William followed in one of the stage-coaches. On entering London the spectators were disappointed by the carriage taking an unexpected route. It was contrary to his principles to avoid them, as he said more than once it was "part of a Sovereign's duty to exhibit himself if it pleased anybody to see him;" but it was now due to the unpopularity of the Prince Regent, who was blockaded in Carlton House by a menacing mob during a great part of the morning, and afraid to stir out to meet his guests; but in the course of the afternoon he left the palace quietly and joined them on the road, returning to London in the same carriage with the Emperor, and giving orders that it should drive by a most circuitous way to Pulteney's Hotel in Piccadilly, where Alexander was to lodge. Rooms were prepared for him at Cumberland House, the residence of a prince he particularly disliked, but he only used them for holding levées and audiences. He had stated his wish to put up at the hotel where his sister was residing; and his suite, including Prince Leopold of Saxe-Coburg, had lodgings found for them in the neighbourhood at his expense. He thought he should be less trammelled by State etiquette, and be able to visit the useful public institutions, and observe the working of English law and the Constitution; but a series of fêtes and entertainments were arranged while he stayed; and no fashionable réunion was thought complete without his presence; so that he found to his regret he had small leisure for more serious undertakings, and was obliged to be satisfied with a superficial view of merely the upper classes of Great Britain.

"These great people," wrote a lady from Dover, "have so inured themselves to hardships that they travel without a respite, and their greatest indulgence is a truss of straw when they stop to collect their followers. The Emperor would have no other bed; and his sister desired not to have a bed, but a sofa, to sleep on." Yet the fatigues of the two years' campaign were almost equalled by a London season; and wild-looking Cossack messengers continued to arrive during his visit, bringing despatches and other correspondence from Russia, which more than once occupied their Imperial master throughout the whole night.

The next day Alexander walked in Kensington Gardens,

visited Westminster Abbey and the British Museum, held a levée, and attended the Queen's Drawing-room; afterwards dining with the Prince Regent. On the 9th he rode before breakfast through the City and Southwark, and in the course of the morning drove with his sister to the London Docks, when the mob took the horses out of the carriage and drew it themselves the whole way. In the afternoon he attended a Chapter of the Order of the Garter, where the ceremonies were completed which had been provisional at Toplitz; and when he walked in procession by the side of the Prince Regent, with the train of his robes borne by Lord Yarmouth, it was observed he seemed embarrassed by his novel dress. On the 10th he went to Hampton Court and the Ascot Races, where the Prince Regent, wishing to show him the ceremony of ordinary knighthood, conferred the honour on his physician, Dr. Wylie. The aged Queen Charlotte with her daughters were present, and the Emperor afterwards dined with them at Frogmore, and visited Eton. On the 11th he went to the Bank of England, and received an address from the Lord Mayor, to which he replied with a fluent speech. " His English is as good as my own," wrote Lady Malmesbury. In the evening he dined with the Prime Minister, to meet the Prince Regent, with whom he adjourned to the opera. They had scarcely seated themselves when the Princess of Wales appeared with her suite in a neighbouring box. Alexander immediately rose and bowed to her, the King of Prussia did the same, and the audience cheered them; upon which the Regent bowed to the audience; so what was feared might be an awkward coincidence went off very well.*

On the 12th, being Sunday, Alexander attended mass at the Russian Chapel in Welbeck Street, and afterwards received Wilberforce, who had requested an audience on the subject of the abolition of the slave trade, Alexander having advocated the previous emancipation of the slaves in those colonies restored by the Treaty of Peace to Holland and France, and also desiring to pass an international law declaring the slave trade to be

---

* "The nobility," says Rush, " gave parties after the opera at twelve. They lasted until two and three. Most of those who have been at them do not rise till noon next day. About two P.M. commences the roll of carriages. At six P.M. the morning ends."—Recollections of Residence at the Court of London, 1818-24.

piracy. But in this measure he was opposed by the English ministers and all the Allies. In the afternoon he rode in Hyde Park, dined with the Prince Regent, and closed the evening at a party at Lord Salisbury's.

The 13th was spent in viewing the Woolwich Arsenal and other objects, and on the 14th the Sovereigns and Princes drove to Oxford to attend the commemoration festivities, which that year were particularly grand. Greek and Latin odes were recited in honour of the Czar, who was made a Doctor of Laws, but he left the next day, inspecting Woodstock and Blenheim on his road. He travelled in an open carriage, and arrived in Piccadilly, soaked through by a thunder-storm, between two and three A.M., when, after changing his clothes, he immediately repaired to an evening party at Lady Jersey's, to which he was engaged, and left it again at six. At 11.30 he went incognito to St. Paul's, to hear the annual service for the Charity Schools, and declared it was the most interesting sight he had yet seen. At three P.M. he inspected the Mint, and in the evening dined with Lady Castlereagh, after which he went in State to the theatre at Drury Lane, and at the conclusion of the performance to a ball at Lord Hertford's, not leaving it till 5.30. "The Emperor's manner is certainly very pleasing and easy; he waltzes well," writes the Hon. Mrs. Robinson : " his mouth and smile remind me of the Empress Catherine." At eleven A.M. he went to Chelsea Hospital and the Military Asylum, then to Greenwich, and afterwards dined with the City merchants and bankers at the Merchant Taylors' Hall, where the Duke of York presided. At eleven P.M. he went to Covent Garden Theatre, where a performance was being held in his honour.

On June 18th he accompanied the English Princes and the allied generals in a State procession to the Guildhall, where they were entertained by the Lord Mayor. The next day, being Sunday, he attended an early mass, and gave an audience to a Quaker deputation. He expressed a wish to see one of their meetings, and was conducted to the same house where Peter the Great had formerly witnessed a similar service. In the afternoon he received deputations from the Foreigners' Aid, the Bible, and Humane Societies ; and afterwards went to a party held by the Queen. On the 20th there was a review in Hyde Park, and the next day he gave an audience of an hour to the Friends, William Allen and Grellet, standing all the time, and asking them many questions about their doctrines and practice. "His conduct throughout," writes Allen, "though kind and familiar, was dignified;" and he shook them each by the hand as they withdrew.

After a dinner at the Russian ambassador's, Alexander attended an evening fête at Carlton House, where he said adieu to the Queen and the Royal family, from whom he had received visits in the course of the day. At night he attended an entertainment at White's Club, where he again met the Regent, and is described as being attired in plain clothes, not even wearing an order or star. He danced till five A.M., and returned to his hotel to receive early visits from some Russians who were remaining in England, and at nine A.M. he drove to the Tower of London, and thence to Portsmouth. Sir John Sinclair had also waited upon him before he left Piccadilly, and when introduced told the Emperor he had seen him before. Alexander asked if he should have known him again. Sir John answered "hardly," and then told him it was at his grandmother's Court, where he was presented twenty-eight years before, when Alexander was only eight years old. "The Emperor did not seem in the least affected by all the fatigue he had undergone." On the 23rd there was a naval review at Portsmouth, and on the 25th the Imperial party left for Dover, driving through Brighton, Chichester, and Hastings, the crowd being enormous in every town they passed. At Dover they embarked for Calais on their way to Holland, and the Emperor seemed pleased by the acclamations of the people, keeping his glass to his eye in the direction of the shore till the vessel was out of sight.

Yet, notwithstanding the cordiality of his reception, there was no period less calculated to impress a foreign prince with the advantage of the English form of government. The Regent,* untrammelled by the responsibility of the supreme authority, had given himself up to excesses which had brought

---

* "The troubles of the worthy Regent thicken," writes Lord Brougham, May, 1814. "He has had an intimation that Alexander means to call on the Princess of Wales when he comes, and this makes him furious. They say Sir T. Tyrwhitt is gone to prevent it."

upon him the contempt of his subjects, and at that moment it was particularly displayed. His wife was regarded as a victim, and her foibles supposed to be exaggerated to induce the Houses of Parliament to grant him a divorce. He steadily refused to meet her in public, and she was forbidden to appear at the Queen's Drawing-room to receive the King of Prussia, who was nearly related to her, or any of the other foreign princes then in England, on the ground that etiquette obliged the Regent to be present, and that if she came he must stay away. The mob took up her cause, and the old Queen, who was nearly seventy, and the mother of a numerous family, was hooted and even spit at when she drove along the streets. The Prince had the same reception, except when he appeared in company with the allied Sovereigns, and even then his carriage windows were once plastered with mud; but although it vexed him to see their popularity, he was certainly better received after their visit. A free press indulged in lampoons and caricatures of its reigning Prince, and the Grand Duchess Catherine was not spared when it was thought she interfered·between the Princess Charlotte and the Dutch Prince. There was not much in common between the elderly beau and his guests, and he was glad when they were gone. The rough, ungainly Blucher, whose conversation made even the German officers blush, seems to have been more congenial to him, as he liked sitting long after dinner; an English practice Alexander abhorred, and which was then carried to excess. A State dinner in St. Petersburg seldom occupied more than an hour, and the Emperor was accustomed to drink but one glass of wine. He grew impatient under the infliction of sitting three or four hours at the dinner-table at Carlton House, at a time that he was anxious to utilize each moment of his English visit, and when on ordinary occasions all his time was employed. The Regent more than once became very confidential, and complained of his wife, abused his daughter, and requested the Emperor to use his influence in persuading her to accept the Prince of Orange. With regard to his disputes with his wife, the Regent did not find the support he had expected. Alexander tried to convince him he would act wisely in showing her more outward courtesy. "No one," the Czar is said to have asserted, " could love his wife less than he loved the Empress, but he did not consider that would justify him in slighting her publicly, or withdrawing the protection a woman should always receive from her husband. The Prince should remember their wives were as much to be pitied as themselves : they perhaps might have married more suitably if left to their own choice ; and Caroline and Elizabeth might have found more affectionate husbands. To which the Prince replied, they could have found no other husbands who could have created the one Empress of Russia and the other Princess of Wales. The Prince used to relate that, when he was driving out with the Emperor, a man put his head into the carriage, and shouted out, " Where's your wife ?" Upon which he turned it off by telling Alexander, " That was intended for your Imperial Majesty."

The Russian suite thought their Sovereign was insulted by " Rule Britannia" being played on all occasions in his presence, but never the Russian national hymn. A few annoying incidents occurred, such as the Regent being more than half intoxicated when he entered the same carriage with the Emperor ; and Alexander's conferences with the British ministers on the subject of the Duchy of Warsaw, and other points to be discussed at Vienna, had not ended satisfactorily, as both sides adhered to their own views. He admired the system of an organized opposition to the Government, which he saw was an open and wholesome check upon the possible abuse of power. He was surprised to see the comforts of life so generally spread through all classes of society, and thought the position of an English squire the most desirable in the world. The richness of the country, and the number of cannon and other military appliances in its arsenals after so long a war, gave him a high idea of her power and resources. Yet his after reflections on his visit seem to have been not altogether pleasant.* In 1818 his aide-de-camp,

---

* Nothing of dissatisfaction at the time was observed by his English entertainers. "There is a striking contrast," writes the poet Moore, "between the natural manners and simple dress of the Emperor of Russia and King of Prussia and the artificial dignity and manufactured appearance of the Regent." "We are all Emperor mad," writes a young lady who had stationed herself with her friends among the crowd on the staircase at Pulteney's Hotel to see him. " His head is bald, his hair light, his complexion blonde and beautiful, his eyes blue, his mouth very small, his lips thin, his chest and shoulders broad and finely formed,

Czernichef, inquired from an English officer "if he knew how the Emperor stood in the personal estimation of the Prince Regent. There were untoward circumstances during the Emperor's visit in London which he feared might have led to some coolness; the endeavour of the Grand Duchess to disturb the prospect of an alliance with the Prince of Orange, and her insisting to go everywhere with her brother, which he humoured her in, might lead to this, together with the Emperor's not going to the apartments prepared for him, and disliking late hours of dinner; the Prince had never visited the Emperor in his hotel, which had hurt him at the time, but the Emperor regretted these circumstances, and feared he had left an unfavourable impression on the mind of his Royal Highness."

Twelve Cossacks of the Guard accompanied Alexander to England, and collected a curious group around them as they stood outside Sir Thomas Lawrence's house in London when their Hetman was sitting for his portrait. The Prince Regent was anxious to obtain the pictures of all the chiefs connected with the late war; but the Czar was too much occupied to spare the time, and for the same reason never sat to a painter from the day he ascended the throne. Gerard and Isabey took several portraits of him in Paris, the result merely of close observation when he appeared in public, and the painting of Alexander by Gerard in the Commemoration Hall at Oxford, that by Bazin, a Russian artist, and the portrait, also by Gerard, given by the Emperor to La Harpe, and now in the Museum at Lausanne, are three of the most correct likenesses existing of him. In the portrait by Sir Thomas Lawrence in the Waterloo Chamber at Windsor Castle, painted in 1818, the figure is like, but the face too broad; and there are three portraits, taken at very different periods, in the gallery at Versailles, said to be good. A medal was struck by Wyon at the Mint, which his sister thought very like him, and it bears

his manner graceful and dignified. I was squeezed so close to him that I took hold of his hand: it was so soft. Two young women in the crowd pressed forward, one on her knee, and kissed his hand, which he drew back as if shocked or ashamed. His sister is very like him, but her nose plainer than his." Lady C. Davies described him as "a remarkably handsome man both in face and figure." Miss Berry as "a tall, fine, manly figure, with a clear complexion and good open countenance." Lady Malmesbury as "making a perfect contrast with the Regent."

a strong resemblance to the Empress Catherine. He refused to give the world-renowned Canova an opportunity of taking his bust, but Thorwaldsen obtained one sitting from him when he visited Warsaw in 1820. Thorwaldsen was fond of describing the Emperor, and said he " had talked to him just like anybody else."

Alexander arrived at the Hague, July 2nd, and after remaining there a day left with the Royal family for Haarlem and Amsterdam, whence he paid a visit to Zaandam to see the house where Peter the Great had lived. Sixteen daughters of the magistrates, dressed in the picturesque national costume, received him. The house is a small wooden cottage in the old Dutch style, containing two rooms and a very little closet, where Peter slept. One of the rooms was used as a chapel, and the other as a kitchen and salon, for he lived here like a hermit; and Menzikof and other members of his suite occupied a comfortable abode in the neighbourhood. The King led the Emperor into the hut, and requesting him to leave a memorial of his visit, offered him a square tablet of white marble and a silver trowel to place it in a space in the chimney-piece already prepared. The tablet was engraved with the words, in gold letters, " Petro Magno—Alexandro."* The same evening Alexander left Amsterdam for Bruchsal, to meet the Empress, whom he had not seen for more than eighteen months. Madame Svetchine received an account of their interview in a letter from Mdlle. Stourdza, sent by the Emperor's own hand to St. Petersburg. She wrote that her correspondent's details touched her deeply. " How many sweet tears it has made me shed! For more than a month my mind was concentrated on that point, and I waited, foreseeing in my hopes and wishes the moment which might realize them. I mingled fears also, but how much I now enjoy the perfect confidence this portion of your letter gave me! In that réunion, so much desired, I see the only triumph left for virtue to obtain, the evil conquered in its last entrenchment and under its last form, and the opening of a new day of pardon and blessings for Russia. You are right to exclude me from the number of those who waited for a marvellous circle of unexampled prosperities to

---

* The house has been cased, to preserve it from the weather, by Alexander's sister, the late Queen of Holland.

render justice to the Emperor. I have felt no surprise at current events, and his finest actions have not aroused it."*

Alexander's return was awaited with impatience at St. Petersburg, where, De Maistre writes, "abuses are enormous, because the nation is enormous." Religious controversies and political disputes occupied the best classes of society, but the Emperor's old tutor, Marshal Soltikof, the virtual Regent of the Empire, had suffered from more than one attack of paralysis, and changes were expected in the ministry. "I am very curious to see what ideas will arrive in this crowd of young heads who return to Russia. The interior will give immense occupation to his Imperial Majesty, for during so long an absence business has much accumulated. In Moscow the merchants only are rebuilding." St. Petersburg was elated at the national triumph. No Muscovite town had delivered up her keys to a French conqueror, but Alexander had received the submission of the city of Paris, and the fate of her inhabitants, and of Napoleon himself, had depended on his will. The European supremacy Napoleon strove to obtain throughout his career, and failed to acquire in the Russian campaign, had fallen into the hands of the Czar, and the moral supremacy Alexander exercised over France herself had been greater than any Napoleon gained over any other prostrate people. The Czar returned the acknowledged leader of the continental Powers, the object of dread to his allies. Had not Napoleon been greeted, after a far less victory, with all the pomp that the civil and military authorities of Paris could display? Had he not delighted to exhibit trophies of his success, and to represent in painting and sculpture, like the barbarous monarchs of old times, a humiliated prince

* Sir Robert Wilson, writing from Bruchsal, the residence of Alexander's mother-in-law, July 10th, says: "This morning I saw the Emperor; the reception amply repaid me for the visit. He took me by the hand, led me to the Empress, and told her to regard me as his faithful companion in arms. I dined with the Emperor, the Empress, the Grand Duke and Duchess of Baden, the Queen of Sweden, the Prince and Princess of Darmstadt, the young Prince of Sweden, &c. &c. I had much interesting conversation with the Emperor on general politics and England. Some of his observations were worthy of record in the golden book of philanthropical and philosophical legislators. . . . Our dinners, both as to length and quantity of wine drunk, our healths and our toasts, were not characteristics of English hospitality, which the Emperor and those who accompanied him to England cite with the greatest satisfaction."

offering homage at the feet of the conqueror? The arch between the Louvre and the Tuileries was still adorned with bas-reliefs, showing the father of the French Empress standing bareheaded before Napoleon (who kept his hat on), submissively asking for peace; and had not Napoleon in his turn begged for peace from Alexander, and offered every concession he could name if he were only permitted to keep his throne? There was not a town in Europe that could have remained unexcited on receiving back its prince with such laurels. London was illuminated for three nights when she received him, and how could St. Petersburg do less? The Senate deliberated for three days on the mode in which they could reward him, and they agreed to give him the title of Béni du Ciel (the Blessed of Heaven), and to send a deputation to Weimar to meet him on the road, with a golden cup engraved with the names of his battles. But Alexander showed as much moderation in his triumph as in his treatment of the conquered, and was, moreover, weary of honours and display. The admiration of a fickle multitude was not the novelty to Catherine's heir that it had been to Napoleon. He had no need and no desire to seek popular demonstration. "The Emperor," writes De Maistre, "who is simplicity itself, is very much averse to all honours rendered directly to his person. He does not like being put, as they say, in face of himself." The four million Frenchmen whom Napoleon sacrificed to his ambition seem to have borne no part in his subsequent regrets, but Alexander was a Russian by birth, and the loss of the thousands of his fellow-countrymen in the war weighed heavily on his soul. His religious feelings also deterred him from accepting the glory of the campaign, and allowing scope for the adulation people are always apt to heap on a successful general, especially if that general be their king; but De Maistre thought it was a mistake to check such an effusion of loyalty.

The deputation consisted of Prince Kurakin, Count Alexander Soltikof, and General Tormassof. When they were presented they asked Alexander to accept the title, and to allow a monument to be erected to him in the Isaac Square. He replied, "I have always tried to give the nation an example of simplicity and modesty. I cannot accept the title offered to me without deviating from my principles, and as for the monument, it is for posterity to erect one to me if they think me worthy of it." He also begged they would reserve their money for the widows, orphans, and wounded in the war, instead of expending it in illuminations. He wrote to the Governor of St. Petersburg, "I am informed that various preparations are making for my reception. I have always disliked these things, and disapprove of them still more at the present moment. The events which have put an end to the sanguinary wars in Europe are the work of the Almighty alone. To Him we must give the praise. Make known this unalterable resolution, that no preparations whatever may be made to welcome me." He even declined the request of the Senate to bestow upon himself the first class of the military Order of St. George.

He arrived in the neighbourhood of his capital several days before he was expected, as he did not stop in Berlin; and went straight to Paulovsky to see his mother, who had thrown off her mourning for Paul on hearing of the capture of Paris. "What a return, and what a triumph!" writes De Maistre.* "I enjoy his happiness as if it belonged to myself. After a long and glorious absence, he arrived last Monday at St. Petersburg at seven A.M. He surprised everybody, coming without noise and without escort, descended at the Cathedral of Kazan to say his prayers, and went back to his palace as if he had only returned from Czarco-Selo or Peterhof." The next day there was a public thanksgiving at the same church, attended by the Empress-mother and her daughter, Constantine, the diplomatic body, and a vast congregation. The Emperor rode to the cathedral on horseback through a joyful crowd, with all the bells in the city ringing and salutes of artillery. "He is not much altered by his campaigns, except being rather sunburnt, but this military colour suits him very well. . . . As to those sort of honours which do not require his presence, I believe he would allow them willingly, but he does not like anything forced; and who can be astonished? In an autograph letter, very elegantly written, so say good judges, the Emperor renders the Governor of St. Petersburg personally responsible for everything done in this way; a light sarcasm, for in the

* Correspondance Diplomatique.

manner in which the sums would have been levied for all these projects there would not have been the voluntary action which is their charm, his pride would be offended by it, and this induced him to refuse everything." But as the Senate and other corporations continued to press his acceptance of a title and a public monument, he answered that these loyal wishes gave him great pleasure, and that his whole efforts were directed to implore by fervent prayer the blessing of God on himself and his faithful people, and to be blessed by them and by the whole human race. "This is my most ardent wish and my greatest happiness. But with all my endeavours to attain it, I cannot as a man allow myself to be so presumptuous as to accept this name, and to imagine I have already obtained this happiness. I consider it as the more incompatible with my principles, because I have at all times and on all occasions exhorted my faithful subjects to modesty and humility, and I will not give an example which would contradict these sentiments. While expressing my gratitude, I beg the public bodies of the empire to abandon all such designs," &c.

One of Alexander's first acts was to appoint a committee, composed of several generals, to confer pensions on the invalid and wounded officers, and provide for the widows and orphans. On the 30th August, the anniversary of Kulm, he published an address of thanks to his army "for their great services and cheerful endurance; their heroic deeds had incessantly attracted his attention throughout the campaign; and he invited all who had returned crippled or wounded to come to him, to receive the rewards they deserved."

This promise was carried out, and a free pardon granted to "all persons misled to hold intercourse with the enemy." All debts to the Government not exceeding 2000 roubles were excused, and a general mitigation of sentences passed upon criminals. In the provinces which had suffered from the war the peasants were exempted from the poll-tax, as well as all arrears throughout the empire since 1812. Notice was given in the German newspapers that, as the inhabitants of Germany who had received Russian bank-notes during the war might find it difficult to dispose of them at their true value, offices were established in Berlin and Königsberg, where all persons who applied with such bank-notes should receive their value according to the actual rate of exchange.

Among the nobility who arrived from all parts of the empire to meet Alexander, Rostopchine came from Moscow to give up his accounts, and to resign his post. He wrote to his wife a few days after the Emperor's return—" When I saw the Emperor, and when I dined with him, he only spoke to me of indifferent things. I shall wait another week, and then ask for an audience to demand his orders on the subject of extraordinary sums I have had at my disposal, and to request my complete dismissal." It has been shown that his interviews with the Emperor had been rare, and that for years he refused to accept office. There is no reason to suppose he wished for anything further now, except a public approval of his conduct during the invasion. But on this subject Alexander was always silent, though he refrained from dismissing him at the demand of the commissioners who joined the citizens of Moscow in their complaints, nor had he shown his displeasure in any other way. Yet Rostopchine felt he was coldly received. He attended a levée held for the wounded officers, where Alexander spoke feelingly and gratefully to each of his services and hardships,* but he accepted Rostopchine's resignation, though he summoned him to the Congress of Vienna, and made him a member of the Council of State. The ex-governor refused to take any compensation for his losses in Moscow, and during the rest of his life occupied himself with religious meditations, like many Russian politicians who had gone through a lifetime of labour and cares in the last twenty years, and now relinquished diplomacy to instruct themselves in German mysticism, or to find the gold still left in their own Church, loaded as it was with rust through many centuries of subjection to Mahometans. The moment was seized by the Jesuits to make conversions in the empire. They were repre-

* Among many purely invented stories of Alexander, it has been said on this occasion he turned so red and addressed the Count so rudely that Rostopchine thought it best to retire at once. The Emperor may have coloured when he saw him, as recalling a great catastrophe to his memory, but that he said anything but a few courteous words, such as are usual at a levée, has been stoutly denied by one who was present and standing close by them. General Tormassof was appointed Governor of Moscow in his place.

sented by learned and worldly men, too powerful in subtle argument for the simple Russian priesthood to meet them at all on equal terms in the arena of polemical strife. Hitherto they were an exiled band, seeking refuge under the protecting wings of Russia; but Pius VII. took the earliest opportunity to display his recovered independence in an edict, published 7th August, 1814, which re-established the Order of Jesuits in "the Empire of Russia, in the Kingdom of the Two Sicilies, the Ecclesiastical States, and all other States." He gave as a reason that "some thirteen years before he had been called upon by the Emperor Paul and King Ferdinand of Naples to allow of the establishment of the Jesuits in their dominions, and he now diffused that which their enlightened minds esteemed so great a blessing over the rest of Europe." Those who recollect the excitement caused in England in 1848 by the Papal aggression, as it was termed—the establishment of Roman Catholic bishops—will understand the alarm raised by the restoration of the Jesuits among the votaries of the Greek Church; particularly as the favours Alexander and Paul granted them had given general displeasure. Apart from the enmity existing for centuries between the two great divisions of the holy Catholic Church, the Jesuits were accused of being political intriguers and foreign spies. "The Sovereign of this country," writes De Maistre in September, 1814, "has great religious ideas, so much the more estimable that he only owes them to himself, for his education pushed him in a completely contrary direction; but I have no motive for thinking he has taken up the questions dividing our two Churches, only he is tolerant, and that is much. The Greek rancour tried to move more than one machine about him to injure us, but has not succeeded. The existence of the Jesuits in Russia is one of the most luminous proofs of his astonishing power over himself; for they inspired him with violent prejudices against them, and he was daily surrounded by those who hate them. However, they endure. The Chancellor has retired (October 8th). It is said he wished to attend the Congress at Vienna, but in a tête-à-tête of nearly two hours the Emperor was inflexible, knowing the foreign Cabinets cannot bear him. He is not an easy man to replace. He displeased everybody by not asking favours for his subordinates when he retired—the usual form. He said the Emperor knew as well as he which of his servants deserved favour." De Maistre speaks of Nesselrode, who succeeded him, as not having sufficient weight with the Emperor to influence him. "I doubt, however, if the Emperor can be influenced; I believe he will remain perfectly independent." Lord Walpole refers to the same subject, August 9th: "Nesselrode has received the portfolio of Foreign Affairs. He enjoys no consideration whatever, but is merely considered as the Emperor's *secretary*. . . . The intimacy between the Emperor and the celebrated Madame Narishkine is about to be broken off, and she will leave this country for some years. I believe her true reason is the fear of what she foresees likely to happen from the great oddness of the Emperor. This was suspected in very early age, and medical men now here were brought over on that account. . . . She excused her resolution to the Emperor by remarking the strong feeling of affection manifested by the public for the young Empress upon her leaving St. Petersburg, her dread of being at some time the victim of that sentiment, and that going away she would at least show she was not the obstacle to a reconciliation which she advised between them. Should any change ever take place, the Empress would be the popular choice."*

Her departure coincided with Alexander's desire to lead a more religious life, though she carried with her the only child remaining to him, who was brought up with the three daughters of the Grand Huntsman in ignorance of her birth. Even the Imperial munificence had not sufficed to keep Narishkine and his wife out of debt, and the husband was at this time a ruined man. Alexander settled on her a pension of (one account says) 8000*l.* to suffice for the education and maintenance of his daughter, who was five years old; but the lady continued to be constantly embarrassed. Alexander eventually paid all her debts.

As to Romanzov, his failing health often incapacitated him from business in 1812, when Nesselrode filled up the vacancy; and not being favourable to the Emperor's views as to Poland, he threatened to resign unless he accompanied him to Vienna, in the hope perhaps of modifying them. Finding Alexander

* Castlereagh Correspondence.

was determined not to take him, he retired at once. He received a kind letter from the Emperor, expressing a hope that his love for his country would not allow him, when his health was restored, to withhold from it the benefit of his talents and experience. The bond between them was his literary and scientific tastes, his integrity, and his desire to promote education among the lower classes. Yet no minister was ever more abused by foreign statesmen. He was personally acquainted with the distinguished traveller Humboldt; and at the end of 1811, when he still hoped to avert a war, he invited him to take part in a Government expedition for exploring the resources and establishing diplomatic relations in Kashgar and Thibet. Humboldt seemed pleased with the idea, provided his services would not be required before 1814, when he would have completed a work he had on hand. "I should think it," he writes to one of his friends, "no humiliation to offer my services to a Prince under whose government the arts and sciences have flourished throughout the length and breadth of his vast dominions, did not my position entirely prohibit such a step." He wished to undertake the journey at his own expense; but although the war and the heavy cost it involved delayed the expedition, and when it was carried out there was such a strong feeling in Russia against foreigners that he was not employed, still he ended by overcoming his scruples, and in 1827 made a journey to the Altai Mountains at the expense of Nicholas.

Romanzov gave up all the presents he received from foreign princes to the fund for the benefit of the wounded, and refused to accept the pension Alexander assigned him. His private fortune enabled him to support schemes for the public benefit with princely liberality. In 1814 he despatched Captain Kotzebue on a voyage round the world, and defrayed the cost of the publication of a Russian "Codex Diplomaticus," printed at Moscow in 1813, of a History of Leo the Deacon, and of a Russian translation of the History of the Monguls and Tartars, by Abdul Ghazi, Prince of Carizme. In 1817-18 he made several journeys to collect historical manuscripts, which he published; and formed a museum of Oriental medals and coins, at the time considered far the richest in Europe. In 1817 Canova executed by his order a colossal figure of

Peace, to commemorate three treaties concluded by his father, his grandfather, and himself, 1743, 1774, and 1809. He also gave 25,000 roubles to the Imperial Academy of Sciences towards the printing and publication of ancient Russian records. He survived Alexander exactly a month.

Admiral Tchichagof* was made a member of the Council of State, having resigned his public duties and lived in retirement since 1813: he now went to reside in England, still inconsolable for the loss of his wife, and for the blame attached to him in the salons at St. Petersburg and among foreign diplomatists at having failed to intercept Napoleon in the marshes of the Beresina. Alexander took an early opportunity to visit the widow and daughters of Marshal Kutuzov, and ordered a pillar to be erected on the site of Moreau's fall at Dresden, inscribed with the words, "The Emperor Alexander to his friend Moreau." He established several committees to draw up plans for the retrenchment of expenses in the various Government departments. The merchants at St. Petersburg gave a dinner to Constantine and 200 officers of the Russian Guard, and the Grand Duke in his turn entertained and rewarded the subaltern officers and privates. But the Emperor's departure to the Congress of Vienna was a drawback to the national joy. He publicly explained that his absence for a short time longer was necessary to secure the fruits of years of contest in a lasting peace. He knew well the opposition organized against Russia, and would probably never have raised Germany, or given the chief command of the armies to an Austrian, if he had then formed an idea of the European jealousy towards him, or the fear excited by the Russian conquests in the last century. But having fallen into that error once, and seen how that jealousy prolonged the war, he was the more resolved to extend his own frontiers till Moscow was protected against any future invader. The reasons Napoleon gave for not desiring to restore the independence of Poland, even if he had possessed the power to do so, applied much more strongly to Russia; and it was obvious that if the Duchy of Warsaw was left in the position it held before 1812, it would serve, as it did then, for a perpetual site of conspiracy against her moral and material influence. Alexander was

* He lived at Brighton, where he published his defence. He died 1852.

taught by the invasion in what points lay the strength and weakness of Russia, and that knowledge was the ground of his diplomacy throughout the Vienna Congress.

Besides the political side of the question, there was his old promise to Czartoriski, when he was but seventeen, that sooner or later he would unite the severed limbs of the Polish territory, and that Poland should again form one nation. It was in his power to fulfil this promise, and his honour was dear to him. If conquest ever gives a right, that right had been conquered by his armies now occupying Poland. He was not called upon to refer the matter to his allies, but he wished the constitution he intended to give her to be additionally guaranteed by a treaty with all Europe. No one knew better that he might prove but a " fortunate accident " in the line of autocrats of Russia, but this wish to make the reconstitution of Poland a European matter, and not merely the gift of Russia, was very unpopular among his countrymen. Moreover, they thought the Poles deserved chastisement, and not rewards and privileges, for the active part they took in laying waste the empire.

So Alexander and the Poles were opposed by all Europe, including Russia. The King of Prussia was his friend, but Frederick William's personal opinion had little weight in the councils of his ministers. Jackson, writing from Berlin to Lord Castlereagh, 19th August, 1814, speaks of " the King's dislike to business, which devolved everything upon his Chancellor (then Prince Hardenberg), and prevented his other ministers having access to him." He mentions, indeed, " the unbounded confidence of the King in the Emperor of Russia, which it is rumoured is likely to be still more closely cemented by the marriage of the Princess Royal ;" but the Chancellor was Alexander's enemy, and influenced by the English ministers. Prussia had always found Warsaw a troublesome province, and did not wish to possess it again; but she would have preferred a neutral State to intervene between her frontiers and Russia. She would coincide with Alexander's views if she could obtain a part of Saxony, but in no other way. Austria throughout fearing Russia more than France, was alarmed by the projected marriage of the Duc de Berri, and Metternich endeavoured to prevent it. The marriage between the Grand Duchess

Catherine and the Archduke Charles, proposed years before and now renewed, fell through because it was contrary to the rules of the Greek Church for two sisters to marry two brothers, and her deceased sister Alexandra had been the wife of the Archduke Joseph. As to France, mere vindictiveness induced Louis to forget his own interests and oppose Alexander's plans. Talleyrand and Napoleon between them were fated to bring upon the unfortunate country a second invasion, and the dire retribution for all the blood shed since the death of Louis XVI.—a retribution suspended after the first invasion, owing to Alexander's generosity—but falling with accumulated weight when the Allies marched once more on Paris. No one but Louis and his advisers were ignorant of their perilous footing, and yet they wished to sever the ropes which kept them floating on the waters, disregarded Alexander's counsel, and encouraged disputes with all their continental allies. Talleyrand went to Vienna with orders from his master to foment quarrels and prolong the Congress in every possible way. An army was marched to the south of France to enforce a demand for Murat's deposition, while the French minister boasted that of all the Powers France was the most capable of carrying on another general war. Napoleon's emissaries kept him well informed of these transactions, and he imagined that Louis was isolated, and would not again receive support from the Allies. Louis even refused to keep a verbal promise to Prussia, that if the Allies would not openly strip the galleries and museums in Paris of their ill-gotten spoil, he would restore the works of art stolen from Potsdam and Berlin. Napoleon opened a secret negotiation with the chiefs in command of that French army which was approaching his island territory, and where every officer and private detested the dynasty that preferred noble birth to military exploits. Once in reach of that army, what should prevent him from placing himself at its head and overturning Louis, who, in trying to identify himself with his kingdom, had treated those who had restored him to it as enemies? So, in the belief that another coalition was impossible, Napoleon broke his word and returned from Elba, and the result was the utter humiliation and prostration of France.

And England, after opposing Talleyrand's policy through

years of war, now combined with him against Russia, and was drawn by his schemes to forsake her usual open diplomacy, and to sign a secret treaty to support each other with arms if necessary in counteracting her views, which after all were carried out. Was it likely that a minister, whose course was marked with broken pledges, should become the sincere colleague of any ally, and not turn directly it seemed to his advantage against his new friend? Castlereagh soon found himself called upon "seriously to remonstrate with Talleyrand," because, instead of following his master's instructions to unite his efforts with the Allies to curb Russia as regarded Poland, he attacked every arrangement. He said it was not for the Bourbons, restored by the Allies, to assume the tone of reprobation or throw odium upon the arrangements which had kept the Allies together, &c.; and even the courteous Alexander declared that Talleyrand tried to play the part of a minister of Louis XIV.

Wellington wrote from the embassy in Paris to Castlereagh (August 18th, 1814), that "the situation of affairs will naturally constitute England and France as arbitrators at the Congress if those Powers understand each other, and such an understanding may preserve the general peace."

Sir Charles Stewart informed Lord Castlereagh* (Paris, August 1st, 1814) that Talleyrand "said he had witnessed with satisfaction the feeling not only Austria, but even the Russian nobility, expressed respecting the plans the Emperor of Russia is supposed to meditate in Poland. He observed that so long as the Polish question was confined to a definition of frontier, it could not produce any material effect upon the affairs of Europe; but that the instant the principle of independence should be set afloat, and the possible establishment of a Polish kingdom, with its corresponding forms and institutions, should be contemplated, though its limits should not reach the present frontier of the Russian Empire, a germ of discord both in Russia and in the rest of Europe would be formed, by which the interests of all parties would eventually be more or less equally affected. He said the probable substitution of Polish authorities for the Russian governors, &c., in all the provinces successively dismembered from that monarchy, had

* Castlereagh Correspondence.

already created a feeling which rendered the Emperor's return to his own dominions very necessary; and if the influence derived from the late auspicious events should enable him to overcome this feeling, it would only lead to a more difficult struggle at Vienna with the ministers of all the principal Powers in Europe. He considered France and England alike interested in keeping Russia from maintaining a weight in the affairs of North Germany." Again, on August 8th, Sir Charles Stewart writes: "This Government expects with very great anxiety the account of the Emperor of Russia's arrival at St. Petersburg. The Prince de Benevento (Talleyrand) told me yesterday that he considered the old divisions (of Poland) to form so essential a part of the politics of Europe, that he was anxious to ascertain if my Court coincided in the same opinion. He said the immediate interests of France would point out that the King of Saxony should be King of Poland, but the discord which must inevitably follow the establishment of a Polish kingdom, however inconsiderable, was so dangerous to other States that he had no hesitation in abiding by the old arrangement, which he considered to be infinitely better calculated for the preservation of general tranquillity. He thought the question had been lightly considered by the Emperor of Russia, whose mode of viewing Polish affairs was the greatest proof of youth manifested by that Sovereign during his stay in France. He conjured the British Government to make Polish affairs a mere question of limits at Vienna, in which endeavour they would be assured of the support of all the great Powers, and but a feeble opposition on the part of the Russian ministers themselves, who do not consider the re-establishment of a Polish kingdom to be by any means a Russian object."*

Louis from the very first preferred the alliance of England to that of Russia, though willing to protract the matrimonial negotiation, to use it as a bribe to induce Alexander to allow of Napoleon's removal from Elba and Murat's deposition. Castlereagh asks Wellington (August 7th, 1814) to "ascertain in what state the treaty of marriage between the Duc de Berri and the Grand Duchess Anna now stands." "It was considered certain in St. Petersburg," the Duke answers, "that the Duc

* Wellington Correspondence.

de Berri told him it would take place on his return to Paris." But at this very time Talleyrand, having found that Alexander would not swerve from his line of policy for the sake of a marriage his mother had much at heart, was directed by Louis to give his final decision to the Czar, that he could not permit it, lest it should introduce insanity into the royal blood of France.* The difficulty about religion had been surmounted, as neither the Pope nor the clergy of France dared object to a Greek chapel in the Tuileries. One of the brothers of the Prince Regent is said to have offered his hand to this young princess, though, as he was more than twice her age, the offer was declined. Ferdinand VII. of Spain was a widower, and a party among the Spaniards, who wished to keep him out of the hands of the priests, proposed his marriage with a Russian bride. The English ambassador doubted if this arrangement would suit England, but the Duke of San Carlos was commissioned to negotiate it. Alexander had a low opinion of Ferdinand, though he hoped he had been improved by calamity. He consented that, in the event of the marriage, his sister should go with the King of Spain to mass, and to all outward appearances conform to the Roman Catholic ceremonies; but he stipulated that she should be allowed a Greek chapel, and on this point the project was broken off.

Alexander left his capital, September 13th, for Moscow, which still presented a melancholy heap of ruins. He stayed there a few days and assembled the principal inhabitants, thanking them for their patriotism, and giving orders to hasten the necessary measures for its restoration. From Moscow he went to Vilna and to Pulawy, the seat of the Czartoriskis, where he had stayed in 1805, passing through the part of his empire most wasted by the war. The elder Prince Adam, having been Marshal of the Polish Diet in 1812, thought it wise not to obtrude himself upon the Emperor, who was received by his daughter, the Duchess of Würtemberg, the Princess Radzivil, General Krasinski, Count Novossilzof, and many others. A deputation of Poles came from Warsaw to offer their homage and to express their gratitude. "I hope," he answered, "that success will justify the confidence

* Talleyrand told Lord Holland that this was the King's real reason, as he believed both Peter III. and Paul to have been insane.

of your nation; the prosperity of the Poles will be my reward. Assure the inhabitants of Warsaw of my friendship, and if I delay my arrival in their town, it is only to consolidate their happiness." At Vilna, where he stayed for one night, he received the principal inhabitants who had returned since he last visited it, during the disastrous period of the French retreat. The nobility had then fled, afraid to meet the Prince to whom they had broken their oath; but now they were anxious to ascertain their position with regard to him. On seeing Count Tisenhausen (the father of Madame Choiseul-Gouffier), he said, "Ah! it is you, Count; the past is forgotten —all is forgotten." "But the accent, the grave air, evidently meant that he was *pardoned*," writes the Count's daughter; "the Emperor could pardon, but he could not forget." The Count felt it so much that he did not again put himself in the way of the Emperor.

Before leaving Russia Alexander* appointed commissioners to ascertain the losses of the nobility and citizens in those towns and provinces overrun by the French, to provide them with indemnities, and to repay every one of his subjects who came forward with contributions during the war. He set out from Pulawy September 25th, and meeting the King of Prussia they entered Vienna together, and were received by Francis at the entrance to the city, where he embraced his allies in the sight of thousands of people. The Sovereigns of Austria and Prussia had returned to their capitals with far more pomp than Alexander permitted in Russia. Berlin and Vienna were brilliantly illuminated, and some of the inscriptions on the public buildings in the last city bordered closely on the profane. Over the principal gateway they read these words: "Five completed the great work. Two in the first line, Alexander and Francis. Two in the second, George and Frederick William. And if you wish to know the fifth, look to the left," and on the fifth, in large letters, was written "God." Frederick William made his triumphal entrance into Berlin August 7th, and gave a banquet to the Russian troops as they paused in his capital on their way to their northern homes. After twenty-five years of battles, the sound of arms had ceased from one end of Europe to another. Even Russia

* Lord Walpole writes: "He is all kindness and flattery."

was at peace on all her frontiers, for the Persian war had ended in the annexation of two important provinces.

The possibility of another war induced the British ministers to hold out an olive branch to America, though they refused Alexander's mediation in 1813, on the ground that "Great Britain could never consent to trust a question involving her maritime rights to any Power, however unexceptionable—independently of that consideration—that Power might be as a mediator." But as many points of dispute were brought forward before matters were finally adjusted, Alexander was eventually appointed arbitrator on the question as to whether the United States could claim indemnity for the slaves carried off by British vessels in the war of 1812. This was in 1816, and by the treaty of Ghent, concluded between Great Britain and America in 1815, it was provided that " all territories, places, and possessions taken by either party from the other during the war, shall be restored without delay, or any slaves or other private property."*

Great Britain contended that this meant, "those slaves only were not to be carried off who, at the time of the exchange of the ratifications, were in the forts and other places where they had been originally taken." This was the question still at issue between the two nations; it was purely a pecuniary one, as the British colonists were then permitted to keep slaves. Alexander's decision was, "that the United States were entitled to claim from Great Britain a just indemnification for all slaves that the British forces had carried away from places and territories of which the treaty stipulated the restitution, and that the United States were entitled to consider as having been so carried away all slaves transported from the above-mentioned territory to British ships within their waters, and who for that reason might not have been restored." The Emperor caused it to be officially made known that he had devoted "all his attention to the examination of the grammatical question, and that his decision was founded on the signification of the words in the text of the article." Nevertheless, his decision certainly did not tend to increase his waning popularity in Great Britain.

* Rush's Recollection of Residence at the Court of London.

CHAPTER III.

1814—1815.

THE CONGRESS OF VIENNA.

ÆTAT. 36—37.

THE attention of the world, once concentrated on Moscow and Paris, was fixed on Vienna at the end of September, 1814, for the most numerous assembly of Sovereigns, statesmen, and generals ever known had gathered in the Austrian city. The Congress, adjourned from Paris, was to have been opened there on July 29th; but the visit of the Sovereigns to England, and the necessity for Alexander to return to his own States, caused a delay, gladly extended by those who thought it to their interest to break up the present unity of Europe. The King and the Czar arrived on September 28th. Alexander had sent forward Nesselrode, Capo d'Istria, Pozzo di Borgo, and Czartoriski with instructions, as he wished to conclude everything as quickly as possible. Yet, though the other Sovereigns and ministers, including Talleyrand, Count de Noailles, Count de Latour, Narbonne, and the Duc de Dalberg, on the part of France; the young Princes of Prussia, Hardenberg, and Baron Humboldt, the Prince of Denmark, the Kings of Bavaria and Würtemberg, with their heirs; Lord Castlereagh, Lord Cathcart, Lord Clancarty, Sir C. Stewart, Blucher, and Beauharnais had assembled by the 13th and 15th, nothing was concluded in a few preliminary meetings, where Nesselrode boldly stated his master's claim of Posen, Cracow, and Kalisch as part of Poland. The discussion on this subject gave them full occupation, and he was beginning to hold out hopes of satisfying France by Murat's deposition and Napoleon's removal to some distant colony, in exchange for Talleyrand's acquiescence with the plans of Russia, when Alexander appeared, and at once refused to depart either from the treaty of April 11th, or from the Polish frontier as he had already marked it out. To the uninitiated, the first period of the Congress was all intoxicating gaiety; but the fêtes and dancing concealed many anxious hearts, cruel disappointment, and suppressed rage; and to Alexander and the ministers of the great Powers it was a time of hard work and incessant vigilance. Even the Emperor's apparent amusements were all to further his object, and the colony of Poles in Vienna were enthusiastic in his praise. The first difficulty rose on the subject of precedence, which he at once solved by suggesting it should go by seniority; and of this no one else could complain, as it placed himself last. His wife met him at Vienna, and they were both guests in the Imperial palace, where his two sisters, Mary and Catherine, and the Kings of Denmark, Bavaria, and Würtemberg, with the Prince of Baden, were also lodged. The Empress Elizabeth received her husband's overtures for a complete reconciliation so coldly, that after they parted at Vienna it is believed they were not renewed, and when she had obtained his support for Baden, which the other members of the Congress wished to diminish in favour of Bavaria, she seemed to have fulfilled her object. She had several conferences with Stein, but was thought to feel annoyed by the presence of her sisters-in-law, of whom the eldest then living, the Princess of Saxe-Weimar, was twenty-eight, and still handsome and attractive. A representative of the diplomacy of the last century was also there in the old Prince de Ligne, whose wit entertained Catherine on her journey to the Crimea, and even now formed a lively element at the Congress. Razoumovski, once accused of admiring Paul's first wife, was another veteran diplomatist, and he took some part in the negotiations, which were officially conducted for Russia by Nesselrode and Capo d'Istria, who held jointly the portfolio of Foreign Affairs. When Alexander ceased to be Francis's guest, they occupied a house connected with his residence. Baron Humboldt assisted Hardenberg, on account of the Prussian Chancellor's age and deafness; and on behalf of Austria there was Baron Weissembourg and the unscrupulous Metternich, the admired of the drawing-room, who courted married women as a means of influencing their husbands.* Constantine arrived at Vienna with his

* Lord Holland, who was no friend to Alexander, says of Metternich,

brother, whom Lamartine styles "the young and modest Agamemnon of this Court of Kings." He stayed there six weeks, and was chiefly remarked for the deference he showed Alexander; "in truth," writes the Count de Lagarde, "one would think him an enthusiast of submission as another might be of liberty." Several others made a similar observation. Gentz writes, that an audience with him left a very bad impression. He says the same of La Harpe, who came to Vienna to obtain his pupil's support to the Swiss Republic, and who, " in a conversation with Pozzo di Borgo and myself, betrayed his bad principles without reserve." The Prince of Würtemberg, always at variance with his father, was employed in courting his cousin, the widowed Catherine. He had been married against his wishes to a Princess of Bavaria, from whom he had obtained a divorce, and two years later she became the fourth wife of the Emperor Francis. The engagement between the Prince and the Grand Duchess was proclaimed before the close of the Congress.

Maria Louisa resided with her son at her father's palace at Schönbrunn, but she called on the Empress of Russia in Vienna, and could not resist joining in some of the fêtes held in honour of her husband's enemies. There was a question of annulling her marriage, but she objected to part with her Imperial title, which in that case she must have lost. The first meeting of the Sovereigns with their ministers was held October 2nd, when Alexander declared his views as to Poland and Saxony. Not one of the foreign Governments except the English ventured to raise objections when he explained them in private audiences with their ministers; but if he had expected opposition from England, his irritation and surprise were extreme when Talleyrand, supported by Metternich, protested in the name of his master against any rearrangement of the Russian and Prussian frontiers, and demanded the removal of Napoleon and Murat. The conference was stormy, and Alexander, " from being usually gentle, became haughty and

"He appeared to me little superior to the common run of continental politicians and courtiers, and clearly inferior to the Emperor of Russia in those qualities which secure an influence in great affairs. Some who admit the degrading, but too prevalent, opinion that a disregard of truth is useful and necessary in the government of mankind, have on that score maintained the contrary."

bitter."* He would not yield a village to Austria, but would dislodge her if necessary from Poland with 400,000 men. They adjourned till October 3rd, to give foreign ministers time to receive further instructions, while Castlereagh undertook a direct mediation with Alexander; and Nesselrode advised Talleyrand also to ask for an audience, and try to soothe the Czar's feelings, wounded at the French ingratitude. His master had long been unable to account for the ill-feeling Louis displayed towards him. What had he not done to spare France's honour? Her very existence as a strong Power was entirely his work. He returned 300,000 prisoners without demanding a ransom or even the usual payment of the cost of their subsistence; but while Louis hastened to present the Prince Regent with the Order of St. Esprit, he had never offered it to the Czar. No one cared less for such honours. He laughed at his own officers if they thanked him with too much eagerness for a decoration, and would not accept the Order of the Garter unless the Prince Regent received a Russian Order in exchange. But it was the studied slight he could not help discerning, and moreover Louis pointedly rejected his counsels, and the result could already be seen in the universal discontent which prevailed in France.

The Czar made Talleyrand wait a few days, and then received him at Schönbrunn with unusual stiffness, abruptly questioning him on the state of his country. "Very good, Sire," said Talleyrand; "as good as your Majesty could desire; better than we could have hoped." "And the public spirit?" "It improves every day." "And the progress of liberal ideas?" "Nowhere is this progress more real." "And the press?" "It is free, except some indispensable restrictions at first." "And the army excellent?" asked Alexander. "We have 130,000 men under the flags; we could have 300,000 in a month." "And the marshals?" "Which?" "Oudinot." "He is devoted." "Soult?" "He has shown temper at first. He was given Brittany, and is satisfied, being most loyal." "And Ney?" "He suffers from the loss of his estates (in Germany), but he depends on your Majesty to put an end to his sufferings." "And your Chambers? It is said they are not with the Government." "Who could say

* Thiers's Congrès de Vienne.

such a thing to your Imperial Majesty? There is, as in every beginning, some difficulty, but after twenty-five years of revolution it is marvellous that in a few months we should have attained so much repose." "And are you satisfied?" "Sire, the confidence and the goodness of the King passes my hopes." At these answers Alexander's face wore an incredulous expression (unfortunately justified), but he said quickly, "Let us finish our business." "It depends on your Majesty," said Talleyrand, " to complete it to your glory and the advantage of Europe." The Czar then expressed his displeasure at the resistance he met with from France, and said he thought the Bourbons owed some consideration to Russia. Talleyrand did not dispute it, but spoke of the rights of Europe, which he ought to respect, above all after overturning a man who was accused of hurling them at his feet. "I am not acquainted," said Alexander, " with these European rights which you now invent to oppose me. Between Powers rights are the requirements (convenances) of each. I admit of no others." Then Talleyrand, who had for years either counselled or aided every scheme of aggression and public injustice on the Continent, turned up his face, and raising his hands above his head, cried, "Unfortunate Europe! unfortunate Europe! what are you going to become?"* But Alexander was in no mood for a theatrical exhibition, and said to him, in a tone that Talleyrand had never known from him, " Ah! well, if it is so—war. I have 200,000 men in Poland; let them chase me from it. Besides, I have the consent of the rest; you only make obstacles and break an almost general agreement."†

It was a saying of Napoleon's, that if Talleyrand were whipped his features would not express that anything unpleasant was going on; and he had learned to maintain the most placid exterior before many an angry and excited orator

---

* Thiers's Congrès de Vienne.
† Lord Castlereagh speaks of the extreme difficulty of making Prussia a useful ally in the present discussion, connected closely as she has been with Russia; but notwithstanding the King's *liaison* with the Emperor, it ought not to be despaired of, under the known sentiments of the Prussian Cabinet, as it was difficult to found a satisfactory balance in Europe, unless Prussia could be induced to take a part. He says, "Talleyrand is very averse to Russia;" and Mr. Rose, writing from Munich, October 10th, speaks of the spell the Emperor of Russia seemed to have laid on the King of Prussia's mind.

in the course of his sixty years' experience. He showed himself more grieved than vexed by this mood in the Emperor, and answered that France did not seek war, but did not fear it; if it was necessary to make it now for the maintenance of European rights, it would be aided by universal sympathy and the help of many allies, for he was convinced the concord the Emperor imagined did not really exist. He bowed respectfully but coldly, and went towards the door. Alexander perhaps felt a little remorse for his anger with so infirm an old man; he immediately advanced and as usual shook him by the hand, though his trembling grasp revealed his agitation.

In a letter from Berlin, Sir George Jackson* observes that " the King of Würtemberg, the oldest of this conclave of Sovereigns, but the last I imagine in point of rank or the extent of his territories, takes the *pas* of Alexander, the youngest in years, but claiming to be the first and greatest among Sovereigns (owing to the mode in which precedence was arranged). His Imperial Majesty is not quite up to the mark just now, from having been thrown by a vicious horse. He is recommended by his physicians to abstain for a short time from his long walks, which he takes in all weathers, from hunting, dancing, and other fatiguing exercises. This, they say, puts him a little out of humour." He seems to have followed this advice only so far as to substitute a long ride on horseback every morning for his usual walk, and constant fatigue added to vexation brought on rather a serious illness. England was just then particularly irritated against Russia by a recent tariff to protect the native manufacturers, who would have had no chance against British goods; for many of them only sprang into existence during the continental blockade. She was alarmed by a prospect of the marriage of Alexander's younger brother and sisters with Austria, Prussia, and France. She could not help admitting that the Czar was acting with toleration by Turkey, who had not yet fulfilled the provisions of the treaty of Bucharest, but in every other quarter the progress and strength of Russia gave her great uneasiness.

* Bath Archives, vol. ii. More than one account, however, says precedence was given by the letters of the alphabet. Their ages were: the King of Würtemberg, born 1754; of Bavaria, 1756; of Denmark, 1768; the Emperor of Austria, 1768; the King of Prussia, 1770; Alexander, 1777.

She therefore claimed the protection of the Ionian Isles, to keep Russia out of the Mediterranean.

Francis opened the Congress with a ball at the Burg Palace, where he danced with the Empress Elizabeth, Alexander with the Empress of Austria, and the King of Prussia with the Queen of Bavaria. "The masters of the world," wrote the Baron Ompteda from the scene of gaiety, "lived for the first time on a footing of intimacy with their equals, and cheerfully laying aside the burden of etiquette abandoned themselves without restraint to a varied series of amusements. Thousands of strangers poured into Vienna, and the sums they spent defrayed the cost of the State entertainments. The Congress was in full activity on my arrival about the middle of October. It was reported it would be speedily dissolved, but weeks and months passed, and the sessions continued, Sovereigns treating each other like brothers." He accompanied his relative, the Prince de Ligne, to a masquerade. "Observe," said the Prince, "that graceful and martial figure who is walking with Beauharnais—that is Alexander. Yonder dignified-looking man, on whose arm a fair Neapolitan is playfully hanging, is no less a person than the King of Prussia. The lively mask, who seems to put his Majesty's gravity somewhat to the test, is perhaps an Empress, perhaps a grisette. Beneath that Venetian habit you see an Emperor. That colossal figure, whose bulk is not diminished by the ample folds of his domino, is the King of Würtemberg. Here is Maximilian, King of Bavaria. Beside him you see a little pale man, with an aquiline nose and fair hair—that is the King of Denmark." At an evening party at the Princess Bagration's, the entertainment consisted in the drawing of a lottery, to which each of the Princes had sent one or more gifts. Constantine won two porcelain vases from the Royal manufactory at Berlin, which he offered to his hostess. Alexander's prize was a box of mosaic work. He gave it to the Princess Maria Esterhazy. There was Prince Koslovsky, the Russian ambassador from Turin, an outspoken man with many bon-mots, a favourite of the Czar, whom he amused by his sallies; Prince Ipsilanti, who had escaped from Constantinople to seek an asylum at Alexander's Court, and lost an arm at Bautzen; Count de Witt, who in the war of 1812 had raised four regiments on his mother's estates.

"Alexander's officers, though most of them were still very young, had already made so many campaigns, that war had become their element, and they spoke of it like veterans reposing on their laurels."

After Alexander's stormy interview with Talleyrand, Castlereagh requested an audience, but the Czar anticipated his visit. The English minister was instructed to yield all Saxony to gain Prussia, but to resist on the subject of Poland. Austria was to receive Lombardy, Illyria, and Venice without opposition. "Unfortunately," says Thiers, "not one of the Powers could give a lesson of moderation to the other, and if Alexander had wished to trace the picture of English ambition since the occupation of Malta to that of the Cape and the Isle of France, Castlereagh would have been embarrassed, but he repressed his indignation, though evidently unhappy."* He explained, that if England had assisted him, the peace he had conquered had been most beneficial to her. He had made a promise to the Poles, and would keep it. He thought the service he had rendered Europe should give her in turn some courtesy towards him. England disposed of Belgium for her own safety, why should not he dispose of Poland for his? Castlereagh said that with a less honourable character than Alexander's, the alarm his project excited would close the Congress at once; and he entreated him, for the general peace and his own glory, to renounce an inadmissible pretension. They parted much dissatisfied.

Alexander was going to Pesth to visit his sister's tomb, and Francis with several princes accompanied him. Those Hungarians belonging to the Greek Church, laymen as well as priests, flocked from the neighbourhood to greet him as their spiritual head. This was unexpected and unsought, for Alexander wished to make the journey privately, but it increased the Austrian Cabinet's fears respecting the extension of the Russian frontier on that side. Before he left Vienna he had another interview with Talleyrand and Metternich, for the first, hoping to make an extra complication, and really more objecting to the extension of Prussia than of Russia, tried to out-manœuvre Castlereagh, and point out that while England abandoned Saxony, but was bent on leaving Poland

* Congrès de Vienne.

in its old divided state, France was willing to give Poland up to Russia for the sake of preserving Saxony. Alexander was more affable, and observed that in Paris he had found Talleyrand entirely favourable to the re-establishment of Poland. "Assuredly, Sire," answered the minister, uttering in a respectful and firm tone a sentiment his correspondence most flatly contradicts, "I, like all Frenchmen, should have seen with real joy the re-establishment of Poland, but of the true Poland. This, on the contrary, interests us little. It is only a question of frontier between you and Germany, so we, the established defenders of European public rights, only interest ourselves in Saxony." But this from Talleyrand, who had drawn up Napoleon's defence of the murder of the Duc d'Enghien, the treaty of Tilsit, and the document for annexing Northern Italy to France, rather lost its effect. Alexander spoke calmly till that moment, when he exclaimed* that rights and treaties were empty words used by each for his own advantage; he was no longer the dupe of them, and here there was no question of principle or of right, but of interests, which each person understood in his own way. He had promised Saxony to Frederick William, and held more to his word than to those pretended treaties. The King of Saxony was a traitor, who had deserted the cause of Europe. Talleyrand showed as much horror for such sentiments as was compatible with the respectful attitude he maintained throughout. "The expression traitor," he said, "ought never to be applied to a King, and above all by so august a mouth. Right is something very sacred, which prevents us from being in a state of barbarism, and your Majesty will reflect more, I hope, before defying the unanimous sentiments of Europe." Alexander abruptly answered, that England and Austria abandoned Saxony to him; his friend the King of Prussia would be King of Saxony, and he should be King of Poland. He cut short the conversation by saying that France might yet need his support, which would depend on her sympathy for Russia. "France," replied Talleyrand, "asks no support; she only maintains principles." Nothing could move Alexander, and the minister only parted from him good-humouredly by treating the question in a light, ironical manner.

* According to Talleyrand's report.

The interview with Metternich was very stormy, for the Prussian ministers communicated to Alexander an Austrian despatch, showing that it was the object of that Cabinet to satisfy Prussia in order to isolate Russia. Alexander had spared Austria most generously, both during and after her invasion of Russia. He had vexed his own people by allowing her general to take the nominal chief command of the Allies, and now her one object was to set aside a treaty for which he was responsible, for she opposed almost every article in it, including the provision for the ex-Empress in Parma. Metternich informed him that his patience was inexhaustible, as he had been accustomed for eight years to similar scenes with Napoleon; but he came away in an excited state, very rare with him, and the same day Alexander set off for Hungary. During the journey Francis took the opportunity to tell his ally, as if to offer himself as a useful example, that he always intrusted diplomatic matters to his ministers, who from habit had more calmness and knowledge of affairs than their Sovereigns, and their opinion might be considered as final. He was forced to sacrifice himself, as he had sacrificed his daughter, for his people. Alexander answered, that his own tried character should reassure the Austrian people; he never wished to quarrel, and hoped peace might continue. But Francis answered, though the character of a prince was certainly a guarantee,[*] yet a good frontier was worth more; and if they were to quarrel, the sooner the better. As to Prussia, Alexander supported her extension, believing the King would keep his promise to his people and grant them a constitution, and his refusal to do so, and the imprisonment of the young enthusiasts who had risen up against the French supremacy in 1813, was the cause of great coolness between the two monarchs in 1817. The Czar also thought the independence of the smaller Powers in Germany was incompatible with its strength, for, as in 1803-5-6, they were open to bribes or any intrigue on the part of France, and were incapable of maintaining themselves. By granting constitutions to those countries imbued with liberal ideas, he hoped to satisfy the republican party, still very strong, and by creating powerful

[*] Thiers, and Wellington Correspondence.

and united monarchies to secure universal peace, and make such aggressions as those of Napoleon impossible for the future. Bribery, he thought, would be out of the question with a representative government. He had every disposition to strengthen England, France, and Austria, but his views were too enlarged for his contemporaries, and he was not supported even by England in the imposition of a constitution on the restored monarchs. Ferdinand VII. had already cast off his, and dissolved the Cortes, which had nobly maintained his claim to the throne. The Duke of Wellington, in a letter to the Emperor, quoted Sicily, where the English had instituted a constitutional government, as a proof of its failure when there was not a sufficient number of educated people in a country to conduct such a form of administration; and the line the English ministers now took as to Poland was to prefer the old divisions of the country under Austria, Russia, and Prussia, to its restoration with a constitution, if under that guise it was to be united to the Russian Empire.

After Castlereagh's interview with Alexander, he addressed a memorial, dated Vienna, October 12th, entreating the Emperor to use his "influence and example to inspire the councils of Europe at the present conjuncture with that spirit of forbearance, moderation, and generosity, which can alone secure to Europe the repose for which your Imperial Majesty has contended, and to your Majesty's name the glory that should surround it." He says it depends exclusively on the Emperor whether the Congress shall prove a blessing to mankind or a lawless scramble for power. He refers to the treaty of Kalisch, February 28th, 1813, in which Alexander says the time will arrive when treaties will no longer be truces, &c. Europe cannot see without alarm his plans for Poland and the annexation of the Duchy, which opens a prospect of renewing those tumultuary contests in which the Poles so long embroiled both themselves and their neighbours, &c. His Imperial Majesty should also weigh how far it can be reconcilable with moral duty to embark in an experiment likely to excite alarm and discontent amongst the neighbouring States, and political ferment within his own dominions. He ends with almost a threat if the Emperor persists in defying the opinion of the Continent.

Alexander replied in an autograph letter, dated October 30th, on his return from Hungary :*—

"I have delayed answering you, my lord, till I had well weighed the force of every argument you oppose to the determination confided to you with regard to the Duchy of Warsaw. I own I had some trouble to understand your motives and their explanation, and to reconcile your proceedings, the sentiments you express, and your words at the opening of the Congress, with the past conduct of Great Britain." He had refuted those arguments in an enclosed memorandum, and merely makes a few comments on its contents. "You say, my lord, you should see me receive, *even with satisfaction*, a liberal and important increase on the side of my Polish frontiers as a pledge of the gratitude of Europe, provided it would not impose on my neighbours an arrangement inconsistent with the obligations of independent States to each other. As I share your opinion entirely in this respect, and the answer in the memorandum proves at length that I am not departing from it, I shall have nothing to add on that matter, except to express my surprise at seeing you take to heart (renchérir) my neighbours' fears.

"I pass now to the article where you remind me of what I can never forget—the free and cordial assistance I received from England when I struggled alone against all the Continent led by Napoleon. He who wishes to recall to another the services he has rendered puts himself in the wrong. If I thought you introduced this into your remarks with the unjust suspicion that I did not sufficiently appreciate the elevated character of the nation, and the enlightened and amicable policy of Great Britain during the war, I should not have answered it. But we are discussing the future, and it is therefore natural to enter into a full explanation of the past. The answer to the memorandum will show you, that all the acquisitions I have made till now had no value except in a strictly defensive point of view. If in the death-struggle I sustained in the heart of my States I had not been easy on the side of the Turks, could I have devoted to the continuation of the war the great means I consecrated to it, and would Europe have been freed? You give me to understand that

* Wellington Correspondence.

England only consented to the acquisition of Norway in favour of Sweden to guarantee to me the previous acquisition of Finland. As for me, I acted more generously, and in soliciting England to consent to the guarantee of Norway I wished to procure one more ally to our cause. I could not lose sight of the great maritime advantage Norway gave to Sweden against me. However, they counteracted each other; my capital was made unassailable, while Sweden, better concentrated, had nothing to fear. In this manner we both gained in security, and all cause of dispute was taken away. If the rules of equilibrium are not found in this case I do not know where they exist. You see, my lord, I have not mistaken the true sense of those acts of the policy of your Cabinet which you recall, and am far from wishing to undervalue them. The future fate of Europe undoubtedly depends on the issue of the present Congress, and the object of all my efforts and of all my sacrifices has been to see the members of our alliance recover or acquire dimensions which shall be capable of maintaining the general equilibrium. I am therefore ignorant how, with such principles, the present Congress can become a hearth of intrigues and hatred, a scene of iniquitous efforts to acquire power. I forbear to turn this phrase against any of my allies, extraordinary as it seems to find it in your letter. The world that has witnessed the principles of my conduct from the passage of the Vistula to that of the Seine, may judge if the desire of acquiring a population of one million more of souls, or of arrogating any preponderance to myself, could have animated me or guided any of my measures. The purity of my intentions renders me strong. If I persist in following them out as regards Poland, I am conscientiously convinced it will be favourable to the general advantage even more than to my personal interest. Whatever shadows you may try to affix to this moral policy, it may perhaps find appreciators among nations which still understand disinterested benevolence. The details in my answer will, I trust, help to calm you for the sinister future you predict for the Powers to whom I am allied by all that friendship and confidence can render most indissoluble. On their part I count on its being reciprocated. When such elements exist, we need not fear whatever brands of discord may be cast among us, but that the Congress will procure a state of things honourable for each member of it and peace for all. As to what concerns my care of my own subjects and my duties towards them, it is for me to know them, and nothing but the honesty of your motives could make me revert to this passage of your letter after the impression it first gave me. I hope that my answer proves my sincere sentiments for you have not changed. " ALEXANDER."

In the reply to Lord Castlereagh which the Emperor enclosed, he says the author " could not introduce his subject with a more suitable preface than the treaty of Kalisch, where the Emperor's State maxims and principles were displayed. It was the first bond for the independence of States. It was Russia who advanced before them, after exterminating the French forces which had devastated her provinces, and who wished that her old allies should recover all their power. The Emperor devoted extraordinary means towards it, and neither Moscow in ashes, nor his desolated towns and fields, could check him in this enterprise, to which his moderation had attracted so many appliances. The author wishes to show that the Emperor has laid aside his first principles, that he despises the faith of treaties, that he threatens the safety of his neighbours. His Majesty has calmly read such strange accusations, though he did not expect them from the person who has entered into the lists. His conduct has already refuted them, and he hopes this answer will serve to allay all alarms, and to render such remonstrances unnecessary for the future." He denies the charge brought by Castlereagh, that he only restored Dantzic and its territory as a *favour* to Prussia, for he gave it up to her spontaneously as soon as it was reconquered. He attacks one by one the other points specified in the remonstrance, and shows the territory claimed by Russia is not out of proportion to that acquired by Austria and Prussia; the first having recovered her old Polish possessions, by far the richest portion, with its mines of coal, sulphur, and salt; and the last obtaining the most advanced and cultivated parts of the Duchy, filled with manufactories such as the rest of the country does not contain; while the portion he proposes to unite to Russia has been ruined by war, famine, pestilence, and emigrations. He states the comparative populations and revenues, and says "that these facts considered, no impartial man can call this acquisition *immense*, as it is styled in the English memoir. Giving quite a new latitude to the Duchy of Warsaw, the author asserts that the Russian power will be established by its means in the heart of Germany. When a reasoning goes into extremes it ceases to persuade. Besides, a few remarks will be enough to annihilate it." He again shows that Sweden's loss of Finland has been more than balanced by the gain of Norway. "As to the frontier line obtained in Persia, it is more easily defended; but notwithstanding this advantage, the safety and peace of that quarter still require very numerous garrisons, which must be renewed every year on account of the unhealthy climate. The acquisition of a part of Bessarabia supplies us with a better defence by means of some fortresses. In every other respect it is an insignificant advantage after a long and murderous war. Now, when everything shows that the Emperor is only anxious to establish a system of defence, not of aggression, when it is remembered that his only means of repulsing the last invasion of the great League was in sacrificed Moscow, how can fears be still entertained with regard to his views and intentions?" Returning to the question of the Duchy of Warsaw, he treats "the animated picture of these uneasy and fickle Poles called to rally round a royal standard, renewing the scenes of the past, conspiring against their neighbours, and destroying all hope of peace and happiness for the future," as purely imaginary. He says, "that Austria and Prussia would not fail to make common cause in case of extremity, and might easily invade his southern provinces, so that the only danger was for Russia." He proves that Vienna was perfectly defensible from invasion on the side of Russia, and that the different Polish fortresses are necessary to secure the navigation of the Bog, Narew, &c., and the Palatinate of Lublin. Lord Castlereagh quoted the old Partition Treaty of 1797: "But when Austria and Prussia have contributed as allies of France to despoil Russia of the greatest part of the Polish provinces, when Russia has been obliged to reconquer them, it becomes really a new division, and the treaty of 1797 exists no more. Suppose the name of Poland is restored, and a part of the Duchy of Warsaw reunited to Russia, what are the dangers which would result from it for Austria and Prussia? None, since the Emperor offers to both those Powers the most formal guarantee of the parts of Poland which remain under their sceptres. None, since this restitution being contrary, according to the author of the memorandum, to the system of Austria, of Prussia, and of the British ministry, the least attempt will unite all these Powers, whom Turkey would readily join, against Russia, isolated and abandoned to her own resources. This avowal is doubtless one of the first of the kind made in diplomacy, but it is worthy of the purity of the Emperor's intentions. It is not a little more or less territory, it is not a few strong posts, which secure the general equilibrium ; it is a similarity of interests, with a common tendency in the moment of danger ; and in this view the balance is assuredly not in favour of Russia."

The Emperor added, that far from the Poles becoming dangerous by the restoration of their nationality, he believed it was the surest means of calming the restlessness with which they were reproached, and conciliating all interests. He was convinced that time and events would prove it. He thought the accusation utterly unfounded, that he had abused the language of treaties or of his engagements with Austria and Prussia, who, freed from Napoleon's yoke, were considerably increased; and he could not imagine how the writer proved that, because the Emperor thought of restoring the title of kingdom to Poland, Europe's deliverance and all the advantages acquired by the Allies would be reduced to nothing. He thought the idea equally absurd that, according to Lord Castlereagh, the whole work of the Congress would be suspended so long as the Emperor adhered to his projects. "If," he continues, "after thinking over the contents of this answer the author adheres to the same opinion, and is not convinced; if he can succeed in dissolving the Congress for one point, while so many other more important remain to be arranged, the Emperor will not have to reproach himself with this misfortune. On the contrary, he will expose to England and to Europe the nature and extent of his demands. Those people who have seen him fight for their liberty and been witnesses of his moderation, will learn the cause which prevented the general re-establishment of order, happiness, and peace, for which so much blood has flowed; though, as to the Sovereigns, his allies, his brothers in arms, nothing should ever disturb his friendship for them," &c. Castlereagh certainly did " go into extremes" when he said " the conquest of Poland was effected principally to bring the Russian nation into closer communication with the rest of Europe, and to open a vast field and a higher and more striking theatre for the exercise of her strength and talents, and for the satisfaction of her pride, her passions, and her interests." This may have been the result, but it was not the cause; and it was moreover Pitt and the English Cabinet who persuaded Russia to descend into the European arena. It was on moral grounds that they induced Paul to take up arms against the French Republic, and Great Britain's representative now objected when Alexander gave moral reasons for claiming a share of the spoil. He ironically proposed that Alexander should give up his own Polish provinces, and erect the whole of Poland into an independent kingdom. "This would be," he says, " it is true, a sacrifice on the part of Russia according to the usual calculation of States; but unless your Imperial Majesty be disposed to make these sacrifices to your moral duty at the expense of your empire, you have no moral right to make such experiments to the detriment of your allies and your neighbours." He also talked of Prussia and Austria signing " their own ruin," if they agreed to make over the whole of the Duchy to Russia; whereas many statesmen asserted it could only be a source of weakness to Russia, and it has certainly proved so rather than a source of strength. England, who had kept Malta after the peace of Amiens, contrary to treaty, for her own interests, not being able to show, like Russia, that the acquisition was necessary for self-defence, could hardly condemn Russia from a moral point of view. Lord Castlereagh answered Alexander's letter, November 4th, again dwelling on the danger and injustice to Austria and Prussia if the Duchy was not shared among them, and condemning the notion that a Power should receive a territorial recompense for great sacrifices. He received a second memorandum on the subject from Alexander on the 21st, written while confined to his room with an attack of fever and erysipelas. " To create suppositions," it stated, "merely to refute them, is not discussion."

"The author of the memoir gives Russia credit for intentions she has never had. She does not reserve the decision of the fate of the Duchy of Warsaw for herself. She desires to regulate it according to the principles of strict equity and in union with the allied Powers. If the Emperor had founded his policy on exclusive and private interests when Napoleon's army, assembled, it may be said, at the expense of Europe, had found her tomb in Russia, his Majesty would have made peace with France, and without exposing himself to the chances of a war so much the more uncertain in its result as it depended on the determination of other Cabinets, and without imposing new sacrifices on his people, would have contented himself on the one part with the safety acquired for his empire, and on the other with acquiescence in the conditions that Bonaparte, taught by a sad experience, would have hastened to propose to him. But the Emperor, in the generous enterprise to which he had devoted himself, made use of the noble impulse of his people to second the wishes of all Europe. He fought for a cause on which the destinies of the human race depended with disinterested views. Faithful to his principles, he constantly worked to favour the interests of the Powers rallied to the common cause, in placing his own in the second rank. He lavished his resources to make their united efforts prosper, in the firm persuasion that his allies, far from reproaching a conduct so pure, would have been assured that he was ready to subordinate all private considerations to the success of an enterprise undertaken for the general good." He shows that his whole aim throughout has been to restore the European equilibrium, that unless Russia was strengthened by the Duchy she would not be on a level with the other Powers, and that it was conquered by her arms without any foreign assistance. He dwells on the extent of the British dominions all over the world, Austria established in Italy and Illyria, which rendered her the mistress of the Adriatic, and assured her a preponderating influence in Turkey. Prussia inheriting the northern part of the old German Empire, and extending from the Vistula and Elbe to the Rhine. " It is of the greatest importance to Russia to put an end to the uneasiness of the Poles. Longer repressed they will react one day under foreign influence, and that reaction must trouble the repose of Russia and of all the north. Experience supports this observation. . . . . The author of the memoir, drawn on by the vivacity of the discussion, seems no longer to appreciate Europe's present independent and happy state, and has forgotten the desperate situation from which she has emerged. . . . . . If all Europe, including Great Britain, would restore everything and return to her condition before the war, the Emperor of Russia would be the first to give an example of such great sacrifices to contribute to this result, but the measure would never be listened to by the rest. Great Britain herself would be called upon to make important restitutions for which she is by no means prepared, however essential they may be to the general good and to the true independence of other nations in external relations. The part of a mediator is no doubt very useful when it serves to bring people together; but, in a contrary case, it is better to leave the interested parties to settle their own differences, particularly when friendship and confidence constitute the most active principle of their negotiations." He considered the statistics of Lord Castlereagh enclosed to be much overdrawn, but concluded by saying, "the true character of a conciliator belongs pre-eminently to Great Britain, and her ministers in sustaining it in all its purity might render the greatest service to the cause of Europe and entire humanity." He quotes several treaties, and refutes the accusation of having broken them, and accompanies the memorandum with a short letter, in which he hopes that this will be the close of their private correspondence, and that Lord Castlereagh will in future send his letter through the usual channel (the ministers). He shows that "England's proposal, far from restoring the balance of Europe, would give a preponderating weight to Austria and Prussia, while France, circumscribed by the excess of a colossal ambition, without a navy or commerce, and Spain were certainly not equal to the rest." When speaking of the combination which would control future Russian ambition, he probably little thought that this prediction would be fulfilled while his minister Nesselrode was still in office, though he himself would have been long in the grave.

He adds a table of statistics that he believed to be more correct than Lord Castlereagh's. The treaty of 1797, which the English minister enclosed to the Emperor, was ratified at St. Petersburg, and engaged the contracting Powers never to restore the name of kingdom to Poland.*

Castlereagh had argued on the same subject with the Emperor ever since he joined the Russian army in 1814. He wrote to Wellington, October 20th : " You see we are still at anchor. The Emperor is beset by the Poles, and has, I fear, embarrassed himself by promises. If I could bring Austria and Prussia fairly to bear upon him, I think we should yet get a tolerably good frontier from him."

Lord Liverpool (the Prime Minister of Great Britain) wrote on the 21st, " that the English must take care not to get the discredit of resisting the Emperor's proposal on a principle of partition." In another letter he complains of the Emperor's obstinacy, and that he has some talent, but no common sense. He believes Poland will be his ruin. " Affairs," writes Mr. Cooke to Lord Liverpool from Vienna, " stick with Metternich, who I believe will never play a great straightforward game but by mere necessity, and when he finds that all little and side games fail.† I think if the Emperor can be brought to bend on the point of Poland, Prussia will not object to preserve Saxony in part. Austria and Prussia are getting closer. . . . . Pozzo di Borgo talked to me in mournful tones," the Emperor having had a warm dispute with him and Nesselrode : " when he finds Prussia fall off he will be furious." In the mean time, the Hanoverian minister had procured a better frontier for Hanover, and the King of England exchanged his title of Elector for that of King, which, Count Munster wrote to the Prince Regent, was " formally recognized by Austria, Prussia, and all Germany, except Baden, who was silent, because excluded from the meeting. The Emperor of Russia, though present, made no answer. I have begged Nesselrode to explain this silence. He assures me he will make the Emperor's answer on his return from Hungary, for which Alexander had set out on the 24th, meaning to return at the end of the week ;" adding that, " the adoption of the royal title caused some embarrassment

* Cooke says Alexander did not show this correspondence to his ministers till he had sent his answers.

† Wellington Supplementary Despatches, vol. ix.

to the ministers of Russia, since the Poles would appeal to it as a precedent."

In a memorandum by Mr. Vansittart,* giving the opinion of the English ministers, they are said to be running the risk of being left alone by Austria and Prussia, who were wavering in their resistance to Russia, of incurring the jealousy of Russia, and being looked upon at home as the advocates of a system of partition. It was feared Russia might revenge herself by bringing forward the question of maritime law at the Congress. The Emperor said to Castlereagh, that Russia would gain more power by acquiring half the Duchy of Warsaw as a province than the whole as the kingdom. The English ministers were also of opinion that "a minority in Russia, or a weak reign, might bring about a separation between Poland and Russia which would be supported by all the European Powers." It also became evident that Parliament would not understand another war with Russia for the sake of maintaining Poland in its divided condition, and to prevent the Emperor from giving it a separate government and constitution. The partition of Saxony was also opposed by the English press. A pamphlet by a Pole, published in England, called "An Appeal to the Allies on behalf of Poland," had a large circulation, and was presented to the Princess Charlotte. The Poles themselves were almost unanimous in supporting Alexander's views; so the opposition to the Czar must be raised on the question of Saxony, and the wickedness of dividing an independent sovereignty, if the British ministers then in power expected to keep their posts.

Wellington wrote from Paris, November 5th: "M. de Blacas is very much displeased at the continued obstinacy of the Emperor of Russia respecting Poland and Saxony. He said the King, and most probably the Prince Regent, would withdraw their ministers from the Congress, declaring they would not acknowledge these arrangements, and Europe would remain in a feverish state, which sooner or later must end in war."† Talleyrand also declared at the Congress that

* Wellington Correspondence.
† A letter from Prince Maurice de Lichtenstein to the Duchess d'Abrantès, dated October 12th, gives another aspect: "The Emperor of Russia is always amiable and good, as you have known him. He often speaks to me of Paris. Believe me, that you have not deceived yourself, and he is really a man truly good and very excellent."

"France was better prepared for war than any country in Europe."

Yet the Sovereigns met daily at hunts and reviews, at one of which the Emperors and Kings assisted on horseback, while a carriage drove on to the ground containing the Empresses of Austria and Russia, with the Queen of Bavaria and the Grand Duchess Catherine sitting in the back seat, and the rest of the Court ladies in various vehicles. A lively writer enters into a personal description of these celebrities—the strong-minded Austrian Empress, who liked shooting hares; the Prince of Baden, with a kleptomaniac inclination; the handsome Princes of Saxe-Coburg; the sad-looking but sharp-tongued Empress of Russia, who was dancing in the same polonaise with her husband, where nobles, Kings, Emperors, generals, Greek chiefs, and Turkish pashas were jostled together with subalterns and commoners. All at once the dance stopped, though the music proceeded, and the restless Alexander leaned over the head of a rather short dancer in front of him, and somewhat impatiently asked his wife, who was two couples in advance, if she could not proceed. "Always polite," she answered, in a voice loud enough to be heard by many others than himself, and in an indescribably sarcastic tone. He said nothing, but coloured and bit his lip as he caught the eye of another dancer, and a moment afterwards the march continued. "Impressionable, but skilful as an Asiatic, most amiable, good, and fond of pleasing, Alexander could not long sustain the part of an irritated man," writes Thiers. "He went on foot in the streets, frequented the drawing-rooms of Vienna like a private person, carefully set his rank aside with the Princes who crowded to the Congress, and succeeded in gaining them, for few men possessed the talent to the same degree." Francis had no personal objection to the reconstitution of Poland under Russia, but he wanted to keep Cracow, and also to obtain the circle of Tarnopol; for as long as it remained in Russia's hands it was a living memorial of Austria's humiliation. He was more easy for his future safety when he learned the marriage was broken off between the Grand Duchess Anna and the Duc de Berri, but he was vexed at the Czar opposing himself to Lorraine and Alsace being seized by Austria. He was piqued at a matrimonial alliance with Austria being rejected for the second time* by Russia, and he disliked Alexander's liberal views. On the other hand, his daughter was appealing to the Czar, both in person and by letter, not to let the Congress deprive her of Parma, claimed by Ferdinand VII., and the Empress Beatrice presented him with a flag embroidered with the words, "Indissoluble union between Francis and Alexander." The Vienna Cabinet was of opinion that war was necessary to restore the prestige of the Austrian arms and also her position in Europe; but in this respect Francis, from family considerations, had placed his empire below that of Russia by renouncing his ancient title and adopting a new one, for this act at once made Alexander the senior Emperor in Europe.

On October 30th the ministers assembled again, when Talleyrand delivered another message from Louis on the subject of Napoleon's removal from Elba, as it was only four hours from Italy and forty-eight from France. He asked for him to be transferred to the Azores. Francis approved, as he would there be far away from Murat, but Castlereagh doubted if the British opposition would stand such a measure, and advised the French Government to pay the 2,000,000 francs stipulated by the treaty of April 11th. Alexander, Hardenberg, and Metternich all pressed the same advice on Talleyrand, though the last two, like their Sovereigns, willingly agreed to Napoleon's removal. "Alexander raised the only obstacle. He was the true author of the treaty, and too often reproached with it to make it possible for him to forget it. Nevertheless, it was a point of honour with him that it should be observed, either as to Beauharnais, Maria Louisa, or Napoleon's pension. He was astonished at Austria's conduct in trying to get rid of her former neighbour, so nearly connected with her Emperor;"† and Thiers says his language was very imprudent since his recent irritation against Metternich. "If it was

---

* Three connections between the Imperial houses of Austria and Russia had been prematurely cut short, so that the Empress-Dowager had become superstitious on the subject. The wife of the Czarovitz Alexis was sister to the Empress of Germany of that day; Alexander's aunt had been Francis's first wife, and died within a year; and Alexander's sister, already mentioned, who died in 1801.

† Thiers, Congrès de Vienne.

necessary they would unloose the monster who seemed to give so much alarm to Austria and her allies." This speech, though only the unreflecting utterance of a hot-tempered man, made a painful impression. "But we should calumniate," adds Thiers, "one of the noblest characters of modern times if we believed this was Alexander's only motive for opposing a violation of the treaty with the prisoner of Elba. His honour, his generosity, would never have consented to it, and his colleagues were so certain of this that no one tried to reason with him, though it was a measure of prudence which all the rest wished to carry out." One of the first measures passed in the Congress was to secure the throne of Sardinia to the house of Carignan* in case of the failure of heirs to the house of Savoy, as Victor Emmanuel I. had no sons. Genoa had surrendered to Lord William Bentinck on the promise of being restored to her ancient independence as a Republic, but she was transferred by the English to Sardinia, and Alexander's influence alone preserved the integrity of Switzerland.

Between the meetings of the Congress, Castlereagh tried hard to detach Prussia from Russia, and easily alarmed the ministers and the military, who, with full confidence of the support of England as to Saxony, in their turn alarmed the King, and persuaded him to reclaim Warsaw. But Alexander's recent journey to Moscow and Vilna kept fresh in his mind the losses and sufferings of his country during the war, and the flatteries of the gay world in Vienna were unable to extinguish them from his remembrance. He felt he could not return to Russia without some fruit of the campaign in Germany and France, undertaken contrary to the wishes of his subjects, or without even procuring for them a well-protected frontier. He invited the King to dine alone with him at the Russian Embassy, where he had removed with the Empress, and then he spoke with the greatest warmth, recalling the friendship they had vowed for each other in 1813, when they met on the Oder, after years of coolness, and had promised to fall together or to restore independence to Prussia and Europe. He reminded Frederick William that his most faithful Russian subjects advised him to remain on the Vistula, and to accept Napoleon's offers of peace, leaving ungrateful Germany to her

* Now reigning over Italy.

fate. Nevertheless he held out his hand to the Germans, and without this devotion on the part of Russia, Prussia would still contain only her reduced number of 5,000,000 subjects, and Germany be yet enslaved. The union of Prussia and Russia produced the change of fortune which at the present moment enabled Germany to hold her head high in the councils of Europe. But now the allied Powers all strove to profit by this change of fortune, excluding the Russians, to whom they were indebted for it. To confine them to the Niemen was to leave them without reward for the blood they had poured from the shores of the Oder to the Seine, for after the disastrous campaign in Russia, Napoleon offered her the Vistula as a frontier, and there would have been no fear of his ever renewing the invasion: it was such as a man only undertakes once in his life. The Russian army might have returned home without exposing itself to new risks, without sacrificing more than 200,000 soldiers to continue the campaign of 1813, when it had already taken possession of Warsaw. Yet the great resolution (wisely opposed by Kutuzov) to cross the Vistula was forgotten. The Allies, like Austria, whom notably it was necessary to force (violenter) to draw them into this European crusade, and who had not expended a quarter of the blood shed by Russia, wished to obtain the sole fruits of victory. Not an Austrian village had been burned, yet they refused to the Russians the price of the ruins of Moscow. The diplomatists only followed their trade, but honourable Princes like Alexander and Frederick William ought not to allow ingratitude to embroil them with each other, but for the benefit of their people, for their private happiness, they ought to live and die attached.

Frederick William felt strongly the obligations of Germany towards Alexander, and that if the Czar had treated with Napoleon after the Beresina, the present position of Prussia would have been widely different. He yielded to Alexander's impassioned eloquence, embraced him, and swore to remain faithful. But Alexander said this was not enough without the word of his ministers. He had no confidence in them. Frederick William called Hardenberg, and the explanation begun with the King was finished with the Chancellor. Above all, Alexander wished to possess the town of Warsaw; without it he could not fulfil in any measure his promise to the Poles; and when Hardenberg related this scene to Castlereagh, he said he never saw anything like it, and that before such vehemence resistance was impossible. He was obliged to yield the point of the Duchy, and engage to support Alexander's policy, on which the Emperor sent an order to Prince Repnine, who still occupied Saxony with a Russian army, to march into Poland, and unite with the troops concentrated on the Vistula; and he invited Frederick William to replace that army with a Prussian force, and at once possess himself of the country. Repnine had governed Saxony provisionally, and left his name in the grateful recollections of the inhabitants, where his army was found less oppressive than the presence of even their native troops. An immediate outcry was raised against this measure, especially by the smaller German States, who, influenced by Talleyrand, and led by the Prince of Saxe-Coburg, were opposed to the partition of Saxony. They accused Austria of weakness, and Metternich adroitly answered that, far from being displeased, he was rejoiced to see the Russians return to the North. They even went so far as to draw up a protest against the two usurpers, but the Prince of Würtemberg, fearing to imperil his matrimonial hopes, stopped its being presented, and the Prince of Saxe-Coburg was persuaded to withdraw for having displeased his chief protector, Alexander; it was feared by his family that his Duchy would not be extended to the proportion of their demands. Count Munster wrote to the Prince Regent that Alexander had a violent scene with the Prince of Saxe-Coburg, and among other things said he counted dynasties and so-called hereditary rights as nothing compared with the interest of States—a sentiment considered most shocking and revolutionary by the politicians at Vienna. Prince Leopold undertook to conduct the negotiation in his brother's place, and though a grant of territory was conceded to him he never obtained the whole, as it depended on an exchange of lands with Prussia, which, with " remarkable bad faith," he writes, she afterwards refused to give up to Coburg when the Congress was dissolved and the affairs rested only with the Prince and the King. The Austrian Cabinet now deputed Schwartzenberg to try his personal influence with Alexander, who had been very civil to him since he came to Vienna. As flatteries had failed, the marshal tried to work upon him by appealing to his sensibility or his fears. He told him he once had a blind faith in him, but now repented of it, or that he ever commanded an army in alliance with Prussia and Russia, wishing, in fact, that Austria was still merely the satellite of France. He was almost as positive as the Czar; but Austria, who had quietly obtained Lombardy, Venice, Illyria, and Dalmatia, and was negotiating for the restoration of the Tyrol from Bavaria, and the Valteline from Switzerland, could not consistently advocate moderation. When Castlereagh received his orders to make a stand on the partition of Saxony instead of on the union of Poland, the Prussian ministers in their turn were enraged, and wished to declare war with Austria and France. Here Alexander was a peace-maker, for it was really the last thing he wished, and he saw that neither of the three was averse to it. He checked their menacing language,* and saw Talleyrand, who again urged the peace of the world, the glory of Europe depended on the re-establishment of legitimacy to its full extent, and he might satisfy Prussia by restoring the Duchy of Warsaw to her. "You wish," answered Alexander, "that I should despoil myself in order to satisfy you." He asked the reason of the extensive armaments France was preparing, and what use Louis proposed for them. Talleyrand would not raise his voice in his reply, and secretly enjoyed obliging Alexander to sit down close to him to catch his words, which were to the effect that old soldiers returned from abroad were enlisted (the very soldiers Alexander had freely restored), and these were at the service of England and Austria if there was war on account of Saxony and Poland.†

All this time Murat manifested great uneasiness in Naples. He was refused admission to the Congress, owing to Beauharnais, who hated him, revealing his offer to the Viceroy to help him to the throne of North Italy after his treaty with Austria,

---

* Thiers.

† Thiers. At this very time, from the Duke of Wellington's Correspondence, it appears that an outbreak was daily expected in France, owing to the unpopularity of the Royal family. Even the Duke's own life was in danger; and the British Government transferred him to Vienna, for the sake of removing him from Paris. As the agitators were Bonapartists and agents of Napoleon, if he did advocate Napoleon's removal from Elba to St. Helena, it was merely a matter of self-defence.

because he feared Alexander's proclamation of March 31st might include him among the proscribed members of Napoleon's family. Hitherto Austria was the only Government which had concluded peace with him, but she was inclined to cast him off to please France. Oldenburg once more became a subject of discord, but Alexander said if he had quarrelled with Napoleon rather than abandon his uncle's States to France, it was not likely he should yield it to any other Power. Westphalia was dissolved, and the Grand Duchy of Berg and the Rhine provinces made over to Prussia; Baden and Bavaria, Bavaria and Austria, and Prussia and Coburg, disputed over their frontiers; but of all the Sovereigns and ministers present, Alexander alone regarded the feeling and interests of the populations, and studied to adjust them according to the national sentiments. If Norway was an exception, he at least secured her the most really liberal constitution in Europe. His health had been disturbed since the beginning of October, and early in November he took a chill which soon confined him to his bed with an attack of fever and erysipelas. The foreign ministers hoped this would lead to his affairs being trusted to Nesselrode and Czartoriski for the future, as they might find them more pliable than their master. Munster writes to the Prince Regent, November 27th, that he had recently invited them again to his presence, " and expressed regret to Metternich that his temper had carried him away." Talleyrand, among other awkward revelations, quoted a letter from Metternich to Napoleon as late as March 23rd, 1814, inviting him to renew negotiations for peace. "Hardenberg has now taken charge of the Polish question, and had a long conference on Wednesday last with Alexander, who is confined to the house with erysipelas in the foot. He represents to him all the misery a new war would bring on Europe, the light in which Alexander would appear as the cause of this war, while hitherto he has been admired as the restorer of continental liberty. Finally, with the consent of Austria, he proposed to the Emperor to cede to Austria Zamosk and its district, as well as Cracow as far as the Warta. Prussia asks for herself Thorn and the territory as far as the Warta (thus joining the Austrian Empire, and forming a belt between Russia and Germany). He had great hopes from the manner in which the Emperor listened to him, and to-day he expects an answer."*

Castlereagh writes, November 21st, that Czartoriski promised him to urge the Emperor to make some concessions. "The Emperor's illness is an erysipelas brought on by over-fatigue and cold. He had danced without intermission the whole night, and almost every night since he came to Vienna, in the hottest rooms, and been on horseback early the following morning. The disorder will probably confine him for ten days or a fortnight." On November 25th he writes to Lord Liverpool, that he had exhausted arguments with the Emperor on the subject of Poland; and Wellington afterwards stated that language could not be stronger than was used both verbally and in writing to Alexander to give up his Polish scheme; but the Czar continued as obstinate as before. "The general sentiment of dissatisfaction and alarm occasioned by his conduct," writes Castlereagh, "is becoming too strong and universal to be any longer a secret from him. It exists extensively among his own subjects, and I have reason to believe this fact has not been concealed from him. Under these circumstances, and profiting by the reflections for which his illness has afforded an occasion, perhaps his Majesty may moderate his pretensions." On December 5th, he adds, "the Emperor of Russia visited the Emperor of Austria immediately he was recovered, and seemed more conciliatory with regard to Poland." Again, on the 7th, "the Emperor of Russia has recovered, and as usual in the ball-room;"† having accompanied the Empress to a dance at Sir C. Stewart's. The Congress was again adjourned, as the Powers apparently hoped to weary out each other, but all the Russians, including the Sovereigns and Constantine, were particularly civil to the English. Hardenberg, having been compelled to submit to Alexander, revenged himself by abusing him violently behind his back, calling him a perfidious usurping character, infinitely more dangerous than Bonaparte.

On December 17th Castlereagh‡ sends an account of an explosion between Austria and Prussia, which produced a very animated discussion. The Prussians were so much exasperated by Metternich refusing Saxony to them, that Harden-

---

* Munster's Political Sketches. † Wellington Correspondence.
‡ Wellington Correspondence.

berg* sent to Alexander parts of the confidential correspondence on Poland between himself and Metternich, showing their *liaison* against Russia to prove to him that Austria now broke faith with Prussia upon the point of Saxony, because Prussia refused to declare war with Russia. Alexander at once went to Francis and reproached him with desiring war. Francis replied, if his minister wrote such a letter, it was without his knowledge, and he must be called on to explain. Metternich, to justify himself, showed Alexander one of Hardenberg's letters, where, to escape an opposition to Russia in which he found himself disavowed, he pointed out that the Czar must be ruined by his own politics; in a few years his military power would become comparatively feeble, then the Allies might seize the occasion of doing themselves justice. "The whole made for two days a great sensation, but the result may prove what I have before alleged, that the climate of Russia is often the more serene after a good squall." Metternich's interview with Alexander "was not the less stormy from a little *private* note of the first, most unaccountably or most ungenerously among the papers sent, denying in terms not very measured a conversation between them, as reported by Alexander. The audience terminated by his Imperial Majesty saying he should give his answer to the Emperor in person. The interview took place the following morning, and according to report was marked by peculiar conciliation on the part of Alexander—a wish to settle all differences—regret that he could not meet the Emperor of Austria's wishes about Cracow, which the Poles could not bear to alienate as the tomb of their kings, and that in lieu thereof, as a proof of his regard, he would cede the circle of Tarnopol which he received from Austria. This district contains a population of not less than 400,000 subjects, and although the cession will not serve Austria in point of frontier, it is the most substantial proof of a disposition to treat à l'aimable which his Imperial Majesty has yet shown. The Emperor expressed his hope that Prussia would also accommodate, and that all might be arranged. I cannot but infer that this disclosure has produced rather a salutary impression on the

* It is supposed Hardenberg was stimulated by one who wished for his post.

Emperor's mind. . . . . In this correspondence the Emperor clearly perceives that I had not been mistaken in representing to him the real feeling of his allies, and I have no doubt they made their impression even after the concert had failed."*

Other versions of the same affair assert that, in Alexander's first warmth at seeing himself accused of telling a falsehood, he sent Metternich a formal challenge by an influential person, who carried it to the Archduke Charles, entreating him to prevent it being delivered. Francis asked for an interview with the Grand Duchess Catherine, which she refused till ordered by her brother to see him. The Austrian princes represented the unequal rank of the two parties rendered such a meeting incompatible with the Emperor's dignity, and he ought to appoint an aide-de-camp to take his place. If the Czar shot Metternich, no blame would attach to him; while, if it was the other way, there would be a war. And after two days' negotiation the Czar consented to a personal explanation with Metternich, who extricated himself by saying the Emperor's deafness caused him to mistake what was said in a conversation. Alexander accepted the excuse, but it was not considered a satisfactory one by even Metternich's supporters. Lord Liverpool wrote to Wellington: "Austria has a minister in whom no one can trust, who considers all policy as consisting in finesse and trick, and who has got his Government into more difficulties by his devices than could have occurred from a plain course of dealing."

"I have not the alarms," writes Lord Liverpool to Lord Bathurst, December 15th, "about Alexander which you entertain. He is forming a sea of troubles for himself, and this question of Poland cannot now be decided in any manner without his making either the Poles or the Russians his enemies." Cooke writes, that the Russians cannot brook the idea of separating the Polish provinces acquired by Catherine; he believes the Polish leaders to be false to the Czar, and it was supposed he could only erect the Duchy of Warsaw into a kingdom. He had never mentioned the correspondence between himself and Castlereagh to Nesselrode, whom Metternich informed of it, declaring that he would rather see

* Wellington Supplementary Despatches, &c., vol. ix.

Cracow belong to Russia than form an independent Republic, much as he condemned the first alternative. But in the end Alexander obtained the cession of the Duchy to Russia, and the separation of Cracow from Austria, with a radius of 450 square miles and a population of about 142,000, which was erected into a Republic under an independent government.* The province of Posen, containing the important town of Thorn and about 500,000 inhabitants, was to be restored to Prussia if she would moderate her demands on Saxony, and leave Dresden and Leipsic with an area of 6777 square miles to the dethroned King. This concession, which Metternich, Talleyrand, and Castlereagh could not obtain from Alexander, was yielded at the personal solicitation of the unhappy Frederick Augustus, who pleaded that it was only fear which induced him to join Napoleon. As far as territory went, the exchange was more than an equivalent to Prussia, and while it quieted her fears on the side of Russia, it appeased Austria, by placing a neutral territory between the two German Empires; as the possession of Saxony as well as Silesia would have given Prussia the command of Bohemia, containing only insignificant fortresses. Alexander hoped that reducing the causes of alarm would increase the probability of a prolonged continental peace; but the Prussian party, led by Stein† at Vienna, were much excited, threatening immediate war, and it was only through Alexander's representations, and on the news of a peace between England and America, that it was abandoned; for the British minister said his country had made peace with the United States to place her armies at the disposal of Europe.

Castlereagh wrote from Vienna, November 11th, to Mr. Vansittart, that he will " not call on the Dutch for the remainder of the loan they owe to Russia if the Emperor persists in his demands, as he would rather give the Prince of Orange something more to fortify the Low Countries than assist the credit of a Calmuck Prince to overturn Europe." He recommended an armed mediation on the part of Great Britain, France, Austria, Bavaria, the Netherlands, and Hanover.

---

* It was annexed to Austria in 1846.
† Stein was only permitted to come to Vienna by the Czar, not by his own King.

Czartoriski told Lord Castlereagh, and Prince Radzivil the Duke of Wellington, that the Emperor would be unable to carry out his views as to Poland, on account of the Russian nobility; but before the Congress met again Castlereagh had returned to England to assist at the opening of Parliament, and the Duke left France (with whom he counselled a strict alliance) for Vienna to take his place. Alexander went to Gratz on December 20th, and then to Venice for a day or two, but he returned to Vienna on the morning of his birthday, when Francis gave a concert in his honour, and he appeared in Austrian uniform. He displeased the British representative by arranging the question of Poland entirely between himself, Austria, and Prussia, and when a memorial was presented to him by the Austrian Cabinet requiring a guarantee if it acquiesced in his wishes, he wrote at the top of the document that his word sufficed. He said he wished to form a strict alliance between Austria, Russia, and Prussia, so that not a cannon should in future be fired without the permission of the three Powers; but while not venturing to dissent from this proposal, Austria formed a secret treaty of alliance with France, England, Spain, and Bavaria against Russia and Prussia; and Stein* asserts that Francis, flushed with pride at having at last formed a member of a successful alliance, was anxious for another war; but this time it would have been in the hope of pushing back his late ally of Russia, and to establish the Austrian supremacy in Moldavia and Wallachia, so as to secure a firm footing at the mouth of the Danube.

Constantine left Warsaw, December 9th, to take command of the army in Poland. During the entire campaign of 1813–14, when he was seldom separated from his brother, his conduct was irreproachable, brave in the field, obedient to orders, and, if not admired by his officers, still popular among his men. "The worship of his brother," which the Prince de Ligne said at Vienna, "seemed to be his only fixed prin-

---

* General Knesebeck (whose mission to Russia was mentioned in 1812) addressed a memoir to Stein, September 28th, 1814, setting strongly before him the danger of Russia crossing the Vistula. "It would render life itself worthless," he said. "There is no security for Prussia when a large portion of the Russian territory protrudes into her own; none for Austria as soon as Russia crosses the Vistula. He goes so far as to lay before Stein a plan for an alliance with England, Austria, Persia, and Turkey in case of a war with Russia."

ciple," was thought by some not to be without design, as he now aspired to the Viceroyalty of Poland. However, Alexander determined to confer this on a native Pole. Constantine arrived at Warsaw about the middle of the month, and presided at a solemn meeting of the Senate on the 24th. He caused the new constitution to be read, and issued a proclamation to the Poles, followed in January by the formal nomination of Alexander as King of Poland. "Unite yourselves round your flag," he said; "draw your swords to defend your country, and to maintain its political existence. While the Emperor Alexander prepares its happy future, show yourselves ready to sustain his efforts. The chiefs who for twenty years have conducted you on the field of glory, will enable the Emperor to appreciate your valour. In the midst of the disasters of a fatal war, he has seen your honour survive events which did not depend on you. Great feats of arms have distinguished you in a struggle of which the object was often foreign to you; now that your efforts will be consecrated to your country you will be invincible. Soldiers and warriors of all ranks and battalions, be the first to give an example of the order which ought to exist among all your countrymen. Loyalty to the Emperor, who only desires your welfare, obedience, concord, these are the means of assuring the prosperity of your country, which finds itself under the powerful ægis of the Emperor. You will thus arrive at the happy position which others may promise you, but which he alone can give you," &c.

This proclamation was regarded by the Congress as a threat; but the representatives of England misjudged their ally, as was afterwards proved, when they gave him credit for vindictiveness, and supposed he would now turn against her at the earliest opportunity. He was naturally unwilling to sacrifice the vital interests of Russia merely to please an English Cabinet, whose measures might be altered by a change of ministry as soon as Parliament met. He had sufficiently set aside his personal advantage for that of Europe, and he felt it was now time to consider his own empire. A naïve remark of the Emperor Francis showed how little Austria could ever be depended upon as an ally if an enemy offered a higher price for her friendship. He asked Alexander if he would not have willingly granted all the points under discussion if they had been demanded when he was canvassing for the adhesion of Austria in 1813; to which the Czar answered, he could not say that he might not have done so, but that circumstances had considerably changed. Now, in consequence of a dispute with Talleyrand, the Austrian Cabinet encouraged Murat, and to Louis's annoyance permitted him to buy 25,000 muskets in Austria, and occupy the Italian frontier with his army. "While every morning we are expecting the Emperor," De Maistre writes from St. Petersburg, February 2nd, 1815, "we receive the news that he may not come for months, as his prescuce will be necessary for some time to avoid a war."

The fêtes continued through the autumn at Vienna. Alexander held a series of entertainments, chiefly tableaux vivants, and a large military fête at Prince Bagration's country seat, while two of the Russian nobility gave balls in honour of the Empress Elizabeth.* When Beauharnais arrived at the Congress, a difficulty was raised as to what rank he should take, till Alexander said he ought to have the same precedence as any other son-in-law of a King. He was the only good pedestrian, except Alexander, among all the princely guests at Vienna; and as soon as the last was sufficiently recovered from his illness, he used to call at Eugene's house every morning, and they took a long walk together. "Alexander," writes Ompteda, "was adored by those who enjoyed the honour of his intimacy, and the simplicity of his manners with his easy politeness and gallantry won all hearts at Vienna." He introduced an Austrian officer walking with Ompteda to Eugene, as the youngest knight of St. George. Hearing the name of my companion, Lucchesini, he asked if his father was a plenipotentiary to the Congress of Listow in the reign of Frederick II. "He was, Sire." "And where is he now?" "Living on his estate near Lucca." "If," said Alexander, "he amuses himself

* "The Emperor Alexander's departure will be regretted more than that of any of the royal visitors," writes a Vienna correspondent to Sir George Jackson, "for he is very popular and altogether the chief star of that brilliant throng. He seems to find far more enjoyment in a *sans façon* mode of life than in the ceremonious life of the Court. He and Prince Eugene are extremely intimate. . . . Sometimes they go over to Schönbrunn together, and breakfast alone with Maria Louisa, who is said to be very little saddened by recent events."

by retracing the recollections of his past life, they must be deeply interesting, for few men have seen so much." Ompteda again met the Emperor, " in his usual neat morning dress," accompanied by Ouvarof and his shadow, Eugene, in the picture gallery belonging to Duke Albert of Saxe-Teschen, the Austrian Emperor's uncle, and heard his remarks on the various battle-fields, portrayed in a most complete collection of maps and plans. He passed alternately from the campaigns of Italy to those of Germany, avoiding any allusion to that of Russia. "After all," he said to Eugene, "here are glorious scenes, reviving recollections which ought to please you." "Ah, Sire," replied Eugene, "you see how this glory has ended. We labour to obtain it, and then it is envied, attacked, doubted, and at length forgotten." "It is not so with regard to yours and that of your family, Prince, which already belongs to history." "And it is an inheritance, Sire," said Eugene, "to which no one can have more indisputable rights than your Majesty. The conqueror overthrows and destroys, but the statesman raises and founds national prosperity on solid bases." This dialogue, writes Ompteda, " reminded me of Peter the Great entertaining the Swedish generals after the battle of Pultowa, and drinking the health of his masters in the art of war."

All the Sovereigns in Vienna paid a visit to the catacombs and Imperial tombs in the church of the Capucines. Constantine went several times. Alexander was also conducted over the various points of military interest around Vienna, and to the battle-field of Wagram by the Archduke Charles, where, he observed, that nothing in Napoleon's character was so extraordinary as his ability to sleep at any moment when he required it, even though he might be leaving his army in the greatest danger, as was displayed particularly at Bautzen, and after the lost battle of Laon in France.

Ompteda had a conversation with Czartoriski's friend and relative, Novossilzof, on the subject of Poland, which shows no attempt was made to deceive her with the idea that the partial independence was to lead to complete self-government. "The Poles," said he, " are ever carrying back their thoughts to the brilliant times of their history, and they want their country to reassume that proud attitude of independence it enjoyed under the Sobieskis, without thinking of the immense changes the political condition of Europe has since then undergone, and their peculiar geographical position, which makes it impossible they should stand again on the same footing. If we allowed her to become completely independent she would make an Asiatic nation of us, and we are not disposed to recede. If you read this MS., with the margin full of notes, written in Alexander's own hand, you will find how we wish to satisfy the Polish nation. This is the constitution intended for them. Their institutions, hereby fixed upon a solid foundation, will become the means by which the peace of Europe may be ever maintained."

The Count Zavadovski, who was not twenty-three, lost two millions of roubles in one night at play. Ompteda went to his opponent, but could obtain no redress, though he pointed out he ran great risk if the affair should reach the ears of the Emperor, whose aversion to gambling was well known. Alexander did hear of it, and withdrew his favour from the winner, who subseqently asserted in Paris that he would rather have lost half his fortune. Some time later the son of a wealthy Russian prince lost a large sum of money at play to one of his brother officers. His father complained to the Emperor that his son had been pillaged. After making inquiries, Alexander said, "Pay the money, which you can do with ease; your son is old enough to take care of himself, and no one obliged him to play. He must therefore take the consequences."

The death of the Prince de Ligne cast a shadow over the festivities at Vienna, as his illness was not at first supposed to be serious. The circumstances were a shock to his associates. He fancied he saw death enter his room in the shape of a ghastly spectre, and in a tone of the greatest agitation exclaimed, "Close the door; see, he is coming in; turn him out!" and called for assistance. He became convulsed, and sank into a state of unconsciousness. Prince Eugene and Ouvarof were among the mourners, and Alexander and the King of Prussia watched the funeral procession from that part of the ramparts formerly razed by the French.

To please the French Legitimists and get up a novel excitement, Talleyrand proposed a funeral service for Louis XVI. on the anniversary of the day of his execution, when the ceremony of tranferring his ashes to St. Denis was to take place. All consented except Alexander, who, without actually opposing it, said no one could doubt of the sentiments that Europe bore to the unfortunate Louis XVI., but a public service would be a party spectacle, very impolitic in Paris, and merely an awkward imitation in Vienna; nevertheless, if they persisted in it, he should attend the service, as the French Legation only could judge of what was agreeable to its Government. The Sovereigns resorted to St. Stephen's Cathedral in deep mourning, and French priests read the funeral oration; during which Talleyrand wept! a week later they heard of the scoffs which greeted the ceremony in Paris, and the incident of the crown rolling off the top of the bier.

While the subjects of Saxony and Poland were agitated, a variety of minor interests were also discussed. Sir Sydney Smith came to advocate the cause of the ex-King of Sweden, and Bernadotte claimed Swedish Pomerania in addition to Norway; Ragusa, Genoa; Venice and all the other Republics their independence; the Queen of Etruria, Tuscany; France and Spain, Parma; the Pope, Ferrara; Baden, Hanover, and Saxe-Coburg an increase of territory; and all the Italian principalities required Elba.

Wellington writes from Vienna, February 25th, that Alexander " is certainly embarrassed by his situation with the Poles, and is excessively anxious the assembled Powers should concur in immediately urging the Government of the Porte to act with more moderation towards the Servians, which, contrary to the stipulations of the treaty of Bucharest, his Majesty alleges is treating that people with great severity. I have urged Count Razoumovski, who spoke to me upon this subject, to delay the mention of it to the other Powers till the period at which the Powers should guarantee the dominions of the Porte." The secret alliance had already been signed on February 3rd, 1815, between Great Britain, Hanover, Spain, France, and Austria, and was soon joined by Würtemberg, Bavaria, and Holland. It was concealed at Vienna, though Hardenberg discovered it, and informed his King, who dared not tell Alexander. Stein suspected it, and imparted his ideas to the Czar, who would not believe Francis could be so treacherous towards a guest. On the arrival of Wellington,

Hardenberg again raised the question of Napoleon's removal, and proposed St. Helena, and it is said the Duke brought instructions from his Government to accede to it. Alexander still refused to break his word, but as he was to leave for Russia on March 13th, the rest meant to revive the measure as soon as he was gone. Napoleon anticipated them in a breach of the treaty, and secretly left Elba, February 26th, for the coast of France.

The history of France during eighty years shows there is no country in Europe, perhaps in the world, where an administration can be more easily overturned by a well-organized conspiracy. The mass of the people are too much absorbed in private interests to care for any particular dynasty if it leaves them in peace, and France therefore has been ruled by an ambitious minority. Napoleon's family were practised revolutionists, and their experience in 1792 had taught them the art of working on the people, and fomenting any germ of popular discontent. The army was as great an embarrassment to Louis as to Louis Philippe and Napoleon III.* The last conscription under Napoleon had brought thousands from their homes, who, after being initiated into military licence and pillage, were left to wander about the country or return to their villages without work, and longing for another revolution to enable them to seize on the property of the rich. There was nothing Alexander had not done to strengthen Louis, or to keep out of view of the people that he had been in reality imposed upon them by their enemies. Their monuments and museums were left intact, and their only burdens a portion of the same taxes they had paid for years under Napoleon; while now the gates of France were opened, strangers flocked into the country spending money, and she was enabled to carry on an unrestricted commerce. But Louis, Talleyrand, and Blacas spoiled all by their bad policy and want of foresight. The pensions settled on Napoleon's

* "The Cossack pike, which represented the constitution," writes Wilson during a journey through France in the previous August, "and the bayonet of Russia raising the throne of Louis, are images which will sooner or later fret the people to madness. . . . Enmity to the Allies, wounded *amour propre*, the view of desolation, and the want of employment, seem the chief moving causes of discontent." This was kept alive by the busy agents of the Bonapartists, hired to sow the seeds of revolution in all parts of France.

family were intended as not only a provision, but a means of attaching them to the Bourbon Government. But these pensions were withheld till the end of the first year of the new reign; and when, contrary to Alexander's advice, the Duchesse de St. Leu obtruded herself on the French Court, she was received with such contempt that she never appeared there again; and, after making her house in Paris a centre for the meeting of the Bonapartists, she joined her brother at Baden to carry on the same intrigues. Ney and the military chiefs who for years in foreign countries held the power of life and death over those beneath them, now found themselves reduced to comparative insignificance, and their rough exterior and unpolished manners unfitted them for the Court. They had little in common with the King, who was a literary wit, and liked to surround himself with clever men; and they sighed in idleness while thousands of subalterns were on half-pay, a system hitherto unknown in France. Although M. de Blacas had for years been a pensioner of Russia, his only idea of satisfying the military was to declare war against the Czar. Napoleon's two campaigns in 1807 and 1812 were accompanied with as much disaster to the French as to the enemy; therefore a really successful war with Russia would exalt the military prestige of the Bourbons above that of the Bonapartists. Austria and Prussia, on the contrary, were thoroughly beaten by the French, so there was nothing further to gain by attacking them. For the sake of recovering her position as a first-rate Power, and enforcing her opinions at the Congress, the armies of Napoleon, which surrendered so unwillingly to the Allies, were kept up just as before, as if they were inanimate bodies with no opinions or recollections of previous rewards. The reaction of feeling which always occurs more or less after a public event soon took place, and, in pity for Napoleon's fate, they forgot the ruin he had brought on France. The returned prisoners were incorporated in the ranks, convinced that they were joining them for the sake of restoring him when the proper time should come; and as there was an open communication between Elba and France, his income was lavished on purchasing adherents, and notwithstanding the large sums he carried away with him, he was already embarrassed. Half of his Guard was sent to

France ostensibly on furlough, but really to gather partisans; and yet, while clamouring at Vienna for his removal from Elba, the French Government took no precautions against the danger they feared. The army, ready to receive him, was marched towards the coast, while the ministers stated their intention to get rid of the treaty; and Louis made no secret of Talleyrand's correspondence, carried on in a series of gossiping letters to the King, all showing disunion among the Allies. The Prince of Baden was not admitted to the meetings at the Congress, but gained information from his sister, the Empress of Russia, and transmitted it to his wife and mother at Baden, while Hortense was there. The King of Bavaria was admitted to the meetings, and was a member of the secret alliance, and through him Beauharnais heard of the desire of that alliance to remove Napoleon and oppose Russia, and he told it to his sister, who corresponded with Napoleon. There was consequently no need of treacherous agents, which he nevertheless possessed, to make the deposed Emperor thoroughly acquainted with the whole state of affairs. The disunion was very evident from the Congress being so much prolonged, and he believed his reappearance would be hailed by one party or the other as a support. He was not a prisoner in Elba. It was his independent territory. When matters were more settled he would have been free to visit the Continent like any other sovereign: he was kept in the island by his word of honour, and nothing more. He embarked in his largest vessel with 400 guards, giving out that he was going to attack the pirates on the coast of Barbary, but landed instead on the coast of Provence.

A part of the garrison of Grenoble was under the command of Colonel Labedoyère, who had engaged before Napoleon left Elba to join him directly he heard of his arrival. The plan succeeded. The civil governors, when faithful to the King, could make no stand against the military; and Napoleon entered his late empire with far less risk to himself than the Comte d'Artois and the Duc de Berri when, before his abdication, they returned to France. He always loved a theatrical scene, and he knew on this occasion it would be repeated and have effect in all parts of France. He therefore acted one before the troops, otherwise unnecessary, as they were already secured. Ney was appointed by Louis to the command of a fresh army collected at Lons-le-Saulnier, to stop the progress of the Bonapartists. He told the King when he took his leave that he would bring back Napoleon in an iron cage,* and this exaggerated expression alone might have excited doubts of his fidelity. He afterwards stated he was faithful to the King when he actually left Paris down to March 13th, when Napoleon's proclamation was put into his hands; but though he may up to that moment have committed no overt act of treachery, he left the capital, it was proved, with the full intention of returning to his old master, having made various preparations, and carried with him an eagle and the marshal's uniform he wore under the Empire. Châteaubriand proposed to defend Paris instead of abandoning it to the insurgents. "Let us," he said, " line the quays and terraces of the palace with cannon. Let Bonaparte attack us if he dare in that position; let him bombard Paris if he chooses; the King defending himself in his palace will awaken universal enthusiasm. If he must die, let the last exploit of Napoleon be the murder of an old man." But, as usual, the National Guard took the side it believed to be the strongest, and a courier from La Valette, the post director, who was throughout Napoleon's secret emissary, informed the ex-Emperor at Fontainebleau that the King left Paris on the evening of the 19th, and the citizens awaited his entrance. However, he did not venture there till it was dark, lest he should be badly received; and the next morning tried to form a ministry. He resorted to the turncoat Fouché for the Police, and Caulaincourt only accepted the office of Foreign Affairs from compulsion, not wishing to parade his treachery in the face of Europe. Others hung back in the same way. In vain Napoleon, having perceived the good effect Alexander produced by his conciliatory measures, now tried the same plan. He granted pensions to the invalid Duchesses of Orleans and Bourbon; he promised to continue the constitution. "It is not so easy to govern with one as some suppose," he said; "give me your ideas, public discussions, free elections, responsible ministers, the liberty of the press,—I have no objection to them. I am the man of the people; if they really wish for liberty I will

* This expression has been denied, but Ney owned to it on his trial.

give it them. I am no longer a conqueror, I cannot be so. I have now but one mission, that of restoring France."

The Government of Louis left the finances in admirable condition, and the army was newly equipped and mounted, and as Talleyrand boasted, in most excellent order for sustaining a war. But Napoleon hoped for an ally in either England or Russia. On April 1st he addressed a circular note to each of the foreign Governments. "Sire, my brother," he began, "the true nature of the late events must now be known to you. They were the work of the unanimous wish of a great nation," &c. He pleaded the unsuitableness of the Bourbons, the love of the French for himself, his desire to repay so much affection. It was time nations exhibited no other rivalry but the advantages of peace, no other strife but that of their welfare. As these letters met with no reply, for the couriers who took them were all stopped on the frontiers, he made England the offer of taking the whole burden of her national debt upon himself; but, like a fraudulent bankrupt who borrows at 20 per cent., such proposals only showed the trembling ground on which he stood. His ministers even assumed a dictatorial manner towards him; but he still hoped for at least the neutrality of Russia, as Louis left a copy of the secret treaty on a table at the Tuileries. Napoleon charged Caulaincourt to transmit it to Alexander through the Russian chargé d'affaires, M. Budiakine, who was still in Paris. He accompanied it with an autograph note, in which he said he need make no further comment on the contents. At the same time he wrote to Maria Louisa by Baron Vincent, the Austrian ambassador, requesting her to acquaint her father with his sincere desire for peace.

Budiakine received the copy of the treaty with diplomatic coolness, but Caulaincourt thought he was inwardly enraged. He promised to make known to Alexander Napoleon's sincere wish to maintain peace with him, and to become again his friend. When the Allies once more entered Paris, Caulaincourt heard from Alexander himself that Budiakine had carried the message faithfully. "I was only half surprised at the treaty," he said; "between my brother of France and me there was not much sympathy." Yet it gave him a feeling of insecurity in the peace he had sacrificed so many personal advantages to obtain for Europe. The hopes Castlereagh and Hardenberg expressed of some future weak reign, or a minority, enabling the Allies to revenge themselves on Russia, rankled in his mind, and perhaps accounted for his refusal to reduce his enormous army, which has since been maintained in the same strength by his successors.

Napoleon intercepted a letter addressed to La Valette from Vienna, enlightening him considerably as to the sentiments of Maria Louisa. Far from being anxious to favour his interests, she openly expressed her hatred of him, supporting all measures against him, and opposing any likely to end in their living together again.* The writer intimated that she had formed an extraordinary attachment in another quarter (probably to Count Neipperg, her chamberlain, whom she afterwards married), and La Valette says Napoleon believed it was true. Certainly no pressure on the part of her family prevented her from sharing her husband's exile. Like her father, she appeared unable to live single, for on the death of Count Neipperg, her second husband, and at the age of forty-eight, she married M. de Bombelles. The Duchesse de St. Leu hastened to Paris, and appeared at the Tuileries the night Napoleon arrived, to preside over his Court in place of his wife. He said he did not expect to find her there. "I remained in France," she replied, "to take care of my mother." "But after her death?" he said. "I found in Alexander a protector for my children, and I tried to secure their prospects." He desired her to write to Eugene, and tell him he counted on his support. She accordingly wrote, entreating her brother to appeal to the Czar's peaceful sentiments, and induce him to prevent war; but a principality in Bavaria was secured to Eugene through Alexander's interest, and though he transmitted his sister's message, he abstained from returning to France.

The news of Napoleon's departure from Elba reached Vienna through two different sources on March 5th, and Alexander was at once attacked by his allies for having refused to permit his removal, and for the treaty of April 11th. He

---

* The day she heard of Napoleon's death she appeared in public, as if to show that the daughter of the Cæsars could only feel contempt for an ex-sub-lieutenant.

alone had received the intelligence with perfect coolness,* and three hours afterwards sent a messenger to his generals in Poland, to stop the homeward march of his troops. But it was neither against Napoleon personally, nor for the restoration of the Bourbons, that he said he should declare war. Napoleon had broken his pledged word; he was freed from any ties with regard to the treaty he had formed with him, and should conclude no truce with France so long as she adhered to him; but as for the Bourbons, they had prepared the ground for the return of the Bonapartes by their own measures. He could not employ the time of his reign and the forces of his empire on their behalf. The country must be placed in such a position that the revolts of her Prætorian Guards could no longer agitate Europe; but for a house which neither knew how to fight nor how to reign, he would draw his sword no more.

"You see, Sire," cried Francis, "what has occurred in consequence of your protection of the Liberals and the Bonapartists." Alexander meekly accepted the responsibility his colleagues cast upon him, and promised to assist in repairing his fault. But he asked if it would not be wise to substitute the Duke of Orleans for Louis, who, in quitting France without appointing a successor, had left the nation or his allies free to choose one more capable of keeping his place. The very age and infirmities of Louis would have protected him if he had remained in Paris, for even Napoleon could not have put him to death, and the spectacle of their old King willing to risk the loss of his few remaining years of life at the head of his troops, rather than take an ignoble flight, might have restored loyalty to his cause. Alexander had

* "Many fanciful accounts have been given of the reception of the first news of Napoleon's flight at Vienna. Among others Scott says that the announcement was made to the Congress on the 11th by Talleyrand, and that general laughter was the first emotion. In the Recollections of Rogers we are told that Wellington said he first heard it from Lord Burghersh, then minister at Florence, and that the instant it came he communicated it to the members of the Congress, who all laughed, the Emperor of Russia the most of all. Sir W. Erle called the Duke's attention to this statement. He said, 'Laugh! no, we did not laugh. We said, Where will he go? and Talleyrand said, ' I cannot say where he will go, but I'll undertake to say where he'll not go, and that is to France.' Next day, when we met, the news had come that he had gone to France, and we laughed at Talleyrand—that is the only laugh I can recollect."— Hayward's Essays.

certainly a right to speak in this strain, for the Romanofs have always been ready to face an insurrection, not to fly from before their own people. Lord Clancarty said he had no power to decide on so grave a question, and then Talleyrand stood up, and knowing the jealousy of his allies towards Alexander, skilfully procured their sympathy for Louis, by laying the blame entirely on the generous conqueror of France. "The Allies," he said, "completely tied the hands of the restored Government, and the fault lay with them. We are far from accusing that greatness of soul which treated a conquered Power almost like a conqueror; but at least we cannot accuse ourselves of the imprudent generosity we admired but could not prevent, though we have now become the victims of it." The Austrian, English, and Prussian ministers secretly enjoyed this aspersion on Alexander.* "See Poland," continued Talleyrand; "where the spirit of independence ever nourishes revolutions. The revolutionary spirit only is formidable in France; but to repress it you must repress the spirit of independence."† Alexander afterwards told Talleyrand he believed Napoleon would not have left Elba if the payments had been made as stipulated. Talleyrand asked if he would pay in March what was not due till May. Alexander's reply to Eugene, and to another urgent letter from Hortense, was "No peace, not even a truce, with Napoleon;" and Wellington expressed himself very well satisfied with the Emperor, both on this point and on that of his prompt co-operation in the new campaign. All the Powers began to feel some uneasiness lest the secret treaty should be divulged, and cause him to break off from their alliance. Castlereagh wrote to the Duke from London,‡ March 27th, that in their hurried departure the French King's ministers might not have carried off the contents of the Foreign Office, and "our secret treaty with France and Austria, as well as all Prince Talleyrand's correspondence, will fall into Bonaparte's hands. He will of course try to turn this to account, first in private, by sowing discord, and if he fails in this, he will expose the whole in the *Moniteur*. I leave it to your judgment to take such steps as you deem most suitable for

---

* Lamartine's Histoire de la Restauration. † Châteaubriand.
‡ Wellington Despatches.

counteracting any unfavourable impression. After all he knew long since, it cannot produce any unfavourable impression upon the Emperor of Russia's mind. He must feel the whole grew out of differences now settled, and a most indiscreet declaration of Prince Hardenberg's. The treaty is, upon the face of it, purely defensive, and all our proceedings since have proved this beyond a doubt."

Lord Cathcart writes from Vienna, March 25th, that Alexander's field equipage and horses are ordered from Warsaw, to join the head-quarters of the Russian army at Prague on April 14th, and that he is to be attached to the Emperor's head-quarters as before. On March 30th he attended a meeting at Schwartzenberg's house in Vienna, where Alexander, the Prince of Würtemberg, and the generals met to decide on the military movements. "The Emperor of Russia," writes Wellington, "is quite reconciled to the old notion of managing the concern in council between him, the King of Prussia, and Schwartzenberg." The Allies were to cross the Rhine once more, the English and Prussians through Belgium, the Austrians and Russians by Mayence; and nothing could be more conciliatory and more apologetic than the Powers who had formed the secret treaty now became to Russia. Alexander's advice in the councils of the Congress was no longer opposed. Bavaria was forced to waive her claim on Baden, and the reconstitution of the German Federal Union, with the boundaries of the smaller States, was arranged according to his views on a strict principle of justice and mutual advantages, combined with the recognized wishes of the people.

Alexander received the communication from Budiakine, who was detained in Paris, April 8th, and he opened it in Stein's presence. He turned exceedingly red as he perused the contents, and the Baron said he fully expected a storm. He sent for Metternich, and showed it to him. This diplomatist for once could make no reply, but recovering himself eagerly began upon some other business.* Alexander informed him he desired never to hear anything more of it again, and put the document upon the fire. Under the circumstances the alliance ought to be firmer than ever. "Il ne s'agit pas de moi, mais du salut du monde." Talleyrand, with cool effrontery,

* Memoirs of Stein.

first denied it to Nesselrode, and then said he was about to abandon it—"the villain," writes Stein. To his brother-in-law of Bavaria, Alexander said much what he had said to Metternich, and when the King excused himself, added, "I see you were drawn in; I will think no more of it." Still for some days there was great fear expressed by the other Powers lest Russia should eventually remain neutral, and Hardenberg advised the members of the Congress to yield everything to Alexander, and to look for a limitation of the Russian power at a future day. In the middle of April he was tacitly allowed the title of King of Poland, and the Dukes of Saxe-Weimar, Oldenburg, and Mecklenburg-Schwerin all assumed that of Grand Duke. Alexander wrote to Frederick William, that the political position of the world made a bond necessary between the German princes, but Hanover was averse to this bond, or Zollverein, and it was not effected for many years.*

The Greek Lent put a stop to the festivities at Vienna, and the Empress of Russia left in the middle of March for Baden. Alexander remained till May 26th, the last point of dispute being the succession of the Duchies of Parma and Piacenza to the son of Maria Louisa. They were claimed by Spain, and Lord Clancarty having taken the place of the Duke, re-

* "I had not till yesterday," writes Cathcart to Castlereagh, May 19th, 1815, "an opportunity to deliver your message, marked 'Private,' to the Emperor of Russia, who received every part of that communication in the most satisfactory and gracious manner. He desired me to say to you everything most civil and kind. He added that he had always found you frank and open, and had the highest opinion of you; he had looked upon your position here to be one of great delicacy and high responsibility, and any animosities which had arisen in the course of the negotiation to have proceeded from misapprehension, the clashing of different interests, too much heat, and causes of a like nature, which had not made much impression upon him, as he had trusted they would cure themselves. Speaking of the march of the army and the length of time it requires to remove troops, even from the nearest provinces of the Russian Empire to the centre of Germany, he said he hoped the time was come when it would be found that the power of Russia might be useful to the rest of Europe, but not dangerous to it. . . . I have not any ground for supposing that the Emperor of Russia has a wish to set up any particular dynasty in opposition to the Bourbon, in the event of getting rid of that of Bonaparte, but I think that now, as in 1813, he doubts in his own mind the probability of the restoration of the King. He has not spoken to me of the Duke of Orleans, but has frequently expressed his determination not to interfere, except for the removal of Bonaparte, and that he should not be succeeded by any of his generals or marshals, among whom he did not fail to name the Crown Prince of Sweden. I never heard him speak of a regency," &c.—Wellington Despatches.

called to command the British troops, stoutly declined to sign the most trifling document till this was settled against the ex-Empress. She appealed to Alexander, the Austrian Cabinet being also against her, and he effected a compromise by which she kept Parma for life, after which it returned to a Bourbon and not to a Bonaparte. Murat protested that he meant to keep his treaty with Austria, but settled the difficulty respecting Naples by entering Rome and calling on all Italians to rally round him and erect their country into a united State. The Austrians in Lombardy marched out to meet him, his troops fled, and he escaped in a fishing-boat to France; but Napoleon refused to see him in Paris, and at last hoping to reinstate himself in Naples, where the Bourbons were re-established, as Napoleon had reseated himself on the throne of France, he landed with a few followers, but met with less merciful foes than his old master found in the Allies, and was seized and shot in accordance with his own law, directing that any person landing in the country without a passport, or with intent to disturb the public tranquillity, should be executed. Napoleon's partisans at Vienna made an attempt to carry off the King of Rome, but when the plan was detected Francis dismissed his daughter's French attendants, and made her drop her title of Empress.

While Napoleon employed every mode of conciliation towards the foreign Powers, he placed Paris in a complete state of defence, and lost no time in preparing the country for the now inevitable campaign. With the system which formerly succeeded in crushing Austria and Prussia, he resolved to pounce on one of the allied armies before it was joined by its colleagues.

Wellington had orders to avoid a battle till united with the advancing Russians, and only three days before Waterloo wrote to Alexander: "I see with the greatest satisfaction that we are quite agreed on the general base of the plan of operations—that is to say, to limit our extension by the necessity of means of subsistence for armies so immense; that the army of Italy ought to co-operate with the others, but upon a different basis; and that the centre of the Grand Army of operation, that which will extend from the sea as far as Switzerland, ought to support either the right or the left, according to circumstances. This centre will be composed of the whole of your Majesty's troops; the right of Marshal Blucher's army, and of that under my orders; the left of that under the immediate orders of Prince Schwartzenberg. As to what concerns us here, I believe we shall be obliged at least to lay siege to Maubeuge. . . . . Blucher thinks that the position of Givet will be of no utility to him, but I believe we shall have means sufficient for all that it will be necessary for us to do."

CHAPTER IV.

1815.

ALEXANDER'S SECOND CAMPAIGN IN FRANCE.

ÆTAT. 37.

THE Evangelical movement in Germany and Switzerland in 1810, in which Jung Stilling took a prominent part, made rapid progress among those on the Continent reduced to extreme misery during the long war. The charitable exertions of the Moravians and other Christian communities were never more welcome than in that period of calamity, nor more useful to civilization itself, as they checked the brigandage and highway murder frequently prompted by despair. In the Vosges mountains the good pastor Oberlin formed at Ban de la Roche a city of refuge from the despoilers, an oasis for those to whom the world had been rendered a desert. Alexander sent forward a guard of Cossacks to protect this village from marauders when the Allies entered France, and some time afterwards the pastor sent his formal blessing to the autocrat.

Among those persons of distinction who gave up rank and fortune to devote themselves to the cause of charity and religion, was the Baroness de Krudener, who entertained Paul and his wife at Mittau, and was presented at Catherine's Court, when Alexander was six years old, on her husband's appointment to the republic of Venice. Her portrait was painted by Angelica Kauffmann, and she was acquainted with most of the literary and political celebrities of the day. Her charms caused the young Russian secretary to the embassy to commit suicide in despair; an event which had a lasting effect on her, and forms the subject of one of her novels, for she was an authoress of some repute till she adopted a religious life.* Her

* Madame d'Oberkirch, writing in 1789, says: "The public attention is entirely turned to the Baroness de Krudener, a young woman of brilliant and exalted imagination, who undertakes to reform the present philosophical belief according to the fantastic notions of Swedenborg and other

husband and son's posts at Berlin made her intimate with Queen Louisa, whom she accompanied throughout the sad year of 1806-7. They visited the hospitals together, and she exerted herself to console her royal friend. "Ah, I have dwelt in palaces," she said to a young girl who was an eager listener, "and if you did but know what trouble and anguish they conceal! I never see one without feeling a pang at my heart." Alexander must have met her at that time, but since his accession she had not revisited her native country. In 1808 she went to Baden, where she became acquainted with the mother of the Empress of Russia; and as the Margravine often received visits from her daughters, the Queens of Sweden and Bavaria, the Electress of Hesse, and the Duchess of Brunswick, Madame Krudener met them all at her table, and the same year was introduced to Queen Hortense, who tried to persuade her to settle in Paris. She refused on the ground that she had a horror of Courts; but they corresponded, and both Hortense and Stephanie were able to serve her when the King of Würtemberg made her the subject of an annoying surveillance in his States.

Baron de Krudener died in June, 1802, and his widow preached celibacy and the superiority of a religious over a domestic life. The room she inhabited was bare of furniture, except a large wooden cross, and she lived as plainly and strictly as a nun, exhorting both rich and poor, and attracting large congregations. In 1814 the Empress Elizabeth came to Baden, and Mdlle. Stourdza was much charmed with the Baroness, whom she persuaded with some trouble to seek an introduction to her mistress. In her correspondence with Madame Svetchine, she is warned against her friend's tendency to cast off dogma and draw her away from the discipline of the Church* (the religion of the Pope and the Czar, as Madame utopian theorists. She explains her doctrines in her own drawing-room, and gains many proselytes. She is sincere and warm-hearted." "A person both extraordinary and interesting," writes Madame de Genlis; "two things which when united are very uncommon, especially in a woman. She was certainly most sincere; she appeared to me amiable, clever, original, and piquant, and inspired me with a genuine interest in her."

* "Remember how pure our faith is; do not let yourself be indifferent to dogma, which would be truly culpable. Think what would have become of religion if the first faithful ones had not preciously preserved its deposit."

Krudener rather contemptuously styled the Latin and Greek Christianity). The enthusiastic Mdlle. Stourdza's warm admiration for her Sovereign gave Madame Krudener, formerly prejudiced against him, a desire to see him. She also heard much of him from Jung Stilling, with whom she stayed at Carlsruhe, and whom Alexander visited during his brief sojourn at Bruchsal. She tried to make a religious impression upon the Empress, after condemning her for harshness to Hortense and Stephanie, and counselling her to adopt "the charity which thinketh no evil." She was satisfied with the result, for she wrote, Sept. 7th, 1814, " The Lord has deigned to conform the soul of the Empress to my ardent wishes. I have had more than one *travail* with this angelic woman, and at last seeing her set out [for Vienna] I felt myself free. I have been ceaselessly occupied with souls, having been able to preach to the Queens and to the Empress, to the Queen of Holland, and to the Viceroy, in announcing to them the great approaching events." She presented herself to Hortense as soon as the ex-Queen arrived at Baden, and strongly advised her not to return to France, assuring her that 1815 would be a terrible year; Napoleon would come back, and all who adhered to him be persecuted. She told her to go to Russia, where Alexander was the refuge of the unfortunate. Hortense introduced her to Eugene and his wife, who were chiefly impressed by her haggard, emaciated appearance and grey hair; but there is little doubt they repeated the prophecy to Napoleon, who was inclined to believe it. He had formerly consulted Mdlle. Le Normand, a sibyl without Madame de Krudener's rank and talent; and had encouraged superstition to work upon his subjects till he began to imbibe a small share of it himself. In a long letter from Strasburg to Mdlle. Stourdza, during the Empress's visit to Vienna, she speaks strongly against the fêtes and entertainments at the Congress. "Do they never shock you? Can they dance and clothe themselves in rich draperies when dark hatred tears the human race?" She regarded concerts and dancing at all times as "voluptuous amusements," and a theatre as the house of Satan; but now above all she felt their incongruity when contrasted with the mourning produced by war, a war which she felt would shortly be renewed. "Guilty France will yet be punished. The storm advances. Those lilies the Eternal preserved, which ought to have been called to purity, to repentance, have appeared to disappear. You wished you could tell me of the great beauties of the Emperor's soul. I seem to know him already. I have known for a long time that the Lord will give me the joy of seeing him. If I live it will be one of the happy moments of my life. There is no terrestrial duty sweeter than to love and respect him whom one ought to love and respect by the order of God Himself. I have great things to say to him, for I have felt much on his account. My business is to be without fear and without reproach, his to be at the feet of Christ. Ah, that it might be on his knees that he may receive from Christ those great lessons which astonish the human heart, and will fill with holy joy that heart filled now with holy uneasiness! Prince Galitzin has sent me 1000 crowns for our old Jung. I guess the hand which sent them, but I am silent. May the Most High bless that hand, and may the fear of Him who carries peace march before him." At the same time she wrote to one of Hortense's maids of honour: "The Viceroy will learn many things at Vienna. Peace cannot be arranged till they see it is not man who has the power to make it." She expressed a wish to be at Vienna on account of "an old sinner," as she calls him, the Prince de Ligne, who had formerly loved her, and "once possessed a conscience." He styled her the Grey Sister of Hearts, and she hoped to rouse him. This letter arrived at the very time of his sudden death, and Mdlle. Stourdza showed it to the Empress, and she in her turn to the Emperor, who said he should like to meet the writer. Her allusion to the Bourbons coincided with his own opinion that they would never maintain their place in France. "I do not know," he said to Eugene, "if I shall not some day repent of having put the Bourbons on the throne. They are a bad set of people. We have had them in Russia, and I know how little they are to be depended on." Again Madame de Krudener wrote to her friend: "I spoke of my respectful and profound admiration for the Emperor. I have immense things to say to him, and though the Prince of Darkness may do all in his power to prevent it, and to thrust away those who might speak to him of Divine things, the Eternal will be the strongest." In February, 1815, she went to a mill at Schluchtern, in Hesse, and there waited for an opportunity of meeting Alexander. Crowds followed to listen to her preaching, and she persuaded whole villages to sell all their property and establish themselves in the Mahometan districts of Russia to convert the heathen.

It has been thought, but perhaps unjustly, that the religious influence she acquired over the Empress induced her to refuse a thorough reconciliation with the Emperor, and prefer a secluded life of prayer. Madame de Krudener used to quote from St. Paul : " The unmarried woman careth for the things of the Lord, that she may be holy both in body and spirit ; but she that is married careth for the things of the world, how she may please her husband ;" and her exhortations were not calculated to strengthen matrimonial ties. But the Imperial couple parted affectionately at Vienna.*

Alexander had a slight return of fever and erysipelas in April, and the extremely lowering treatment prescribed at that time, as a means of warding off such attacks, made him feel the fatigue of his journey more than usual when he left Vienna to join his army at Heidelberg on May 26th. He declined an invitation to rest at Munich, and was distressed by the brilliant reception the Bavarians gave him in every town he entered. He had an interview with Kosciusko, at Brunau, and could not avoid spending a day with his uncle at Stuttgart, but he then pushed on to Heilbronn. He was in no enviable state of mind. He had trusted in Napoleon's honour, though all precedent told him that the man who marked out officers for especial distinction when they broke their parole was not likely to keep his own; and on all sides he was now accused of plunging Europe into another war. The revelation of the secret treaty exhibited the ill-feeling of

* " What you tell me of the Emperor gives me great pleasure," writes Madame Svetchine to Mdlle. Stourdza. " At last from all parts they do him justice. It cannot be concealed that happiness only gives a spirit of equity to great masses, and the vulgar will never have a heart for anything but success. . . . Though we know nothing positive about the plans on which you depend, I presume that the Emperor setting out again in a short time, you will remain in foreign countries all the time which will elapse before he returns to us, a time which the affairs of Europe, where the Emperor is truly the advocate-general, may make indefinite. The sojourn in Germany will prolong to you that life of enchantment which never counts too many pages. Also this prolonged absence appears to me a favourable chance to the return of the angel's happiness. Far from hostile and jealous looks, from the devices of ingenious intrigue, fewer obstacles may perhaps be opposed to a change in her fate."

his allies; that France ignored any obligation for his extreme moderation, and was still his enemy; while even England lent herself to the fickle policy of the Continent, and had declared against him. How much more advantageous it might have been for Russia if, leaving France to carry on her quarrel with England and Germany, he had originally followed out the wishes of his people, and concentrated his strength against Turkey! This may have passed through his mind, for nothing was more discouraging than the accounts from Russia, where his prolonged absence was exciting universal discontent, and the want of money had put a stop to all mercantile undertakings in St. Petersburg. Lord Walpole, writing in March from the Russian capital to Lord Castlereagh, says: " Those hitherto most loud in praises of the Emperor have lately changed their tone. His refusal to reduce any part of the military establishment has caused a strong sensation; the whole revenue of the empire is unequal to it. Bonaparte's evasion has caused a strong sensation, and we are accused as the authors of it." A new tariff was being drawn up by order of the Emperor, but it was unpopular, as too liberal. A committee was called to revise it. Again, in May, he writes, that owing to the destruction of Moscow and other causes, the price of houses has become enormous, and that during the last ten months every necessary of life—corn, wood, forage, &c.—is more than doubled. A new issue of Government paper and a forced loan were proposed, but the Emperor rejected them, and preferred the alternative of new taxes. " Aratchaief does not join the Emperor. His place as Général de Service is filled by another. He is the only man supposed to have had power over his master's mind. The kingdom of Poland very much displeases here. Silver again rises in price; it is nearly five roubles the silver rouble, ducats $14\frac{1}{2}$ roubles." And this at the commencement of a new war.

Alexander arrived at Heilbronn June 4th, having travelled throughout several nights since he left Vienna. He received the authorities of the town, and after an exciting day, sought his quarters for the night. He took up a book, though too much tired and depressed to read, when Madame de Krudener was suddenly announced; Prince Volkonski having vainly tried to keep her from insisting on an audience. Her language was as uncompromising to her Sovereign as to his meanest subject. She accused him of pride, and told him he could never expect peace till he had humiliated himself with the prayer of the publican; that he should listen to her, who had also been a great sinner, but had found pardon at the foot of the Cross. Then perceiving that she had touched an open wound she expressed regret, but he desired her to go on; and afterwards wrote to his wife, that she had calmed the trouble which had overshadowed him for so long; and Madame de Krudener on her side stated that she had inspired him " with a holy contrition and durable repentance, in the place of discouragement and remorse."

The next morning Alexander joined his army at Heidelberg. Madame de Krudener resided in a labourer's cottage about half a mile distant, with her son-in-law, the Baron de Berckheim, and an evangelical pastor named Empaytaz, where, every second day, the Emperor came to their prayer meeting at ten P.M. and often conversed with them till two A.M., but was always alone. No one disliked ridicule more than he, and a man educated by the disciples of Voltaire could not fail to perceive that the fact of joining a prayer meeting in a labourer's cottage might be a subject for ridicule to many of his contemporaries. There never was an age in which religious laymen were looked upon with more contempt in England as well as on the Continent, and Alexander showed his sincerity by incurring it. He seems to have had doubts as to the duty of sacrificing his army in a cause which did not concern Russia; and said to Madame de Krudener, as he had said at Vilna in 1813, that he would thankfully give his own life to accomplish his object of procuring peace to Europe.

The Allies, accustomed to Napoleon's system of war, waited to begin the campaign till their forces were concentrated, and not offer him the chance of dealing singly with the first in the field; and Alexander stayed at Heidelberg, under cover of the Rhine, for the arrival of his Guards, and till the British and Prussian armies should have advanced nearer to the point of rendezvous. Then the news came that Napoleon, masking his movements, had poured suddenly upon Belgium, and was about to engage the British and Prussian troops. Lord Cathcart wrote from Heidelberg, June 18th: "The Russian army, if not in time to take the lead in this operation, will at least have troops enough present to support and follow it up." He then refers to the affairs of Switzerland, where M. de la Harpe " had been holding very injudicious and unfit language, perfectly unauthorized by the Emperor, who sent a practical disavowal in a treaty with the Swiss. Nesselrode is at head-quarters, and has been with me for some time this evening." But that very day a decisive battle was fought at Waterloo, and Napoleon, outstripping the ministers and civil functionaries who accompanied him on the field, abandoned his army, and even his private papers and carriage, to secure the swiftest mode of flight. He had twice left his troops to save themselves—in Egypt and Russia, but on this, the third occasion, even his brother Jerome exclaimed, " Can it be possible that he will not seek death? Never will he find a more glorious grave."

The news was received by Alexander with the greatest joy, and he was bold enough to say he felt very thankful the campaign was decided without the loss of any of his own troops. He crossed the Rhine on June 25th, and proceeded with little opposition to Paris. The French made a slight stand at Châlons; but the war did not cost him above forty men, and he arrived in the French capital on July 10th. Very different from his march, distributing money as he went along among the peasants stripped by the French conscripts, was that of the avengers of blood who entered the country by the Belgian frontier. " The Prussians of our time," writes Scott, who visited Waterloo and Quatre Bras a few weeks after the battle, " will never forget or forgive the dreadful injuries inflicted by the French upon their country after the defeat of Jena. The plunder of their hamlets, with every inventive circumstance which evil passions could suggest—the murder of the father or the husband, because he *looked dangerous* when he beheld his property abandoned to rapine, his wife or daughters to abuse, and his children to wanton slaughter. The officers thought of the period when Prussia had been blotted out of the book of nations, her Queen martyred by studied and reiterated insult, and her King only permitted to retain the name of a Sovereign to increase his disgrace as a bondsman." They resented not being permitted to exact a thorough retribution in 1814, and they were now resolved to have their revenge.*

The British army behaved with its accustomed chivalry; but both French and Prussians disgraced themselves at Waterloo by many acts of barbarism. "Most of the prisoners," writes Scott, "whom the French took from our light cavalry were put to death in cold blood, or owed their safety to concealment or a speedy escape. Even the British officers who were carried before Bonaparte (after Quatre Bras), although civilly treated while he spoke to them, were no sooner out of his presence than they were stripped, beaten, and abused. Their lancers rode over the field during the action, despatching the wounded British with the most inveterate rancour." The Prussians, having taken less part in the great battle of June 18th, were intrusted with the pursuit; and they carried it out with such vigour that many of the fugitives traversed a space of 100 miles in forty-eight hours to effect their escape.

Napoleon said at St. Helena that there was no cannon-shot for him at Waterloo, wishing to convey to his auditors the idea that he was much exposed; but the accounts published by those who were with him during the day, prove this was by no means the case. "From 2 till 6.45," wrote a member of his staff,† "Bonaparte commanded the operations and movements from a position where he remained without any danger whatever to his own person; he was at least a cannon-shot and a half off. When convinced that the corps d'armée he had so long and so obstinately mistaken was a Prussian corps, he seemed to think affairs were desperate, and that he had no other resource than to make a great effort with the reserve of his Guard, composed of 1500 men. He ordered them forward, and accompanied them nearer to the battle, but halted himself under the broken ground of a sand-pit or ravine, and a little on one side, out of the direction of the cannon-balls. It was at this moment the decisive crisis of the battle began. Bonaparte had six persons close to him: his brother Jerome, Generals Bertrand, Drouet, Bernard, Daubers,

* Sir Walter Scott's Paul's Letters to his Kinsfolk. 1815.
† Published in the *Gentleman's Magazine*, September, 1815.

and Labedoyère. At every step he took, or seemed to take, to put his own person in front, Generals Bertrand and Drouet threw themselves before his horse's head, and exclaimed in a pathetic accent, 'Ah, Sire, what are you going to do? Consider the safety of France and the army is lost if any accident happens to you.' Bonaparte yielded with a real or affected effort. But it was singular that the men who knew so well how to moderate his ardour were the only persons he never sent out to reconnoitre the battle; while he sent the rest twenty times into the midst of the fire, to carry orders or bring him information. Jerome having taken aside and whispered with one of his brother's aides-de-camp, Bonaparte sent him several times into the middle of the fire, as if to get rid of such a critic. Jerome, in fact, took it greatly to heart that his brother did not profit by this occasion to die in a glorious manner, and I distinctly heard him say so to General Bertrand. . . . . Bonaparte disappeared from us under pretext of going himself to ascertain the state of things, and to put himself at the head of his Guards to reanimate them, but before effecting his personal retreat, to get rid of impertinent witnesses, he directed all those round him to carry different orders at once, and to bring information, the result of which could not concern him in the least." When he saw his Guards bending before the English cavalry, he turned to Bertrand, saying, "All is over; let us save ourselves;" and leaving his generals to sustain the battle till he was out of reach, he put spurs to his horse, and first drew bridle in a field near Quatre Bras, where he took some refreshment, and then rode on all night till he reached Charleroi. At Philippeville he met his secretary, and they wept together over his defeat.* He was, in fact, the first to bear the news of the battle† to Paris, where he arrived on the 21st, and alighted at the Elysée. Caulaincourt soon joined him, and listened to his abuse of the

---

* Fleury du Chabaudon.

† The account he brought was, however, as false as most of his bulletins. He pretended that he had beaten the English, taken six standards, and the day was decided, when on the approach of night some disaffected persons spread an alarm, and occasioned a disorder which his presence could not, on account of the night, recover. He returned to Paris to order a levy *en masse* of the National Guard and ask for more *matériel*. It was the officers flying from the battle who first brought the truth.

brave generals who had risked everything for his glory. He still hoped to save his throne, and his brother Lucien pleaded his cause uselessly in the Chamber of Representatives. He was told that unless he abdicated his dethronement on the motion of Lafayette would be carried, and he made a last attempt to secure his dynasty by proclaiming his son, as he imagined that Russia at least would not restore Louis. The more his hopes were excited of Alexander's assistance from the opposition he met with at the Congress, the more bitter he felt against him when those hopes were entirely crushed, and he ever afterwards declared that Alexander was the soul and promoter of the campaign of 1815, for he imagined the British Opposition, who had spoken strongly against it in both Houses of Parliament, would have inclined their Government to peace if left to itself. He retired to Malmaison, where, far from occupying himself in reveries on the wife whom he had discarded for the sake of a bride of higher birth, he was busied in securing and packing up any object of value he could carry away, among other things a clock of Frederick the Great, which he had brought from Potsdam. He offered the Provisional Government to place himself at the head of the French armies still on foot, as a simple general in their service, to oppose the advancing forces of the Allies, and to defend Paris, but the offer was coldly declined : they preferred to trust once more to the mercy of the enemy than carry on a prolonged and probably hopeless war.

On June 29th, when the English and Prussians, bearing down all opposition, were within three days' march of Paris, Napoleon had completed his preparations for a flight, which was hastened by a peremptory order from the Assembly, and Davoust threatened to arrest him if he refused to obey. Napoleon spoke to Caulaincourt of going either to England or the United States. "I tried an insinuation," writes the Duke, "of which he seized the spirit." "No," said he, warmly, "that would not do. Between the Emperor Alexander and me there are old remembrances which would render a step towards him impossible." He set out for Rochefort with a train of carriages laden with all the plunder he could collect from the French palaces, and arrived there July 3rd, corresponding with his army till the 14th, as the vigilance of the British cruisers prevented him from embarking for the United States.

In the mean time the English and Prussian troops entered Paris; and Louis, following them, was again proclaimed. The allied Sovereigns were all in Paris on the 10th, and any moment active steps might be taken to arrest the ex-Emperor. He began to negotiate through Las Cases and Savary with the captain of the *Bellerophon*, a British man-of-war stationed on the coast. His friends tried to persuade this officer that as his departure from France was voluntary, no one ought to interrupt his passage to any point he chose; but the captain answered, he had strict orders to prevent Napoleon's escape, and convey him to England if he obtained possession of his person. He entered the *Bellerophon* perfectly aware that he was merely throwing himself on England's mercy. But he had no other choice, unless he wished to fall into the hands of the Allies, and Blucher had stated that if he caught him he should shoot him at once.

On July 13th Napoleon wrote a letter to the Prince Regent, comparing himself to Themistocles, and claiming his protection "as the most powerful, most constant, and most generous of my enemies." He went on board the *Bellerophon* with his suite, and took the greatest pains to conciliate the English officers. At Plymouth crowds of people came from the shore in boats and warmly cheered him. He seemed much pleased, and, though not allowed to land, ordered anything he liked from the town; and procured quantities of wine, fruit, and other luxuries at the English expense. He passed most of his time in playing at chess; but his partner, Montholon, who was the better player of the two, made obviously bad moves when he was having the best of the game, so that Napoleon might always win it. On July 31st it was announced to him that the British Government had decided to send him to St. Helena, as a place where he would be secure, but at the same time allowed personal freedom. He dwelt more on the term "General Bonaparte" being used in the official document than anything else, but protested he would not go to St. Helena—he would die first. The climate would kill him in three months. He asked to reside quietly in England, and become a British subject. "Otherwise," he said, "why should I not have gone to my father-in-law, or to Alexander, who was my personal friend? We have become enemies because he wanted to annex Poland to his dominions, and my popularity among the Poles was in his way. But otherwise he was my friend, and would not have treated me in this way. . . . . When I was at Elba I was at least as much a Sovereign in that island as Louis on the throne of France. We had both our respective flags, our ships, our troops. Mine, to be sure, were rather on a small scale. . . . . I made war upon him, defeated him, and dethroned him. But there was nothing in this to deprive me of my rank as one of the Sovereigns of Europe." He repeated this pleading and his protest that he would not go to St. Helena, and his manner was so persuasive that the English officers said if he had had a personal interview with the Regent, in half an hour he would have converted him into his friend. He inquired from Lord Keith, privately, what measure he could take to avert it. Lord Keith asked him if it was not surely preferable to being sent a prisoner to France, or perhaps to Russia? "Russia!" he exclaimed; "God preserve me from it."

Mr. Lyttleton and Lord Lowther saw him on board, when he talked incessantly upon every political subject. He tried to please the English by speaking highly of the Prince Regent. General Bertrand put in that Alexander was a good man, his heart better than his head, but he did not think him a great one. The English Liberal newspapers asserted that Napoleon added, "Nor do I;" but Mr. Lyttleton formally contradicted it, and said Napoleon was taking a pinch of snuff, and made no reply. He was permitted to take three general officers and their families, with twelve servants, to St. Helena, whither, in spite of continued, though good-humoured remonstrances, he was landed on October 15th. On the way he became more reconciled to his fate, and, after minute inquiries about the climate, he said he thought he should be more comfortable there than in Austria, and that he had never been ill more than twice in his whole life. Indeed, no small part of his success might be ascribed to his excellent health.

Two officers on board the *Bellerophon* gave similar descriptions of him, and they thought he looked less than his age, which was forty-six or forty-seven. He was extremely curious, inquiring into everything, with grey eyes, a very penetrating glance, little or no eyelashes, no eyebrow, dark brown hair with no appearance of grey,* a sallow or southern complexion, only five feet two inches in height, and very corpulent, but otherwise symmetrical, and giving the idea of great strength. His hands small, but square and brown, for he never wore gloves; his feet also small, but broad. His attitudes were ungraceful, but he was as active as a sailor in springing up the side of the vessel. He was very deep-chested. His dress was a green uniform faced with red, and he wore the Legion of Honour. He rose at seven o'clock, but seldom appeared before half-past ten, as he was very particular about his toilet; though during the day he took so much snuff that his face was usually stained with it. He read a good deal, talked to the sailors, and retired to bed about eight. He was transferred to another ship, handsomely fitted up to convey him to St. Helena, and the Prince Regent gave personal orders that he should be supplied with every comfort.

It is difficult to comprehend the philanthropy which considered the murder of the Duc d'Enghien, of Palm, of Hofer, of the Prussian patriots, of the Russian prisoners, of the sick at Jaffa, of the garrison of Acre two days after they had surrendered their arms, of Toussaint l'Ouverture the negro chief, sent to perish of cold and starvation in the snows of the Jura, and the forcible abduction and imprisonment of the Pope and the Spanish princes as venial offences, yet could blame the British Government for its conduct towards the man who caused the ruin of so many of her citizens by forcibly detaining them in his dominions, contrary to the usages of civilized nations; and had only lately, by a glaring breach of faith, headed an insurrection in France which cost the English at least 22,000 men. The French Empire conducted its measures from the very first with as little regard to international law as the pirate vessel which enriches itself by murder and rapine; and its chief could plead no

* "Las Cases relates that at St. Helena Napoleon observed one day that on his return from Moscow it was reported in Paris his hair had grown grey. 'But you see that is false,' he said, showing his head, which did not contain a single white hair; 'and I hope that I shall know how to support many more of them.'"—Mémorial de St. Hélène.

"rights," which he had always systematically disregarded, but had incurred the same penalties as the brigand or buccaneer. Yet even the brigand or buccaneer has been known to submit philosophically to his fate, and to feel some remorse on account of the confederates whom he had led to their destruction, and a desire to mitigate their punishment. But the insensibility to anything but his own self-aggrandizement, or personal rancours, which Napoleon exhibited throughout his career, adhered to him to the end of his life.* While France lay tremblingly awaiting the sentence of her conquerors, and Ney, Labedoyère, and others who had assisted him were doomed to death, his mind could dwell on small personal grievances—being refused the title of Emperor, and being obliged to let an English officer see him once a day, in order to be assured of his security; and could plead his own cause to the British officers with the greatest vehemence, without a word for the hapless country he had brought to the verge of ruin. Far from troubling himself about her, he was soon absorbed with the idea of writing his memoirs, falsifying history, and to show that in every instance in which he had failed it had been through the fault or treachery of his subordinates, or that his virtuous simplicity was deceived by the double nature of his opponents. The Marquis de Chambray spoke truly when he said that the character of Napoleon was far below his fortunes and his fame.

The admirable order preserved by the British troops made the rumour that their Government intended to reclaim Normandy very acceptable in the north of France. But the Prussians were no longer kept in check by their Russian allies,† and Paris was perhaps saved from destruction by resolving to open her gates. Louis retired no further than Ghent when he left Paris, and there he wrote to Alexander, who replied rather laconically, but told Pozzo di Borgo, who assisted at the

* At Elba Sir Neil Campbell was of opinion that his only feelings were vanity and revenge.

† Napoleon, for political motives, had instilled such a dread of the Cossacks into the French people that, as a matter of course, every depredation was attributed to them. Count Beugnot gives a story of Louis XVIII.'s indifference when he passed a cottage on his road from Ghent just destroyed by "the Cossacks," whereas no Cossack had been near his route during the campaign of 1815, and he travelled in the rear of the Prussian army.

battle of Waterloo, that it was his wish the King should be restored, on which the Russian ambassador sent to advise him to come back to Paris, " lest his place should be filled up ;" so Louis drove into his capital the day after the British and Prussian troops made their triumphal entrance. He tried to act with a high hand towards the Legislative Body, and dismissed both Houses; but a hundred of them protested, and continued to hold their sittings. The Prussians coerced the disaffected by quartering from ten to fifty soldiers upon each, and Louis ordered the names of twenty-nine of Napoleon's nobles to be erased from the Peerage, including Ney, Latour, Maubourg, Ségur, Casabianca, the Duke of Dantzic, Albufera, and Montesquieu. By a second ordinance nineteen officers were tried for waging war against the Government, including Ney, Labedoyère, Lallemand, Drouet, Bertrand, Savary, Grouchy, Lefébvre, and La Valette. Caulaincourt was pardoned at Alexander's request. Soult, Bassano, Durbach, and thirty-two more were to quit Paris within three days, remaining under surveillance till the Chambers settled their fate. Talleyrand, returned from Vienna, was received with favour by the King, and by his advice the infamous Fouché was retained in office.

Blucher announced his intention of laying a contribution of 4,000,000*l*. sterling on Paris, as Napoleon had done on Berlin, and pulling down the Vendôme pillar and the Bridge of Jena, as Napoleon had destroyed the monument of the victories of Frederick the Great. Wellington wrote to advise him to wait till Alexander arrived, as during the previous occupation he had thought fit to let them stand ; but Blucher began to undermine the bridge. The Duke and Lord Castlereagh sent Pozzo di Borgo to meet Alexander on his road, with copies of the reports of the battles and all that had since passed ; and the Emperor quickly stopped the destruction of the bridge by stationing a regiment upon it. He arrived in Paris at 8.30 P.M. of July 10th, and Louis at once visited him at the Elysée, and remained three hours* in a very different mood from that in which he met the Czar in 1814. He was now

---

* Alexander's march was Spires, June 27th; Rheinzabern, 28th; Weissenburg, 29th; Hagenau, 30th; Savern, July 1st; Saarbourg, 2nd; Hall, 3rd; Vick, 4th; Nancy, 5th, &c.

full of apologies, and ready to take his advice in the hope of obtaining some relaxation in the conditions of peace. On one point Alexander was inflexible. Louis must dismiss Blacas, and must not replace him by Talleyrand, for both were enemies to Russia and to the constitution which was necessary to maintain the repose of France. Talleyrand had proved that he could forego the real interests of France for personal reasons, and had practised fraud and trickery too long in his diplomacy to alter now. It would be impossible for Russia to place faith in the professed principles of a French ministry while he formed part of it. Louis at first resisted this demand, but the Czar told him he would not oppose the partition of France unless a Cabinet was formed to reconcile opposing factions, and keep France from agitating all Europe; and he proposed the Duc de Richelieu, who had been governor of Odessa for eleven years. The Duke was inclined to remain in Russia, but Alexander said his first duty lay with his native country, which now absolutely required him; and Louis felt himself obliged to yield, and dismissed the two ministers from their posts, although Talleyrand tried to please the Emperor by proposing to place Pozzo di Borgo in the new Cabinet.* A paragraph in an English newspaper (July 21st) says, "The Emperor of Russia seems to be a great favourite with the people, who hope through his interest to avoid the evils of war."

Lord Liverpool writes to Lord Castlereagh, July 15th: "It is satisfactory to find the Emperor of Russia in so reasonable a state of mind, and so likely to co-operate with us cordially in the great objects we must all equally have in view." He goes on to say that forbearance towards France would be weakness, not mercy, and pressed that Paris should be stripped "of the trophies she had acquired in her campaigns, as the Allies had as much right to take possession of them by right of conquest as she, and leaving them would only foster her vanity," &c. Lord Castlereagh answered: "I have nothing to complain of; on the contrary, much to acknowledge, in the spirit of conciliation hitherto shown by the Emperor of Russia, but I think you must not expect him to go all your lengths. . . . . The Emperor, expressing his wish to act in concert with the Prince Regent in consolidating the peace of Europe, asked me

* Beugnot's Memoirs.

in confidence if anything passed when he was in England on his part which had given umbrage to his Royal Highness, expressing himself at the same time in very proper terms on the subject. I beg you will mention this conciliatory overture; and as any personal coolness between two such personages can be productive of no advantage, perhaps his Royal Highness will authorize me to say something civil on his part to the Emperor, who takes great pains to show attention to the Duke of Wellington and to the British army here. I should also wish to receive the Prince's commands upon the invitation to be given to the Emperor of Austria. I delayed it till I knew whether the Prince would wish anything to be said to the other Sovereigns. I can venture to say all will decline. The Emperor of Austria is most impatient to go to Italy. The Emperor of Russia not less so to return home."*

Lord Liverpool wrote to Castlereagh, July 28th: "I read to the Prince Regent that part of your letter which alluded to the conversation his Imperial Majesty had with you. . . . The Prince wishes you to express to the Emperor of Russia that his Royal Highness is perfectly satisfied that if there was any misconception it was perfectly unintentional, and that he can never entertain any sentiment but cordiality and friendship towards his Imperial Majesty." An invitation was sent to the three Sovereigns, which they all declined.

Alexander again opposed the dismemberment of France, though Lord Liverpool, on behalf of his Government, strongly urged it.† The Prussians demanded Alsace and Lorraine, Austria part of the ancient Burgundy, the Netherlands a portion of Picardy, and every nation an indemnity for the expenses of the whole war. Castlereagh writes on August 17th to his chief, that he thinks "it would be unwise to reduce France too much; and though Great Britain's interests are more identical with the interests of Austria and Prussia than Russia, yet those two Courts require to be watched lest they should push their selfish policy to the detriment of the general interests." He had "received much support from the Russian minister, and the Czar acted very liberally, in the management of his troops being as little open to reproach. He put his second army in motion before he had received even the smallest

* Wellington Supplementary Despatches, vol. ix. † Ibid.

assurance of any assistance, and he stopped their march and sent them back to Russia when their advance was no longer necessary. He now urged "a prompt settlement with France for economy's sake, as he wanted to send back all his troops except the stipulated contingent as early in the next month as possible."

On his march to Paris Alexander brought magazines of bread and forage for his troops, so as not to exhaust the last provisions of the inhabitants, and, although much has been said about the Prussian inhumanity, yet Lord Palmerston was told at Le Mesnil (September 18th, 1815) that the country had suffered as much from the French troops the previous year as from any excesses of the Allies.

Castlereagh writes* to Lord Liverpool, August 24th, that "amongst the Powers which border on France, there is an evident desire for strong measures, even to the extent of partial dismemberment. This is the tone of the King of the Netherlands, of the Prussians loudly, of the Bavarians and Würtemberg. Russia, on the contrary, being remote, rather inclines to protect France, the Emperor's principles not leading him to this line. In a long conversation with him the day before yesterday I could perceive he was averse to any permanent reduction of the territory of France, and that as a measure of security he looked with more favour to dismantling than temporarily occupying certain of the fortresses. . . . ." The Prussians openly said of Alsace and Lorraine, "Instead of negotiating, let us take possession and hold fast." A Prussian discussing politics before Alexander said, "We have bayonets." "And I also," said the Emperor irritated; "I have bayonets;" and he left the room.

Castlereagh wrote, August 10th, that he had talked to the Emperor on the approaching marriage of the Prince of Orange with the Grand Duchess Anna, and hoped the connection with the King of the Netherlands would give his Imperial Majesty an additional interest in watching over the independence of that most important part of Europe. The Emperor expressed in strong terms the pleasure he should feel in co-operating with the Prince Regent in promoting the security of the Netherlands. The Emperor refused to keep his army in

* Wellington Despatches, &c., vol. ix.

France after September, for fear of exposing it to a winter march. The Prussians were becoming very vociferous in their demands, and determined to change their position in Europe. They wanted to make the indemnity twelve hundred millions. Castlereagh complains that Richelieu's appointment will give the new French Government a strong Russian tinge. It was soon attacked on this ground, and the wits reported that the Czar was appointed President of the Cabinet. The English Foreign Minister adds, that he will lose no time in concerting with Wellington to bring Alexander to a salutary decision as to the dismemberment of France and the fortresses, " which, if we succeed, the difficulties in other quarters may be comparatively easy to surmount."

The Prince of Orange took an active part at the head of the Dutch army in the battle of Waterloo, where he was wounded, and as, in spite of six or seven offers, including Napoleon's, the Grand Duchess Anna still remained single, Alexander wrote from Paris to the King of Holland to thank him for recent congratulations, and to propose a marriage between the Prince and the Grand Duchess. " Whilst I was in uncertainty," he said, "as to whether his old engagement with the Princess Charlotte of Wales continued, I abstained from discussing the matter, but having learned that it was entirely concluded, I may mention it without reserve. It would give much pleasure to my mother and myself," &c.*

This letter was sent to Wellington by the King, who asked him to inform the Regent, giving as a reason for accepting it the hope of Russia's support, whom he should be afraid to offend by a refusal: but it seems to have gratified the Prince,† since Sir James Riddell complains two months later of the change in his disposition towards England, and his devotion to the Emperor. It is curious to observe the alteration in the British policy during the next fifteen years, which made this Russian alliance the cause of the Dutch King's unpopularity in Great Britain and France in 1830. The Emperor Nicholas, being tied by an insurrection in Poland, England united with Louis Philippe to separate Belgium from Holland, and undo her own work, for the British share of the French indemnity was spent in restoring the fortifications of Breda

* Wellington Despatches, &c. † Bath Archives, vol. ii.

and Antwerp, and strengthening the positions on the Moselle, which France ceded to the Netherlands by the treaty of 1815.*

Prussia declared that her safety depended on the possession of Alsace and Lorraine, and was determined in her claims. Her King listened to Alexander, but had little control over his own generals; and Talleyrand was awakened to the fact rather late that Prussia and not Russia was the enemy France had to fear, and that he had made a grand mistake at the Congress in trying to alienate Louis from the Czar. In vain Louis and his ministers protested, that rather than sign away the French provinces they would encounter another twenty-five years of war. It was empty boasting when 800,000 troops of the Allies were quartered on the French soil. All Prussia seemed to have poured into France; Austria had sent a stronger army than in 1814, not to share in the battle—that was over before she arrived—but to divide the spoil. Even the Spaniards crossed the Pyrenees and claimed Roussillon and Bearn. The British army was quartered in the Bois de Boulogne, and the soldiers cut down the trees for fuel. But again Alexander showed himself the friend of national rights, and able to take a just view of the situation of affairs. If

---

* On the 24th of August Count Nesselrode forwarded to Lord Castlereagh, on the part of Alexander, the following proposal as to the guarantees to be obtained from France:—

"After having well considered the ideas put forth in the various memorials issued on the present negotiation with France, his Majesty the Emperor of Russia is of opinion that the following project will be most likely to combine the future security of Europe with the consideration that the Powers owe to the Government of the King whose re-establishment and solidity are to be regarded as the first guarantees of a state of peace and tranquillity.

"1. Occupation of places designed by the Duke of Wellington for five years.

"2. Cession of Landau as an outpost of Germany.

"3. Cession to Switzerland or demolition of Huningen.

"4. Restitution to the King of Sardinia of the part of Savoy united to France by the Peace of Paris, against the cession on her part for the rectification of the frontiers of Geneva.

"5. Restitution of the districts detached from the Low Countries by the Peace of Paris.

"6. Contribution equivalent to a year of revenue of France—say 600,000,000 francs.

"7. To comprise in this contribution the fifty millions actually exacted and the supplies which have been furnished to the Allies.

"8. To employ the third of this contribution in the construction of some fortified points in Belgium and in the south of Germany.

"9. The contribution to be payable in three years."

Austria showed an "enormous ingratitude" when she took part in the Crimean war, what can be said to the conduct of France? Could she expect Russia, for a third time after such a return, to come forward and help her in her distress in 1870-71? He pledged himself to the old King that France should keep Alsace and Lorraine, and incurred the lasting enmity of the young Prince of Prussia (Frederick William IV.), who was imbued with the aggressive spirit of the Prussian youth, elated by their recent success. When Louis heard the Prussians were going to strip the museums of the pictures and statuary wrested from foreign towns, some, like Aix-la-Chapelle, actually allies of France, he wrote to ask Alexander's interference, as he had just saved the bridge of Jena; but the Emperor called upon him, and said he had promised his support with regard to the provinces, but he could not prevent people from reclaiming their own property. "You must allow me to serve you in more important matters," he added. Blucher made little ceremony in taking possession of the Prussian objects of art, and wrote to the Prussian governor of Paris, October 19th, 1815 :—

"As my conduct has been publicly censured for not allowing the property plundered from Prussia by a banditti to remain in the Louvre, I must remark that, ably supported by the illustrious Wellington, I pursued thieves who had despoiled many of the nations of Europe, I attacked and dispersed them, and restored to my country the plunder they had unjustly taken, spurning the idea of negotiating with the French commissioners on that subject.* They may now thank Providence for our not having followed their base example.— BLUCHER."

* Of the works of art Lord Palmerston remarks in his Diary in 1815-18, as one reason among others for the general restitution, that the mere presence of the Allies in Paris might be explained away to future generations "by arrangements and conventions, the payment of sums of money by the French might be the stipulation of a treaty to which the Government of France might consent from motives of policy or justice, but in which it acted, at all events, as an independent Power; but when history shall record that these works of art brought to Paris by victory, and held there by the sword, were sent back to their respective proprietors by an allied army in possession of Paris, there will exist no doubt but that such a measure would not have been submitted to unless enforced." All who are acquainted with the inaccurate and superficial mode in which the French deal with history must see the justice of this observation.

He desired his soldiers not to enrich France, but to save their money to revive the struggling fortunes of their native land, while the Russian officers lavished whole fortunes on the jewellers' shops in Paris. Lord Palmerston writes, that all the French agreed the Russian army had behaved well; and the Prussians and Bavarians very ill. When it is remembered how many wild tribes were comprised within the Russian army, where Sir Walter Scott saw one soldier who had marched with a contingent from his horde near the great wall of China, the extraordinary influence Alexander had gained over his troops must be admitted, even if the discipline he maintained was rather severe. Canova was sent from Italy to reclaim the works belonging to Rome, and a British regiment kept order while the horses of St. Mark, carried off by force from an ally, were taken from the gate of the Tuileries, to be restored to Venice. Prussia had lost in the war of 1806-7 so many pictures, gems, cameos, and other curiosities that the mere list occupied fifty-three closely-printed pages, and she now took back as many as she could find. Antwerp received her most celebrated pictures, and the Vatican was again adorned with the Transfiguration and the Communion of St. Jerome, while the most celebrated existing statues of ancient times were restored to Rome and Florence. Russia and England had nothing to claim, and the first was considered as too apathetic in the cause; but when Alexander heard that the Elector of Hesse was trying to procure the gallery of Malmaison in the same way, without payment, having really sold the contents to Josephine, he bought it from her heirs at a fair valuation, which enabled them to pay her heavy debts. This was the only trophy, if it can be called so, which he carried to St. Petersburg, where they now adorn the palace of the Hermitage. A French author states that he obtained the statue of Napoleon from the column in the Place Vendôme, but this was not the case, as it was sold to an Englishman by the city of Paris.

Besides the works of art, all the smaller continental Powers supported Austria and Prussia in demanding indemnities for the losses sustained during twenty-five years of war, though as most of them had suffered as Napoleon's allies, it was not altogether deserved. The claims were at first beyond all reason, though they proved that France since the revolution had exacted at least 1,020,000,000*l.* from them; but it was agreed by the treaty of 1815, that 29,500,000*l.* should be paid to Austria, Prussia, the Netherlands, Denmark, Italy, and the German free towns and smaller States, besides 28,000,000*l.* to the Allies for the expense of the last armaments. Alexander claimed nothing for the damage sustained by his own empire, observing truly that nothing could repay him for Moscow. In addition, the principal frontier fortresses of France—viz., Cambray, Valenciennes, Longwy, Sedan, Bouchain, Condé, Quesnoy, Maubeuge, Landrecies, Avesnes, Rocroy, Givet, Montmédy, Thionville, Bitche, and Fort Louis, were to be held by 150,000 British, Russian, Austrian, and Prussian soldiers, maintained, paid, and clothed at the cost of France. Versoix, with a small district, was ceded to Geneva; the fortifications of Huningen were demolished, and Landau, Sarrelouis, Philippeville, and Marienburg, with a small territory annexed to each, were made over to Prussia and the Netherlands. But the district of Venaissin, the first conquest of the French republicans, was left to France, so that she still possessed twenty square leagues of territory above the extent of the kingdom of Louis XVI.

The Duc de Richelieu wept when he signed the treaty, and preserved as a memorial of Russia's moderation a map with the provinces marked which were saved by Alexander, who at this period sent a sharp remonstrance to Spain. Ferdinand had thrown over the constitution, re-introduced the Inquisition, and imprisoned many members of the Cortes. In consequence of this remonstrance, it was stated, they were lightly dealt with, but the Sovereigns excluded him from their alliance, while instead of trying to obtain the splendid pictures carried off from Spain to Paris, he seemed only bent on crushing the free spirit that had supported the claims of his family against Joseph.

On August 2nd a treaty was signed between Russia, Great Britain, Austria, and Prussia, by which Napoleon was declared a prisoner of the four allied Powers, who signed the treaty of March 25th at Vienna; the custody of his person was intrusted to Great Britain, but the other Powers might name commissioners to reside at the place appointed by the English

Government for his imprisonment. France was so completely crushed, that even if he had been left at large in Europe, he could never have hoped to set the allied Powers at defiance, but he might, like Garibaldi, have headed disturbances in Italy or other parts of the Continent; and while his accessories were being punished by death or exile, it would have been contrary to all the rules of justice to allow the principal to go free. Alexander counselled mercy so far as sparing the lives of those who aided Napoleon in his late attempt, and the list of condemned and proscribed, originally very numerous, was reduced to the proportions already mentioned at his request. But he urged Louis to disband at once the whole French army, and entirely reorganize it. The presence of the Allies would prevent disturbances arising from this measure, which would also save the French Government much expense; and as Napoleon had again emptied its treasury, this was a very important point. The King felt himself wholly at the disposal of the Allies: if he had imagined in 1814 that the majority of the French really wished for him, he was quite undeceived in 1815. Pressed between his people and their enemies, he could only hope for moderation from "the most generous and the most influential of the princes of the coalition," and Alexander's advice became his law. The French might think over the glory of the reign of Louis XIV., or even of the first days of the Republic, and sadly compare it with the state to which they were reduced through Napoleon's Empire, only owing the last shreds of independence to the Christian forgiveness of the prince who had most cause to be their enemy.

Castlereagh wrote to Lord Liverpool, July 27th, 1815: "The King finds considerable difficulty on the slave-trade point, first, because the colonists are his warm adherents; 2ndly, because Bonaparte has in some degree made the abolition his own measure. You may, however, consider the point as carried, and we owe considerable obligations to the Emperor of Russia for the manner in which he has supported us in this object."

Alexander received innumerable petitions and complaints from all quarters, and Muffling, the Prussian commander of Paris, calls him too partial to the French. This fault could not be alleged against the Prussians. Gneisenau, speaking of the treatment of Napoleon, whom he thought ought to be put to death, an idea which Wellington opposed, said, " Great Britain is under weightier obligation to no mortal man than this very villain ; for by the occurrences whereof he is the author, her greatness, prosperity, and wealth have attained their present elevation. It is quite otherwise with us Prussians. We have been impoverished by him. Our nobility will never be able to right itself again. . . . If others will assume a theatrical magnanimity, I shall not set myself against it," but he asserts that he considers it " weakness." Such the French or Napoleon would have considered it if the case had been reversed, and Alexander and Wellington were before their time. The Prussians had the pleasure of escorting Hortense to the frontier, as she had large sums of money at her disposal, and used them to foster intrigues. Joseph concealed himself for some little time in his sister-in-law's house (the Crown Princess of Sweden), and Alexander was supposed to have connived at his escape, much to Prussia's indignation ; but no object could have been attained by delivering up this most harmless member of the family to vengeance, and the outcry against them was so great at that time that his life would hardly have been safe. The trial of the proscribed officers was an exciting episode in the summer of 1815. Several of these desperadoes, headed by Labedoyère, made a plan to overpower the guards at the different houses of the allied Sovereigns and assassinate them all. A similar plot was to take effect on the 7th of August, at a party at the Duke of Wellington's.* A letter was sent to Alexander, signed " the Captain of the Regicides," in which he was threatened with death if he did not proclaim Napoleon II. A poisoned bottle of wine was also placed on his table, and his cook, who tasted it, nearly lost his life.

But at last the proscribed were one by one hunted down, with the exception of a few chiefs, including Ney, and it was not till after Alexander had left Paris that he was arrested and executed.

No one could have been more guilty than Labedoyère, but his case excited sympathy from the exertions of his wife and mother in his cause, and his frank confession and repentance.

* Despatches of the Duke of Wellington, 1815.

In vain his wife threw herself at the feet of the King to ask his pardon : she was refused, and then applied to Alexander. The Emperor told her he could not interfere with the decision of the French tribunals, though he truly pitied her. He felt, indeed, that Louis was as guilty as his subjects for having deserted the helm in the hour of danger; but his interposition was required on so many important State matters, that he did not consider it advisable to use his personal influence where a man was justly condemned. He said to the Duchesse d'Angoulême, who was known to urge severity on her uncle, "Of what use is such rigour? What can come of it?" "Sire," replied the Duchess, "justice demands firmness, and the enforcing of proper measures." "Madame, if justice has rights, there are also the claims of mercy." "Mercy," said she, "cannot be distinguished from weakness." "I think you are mistaken, madame," he said; "it may sometimes gain hearts, and secure them." But she had no idea of this mode of securing attached subjects, and accordingly Labedoyère with several more suffered death.

Madame de Krudener, her daughter and son-in-law, with their companions the German pastors, left Heidelberg a few days after the Russian army, and followed the Emperor to Paris, where they established themselves in a house at the back of the Elysée Bourbon. There they held prayer-meetings, and the great world and even the clergy of Paris were attracted by the chance of seeing the Emperor, and curious to hear a woman who had given up a palace to live among the poor. She established an association for intercessory prayer from the Baltic to the Mediterranean, which prayed for special persons and occasions at every hour of the day, and " her warmth and enthusiasm impressed if it did not convert the lighthearted people of Paris. Many a Parisian scoffer, going to hear her in her drawing-room, which was open to all, returned," says Sainte-Beuve, "at least thoroughly subdued by her personal magnetism. Those who seriously believe," he adds, " in the intervention of Providence in the affairs of the world, should not judge her too superciliously. 1815 was a decisive epoch, and to religious minds it may well have appeared that the crisis was grave enough to demand a prophet." Historical compilers have much exaggerated her intercourse with Alexander. Capefigue antedates it, and in his History of the Restoration, after passing in review all the persons assembled at the Congress, describes the Emperor of Russia kneeling in an oratory with Madame de Krudener. "It is doubtless," he says, "during this sojourn of Madame de Krudener at Vienna, that she persuaded Alexander that Napoleon was the Black Devil, or the genius of battles, and that he was the White Angel, or the genius of peace." The fact is, she never was at Vienna ; their first meeting took place after the termination of the Congress, and she combated rather than joined in Alexander's vision of peace. Sainte-Beuve says that the religious service on September 11th, in the midst of a review of the Russian troops on the Plaine des Vertus, was dedicated to her, whereas it was only the ordinary service always held on Alexander's fête-day. An English historian* asserts that Alexander "during September and October of this year, spent whole days at Paris in a mystical communication of sentiments with this remarkable lady." Alexander left Paris before the beginning of October, and his religious exercises never drew him away from the business of his empire. They entrenched only on his hours of recreation and rest. His correspondence and the contemporary journals show how all his days were occupied, but he spent some part of every alternate evening at her house during a period of his visit. It had been his occasional habit in St. Petersburg to pass an hour or two of his leisure evenings with some quiet philanthropic family, though he left it off when he found it was misconstrued. He could not imagine that a visit to Madame de Krudener, a worn, haggard woman of fifty, thirteen years his senior, could produce any evil reports; and as a man, sick in body, finding no relief from regular physicians, seeks for cure from a quack, so the Emperor, fatigued and uneasy in his mind, unable to procure consolation from the orthodox ministers of religion, was willing to look for it wherever it seemed likely to be found. His recent conversation with the Quakers in England prepared him for female inspiration, if he had even resisted the superstitions common to his countrymen. He had inquired

* Alison. This is refuted by Madame de Krudener's own correspondence.

how they could reconcile female preaching with the doctrine of St. Paul, and they answered, that a Christian man or woman being one, the gift of the Spirit might be equally bestowed on either sex, as on the day of Pentecost; that it was the practice of the primitive Church, and they quoted the example of the daughters of Philip. Talleyrand, eager to revenge himself on Alexander for his opposition in Vienna and again in Paris, tried to undermine his influence by holding him up to his friends as an object of ridicule for his attention to Madame de Krudener, in whom the old diplomatist of sixty-one seems to have thought there was still something fascinating; and following the good stories with which the ex-minister, who went to hear her, entertained his convivial guests, her thin grey locks have been transformed into luxuriant light hair. He declared that Alexander clothed himself in sackcloth and fasted according to her directions, whereas he kept the numerous fasts strictly prescribed by the Greek Church, and had observed them no less in 1814 than since he made her acquaintance. Others chose to perceive some deep political motive in their meetings. "He is too well informed and able a man to be religious," said one diplomatist, whom it is to be hoped lived to see that the two might be combined. Madame de Krudener is accused of having tried to gain him by flattery. Her first conversation with him is a proof that it was no flattery which procured his confidence. His hope of establishing a lasting peace was no novelty, but the constant object of his policy, as it was formerly a dream of Paul's; and Madame de Krudener always denied having had anything to do with the project of the treaty commonly known as the Holy Alliance. Stein says she had no influence over the Emperor in his management of home affairs, and he soon perceived she was not sufficiently practical. "Your views," she wrote to him after he left Paris, "are great and noble, but you cannot effect them yet; you ought only to think of regenerating yourself to regenerate all around you. Everything will yet pass through a great crisis. Germany, which bears in her the germ of destruction, will be overturned; the Turks will disappear; the English are not safe." Man was to stand by and watch the coming storm and the rescue of the faithful, taking no other part in averting it than constant prayer. Such a course was very proper for a weak woman, but Alexander was aware that more was required from the autocrat of all the Russias. Among her companions in Paris was a girl brought by Fontanes, an Evangelical pastor, who asserted that she had ecstasies and revelations. Madame de Krudener took Alexander to see her at a moment when she was said to be inspired with the gift of prophecy. In her ecstasy, the girl asked for money to found a Christian community in Weinsburg. Alexander drew his conductor into another room, and told her he knew enough of human frailty to be aware that when piety took a mercenary form, it was rather to be suspected, and he advised her to get rid of them both.*

In August, 1815, the Empress Elizabeth paid a short visit to England, and Madame de Krudener wrote from Paris, August 7th, to her maid-of-honour: "Our Emperor's attitude has been that of a Christian hero, which, with the aid of the All-Powerful, I dared to foresee and desire last year. His greatness strikes even the blind. His calm, simple life, compared with the frivolous pleasures which make all the happiness of the world, is a magnificent study, which preaches the long-forgotten Gospel to men. He works much, but in the evening he comes often to see a person who is much attached to you, and who lives not far from him. They like him much here. The people constantly call him by affectionate names. Evil alone flies from him."†

The service at Madame de Krudener's was at seven P.M., but except on one or two occasions, Alexander did not attend it,‡ going there later, and leaving at midnight. But however late he retired, he always rose not later than five A.M., and from seven

---

* Their ultimate career justified his opinion of them.

† On August 30th she wrote to the same correspondent: "He marches in the way of renunciation. I know each detail of his life. When he is obliged to go sometimes to the world, it is never to a play nor to a ball." Both a French diplomatist and Metternich did their best to draw him away with the most attractive female society. "Yesterday the Duchesse de Duras and Châteaubriand talked with me. We spoke of the chastisements weighing on France, and I answered, when they spoke of the power I have over some one, 'That some one is only dust und an arm of flesh. God directs me to tell him the truth. God inspires him with the love of truth, but he can do nothing for France. This country can only make an *amende honorable*, humiliating herself and asking grace at the foot of that cross so long deserted, confessing Christ aloud. I have sinned also in the middle of this Babylon. Let the King, the nobles, and the people also repent,'" &c.

‡ The lively author of the Revelations of Prince Talleyrand has given

to ten inspected his troops. He conducted the affairs of his empire while abroad as well as at home, and a large amount of correspondence continually arrived from Russia, to be answered or revised. The winding up of the French treaty necessitated constant interviews with the foreign ministers; but he refused all invitations, except once to dine respectively with Lord Cathcart, Lord Castlereagh,* and the Duke of Wellington, though he received Talleyrand and the other statesmen at dinner in his own quarters. Sir Walter Scott met the Emperor at Lord Cathcart's, and again at a review, where "the Russian infantry" appeared to him " small men, fine, firm, steady-looking, clean, handsome, and the appearance of the Cossack proper was prepossessing." The Russians were commanded by the Emperor to charge in line, it was thought for the sake of taking down the pride of the English military present, who looked upon it as a peculiarly British manœuvre, and they went through the movement remarkably well. The chief part of the Russian army was encamped this year in Champagne, and on September 11th it was reviewed in the Plaine des Vertus, just before all but the contingent of 40,000 men returned to Russia. An English traveller describes their huts as most picturesque, and crowds came from Paris to see the spectacle. Applications for orders on the postmasters and hotels in the district had to be made to the Emperor through his secretary, so that he supplied Lady Castlereagh and her party, Madame de Krudener and her friends, and every one else who required a billet, with the necessary note. One hundred and sixty thousand men were

the Prince's account of a visit in which the old diplomatist, to make a good story, drew considerably on his imagination. He mentions meeting in the street on his way there the plain " green carriage and unpretending liveries of the Emperor Alexander," who, however, always walked to Madame de Krudener's through the garden of the Elysée Palace, though on that occasion he may have been on his road from another house. The Emperor himself he describes as "dressed in black, with no mark of his high rank save a glittering star of brilliants." The King of Prussia, "with the most perfect nonchalance imaginable, was leaning back in his chair," for "at that time he never left Alexander's side, nor turned his gaze from the autocratical countenance," &c. Jung Stilling, he asserts, was present, and calls him a new illuminé, whereas for years he had been a preacher, and was not then in Paris at all. Five hundred, he says, filled her drawing-room, and all knelt except himself, &c.

* Lady Brownlow met Alexander and his two younger brothers at Lord Castlereagh's.

reviewed and 300 guns discharged, giving to the spectators a rather alarming impression of the power of Russia. On the 12th there was a grand mass for the Emperor's fête. In one tent assisted the Emperor of Russia and his three brothers, the Emperor of Austria, the Prince Royal, and one Archduke, the King of Prussia and his two sons, a multitude of German Princes, and Wellington, Schwartzenberg, Wrede, Platof, Barclay de Tolly, and several other generals—a proof of the extreme liberality and comprehensive nature of the doctrines of the Greek Church, which permitted all shades of Christianity—Roman Catholics, Anglicans, Lutherans, and Calvinists—to be alike present at her most solemn service.* Lamartine observes that Alexander had not only extended, but during his sojourn in Germany and France, "he had popularized Russia." It was on his return from this service in the Plaine des Vertus that he first communicated his plan of a religious union between the Princes of Europe. He was struck at Vienna and Paris by the contempt with which any religious fervour was regarded in society, and that even in London those who objected to profane conversation were insultingly styled Methodists. He hoped to undo, by a more open profession of his opinions, the evil he felt he had tended to increase by his former well-known scepticism, and to induce his Allies to do the same, as if they had not been quite so irreligious in their doctrines as Alexander, their practice had been no better, and their people required an example of faith in high quarters quite as much as the Russians. Stein observes that "Alexander's religion had so far a beneficial effect upon him, that it set bounds to his natural violence and restless activity, which might otherwise have grown very dangerous to Europe. Nesselrode, Capo d'Istria, Pozzo di Borgo, and those around him were glad to see it, and encouraged the Holy Alliance; Capo d'Istria hoped it might be turned to the advantage of Greece." "This act," says Lamartine, "which the Liberal party for a long time fancied was a mutual bond for the slavery of the

* "From this tent," writes Lady Brownlow, "to behold an immense army of conquerors, who all at the same instant fell on their knees in prayer and thanksgiving, seemed more like a tale in the Arabian Nights than an occurrence of real life. The magnificent dresses of the priests and the perfume of the incense were calculated to increase the illusion. The music, entirely vocal, was beautiful."

people, was only in principle an act of faith in Providence promulgated by a grateful prince after the freedom of the Continent; and to substitute morality and equity for arbitrary dealing and force in the transactions between Sovereigns." A project in fact hardly deserves the ridicule it received, which secured peace between the Powers of Europe for forty years—a peace followed by eighteen years of almost constant war.

Castlereagh wrote to Lord Liverpool, Paris, September 28th: "You will receive enclosed, an autograph letter from the three allied Sovereigns, addressed to the Prince Regent, which I have been desired to transmit. To explain the nature of this rather novel proceeding, I have obtained copies both of the letter and its enclosure, deeming it material to accompany it with such explanations as may assist his Royal Highness in making it a suitable reply. I have to acquaint you that the measure entirely originated with the Emperor of Russia, whose mind has lately taken a deeply religious tinge. The first intimation I had of this extraordinary act was from the Emperor himself, who said he had communicated that morning to the Emperor of Austria his sentiments upon this subject, and he would speak to me further upon it in a few days. Prince Metternich the following day came to me with the project of the treaty, since signed. He told me in great confidence the difficulty in which the Emperor of Austria felt himself placed, that he felt great repugnance to be a party to such an act, and yet was more apprehensive of refusing himself to the Emperor's application; that it was quite clear his mind was affected, that peace and goodwill was at present the idea which engrossed his thoughts, that he had found him of late friendly and reasonable on all points, and was unwilling to thwart him in a conception which, however wild, might save him and the rest of the world much trouble so long as it should last. In short, seeing no retreat, after making some verbal alterations, the Emperor of Austria agreed to sign it. The Emperor of Russia then carried it to the King of Prussia, who felt in the same manner, but came to the same conclusion. As soon as the instrument was executed between the Sovereigns, without the intervention of their ministers, the Emperor brought it to me, developed his whole plan of universal peace, and told me the three Sovereigns had agreed to address a letter to the Prince Regent to invite him to accede, of which intended letter his Imperial Majesty delivered to me the enclosed copy. The Duke of Wellington happened to be with me when the Emperor called, and it was not without difficulty that we went through the interview with becoming gravity. I examined, with Prince Metternich, every possible expedient to stop it; but the Emperor of Austria, with all his sobriety of mind, did not venture to risk it. When it reached me, in fact, the deed was done, and no other course remained than to do homage to the sentiments upon which it was founded, and to the advantage Europe might hope to derive from three such powerful Sovereigns directing all their influence to the preservation of peace, . . . that I was confident the Prince Regent would unite heart and soul with his august allies in making this the basis of all his policy, and that I would lose no time in laying before his Royal Highness this solemn pledge of the pacific and moderate spirit which actuated their councils. I ventured to express my satisfaction that the Sovereigns had not given to this instrument an official character, that this might have rendered its production as a State document necessary; that it was better it should pass as an autograph communication of sentiment between Sovereign and Sovereign, binding upon their own consciences in the general management of their affairs, than that it should be exposed to public discussion as an act advised by their ministers. I had, in truth, taken pains, through Prince Metternich, to keep it, if it must go forward, in this channel, foreseeing that as Wilberforce is not yet in possession of the Great Seal, even if I receive the Prince's command to countersign it, it might find some difficulty in passing through the ordinary course of office. The fact is, that the Emperor's mind is not completely sound. Last year there was but too much reason to fear its impulse would be to conquest and dominion. . . . He really appears to be in earnest. It is at all events wise to profit by this disposition as far as it will carry us, and this is peculiarly the feeling of Austria and Prussia. I am desired by the Emperor of Austria, through Metternich, to express his earnest hope that the Prince will not refuse this overture, however much he may feel with him the embarrassment of the proceeding, that he thinks good may come of indulging the Emperor, and that real danger might result to the Alliance from a refusal. My own opinion very much concurs with that; and in weighing difficulties on both sides, I think no person will blame the Prince for not refusing himself to a proposition so made to him, where the objection lies rather against the excessive excellence than the quality and nature of the engagement; but then I think the Prince must take it upon himself, and sign it without the intervention of his ministers, as an autographic avowal of sentiments between him and the Sovereigns his allies, tending to preserve the tranquillity of Europe. To decline doing so after a late explanation, might produce very unpleasant consequences. The Emperor told me that nothing had given him so much satisfaction as to affix his signature to this bond of peace in he believed the most irreligious capital in Europe. I confide this communication to your management, and hope the Prince Regent may find himself enabled to avert disturbing the harmony which at present subsists between him and his allies.—Castlereagh."*

Lord Liverpool in answer to this letter,† says he has laid the treaty before the Prince Regent, and called a Cabinet to discuss it, but wishes it could have been suppressed altogether. He thinks that, though the Regent of Great Britain can be a party to no act of State personally, as he only signs treaties through his ministers, the Prince had better write an autograph letter to the three Sovereigns, stating that he entirely concurs in their views as to making the Christian religion the invariable rule of their conduct in all their relations, social and political, &c.

The letter and treaty which troubled the English ministers so much were composed and written out by Alexander.‡ The

* Wellington Despatches, &c., Supplement, vol. x. † Ibid.
‡ "Sire, our Cousin and Brother,—
"The events which afflicted the world for more than twenty years have convinced us that the only means of putting an end to them is to be found in the closest union between the Sovereigns whom Divine Providence has placed at the head of the nations of Europe. The history of the three last memorable years are a proof of the happy effect this union has produced for the safety of mankind. But to assure to this bond the solidity required by the greatness and purity of the end to which it tends, it ought to be founded on the sacred principles of the Christian religion. Deeply penetrated by this important truth, we have signed the act we

last bound the contracting Powers to govern their people according to the precepts of Holy Scripture, to consider all Christian nations as one family, irrespective of a difference of creed, to lend each other all necessary aid, and after acknowledging the Divine source of all earthly glory, wisdom, and success, made a formal avowal of the doctrines of the Catholic Faith. At this period, so far from all Christians being regarded as brothers, Dissenters from the Established Church laboured under heavy civil disabilities in every European country except Russia, and while the Allies occupied Paris, a serious rising against the Protestants took place in Provence. In England Dissenters had no part in the legislature, and throughout the war were all strong Bonapartists. "The Holy Alliance," writes Count Munster,* "had great political importance." It was a counter declaration to the decree establishing infidelity by the Republic of 1792. Alexander interpreted his own text: that there were no such things as dynastic rights, that the Sovereign was but delegated by Providence to promote the good of his people; and nearly all his allies had verbally promised him, and some in writing, that they would promote liberal institutions among their people. How they kept that promise belongs more to their history than to his, and he was disappointed by the result of the Alliance. No Christian compact could keep Metternich from crooked intrigues, and it was fear of the power of Russia and of the revolutionists which prevented another secret treaty against Alexander, quite as much as this League. However, it was joined by most of the continental States, even by Louis, and it was agreed that the

submit to-day to the meditation of your Royal Highness. You will see its object is to strengthen the ties uniting us in forming the people of Christendom into one family, and in assuring to them, under the protection of the All-Powerful, the happiness and safety of peace in the ties of an indissoluble fraternity. We much regret that your Royal Highness was not with us at the moment when we concluded this transaction. We invite you as our first and most intimate ally to accede to it, and to complete a work consecrated only to the welfare of humanity, and that we ought in consequence to consider as the most splendid recompense of our efforts. We repeat to your Royal Highness the assurance of sincere attachment and high esteem, with which we are your Royal Highness's good brothers, cousins, and allies,

"FRANCIS.
"FREDERICK WILLIAM.
"Paris, September 14th (26th)."   "ALEXANDER.

* Political Recollections.

Sovereigns should meet periodically to consult on the affairs of Europe, and settle any important matter on hand. The Ultramontanes, such as De Maistre, hailed it with delight, as a proof that the most powerful Sovereigns of Europe professed the doctrines of Christianity; (a proof certainly needed,) and as a great bulwark against infidelity and republicanism. "The writer," he says, "is the Emperor of Russia, who writes, as you know, with as much ease as elegance. It is signed by no minister. Some may laugh, others can think. A great religious revolution is imminent in Europe, and it is already much advanced. This declaration is one phase of this revolution; soon doubtless it will become useless, but at this moment it will produce much effect. The King of Prussia at last perceives the moral dissolution of his country. There is no longer a Prussian people, only an army and a military democracy. He has entered this religious fraternity with pleasure, for he feels his principal need."

"The Emperor of Russia for some years has occupied himself much with religion, and the moderation and rectitude of his ideas on this point are in my eyes a perfect prodigy, because they belong to him exclusively, the education he received pushed him quite in the other direction. If I am not deceived, he will require at least all his dexterity to exercise at home the religious supremacy belonging to him with the measures circumstances exact. In fact, Russia knows nothing of religion. The absolute ignorance of the Latin tongue renders her a stranger to all the sources of controversy. She has much mind, but the greatest mind only knows what it has learnt, and the Russian (I speak of laymen) has not yet looked on this side."

Of course the Bonapartists and Republicans took a different view* of a treaty calculated to strengthen their opponents,

* "The Liberals," writes Madame de Genlis, "angry and indignant at the coalition of the Emperor of Russia and the Emperor of Austria with the King of Prussia to prevent the overthrow of thrones and altars, have for some time all joined in the same cry, that these Sovereigns wished for nothing but to divide Europe between them, and that under the pretext of maintaining peace, their object was to invade foreign States. An instance of this ambition was seen in the reign of Napoleon. . . . Yet a great many who make such an outcry against the enterprise of the Emperor of Russia, very far from disapproving of Napoleon's conduct, served with great zeal and courage in the war against Spain, even after Napoleon had carried off the royal family as prisoners, and made known

and after Alexander's death, his old tutor, La Harpe, wrote a defence of the Holy Alliance for that especial faction, which appeared in the *Globe* in 1828. He also intended it as a reply to a book by the Pastor Empaytaz, who was introduced to Alexander by Madame de Krudener at Heidelberg, and now revealed the religious conversations between himself and the Emperor. Words written down fourteen years after they were spoken by an enthusiast, much elated at having talked to a great Sovereign, are not wholly to be relied on, and though a Lutheran pastor may not feel himself bound, like a Greek or Latin Priest, to receive such confidences as under the sacred seal of confession, yet there was a striking absence of propriety, if not of honour, in publishing to the world Alexander's uneasiness with regard to his brother Constantine, and the prayers he offered up for his improvement while Constantine was still living; and as both this pastor and Madame de Krudener tended to bring the Alliance into disrepute, by the exalted manner in which they boasted of it to their followers, La Harpe, who was still a freethinker and Ultra-liberal, tried to account for it while respecting the memory of his pupil—whose real fault in the eyes of his enemies was that he had shown himself stronger than Napoleon. " Although intrepid in the midst of danger, Alexander had a horror of war. Thoroughly aware of the abuses that excite the discontent of nations, he hoped that during a lengthened peace, the want of which was generally felt, the Government of Europe, recognizing the importance of undertaking such reforms as the necessities of the age called for, would seriously apply themselves to the work. For this a state of profound repose was indispensable, and as the confusion of the past

his intention of putting his brother Joseph on the throne. This is surely a strange kind of inconsistency. Did they not say when the Allies entered France that their intention was to seize upon the provinces allotted for their residence during the five years granted for the payment of the expenses of the war? They said, such was the state of the finances it was impossible to pay these enormous expenses, and therefore the Allies would pay themselves by keeping the provinces and partitioning France. Yet these sums were paid without burdening the people, and two years and a half sooner than was agreed on, and the Allies returned home in the most peaceful manner possible. This important business, so speedily terminated, did not even prevent the Government from diminishing the taxes. We must be both very ungrateful and very blind not to admire such things."

thirty years had greatly weakened the old ideas of allegiance and subordination, he thought he provided a remedy in a solemn appeal to religion. At this period, from north to south, from east to west, the eyes of the oppressed were turned towards Alexander I.; but from this moment is to be dated the conspiracy which secretly plotted to strip him of that formidable moral power which gave him for auxiliaries every friend of enlightenment and humanity, the universal co-operation of honest men. Disposed by the natural moderation of his character to consent to anything which might remove fears of his preponderating influence, and willing at any price to dissipate the alarm feigned or felt, he consented to (or in reality proposed) the establishment of a Court of Areopagus, where a majority of votes should decide the measures to be taken in common for the maintenance of the general tranquillity. The genius of evil quickly caught a glimpse of the advantage he might reap from so generous an abrogation of this preponderating influence. Thanks to the troublesome and vexatious turn the members managed to give to the progress of ordinary affairs, the confidence of the nations was impaired, and the magnanimous monarch who had so well deserved it, saw it lost amid the impudent acclamations of the enemies to his glory, who did not hesitate to impute to his obstinacy and absolute will the most unpopular measures which they dictated in their Areopagus." In short, Alexander instituted a constitutional government of the universe.

One more opinion must be quoted before the subject is closed—that of Napoleon, who, as if already transferred to another sphere, was for nearly six years the critical spectator of the progress of events in Europe, still hoping that a change in the English Cabinet might some day enable him to share in them once more. After speaking of his campaign in Russia, and saying that if he could have dictated his own terms of peace to Alexander it should have ended all his wars, he added, with the egotism which adopted every plan he approved as his own, " Satisfied on these great points, and quiet everywhere, I should have also had my Congress and my Holy Alliance. They have stolen these ideas from me. In this reunion of all the Sovereigns we might have treated of our interests as a family, and made up our accounts with our people."*

Before Alexander left Paris, Madame Krudener tried to plead the cause of her friend Hortense, whom she regarded as a brand plucked from the fire. "I frankly own," he said, "I do not like women to busy themselves with politics, and am disappointed with the Queen in this respect. After receiving from the bounty of the King of France the permission to remain in Paris, she ought not to have taken the active part she has done in expelling him from the throne." "Of your bounty, Sire." "It matters little," he answered, "who she accepted it from. She ought not to have remained in Paris on the return of Napoleon." The treaty of April having been broken by Napoleon, its provisions respecting the maintenance of his family were now set aside, except Parma, which Alexander secured for Maria Louisa, and Bayreuth, which was disputed between Prussia and Bavaria, for Eugene. But they had already reaped such a rich harvest that they were still by no means impoverished; some of them emigrated to America, and others went to live in Italy.

The Russian contingent† left in France was placed under Count Voronzov, whose sister was married to the Earl of Pembroke, and the Allies selected Wellington as the commander of the whole force. The Prussians still felt themselves insufficiently revenged; and before quitting Paris Alexander assembled several Prussian officers, including Gneisenau, and speaking to them as to his brothers-in-arms, he tried to calm their angry feelings, and ended by telling them that, while bearing the name of Christians, they could hardly desire to imitate the conduct of those who had been a disgrace to civilization in the mode in which they comported themselves towards Prussia. "Give them," he said, "the

---

* Mémoires de Ste. Hélène. Par Las Cases.
† It appears from the Duke of Wellington's correspondence that the rations then supplied to the Russian private soldier was 3 lbs. of bread a day, salt, and some flour to make quass. In hospital they were even better treated than the English, as appears from the payment made to the French Government for the soldiers of each of the allied armies, which was fixed according to the treatment followed by each: for an English soldier, 2 francs 25 centimes a day; for a Russian, 2 francs 45 centimes; for a Prussian, 2 francs 55 centimes; for an Austrian, 2 francs 20 centimes; &c.

example of pardon; this is the only Christian revenge." He left them, for the time at least, pacifically disposed. He set off for Brussels to see the King of Holland on September 27th, and was conducted over the field of Waterloo by the whole royal family and the Princes of Prussia. He returned to France to inspect his army once more, and reviewed the Austrian contingent at Dijon, being presented by Louis with thirty-four decorations of the Order of St. Louis to distribute among his officers. From Dijon he went to Zurich and Munich, where he saw the Empress, and then straight to Berlin, arriving there October 24th. He had not stayed a night in this city or in Potsdam since, full of youth and hope, he had rested on his way to Austerlitz; and, though he had now realized all the aspirations then premature, and had conquered a permanent peace, the little elation he showed at his victories convinced every one that he thought the results hardly worth the cost. His visit to the capital of his ally was to calm the anger of the young military against him on account of Lorraine and Alsace. They piqued themselves on their battles at Ligny and Waterloo, and pretended that these alone achieved Napoleon's fall; ignoring the sanguinary campaign (because the army under Blucher was half composed of Russians) which had so completely broken Napoleon's power that his last struggle, even if he had conquered at Waterloo, could have been nothing but a prolonged death. There was also rivalry between the Prussian military and their own Government. Every officer, including Blucher, belonged to a secret society, which the ministers regarded with suspicion; and Alexander was now anxious to induce the King to fulfil his promise of religious toleration and a representative Government to satisfy the country and occupy these restless spirits. The King hesitated, half undertook to do so, and ended by yielding to Hardenberg, and rewarding their aspirations by a prison, and obliging many of his non-conforming subjects to quit Prussia. The King of Holland and the Dukes of Saxe-Weimar and Baden were more complaisant, and agreed to Alexander's demand of a constitutional Government.

The Emperor was joined in Berlin by his sisters Mary and Catherine, beside Nicholas and Michael. At a royal banquet the King proclaimed the engagement between his eldest daughter and "the brother of his most faithful ally and friend." Blucher and Barclay sat among the princes, and all drank the health of the young pair. The Princess Charlotte* had been the support of her father, and had presided over the palace since her mother's death, and was more fitted than the shy and retiring Elizabeth to fill the place of an Imperial bride; but there is no reason to suppose that the King was only persuaded to allow his daughter to change her name and form of creed by its being intimated to him that Nicholas was destined to be Alexander's heir. The Emperor was thirty-seven, Constantine thirty-six, and though present appearances were in favour of Nicholas being ultimately an Emperor, still either of them might marry again and leave a son. The King could not refuse his daughter to Alexander's brother any more than Francis of Austria could refuse to sign the Holy Alliance; besides, the young princess was much struck with her youthful bridegroom, and his character gave her every chance of matrimonial happiness.

Alexander spoke to one of her relations on his brother's good fortune in marrying a princess whom he had chosen himself, and whose heart he had gained. "They will be a happy couple," he said, "and I rejoice at the event. My fate was different. My marriage was settled when I was a mere stripling, and scarcely knew what a solemn act it was, and before I had ever seriously thought of such an affair. Indeed, though I was joined to a beautiful and amiable princess, she had not captivated my heart. I had not selected her as my companion for life—that was my grandmother's business, and no doubt Catherine had good political reasons for her conduct; but the Empress and myself have been the sacrifice."

The next day the Princess took her future husband with the Emperor to see the mausoleum at Charlottenburg, containing her mother's tomb; and in the evening Alexander pursued his journey to Warsaw to make his first entry into the city as King of Poland.

Lord Walpole writes from St. Petersburg to Lord Castlereagh, September 11th, "The Emperor's continued absence

* She was goddaughter to Queen Charlotte of England.

has occasioned a more painful impression than any I have ever before observed." In November, "Everybody is much discontented, and the Guards want another foreign war for the sake of crosses, decorations," &c.* De Maistre writes: "The Emperor is looked for like rain after an African summer: one must live in Russia to know what he is for her; his name is a constitution, and who knows if she could have a better? Poland counts on hers, and Russia, without exception, cannot bear the idea. The new Polish armorial bearings are the eagle of Russia surmounted by the eagle of Poland. Even this is criticised, though every Russian province bears its private arms above that of Russia. The Poles ought to learn to marry before anything else (alluding to the facility with which divorces were obtained in Poland). They are not aware that a people who play at marriage is unconstitutionable." September 26th, 1815: "They are very impatient at the absence of the Sovereign, but I should be curious to know how the same men who admire Peter I. in the dockyards at Zaandam can refuse the same feeling to Alexander I., occupied with much more essential things than cutting planks and striking nails. The Emperor must necessarily meet on his road a crowd of European ideas which would not come to seek him. . . . In no other country of 40,000,000 would it be possible for a Sovereign to remain away two years, and no disturbance in his absence. . . . He who demands the freedom of the serfs in Russia, asks for the division of the empire. . . . In Russia we are in the 16th century.† The religious movement agitating Europe has reached her, and gives alarm. In this state of things the Bible Society cast its toils into Russia. . . . A colony offered itself, and was immediately accepted, for the Russian is fonder of novelties than the Frenchman of the old régime, with whom he has much in common, and among the number of very respectable members (of the Bible Society) we find the Russian and Roman Catholic Archbishops. They are there like two courtiers, be-

* Lord Liverpool, writing October 2nd, to the Duke of Wellington, says: "I trust Lord Castlereagh will be able to bring our negotiations to a satisfactory conclusion; and if the Emperor of Russia acts upon the advice of the military council, and halts his army, I have little doubt of it. On the other hand, the departure of the Sovereigns from Paris and the march of the Russian army across the Rhine will, I fear, prevent matters being settled without another conflict."

† "Science arrives, and takes Religion by the collar."

cause they imagine the Society is agreeable to the master. Yet it is evidently only a means for overturning the whole ecclesiastical establishment.* The Anglican Church is alarmed, and some of its bishops have attacked the society. Here they dread no danger. Catholicism plays its part in this general movement, they reprove its natural proselytism. Prince A. Galitzin (the Minister of Religion) is much alarmed. This minister is a very good subject of the Emperor, of a very estimable character. I am curious to know how Alexander's wisdom, enlightened by all he has seen, will unravel these different interests. Foreigners have done Russia much harm, have sold her poison, have calumniated her, seduced, or insulted her. . . . Those in this country who hate Roman Catholics have no fear of Protestants. Prince Galitzin watches the Jesuits keenly, and only awaits the arrival of the Emperor to procure some rigorous measure. . . . The State already contains forty sects, some absurd, others guilty, all fanatical and obstinate. Protestants on one side and Raskolniks on the other, are two files which saw the religion of the country at each end, and they must soon meet. It is sadly amusing to see the Bible Society propagated and sustained in a country where the extravagant interpretation of some text of the Holy Scriptures in the vulgar tongue produced a mad and dangerous tribe of Dissenters. . . . The praises I hear from France of the Russians and their Sovereign give me extreme pleasure, but the eye of the father of the family is wanted here." The "natural proselytism" of the Roman Catholic Church had been carried so far as to cause a panic during the Emperor's absence, and conversions were daily coming to light, having been kept secret for many years by the advice of the Jesuit confessors. As early as 1806 the Countess Rostopchine, unknown to her husband, entered the communion of the Roman Church; as the Count said years afterwards, it was the only trouble she ever gave him. The Roman curé dined at his house once a week in Moscow, lent her books, and in the end received her into his Church; counselling her not to divulge it, and bringing her every Sunday a portion of the consecrated Host when he came to accept her husband's hospitality. Her sisters, the Princess Galitzin, the Countess

* Also Sainte-Maure.

Tolstoi, and the Countess Protassov, who, like herself, had been brought up in ignorance of the first principles of religion in the midst of Catherine's Court, were all converted some years later, and during a long time the Countess Vassiltchikov concealed her own change of creed from her family, but went early every morning unknown to them all to hear mass, and returned in time to join them at breakfast. Madame Svetchine had also just declared herself a Romanist; and the same year a nephew of the Minister of Religion, a boy of sixteen, was converted by his tutor, a Jesuit priest. The Russian Council of State was excited by a rumour that a Jesuit priest, who was an oculist employed by the Empress Dowager, had taken the opportunity to tamper with her faith. They were pleased at the prospect of a marriage with a country so strictly Protestant as Prussia. That of the Grand Duchess Catherine was vexatious to her Imperial mother. Lord Walpole writes that she "is much displeased: she can neither stomach the former divorce of the proposed bridegroom, nor the idea of the arrangement having been made without reference to her." The Dutch alliance was approved, as it would constitute a Russian outpost in the Netherlands, a barrier between Austria and England, and a tower of observation on the future designs of France.

Alexander received the news at Berlin of the almost total destruction of the old Tartar town of Kazan by fire, 1500 houses and eighteen churches being destroyed. "It is thought," writes De Maistre, "that it is the work of incendiaries. Some suspect Dissenters, others serfs. . . . Three days afterwards another terrible fire: one merchant lost 100,000 roubles in sugar. It is certain that Russia contains incendiaries."

The Republicans tried to excite sympathy for Napoleon by saying that, far from being allowed the luxuries to which he had accustomed himself, he was almost without the necessaries of life. This assertion is disproved by a mere list of the goods sent on board the vessel that accompanied him to St. Helena for his especial comfort, and by the account of the fitting up of his cabin from uninterested observers. He was allowed an income of 10,000*l.*, more than any English Governor except the Viceroy of India, and his establishment in the island consisted of about fifty persons. Alexander nominated M. Balmeine as his commissioner to St. Helena, and this gentleman stated when he arrived there that it was the Emperor's wish Napoleon should be treated as well as circumstances would admit, and he never found reason to send home any complaint. An English newspaper of December, 1815, says: "The Prince Regent is not the only one who wished to render the ex-Emperor comfortable; for, about the middle of November, Baron Stumert, a Russian nobleman, landed at Brighton, bringing with him fifty large packing-cases containing presents from the Emperor of Russia to his *ci-devant* Imperial brother. They were immediately forwarded to Portsmouth, to be shipped for St. Helena."

CHAPTER V.
1815—1818.

RUSSIA AT PEACE.

ÆTAT. 37—40.

AS soon as it was decided at the Congress that two districts of Poland were to be held by Austria and Prussia, Alexander required a national organization to be conferred on them, so as not to amalgamate them with Germany, and Castlereagh gave this measure his cordial support; but the affairs of the Congress were hurried to a conclusion on Napoleon's return to France, and Austria and Prussia delayed binding themselves to anything concerning the Poles till Alexander left Vienna, and then evaded it altogether when the treaty was finally signed in June. Cracow was formed into a republic, much to the annoyance of Austria; and Alexander ordered Czartoriski to repair to Warsaw to inaugurate the new régime. He sent him an autograph note with instructions (May 25th); and a month later the kingdom of Poland, under the protection of Russia, was proclaimed. Everything went off well, and ten days afterwards Czartoriski wrote that "The public spirit is good, and becomes better every day. The Russian and Polish Guards have treated each other; the greatest harmony exists among them. Monseigneur the Grand Duke cements it with much amiability, and appears to satisfy the troops." In a second letter, on the 29th, he begins to find fault with Constantine for "speaking jeeringly of the constitution, and covering everything Polish with ridicule. Some of those about him encourage his gloomy and hasty temper. The Grand Duke wishes to accompany the Russian army to Paris, and complains much of being obliged to remain in Warsaw," and he imagines that a large number of the Russian military are resolved to destroy Poland, and make use of him as their instrument. Constantine was summoned to attend his brother in Paris, and at the same time the Provisional Government of Poland sent Count Potocki to claim from France the sums she had borrowed from Warsaw. Czartoriski complained to Alexander that the treaty of Vienna left Poland involved in debts—debts contracted by the French to enable them to carry on the campaign in Russia. It was curious to bring these forward as a complaint to Alexander, but Poland seemed to think she ought to reap nothing but advantage, even when she had chosen the losing side as her ally. It was a hard task for any administration to make itself popular in a country laid waste and drained of its resources like Poland in 1812; and the new Government suffered the odium of the poverty which others had inflicted, as the present Government of France has to bear the burden imposed upon her by the wars of the Second Empire. Throughout the year 1815 the Russian employés were gradually withdrawn from Poland and furnished with posts elsewhere, and the Polish Constitution of 1791 was by degrees brought into force.

This constitutional charter placed supreme power in the hands of the King, and no Sovereign in his senses, looking back at the history of Poland, could have proposed to superintend her government on any other basis. He was assisted and controlled by two chambers, the Senate and the Diet. The direction of the affairs of the kingdom was confided to a council in the absence of the monarch, which was composed of five ministers appointed by the King and the Lieutenant-Governor. The bishops, voyvodes, and chatelains, named for life by the King, formed the Senate. The Diet was composed of the deputies of the nobility and the Commons, and was to be convoked for a month in every year. Every new law must be adopted by the majority in the two chambers, and receive the sanction of the Sovereign. The examination of the budget and public expenses belonged to the chambers, and the revenue was to be exclusively devoted to the maintenance of an independent Polish army and the payment of the Government officials. The press was free; the nobility had the right of electing its own marshals, and a municipality was established in every town. Alexander was careful to confide the direction of affairs to men whose thoroughly Polish character and abilities presented sufficient guarantees to the national susceptibilities. He offered either the Viceroyalty or the command of the Polish army to Kosciusko, but the old patriot refused both. On his visit to Warsaw he conferred the Lieutenancy of the Polish kingdom on General Zaiconzek, an old Polish soldier grown grey in battle, and whose heart and hand, from Kosciusko to Napoleon, never loved and served any other cause than that of Poland. He told the Emperor he was too poor to accept this rank. "It is only one merit more in my eyes," said Alexander, who assigned him a revenue of 200,000 Polish florins, and later created him a prince. The ministers were equally chosen from among the Poles who had assisted in the government of the Duchy of Warsaw; and Constantine, commanding the Polish army, and the relative and former colleague of Czartoriski, Novossilzof, were the only representatives of Russia. Constantine was always popular among the common soldiers, whom he protected from the oppression or dishonesty of their officers; for peculation was as great a stumbling-block in Poland as in Russia. It was decided, after a consultation with Czartoriski and the chiefs of the Poles, that the Diet should not be called together for three years, that the country might have time to settle down after its long wars, and the landowners to restore their fortunes and attend to their estates. Constantine, though commander of the army, was subject to the civil power, and as Alexander was at that time still hopeful of bequeathing a constitution to his own empire, but knew how distasteful such a government was to his heir, he thought it would accustom him to limited authority, and even give him a predilection for a constitution if he saw the benefits accruing from it to Poland; but the event proved there were not sufficient men of education among the Poles to offer constitutional monarchy a fair chance of success, even if the Polish nobility had sincerely striven to assist the union between Poland and Russia.

Alexander arrived in Warsaw November 10th, and appeared in a Polish uniform, with the order of the White Eagle, which he had re-established. "The Poles exhausted demonstrations of respect, joy, and attachment," writes De Maistre. "They erected a triumphal arch, bearing on one side this verse of Horace—

Hic ames dici pater, atque princeps;

on the other from Virgil—

Expoctate veni sacra suosque tibi commendat. Troja penates.

The Emperor perfectly knows the Russian prejudice against Poland and its political existence, which could not be carried further." All the streets and windows were decorated; but he refused to receive the keys from the magistrates, as he did not come as a conqueror, but as a friend, and in that quality accepted instead the usual municipal gift of bread and salt. He was touched with the unexpected enthusiasm they displayed, believing it was only necessity which had made them accept him as their King, and that they would still have preferred Napoleon. The next morning he held a levée, in which he received deputations from various provincial towns. The Palatine Malachowski expressed in the name of his countrymen their love, veneration, and gratitude for the noble conqueror who had given them a new political existence. In memory of so happy a day they had provided for a certain number of indigent labouring families. Alexander answered: "I receive with gratitude the expression of your sentiments towards me. I know this country has supported great reverses, but I hope the traces of them may shortly be effaced: to relieve it speedily I have given orders to the Russian armies to retire. You could not possibly have done anything more agreeable to me than to occupy yourselves with the agriculturists, and everything you undertake in that respect will excite my liveliest interest. I shall be always ready to receive every request presented to me, either by the deputies from the districts or by private people. I shall be informed of your wishes by persons appointed for the purpose, and I will give all my attention to them. I have no other object with regard to you than the prosperity of your country, and the happiness of its inhabitants." The fundamental principles of the constitution, in thirty-seven articles, were published. The Emperor's successor was to be crowned at Warsaw, but, rather to the disappointment of the Poles, he dispensed with the ceremony for himself. He left them filled with loyal enthusiasm, and at Vilna Count Oginski received him at the head of a deputation, and in a long speech spoke of the rapidity of his victories, comparing them to an eagle's flight, at which the Emperor was thought to look rather contemptuously; but when he talked of the gratitude of the Lithuanians and their sufferings, the tears stood in his eyes. He visited his old acquaintances round Vilna, and in conversation with them seemed pleased with Warsaw, but said it was easy to see that the Grand Duchy had suffered much, and required great care and a paternal administration. The Countess Choiseul-Gouffier asked if it was true that he liked London better than Paris. He liked the society better: "The French were in general frivolous and grasping." "The French at least have the merit of appreciating your Majesty's goodness towards them," she answered. "I assure you, madam," he said, reddening, "I have only done my duty; the right of reprisals has always seemed frightful to me." He turned the subject, and spoke of the splendid English parks, where art consisted in developing Nature, and the wisdom of the constitutional institutions of Great Britain.

"Since December 1st," writes De Maistre, "we have seen arrive in turn at St. Petersburg, the Grand Duchess Catherine, the Grand Duchess of Saxe-Weimar and her husband, the Grand Dukes Nicholas and Michael, and lastly her Majesty the reigning Empress returned after all the rest on the 12th. The next day, the 13th (N.S.), the great soul returned into its great body—the Emperor arrived towards eleven P.M. After a short service at the Kazan church, he went to the Empress, his august spouse. Both are gone together to the Empress-mother's, and have returned again together. The Emperor, who only slept two hours, was before eight in his sledge: he has seen the exercising house, the parade, &c., and has gone to see the President of the State Council, who is unwell; he received the Metropolitan at ten A.M.—in short, he returns to his usual course with a perfect precision; he has seized the reins again, and they were rather wavering, with much grace and vigour. Russia must gain much by her master's brilliant absence. However, there is a dissenting voice on this subject, for, as elsewhere, a detracting spirit exists which refuses to admire, and even blames what others admire. The fear and hope agitating the face of every great person in the State is a curious spectacle. No one knows if he deserves favour or blame. We hear whom the Emperor has spoken to first; they tell us he has talked eight hours and three minutes to another; they can inform you of the exact number of syllables he addressed to each, and what expression he wore, &c. . . . Yesterday he went to bed at three A.M., rose at six, and visited all the military hospitals. So active a mind would be useless if it did not command an iron body." "I fancy," writes Lord Cathcart from St. Petersburg, December 28th, " that a more complicated or laborious task,* never presented itself to any Sovereign than that now before the Emperor. Some irregularities to a serious amount have, it is said, been discovered in Volhynia, and occasioned charges of a criminal nature against the governor, which are to be examined by a special commission. The energy with which this matter has been taken up is thought to forebode very strict investigations in other quarters."

But the question most warmly pressed on the Emperor was the expulsion of the Jesuits, who were not only accused of making numerous conversions, but of having publicly declared that "the Roman Church is the only one true and sure religion for salvation." No clergy in the world were more tolerant than those of Russia, but this was naturally more than they could support when added to the wavering faith of the Empress-mother, whose family were Romanists; and they appealed to the Emperor, as the head and sworn protector of orthodoxy, to check the mischievous intrigues which had taken advantage of his absence to undermine the foundations of Eastern Catholicism. Prince Galitzin, the liberal protector of the Bible Society, which was warmly denounced by the Jesuits as well as censured by a Papal bull, and his rival the fanatical Aratchaief, were both agreed in urging their master to take some strong measure against them, and this was not long delayed. On January 2nd, a ukaz appeared banishing them from St. Petersburg. "They have turned from our faith," it ran, "young men intrusted to them for education, and some persons of the weaker sex."† De Maistre wrote

---

* Also De Maistre.
† It ran thus in the original Russian, but was badly translated, "Some women of a weak and inconsequent spirit."

five letters in their defence some years before to Count Razoumovsky, and he now declared it would be as impossible to preserve the Russian religion in the midst of its numerous enemies, as a statue of wax in a volcanic crater. "Those even," he says, "who read the Emperor's ukaz, will find something to praise. He was angry with the Order, every line proves it; but instead of expelling them from his States, he limits himself to forbidding them the two capitals. Of all European princes he is the one who has had the strongest prejudices against the Jesuits, and he has let these fathers quietly remain here during fourteen years, only from mistrust of his own opinion. He may wish to calm excited heads by giving them satisfaction. No minister, no magistrate, no accuser, no advocate appeared in the matter. They were provided with pelisses and warm boots of a very good quality, and sent off in comfortable covered carriages. . . . Who will dare to tell the truth to him who can do everything, and who has never heard it? People well informed pretend that the Emperor, disgusted by the religious scandals he saw at Vienna, has come home strongly prejudiced. In one sense this Prince is right, for there is unfortunately nothing so real as these scandals. But he needs a courageous minister by his side, able to say to him, 'You imagine, Sire, that you see Catholicism here—you only see the absence of it. You see the works of Joseph II. With the impetuosity of a young, inexperienced man, he sapped the power of the Pontiff in his own dominions. You see the result of it, Sire. There is no more religion at Vienna than there is at Geneva, and than there will be soon with you when certain powers you are not aware of shall have come to their full development.'"

The Jesuits had one bold advocate in their new convert, Madame Svetchine, who, directly she heard of their intended banishment, took advantage of the favour the Emperor had shown her since his return, to speak to him on their behalf. Her husband refused to re-enter the public service after Alexander's accession till troubles threatened the empire in 1811: he had numerous enemies among influential men, but in 1812 his wife took a prominent part in the society for the relief of the sick and wounded, which was alone a passport to her Sovereign's goodwill. "I was much touched," she writes to Mdlle. Stourdza at Vienna, " by what you tell me of M. de R—— (the Emperor) relative to me. I believed I was more than effaced from his recollection." As soon as he returned in 1815 he called upon her, and she afterwards received invitations to the palace. Her religious enthusiasm interested him; and when he wished for relaxation from his State duties or his own thoughts, he found it in her amusing conversation. Her husband's enemies took alarm. Aratchaief was devoted to the Emperor, but his jealousy of any one else who received the least attention from him equalled that of a disappointed lover; and those who advised the expulsion of the Jesuits were uneasy lest Madame Svetchine should turn him into a Romanist. These fears shaped themselves into a plot against the general, who was too proud either to complain or to justify himself, but resigned his post, and retired to France. The matter was never explained to Alexander, who expressed much sorrow to Madame Svetchine at this abrupt resolve; and when they left Russia he asked her to write to him, which she did till his death, when her letters were restored to her by Nicholas.

Mdlle. Stourdza,* married to Count Edling, went to live on her paternal estate in 1818. Her brother published a book in Russia and at Stuttgart, for which Alexander gave him 20,000 roubles, entitled "Considerations on the Doctrine and Spirit of the Orthodox Church." It was answered by the Jesuit father, Rosaven, in 1824, with a volume entitled "The Catholic Church Vindicated." In 1823 Alexander conceded a large tract of barren territory between the Dnieper and the Dniester to the Countess Edling, as it bordered on her property in Bessarabia, where she carried on the active work of a mis-

* "Our Emperor," she wrote to Jung Stilling in 1816, "continues to walk in the ways of the Lord. He leads a very retired and very exemplary life, and endures with patience the thorns with which his crown is entwined. Of his difficulties you cannot form an idea. My brother labours much for the service of the Emperor, but he labours also for God. The unhappy events which have troubled so many souls here by means of the Jesuits induced him to write a book upon our Eastern Church, which proves, I hope, in a triumphant manner that we have remained attached as scrupulously as possible to the primitive church, while the Catholics have removed far from it." She goes on to relate an account she has received from a nun returned from Jerusalem of the sufferings of the native Christians, and disputes between the Greeks and Latins. The Russian missionaries had been very successful among the tribes in the Caucasus. The Emperor had assigned funds for the maintenance of twelve churches, and of the priests commissioned to minister in them.

sionary among the Mahometans. With the aid of her husband she established a fruitful colony, called Mansir, covered with villages and well-cultivated fields; and besides aiding in the extension of Christianity among the natives—an idea she had contemplated from her childhood—it became a refuge to the Greek population who were flying from the tyranny of the Turkish Empire.

Alexander sent an edict to the Holy Synod (23rd February, 1816), pointing out the desirability of translating the Bible into modern Russian. Many of the archbishops agreed, or did not venture to differ from him; and copies were bought up so eagerly, even by the Russian Dissenters, that the receipts exceeded the expenditure. The Pope was powerless in Russia itself, but he could not remain quiet and see one of the grand principles of the Roman Catholic Church overturned, and the Bible not only translated into a language understood by all the people, but delivered without any restriction into their hands. He tried to excite a religious ferment among the Poles, and directed an extraordinary bull to the primate of Poland, complaining of the Bible Society. "We are shocked by this most crafty device, by which the foundation of our religion is undermined." He went on to declare that, "to remedy this pestilence, this defilement of the faith, so dangerous to souls," &c. The most prejudiced must allow that the head of the Latin Church yielded the palm in enlightenment to the head of the Eastern Communion, when this bull is compared with the letter Alexander wrote to the governor of Cherson on December 9th, 1816. The Governor had objected to a sect called the Duchobortzi, who opposed war and social distinctions, but were an industrious and well-conducted people. "From reports," said the Emperor, "sent to the Minister of Police, I observe you desire to have them removed, owing to rumours of their alleged wicked lives, anti-social principles, and efforts to propagate the same. The Duchobortzi have sent petitions praying for protection from oppression, and I have ordered the Minister to correspond with you; but at the same time I wish to remind you of their original removal from the Ukraine to the Melitopol district of the Taurian government, which was by my express orders given to Miklashefsky, then governor of New Russia (January 26th, 1802);

on account of the miseries they had suffered, and to protect them from improper and fruitless severities. They are sufficiently separated from intercourse with the rest of the nation, which puts a stop to their extension. For several years the Government has received no complaints from any quarter respecting disorders among them, and it has therefore reason to believe the measures already adopted adequate. The secession of this people is decidedly an error grounded on certain false opinions from a want of cultivation, for they have a zeal for the Almighty, though not according to knowledge; but does it become an enlightened Christian government to try to bring back stray sheep into the bosom of the Church by oppressive means? The doctrine of the Saviour of the world, who appeared on earth to seek and to save that which was lost, can never be instilled into men by force and oppression, and can never justify the infliction of temporal ruin on him whom it seeks to bring into the way of truth. True faith is produced by the grace of God through conviction, instruction, forbearance—and, above all, good example. Severity does not convince, but harden. The harsh measures exhausted upon the Duchobortzi during the thirty years preceding 1801, instead of rooting out this sect, much increased it. . . . Their separation from the Orthodox Church was then the only complaint against them: if again removed they would be punished owing to a mere report, without the truth of the accusation being proved—a course contrary to law. . . . This colony I commit to your own immediate inspection and care, not trusting to the reports of any one: examine impartially into all the circumstances of the case yourself, inquire into their mode of life, viewing them with the eye of a benevolent ruler. All ought to feel they live under the security and protection of the laws. Should you even discover that some of the colonists conceal deserters, or try to seduce others from the National Church into their own way of thinking, then turn the force of the law against such acts only as are contrary to it, and thereby put a stop to the evil. But for the sake of one, or even several, offenders, the settlers who had no part in them should not be involved. On occasions of this kind, when accusations are sent in, an attentive inquiry is necessary to find by whom such accusations are made, and their probable motive. Thus the two Duchobortzi you mention, who on returning to the Church accused the Society of various crimes, may have done it out of anger or revenge, for they may have been excluded from the Society for bad conduct, or left it on account of some quarrel. The mere accusations of such persons hardly deserves attention, and ought never to serve as the foundation of an imprisonment or other persecution of people not yet convicted. Even the very examination into a suspected offence should be conducted in such a way that the innocent can on no occasion suffer from it. You will not fail to conform punctually to these directions, and in the mean time report to me fully concerning your measures and discoveries," &c.—" ALEXANDER."

When the Emperor returned to St. Petersburg he found a Persian ambassador waiting to see him, with presents from the Shah, to induce him to restore the two provinces ceded by Persia to Russia in 1813. During the French invasion an emissary was despatched to Teheran to make a favourable treaty, and Sir Gore Ouseley arrived from India, by order of the British Government, to counteract the intrigues of the French and obtain the same end. The Shah Abbas Mirza was resolved to make another expedition into Georgia, and wrest it from Russia before he would talk of peace, being also persuaded that the Czar would be conquered by his ally of France; but the Persians being completely defeated, the Shah, alarmed for his own safety, agreed to the original terms, the cession of a district bordering on the Caspian Sea, which cut off the Persian access to the north of the Caucasus. According to Dr. Lyall, then in St. Petersburg, the ambassador was by no means conciliatory, but showed dislike of the Russians and partiality for the English. He brought three elephants dressed in black, and red leather boots to protect their feet from the snow, with some horses and Persian manufactured goods. Alexander received him at a Court ball on his birthday, when supper was laid for 800 people. "The Emperor much dislikes ceremony," writes De Maistre, "and receiving ambassadors officially in imperial pomp. He took the Persian ambassador into a small room," where they had almost a tête-à-tête; and the Persian afterwards supped with the diplomatic corps at the imperial table, which was shaded with orange trees; "and the exactness, the quickness, the punctuality of the servants, excites all my admiration in the middle of such a crowd." In the following May "the ambassador had his audience of leave. During his long residence he constantly said if he did not succeed it would cost him his head. He has obtained nothing." But this tragedy was averted by the Emperor sending an ambassador, General Yermolof, to Persia, where he arrived at Teheran, May, 1817. He carried with him as presents from Alexander to the Shah several enormous looking-glasses, rich furs, and ornaments in crystal. The Shah was much pleased with them. He put his hand upon the furs, and when told the Czar selected them, said, " May my hand repose upon the same place that the powerful Emperor of Russia has touched. My friendship is pure and sincere; it will endure for ever." His ministers suggested to Yermolof that this friendship would be cemented if Russia restored the provinces, or at least part of them. "I told them," said the General in the journal of his embassy, " for the last time, that I myself, as commander-in-chief in Georgia, upon whom devolved the care of the frontier, informed the Emperor it was not possible to make the smallest concession, and my Sovereign gave me leave to speak in his name." The General further repeated, that the Persian Government was so corrupt and oppressive that it would be an inhuman act to restore to her those provinces which had once experienced the blessing of a European administration. Wilson,* writing in 1818, remarks upon the extraordinary manner in which Alexander succeeded in attaching foreign acquisitions, such as Finland, Courland, Lithuania, Georgia, and the Tartars to his throne. " But after having conquered them," he adds, " Russia is satisfied to enjoy her conquests with moderation. In every country she respects its customs and its creed, and maintains the laws that she found established there so long as they are consistent with humanity."

The Prince of Orange arrived at St. Petersburg December 22nd, and for the first time met his destined bride. Their marriage took place February 21st. In the interval her sister was married to the Prince of Würtemberg, who before the end of the year succeeded his father. The Prince of Orange

* Sketch of the Power of Russia.

wrote to announce his wedding to Wellington, who had always been his friend: "I have every reason to hope I shall find as much happiness in this union as can be hoped for; the character of the Grand Duchess being a very delightful one, her mind very accomplished, and her person very pleasing." The Princess was certainly without an equal in beauty and elegance; but she was perhaps almost too grave to please a man once attached to the gay, unconventional Princess Charlotte.*

"There is a vast field," writes De Maistre (January, 1816), "for the activity of his Imperial Majesty. He sees many evils; above all, the spirit of infidelity and extravagance, which he tries to repress with all his strength. He is become severe, even hard. He mortifies everybody. His success abroad has given him self-confidence. God grant he may not go too far. I cannot cease to love him; besides, we (that is Sardinia) have no other friend; Austria wishes to possess everything, either for herself, or her princes . . . . and in the state in which he found Russia on his return, there was no remedy but in a more than firm hand." An immense coalition worked to render his reforms non-effective. "The Jesuit fathers have been perfectly well treated. This precaution, which was entirely due to his Majesty, is worthy of all praise. Peter the First would have decapitated them; even in our days, Paul would have sent them to Siberia."

One cause of the prevalent discontent with the Emperor's measures, was that few of the nobility did not feel them in a pecuniary point of view, and retrenchment is always unpopular, however necessary it may be. The farmers of brandy, a Crown monopoly, were 25,000,000 roubles in arrear to the State, and an order was published that they should pay their debts within four months, a term afterwards extended to a year. Many of the nobility had mortgaged their estates to

* The two Russian Grand Duchesses were also the richest in Europe. Alexander bought his sister Catherine's Russian palace and estate for 2,000,000 paper roubles, and another estate with which she had been endowed on her first marriage was made over to her two sons, who were to be educated in Russia. She was accompanied by a Greek priest, and a Russian chapel was erected for her benefit at Stuttgart. The same was established for her sister in Brussels, where the Prince of Orange was to hold his Court.

these farmers, and there was great alarm lest they should be confiscated with the private property of the farmers to defray the amount of their debts. The extension of the term enabled this difficulty in most cases to be surmounted. Another reason for the discontent was the curtailment of the salaries of those general officers in good health who were not actively employed; for, after the war, numbers retired, and in many instances lived abroad. This was an economy to the State of 500,000 roubles yearly; at the same time (March 12th) three admirals and five general officers past active service were made senators, which provided them with an honourable maintenance. Russia had in reality suffered more in material than any other country in Europe during the long war, for during seventeen years she had not known a month's peace on all her frontiers, having previously been engaged in hostilities for thirty-five. Her power of reparation was slower than on the rest of the Continent, from her maritime commerce and agricultural labour being suspended during half the year, and no foreigners came to expend fortunes in Russia as in Italy, Germany, and France. It was therefore vexatious to see crowds of her wealthier classes spending their money at the gambling-tables in Paris and Baden. But the value of paper money, which fell throughout 1816, to the great distress of the officials whose salaries were paid in it, rose suddenly towards the end, and continued to rise from the large exportation of corn, owing to the scarcity throughout Western Europe. "In the midst of general European misery," writes De Maistre, " Russia enjoys the greatest abundance, and feeds other people. Not less than 100,000,000 silver roubles entered the country only for corn sold." In February, 1817, the Minister of Finances announced the payment in silver of a loan of 20,000,000 roubles borrowed for seven years from the Bank of St. Petersburg in 1810. Even De Maistre writes, " All appearances are good." The conscription for 1816 was suspended, and the pay of the subaltern officers increased. The Emperor also bestowed grants of land in St. Petersburg on any military man wishing to build himself a house and made the necessary advances, so that within a very short period 1,500,000 roubles were lent from the Treasury for this purpose. "The Emperor in these sort of cases is an infinitely honest creditor. He has great projects for embellishing St. Petersburg." He drew, and approved of, several plans for houses to be adopted by those who wished to build on Government security, so as to obtain some uniformity in the streets, and exchanged the wooden quays of St. Petersburg for solid granite. The activity infused into commerce, and the credit the Russian Government now enjoyed, restored prosperity to the nation, and already at the close of 1816 it had made a rapid advance towards healing the wounds inflicted by the war.

"The Russian army," writes De Maistre in January, 1816, "consists of 560,000 effective men, and 260,000 reserve; the finest youth in the world, little troubling themselves about the buried million." "Our national levity," wrote Madame Svetchine in 1813, "has alone prevented us from dying of grief." The buried million was indeed forgotten when the Liberal party in Europe, as well as many of his subjects, hurled execrations upon Alexander for refusing to undertake a war with Turkey, single-handed, in order to emancipate the Greeks; but they were remembered by the Emperor, and accounted for his determination to preserve peace to his country till all trace of the campaign of 1812 should be effaced.

The national vanity was gratified by an archway Alexander erected at Czarco-Selo, "to the memory of his brave companions-in-arms," and he placed statues of Marshal Romanzov, Barclay, and Kutuzov in the summer gardens. With his brothers he reviewed 40,000 men on the second anniversary of the entry into Paris. They dismounted, and all the army stood uncovered while the Te Deum was sung, after which the manœuvres commenced, being followed by a banquet of 880 covers, which the Emperor gave to all the officers of his guard who had accompanied him to Paris, and a few other distinguished generals. Lord Cathcart and his son, as well as one German envoy who had taken part in the war, were invited; but no other foreign minister. The diplomatic corps and a number of ladies related to the officers watched the proceedings from a balcony; the presence of ladies at a military fête being a novelty to Russia. "The dessert was on the table, according to the Russian custom: the dinner service was of native manufacture; each plate bore in the centre the representation of a Russian Order; each guest had before him three crystal glasses worked like the facings of a uniform. Everybody was served to turtle soup, sterlet, truffles, patties, &c.; there was no dish cold, and no one wanted a plate. Three healths were drunk—first, to the victorious army; secondly, to the brave Imperial Guard; thirdly, to the allied armies in France."* A fête was also given by 150 generals and Imperial aides-de-camp, when the ambassadors of England, Austria, and Prussia were invited. Lord Cathcart proposed the Emperor's health in English, and said that doubtless all the allied Powers had done their duty, but Alexander was not the less the true preserver of Europe. The admirable perseverance, the dauntless courage, the decisive resolutions, and the ability of the Emperor of Russia has made these discordant elements march together, though as discordant to others as to himself."†

It was said, if peace continued the army would be reduced to 200,000 men; but there was danger in disbanding half of it at once, and turning so many soldiers loose in a country accustomed to serf labour, where freed workmen could find little or no employment. The militia disbanded in 1813 had caused much trouble by supplying brigands and thieves. Many projects were put before the Czar. It was generally thought part would be employed on the public works hitherto executed by salaried workmen, the Crown serfs; and others formed into colonies on the uninhabited Crown lands. The Romans formerly did something similar," wrote De Maistre; " but the Emperor wishes to keep his hand on the soldiers, and only confide the spade to them on condition of retaking the sword at the first signal. A plan of this kind, modified according to circumstances, might be of the highest utility to Sardinia. The Emperor can do without the smallest danger things very dangerous everywhere else." The result of these projects was the establishment of the military colonies, which excited great alarm in Europe. Aratchaief has been accredited with them, but he always declared they were the Emperor's own idea. They fulfilled the double purpose of cultivating waste lands and providing for the surplus soldiers, and of forming a nursery for future armies, to prevent the loss sustained by marching recruits through the country in the

* De Maistre's Correspondence, April 19th, 1816.   † Ibid.

depth of winter, as in 1812. The Cossacks were a most useful part of the Russian army, and the system on which their community was originally organized was made the foundation of the new scheme. The Russian soldier and peasant communistic habits were taken into consideration—their custom of putting their wages and pay into a common fund, and making an annual equal division, and of distributing the lands allotted to the villagers by their seigneurs in the same way; and the tendency of families to remain together in one house, so that it was not unusual to find three or four generations living in perfect harmony under the same roof. The plan would greatly diminish the cost of keeping up a large army, it would avoid the separation of parents from their children when they entered a military career, and would civilize and educate a considerable number of the Russian lowest class. It might have been successful in Germany or Hungary, or in some tribes of the Russian Empire; but the ordinary Russian serf was the most conservative of human beings, and most impatient of anything like system or method. He had learned to look upon labour, even for his own profit, as synonymous with slavery, and to regard utter idleness as the great blessing of freedom. Alexander had marched too long at the head of an army to regard individual interests as compared with the public advantage. He thought the state of the Russian peasant abject and degraded, and that elevating him into the position of a military colonist was a material and moral advantage. Difficulties might be met with at the outset, for what had he ever undertaken which had not met with obstacles? but these would be overcome, and in the end the colonies would furnish the whole military force of Russia, and regular conscriptions entirely cease.

In Georgia the climate was so destructive that another plan was adopted. All the soldiers who served beyond the Caucasus took their wives, that a population might spring up which, born in the country, would be able to resist its effects. Talleyrand once observed, that the difference between the policy of Russia and Europe was, that Russia worked for the future and Europe only for the present; and this was peculiarly the case with Alexander, whose object seemed to be to procure a glorious and tranquil reign for his successor. The French traveller, M. Dupin, wrote in 1822, that in thirty years' time the colonists would furnish Russia with 3,000,000 soldiers; Dr. Lyall thought 5,000,000, while Count Ozarowski went still further, and said that at the ordinary rate of increase the colonies would supply 6,000,000 to the empire. These exaggerated statements gave rise to the belief that Alexander could have no other motive than the conquest of the whole of Europe; and he consequently became one of the most unpopular of princes beyond his own dominions.

A number of villages belonging to the Crown were designated by the Emperor for colonization, and he selected such as seemed most impoverished. Every peasant of fifty or above was called a master-colonist, and in place of his wooden cabin, a well-built brick house, furnished with such comforts as a peasant requires, was given to him, with about forty English acres of land and a few head of cattle. The house was sufficiently commodious to take in a soldier and his family, if he had one, and in return for the soldier's maintenance he was to help to cultivate the land, with other country labour, when not occupied in his military duties, which it was expressly stated would not call him away at the season of ploughing and harvest. No capitation tax was levied on the colonists: the villages were provided with water, a church, a school, a hospital and medical staff, medicines, public baths, a shop, a gymnasium, an exercising-house, and a restaurant and reading-room for the officers, all the buildings being of brick. A master-colonist might choose a son or a friend in the colonized regiment as his partner, but it was plain that an injudicious commanding officer might exercise great oppression. The soldier succeeded to the master-colonist's place in case of his death, and in his turn received a partner in his toils. If a master-colonist had sons, the eldest was made his partner, and enrolled under the name of a soldier-cultivator; the second was put on the reserve, and furnished with a separate house; the rest, according to their age, would be on the reserve, or children of the regiment, who were educated in the public school of the colony and drilled twice a week. The houses were provided with buckets and other conveniences in case of fire; a patrol preserved order or gave alarm; enclosed gardens and yards surrounded the habitations, which were gaily painted and inscribed with the name of their owner; the streets were paved and drained and lined with rows of trees. Even those who opposed the system allow that the cleanliness and embellishment of the military colonial villages was a striking contrast to the ordinary aspect of Russian homes; the schoolboys and cadets (the youths between thirteen and seventeen) fired at a mark and executed military evolutions with astonishing precision, and esprit de corps existed among these children which gave much promise for their future efficiency. At the end of ten years 60,000 men and nearly 30,000 horse were established on the Crown lands in the midst of a population of 400,000 peasants with their wives and children.

The cavalry regiments were colonized in Little Russia, where the abundance of grass made the keep of a horse a comparatively light burden, else that was in some cases added to the establishment of a master-colonist. Every soldier who could not read and write attended an adult school, and the whole colony were supplied with uniforms, and under the supervision of the commanding officer. The two chief superintendents of the military colonies were Aratchaief and Count de Witt; but the first, by his excessive attention to minutiæ, harshness, and economy, soon made the system odious to the people at large; for the master-colonists, who had worn their beards and hair long till fifty, were obliged to be shaven and trimmed like the rest, on the ground of cleanliness. Byron little thought when he counselled Alexander "to wash and shave his Bashkir hordes,"* that it was already being carried out, to the grief of his subjects. Several of these rules were soon modified; but still the peasants, who had elected their own magistrates and formed their own municipal laws, resisted the supervision of the military authorities; and the secret societies, beginning to be very numerous in Russia, excited troubles and insurrections among them. The first regiment colonized was a battalion of grenadiers in the government of Novgorod, and the ukaz on the subject was dated August 17th (N.S.), 1816. Another was established the same year at Vitepsk, and produced in a twelvemonth corn sold for 80,000 roubles, and 144 male children were born to add eventually to its military strength. Alexander spoke of

* The Age of Bronze, 1823.

the colony at Novgorod as an experiment. That province had furnished more than the usual number of complaints, and he wished to see if a military governor over the heads of the civil authorities would meet with more success. " It is impossible," writes De Maistre, " to judge the result of all the Emperor's innovations, for he governs an empire without precedent." In point of territory it was four times the size of that of Napoleon, and neither Cæsar nor Alexander the Great had exercised authority over such an extended dominion or so many different people. " Public opinion is against the colonies. The Emperor has all that is necessary to operate great changes—a great strength of mind, and strength of body, which is quite as necessary to sustain his labours, and a great confidence in himself, acquired by brilliant and well merited success; a great knowledge of abuses, a great wish to repair them, and an absolute independence of every sort of prejudice. Several abuses called for a repairing hand; but what human eye can see into the future?"*

By the treaty of 1815 the protectorate of the Ionian Isles was claimed by Great Britain, though the inhabitants had shown a preference for Russia; and the English officer appointed to govern them made himself very unpopular by his contempt for the native inhabitants. Complaints of his harshness were brought to the Emperor in 1816, by some of those who had formed part of the Legislative Council when the islands were ruled constitutionally, first by Russia and then by France; and Alexander wrote a short letter to Castlereagh on the subject, recommending a constitution. " I rejoice," writes Castlereagh to Wellington, May 13th, 1816, " to observe the good humour with which you have kept the allied machinery together. I persuade myself that Russia means to preserve it. The Emperor recently made a very cordial overture to the Regent in this sense." Still Alexander was viewed with unfounded suspicion, not allayed by a close alliance he formed with the United States. He had made many inquiries about the working of the constitution in the various provinces of America, and read every book he could find on the subject; and it was rumoured an article of the treaty promised him four ports on the Pacific Ocean if America obtained possession

* De Maistre's Correspondence.

of Mexico and California. Louis XVIII. sent this report in great alarm to the British Government, and the next year another was circulated, that Spain had ceded to Russia the port of Mahon in Minorca (the island formerly offered by the British Government to Catherine II.). Lord Cathcart was instructed to inquire about it from Nesselrode, who at once denied it, as such an establishment was quite foreign to the Emperor's views and wishes.* At the same time Maria Louisa resisted settling her duchy on the Spanish royal family in the event of her death, wishing to reserve it for her own heirs; and when her father appealed to the treaty, she threatened to make such disclosures to Alexander as would bring Russia against him. Austria still felt bitter about the republic of Cracow, and her agents were active in fomenting discontent in Warsaw, with the hope that an insurrection in the Grand Duchy might give her a pretext for reclaiming it.

One result of the war of 1812 was an increased feeling of nationality in Russia, and a desire to cultivate the Russian language and literature instead of the French. Russian was established as the Court language, and native tutors began to be extensively employed. As a better style of building and draining was introduced into Moscow, fevers, which constantly prevailed there before 1812, almost entirely disappeared, and the plague has never since penetrated so far north. In 1816 six journals and magazines were being published there, and fourteen in St. Petersburg. "The liberty of the press," said an article in the *Presse du Nord* of St. Petersburg, October 4th, 1816, "protected by our august monarch, has the inappreciable advantage of allowing every truth to reach the foot of the throne: it can displease none but those who wish to isolate the prince from his people, and such men will never be listened to during the reign of Alexander." The feeling became so strong in Russia against the employment of foreigners, that after 1815 no officer not born in the empire could obtain a commission in her army, except to serve in Georgia. The prejudice was warranted by the discovery that many of those who had served with them during the war had been half-hearted friends, mainly bent on procuring their own

* Wellington's Despatches and Correspondence.

interests, or the interests of their native country, by means of Russia.

Alexander's old governor, Soltikof, died June 13th, 1816, at the age of more than eighty, having served as a colonel in the Seven Years' War. Since then he was employed in civil occupations, though the Marshal's bâton was on his coffin. Alexander had bestowed every honour upon him, and visited him frequently during his last illness: their adieu the very day of his death was most touching, and with Constantine he followed the hearse on foot. "The Marshal presided over the Council of State during the Emperor's absence, who created him a prince on his return. He was a sensible man, well instructed in the principles of the country, and understood business well: his good qualities were rather tarnished by his love of money. His eldest son is in all respects one of the most estimable and marked men of this country."

De Maistre describes a fête given by the Empress Dowager at Paulovski, on June 18th, in honour of the Prince of Orange, and a dinner from the merchants of St. Petersburg to the Emperor, the two Empresses, and the Imperial family, on the opening of the new Bank.* "Yet St. Petersburg is not what we knew it in past times. A sad atmosphere overspreads it to such a degree, that foreigners who have not seen this beautiful city for ten years no longer recognize it. The highest class has forgotten what an open house is. . . . The Emperor has shown himself the preserver of Europe, and of Sardinia particularly, by saving France, and consequently the general equilibrium. It will be a calamity to us and to many others if he cannot maintain the attitude he holds now."

The fête-day of the Empress-mother, August 3rd, was celebrated by the annual popular masquerade ball in the castle and grounds at Peterhof, instituted by Peter the Great. Six thousand invitations were distributed, but the admission was

* "The dinner was on the table at exactly two, according to the new order established by his Majesty, and the banquet was very short, for the Emperor has not time to lose. The great hall is very handsome by itself, and was embellished by a profusion of flowers, orange trees, arbutuses, and decorated with the flags of all nations. Another hall was destined to receive the Court on its arrival, and a third contained a chapel, where they sang a Te Deum. The only priest present at dinner was the Metropolitan."

almost unlimited: nobles, merchants, and serfs mixed together in the presence of the Sovereign without distinction or etiquette, and the gardens were brilliantly illuminated. A number of spectators, merchants and their wives, were returning home by water to St. Petersburg, when they were overtaken by a sudden squall which wrecked several of the boats, and nearly 200 people were drowned. The Emperor told his mother this fête should be the last, since they were so unfortunate; for a few years before some horses took fright at the fireworks, and did great damage. Towards the end of August the Russian ship *Suvorov* returned from a three years' voyage round the world, loaded with curiosities in natural history and botanical science. A Russian colony was established in the Sandwich Islands*, but ultimately abandoned, as Sitka was sufficient to protect the fisheries in the Northern Seas.

Alexander left for Moscow with Volkonski and Capo d'Istria, August 27th; it was officially announced to visit those provinces which had suffered most from the war, and to stimulate the measures taken for their relief. They were exempted from taxation for a term of years, the same privilege being bestowed on Kazan, and he subscribed liberally for its restoration. He met his brother Nicholas, who had been to the Crimea, in Moscow, and in a public speech alluded to the sufferings† and heroism of her citizens, and to the stupendous

---

* Vancouver has given evidence of the good treatment which the natives received from the Russians in their American settlements.

† "The journey of his Majesty to Moscow," writes De Maistre, September 17th, "was successful beyond imagination. The presence of this great prince in the middle of his true capital produced a tender enthusiasm. He told his assembled nobility, that among the foreign people he had visited he had found none to compare to his own; he has promised to pass a whole year with them (next year it is said), and in addition two months out of every succeeding year. He left Moscow on the 2nd (14th), not wishing to be there on the 3rd, a day for ever to be deplored. A Russian said to me, 'If the Emperor asked the nobility of Moscow at this moment for two-tenths of their wealth they would give it weeping for joy.' I do not think he exaggerated. It would be disrespect to a prince, equally clear-sighted and impenetrable, to scrutinize his thoughts; but certainly they are very profound. To satisfy yourself on the imperturbable and wise progress of this prince, you have only to look at the establishment of Poland. Read all, Sire, and you will see he has walked invariably to his end, mocking at all errors, all vain-glorying, and all factions, and he has not ended yet."

act of patriotism which must redound to their honour to the end of time. He visited the most liberal of the merchants in their own homes.

Arrived in Warsaw one of the first days of October, he was much pleased with the Polish troops. Czartoriski's repeated complaints of Constantine during the spring of 1816 made him recall his brother to St. Petersburg to answer them; but he was allowed to return after a salutary caution, when it was shown that the instances brought forward were cases where punishment was merited, although he had inflicted it without going through a legal process. The Polish military were accustomed to the license Napoleon permitted to his armies, and the civilians had lived too long under a lawless rule to consider thefts, duelling, assaults, and other offences common in a barbarous state, as crimes; and in a Polish court of justice if a Russian prosecuted a Pole the case was, as a matter of course, dismissed. It was not as if a peaceable, well-ordered people were being restored to a long-established constitutional government, but it was the nation of all others most restless* and most impatient of all law or the control of civilized life who were being allowed as an experiment to undertake their own legislative functions; and never at any period has Ireland proved herself a more troublesome appendage to the British Crown. However, when Alexander visited the Polish capital he was enthusiastically received, and the year of peace in which the revenue was expended upon the country while Russia defrayed the cost of the army was beginning to show effect. During the French campaign in Russia the population of the Grand Duchy was reduced by 800,000 people. Now new houses and new shops were springing up in the towns; the capital was paved, having hitherto been a swamp in wet weather: no regular high road had existed through Poland, and the nearest on the side of Germany was at Leipsic; but several were already marked out for construction as soon as the national finances could afford it. Everything wore a smiling air of prosperity. While Alexander stayed he attended the early parade every morning as in St. Petersburg, and frequented the Polish balls.

* A Polish priest in Warsaw blew out his brains on the high altar in June, 1816.

He visited Vilna, arriving October 25th, his mother's birthday, at Gateschina, and the same night at St. Petersburg.

The property left by the Jesuits in St. Petersburg was a matter of dispute throughout the year 1816. Their last legally appointed general, Father Gruber, had received a sum of 9000 roubles from Paul to build a church and college, and erected them at the cost of 450,000 roubles, thereby contracting a debt which the community was gradually paying off. Prince Galitzin now wished to sequestrate it and sell it for the payment of the debt, and referred to an old law permitting the sequestration of the property of exiles. The Roman Catholic Archbishop in St. Petersburg seconded him, and when the Emperor referred the matter to the Council of State, all the members except two pressed for its immediate confiscation. The Emperor answered, "As this religion is not mine, I ought not to be in haste to decide." Aratchaief said to his fellow councillors, "What does this silly question matter of knowing to whom the house belongs? We wish it, we will have it, and all is said." Alexander consulted the chief lawyers on the subject. They voted for its confiscation. The Emperor at last bought it, and repaid the creditors, who were chiefly Roman Catholics, devoting the surplus to pious works. "What must he have thought," says De Maistre, "of the honesty of his advisers?"

"On December 24th, the Emperor's birthday, there was the usual levée, ball, and a supper laid for 800 guests. The reigning Empress made an effort to appear at the levée in the morning, but not at the fête in the evening. She is mortally afflicted by the death of a Princess Galitzin, a child of twelve, the daughter and relic of a friend who died in the flower of her age. When the young child expired under the eyes of the Empress, who had brought her up, Mlle. Wittgenstein, daughter of the general, whom the Sovereign had also adopted, was at the last extremity at the convent (school) for the daughters of noblemen. I was told that at the beginning of the young Galitzin's illness, the Empress said, ' I interest myself in her. She will die.' Everybody says the Emperor has been wonderful on this occasion. I knew it, even if they had not told me. This birthday was marked by general favours. The Emperor nearly doubled the pay of the military officers.

This increases the expense by 8,000,000 roubles, but he has raised the necessary funds by reducing the number of horses, and economy in the military train. His time is almost absorbed by military details. Prince A. Galitzin sees him and dines with him, but it is as a friend, and almost as a messmate. The council of ministers govern, and the result of their operations is carried to the Emperor, who decides. The great personage who transmits orders to all the departments is Aratchaief, a man of natural ability, who invariably maintains himself. He refuses money because he is rich, and orders because he has no need of them. He modestly contents himself with the Emperor's portrait. Every day he brings to his Majesty piles of papers relating to every branch of the government."*

Since the settlement of Europe foreigners who had obtained honours or fortune in Russia began to return in large numbers to their native countries. To one of these Alexander observed, he was doing his duty in passing to the service of his own master; yet De Maistre thought he saw in " all these hasty resignations a little indifference towards himself. The Emperor pays highly for all talent, but the ordinary foreigner would meet with a poor reception." He fancied he had rather gone out of the imperial favour in the spring of 1817, though the Empress paid particular attention to him, and he pressed for his recall.†

For once in his life, on December 24th, 1816, the Emperor spoke politically at a levée on the subject of the insurrection in the Spanish and Portuguese colonies in the New World. "I am very sorry," he said in a low voice to Saldanha Gama, "for what is passing in America;" and to the Spanish minister, that "after all the efforts made to restore peace, it was being troubled by Portugal and Spain."

---

* De Maistre.
† "No prince is more disposed than the Emperor to pardon things which might have offended him. I have good reason to believe him capable of disregarding personal wrongs and insolence, which under other reigns might have drawn thunder. On this point he is sublime; but by one of those contradictions found in human nature, if once he receives an unfavourable impression there is no remedy. This last quality belongs to temper and sovereign obstinacy, the first to conscience and greatness of soul. I am as sure of his justice as of his existence; but this virtue is not enough for me, as I was accustomed to something more gentle."

But the Ultramontanes were also troubling the peace in Poland, alarmed at the inclination of the Polish Church to break off from Rome, and acknowledge the Czar as its only head. One day, seeing the Emperor pass, the Roman Catholic Archbishop at St. Petersburg said before several people, "that is my Pope." De Maistre thought the Emperor might unite the two Churches, but that it would be possible for no one else. "It would not be the work of a year; but he is only thirty-nine."*

Among other resignations, Paulucci sent in his, to accept a post in the Sardinian Court; but the Czar hearing it was offered, called it "ridiculous to expect a general to take it," and Paulucci remained for a few years longer in Russia. Alexander held such dignities in so much contempt, that he deprived all Court officials of any rank unless they filled some other office, and gentlemen of the chamber were entirely abolished. On Easter-day the Grand Chamberlain was admitted to the customary Easter kiss from the Sovereign after the State Council, the Senate, and the lowest lieutenant among the military. The Carnival was kept in 1817 with especial brilliancy. Three thousand persons were invited to a ball in the Taurida Palace, and outside there was a display of fireworks, representing an obelisk and trees in green fire.† The greatest precautions were taken to avoid danger from the crowd of carriages.‡ In 1816 a steamboat plied daily between St. Petersburg and Cronstadt.

The year 1817 was one of great distress and scarcity in

* "He is at this moment all-powerful in Europe. There are few princes on whom criticism has been more exhausted, even at home. I have never shared the opinion of the critics. My judgment is now justified, and no one doubts this great prince's merits. The campaigns of 1812 and of 1814 were conducted with so much prudence, dexterity, and courage, it is impossible to dispute the glory due to him. In the interior he does what he can, but the material resists the workman. What is most to be feared on his part is the annihilation of the civilian, and the creation of a nation of soldiers, with all the ills resulting from such a state of things. We may also fear his projects in point of religion . . . but, nevertheless, when the Emperor deceives himself, he will not the less be the greatest of self-deceivers."

† This artificial fire is peculiar to the Russians, learned, it is said, from the Chinese.

‡ "In general the respect for human flesh and a tender consideration for mankind is and can not be yet a virtue perfectly naturalized in Russia, but it has a great entry at the Winter Palace, and thence will extend itself to all Russia." . . . "In point of sovereign amiability, royal politeness,

Germany, and as Jung Stilling preached that an earthly millennium was approaching, when the Saviour would reign in Georgia, the cradle of the human race, thousands left Germany, and embarked, without notice or preparation, on board rickety boats on the Danube, to venture across the Black Sea to the Crimea. Some were wrecked, others died of fever, famine, and fatigue. Two of the elders of their community found their way to Moscow towards the end of 1817, to lay their distressing case before the Emperor. They were admitted to an audience with Alexander and the two Empresses, and received a grant of money and an escort across the steppes and the Caucasus into Georgia, where the Governor received orders to allow them to choose a district out of the Crown lands, and they soon formed a flourishing colony. In their collection of hymns Alexander is called " the Protector of the believing flocks in the new kingdom of Jesus on earth." " Providence has chosen Alexander to be the defender of Zion, to prepare a place of security for the Bride, the Church." These religious sects were all looked upon with great disfavour by the German Governments, and Madame de Krudener, who left Paris soon after the Emperor, to return to her missionary labours in Baden and Württemberg, was chased from town to town, and thought by many to be a Russian spy. Alexander was weary of her vague prophecies, and his modesty was distressed by the exalted manner in which she spoke of him in public to her followers; but he protected her as his subject when he found she was expelled from Basle, and at a time when she was suffering from cataract in both eyes, and an operation was necessary to restore her sight. At the end of 1817 she returned to her estates in Russia, but some of her companions were arrested and detained in Prussia till he reclaimed them. A year later she came to St. Petersburg, where her appearance and exhortations excited the greatest interest. A large number of Russians of the old school had become Illuminists and Swedenborgians as early as Catherine's reign, and published a journal, which was suppressed by the Holy Synod. The Bible Society gave them a fresh impetus,

charming and animated conversation, his Majesty cannot be surpassed by any prince, as I have more than once observed; but if he wishes to freeze or chastise by a single word he is quite as superior."—De Maistre.

and Madame de Krudener added fuel to the flame. But the Greek Church had an able champion in the Archimandrite Photi, whose ascetic life equalled the hermits of old times, and who was supplied with large funds for his monastic establishment near Novgorod by the wealthy Countess Anna Orlof. Her father, one of the murderers of Peter III., had been enriched by the spoils of the Church, and in the hope of procuring pardon for his soul, she refused all offers of marriage, and devoted her life to pious works and her riches to the source from which they sprang. The Bible Society had 280 branch establishments through Russia, and the Emperor paid the expense of a Scotch missionary settlement among the heathen in Siberia; but the heads of the Society, not imitating him in tolerance, boasted that they should convert Russia into a Protestant empire, and accused the Greeks of superstition and idolatry. Far from having any special predilection for Protestants, beyond regarding them as people leading moral lives likely to civilize his empire, Alexander was often known to resort privately to the Roman Catholic church, which was always kept open, and there to offer up his private prayers. But Photi took alarm. He possessed enthusiasm and eloquence, and preached energetically in St. Petersburg, calling on the people to repent and amend their lives, and to protect the Holy Orthodox Church. He even penetrated unbidden into the Winter Palace, and entreated the Emperor to stop the innovations of the English heretics. Alexander visited his monástery, an example soon followed by half of St. Petersburg, and prostrated himself by the side of the sandalled monk and Aratchaief in the chapel, where the exact spot is still pointed out to travellers. Nevertheless, he endeavoured to hold an even balance between the contending parties, and was of opinion that in Russia there was room for all. He believed that prayers offered up in English, German, Latin, or Slavonic were alike acceptable to the Almighty if the humility and faith were the same; and he thought this fervour, though wanting in charity, was better than the cold liberality of scepticism.

The new bank for the aid of commerce, opened in 1816 in St. Petersburg, received an advance from the Emperor of 30,000,000 roubles; and by a ukaz, 17th April, 1817, he devoted 30,000,000 roubles annually from the Imperial treasury, and the same sum from his own revenues, towards the payment of the debts contracted in 1812 and 1813. At the same time the expenses of the Court were much curtailed by the diminished number of fêtes. Alexander attended two balls at the English and French Embassies in the winter of 1817, but stayed only an hour at each; for after dancing a polonaise with his mother and his hostess, he left the two Empresses and his brother Michael to represent the Court; and from this period he was seldom known to pass a longer time at any similar entertainment.

Nicholas paid a visit to England in the winter of 1816-17, and his arrival there was made the occasion for more than one lament over the power of Russia by the English press. He returned in the spring to Russia, where his wedding was celebrated, July 13th.

The Princess Charlotte of Prussia left Berlin June 12th, accompanied by her brother William (the present Emperor of Germany). Alexander met her at the last stage from Gateschina. At Paulovski the two Empresses received her; the tall, stately, rather stiff Mary Federovna, now fifty-eight, and the small, quiet Empress Elizabeth, who still bore some trace of the beauty which once made her one of the loveliest women in the mpirce. The frightened Princess looked on Alexander as a protector, for, of all whom she saw, he was the only one she had known from her childhood. The next morning she entered St. Petersburg, and five days afterwards made her public profession of the Greek faith. The Emperor acted as her godfather, and she was named after him when she was rebaptized, appearing for the ceremony before the assembled court between her two sponsors, Alexander and a nun clothed in black. On July 7th (N.S.), Nicholas's birthday, she was formally betrothed, and the wedding, a week later, was solemnized in the presence of all the Imperial family. In the evening Alexander and his wife drove together to the Anitchkov Palace, to receive the young couple in their new abode; and the marriage festivities continued for nearly a week. Prince William of Prussia remained six months in Russia, till his sister had become reconciled to the separation from her old home.

Alexander went to Czarco-Selo after his brother's wedding,

and gave a banquet to the newly married pair, who stayed with the Dowager-Empress at Paulovski. The bride was distressed by the stiff etiquette which prevailed in her mother-in-law's Court. Her husband was ordered about and directed in his most minute occupations as if he were still a child, and the Empress domineered over every one within her reach. Nobody could ride or walk even in the garden unless she pleased; and as this system produced silence and reserve throughout the establishment, Alexandra found it extremely dull, and looked forward from one Sunday to another, when the Emperor came to spend the evening with his mother, and amused her with anecdotes of her native land; but she never could get on with the reigning Empress, and was an object of some jealousy to Elizabeth when she became the envied possessor of a son.

Alexander reviewed the fleet at Cronstadt, and proceeded to inspect the military colonies, while his wife and mother held a masquerade ball at St. Petersburg, in which one appeared as a bat and the other as a sorceress. He met them in Moscow towards the end of September, and the Court spent the ensuing year amidst the ruined city. In consequence of the flattering addresses he received on this journey, he publicly reminded his people that they made use of eulogiums which could only properly be applied to the Most High, and requested the Synod to give necessary instructions to the clergy to prevent his ears being offended by such expressions in future. He paid a visit to the gunworks at Tula, and ordered an Englishman to search for coal in the province, where some was discovered very conveniently situated for the manufactory; but Dr. Lyall says the proprietors of the forests, who would have suffered by its introduction, caused it to be declared unfit for the purpose, and it was therefore not used.

Although traces of the conflagration were visible in Moscow, an almost inconceivable advance was made towards obliterating them, but the palaces of the nobility remained in ruins.* In the suburbs Paul's old favourites, Pahlen, Panine, and Kutaissof, still occupied country seats. The Emperor inhabited the part of the Kremlin where he had stayed for his coronation, and where Napoleon afterwards installed himself; and the Dowager-Empress was accommodated in another palace.

* Macmichael, 1817.

Nicholas and his bride, with Prince William of Prussia, lived in a third.

"In the hospitals and public institutions," writes a visitor to Moscow in 1817, "good order and cleanliness are enforced by the constant unexpected visits Alexander pays to them, for he is liable to appear and go through a minute inspection at any hour of the day, and sometimes in the middle of the night." His sojourn in Moscow was beneficial to its trade, and he was indefatigable in visiting the environs and reviewing the troops in the neighbourhood; but it had a lowering effect on his own spirits, and the melancholy which had overshadowed him at frequent intervals now threatened to become chronic. On October 22nd he laid the foundation-stone of an enormous cathedral, to be erected on the Sparrow Hill, and dedicated to the Saviour, in memory of the deliverance of Moscow in 1812. Four hundred thousand people witnessed the ceremony, and fifty thousand troops. The Emperor laid the first stone, and the two Empresses, Prince William, Nicholas, and the archbishop, each put one in the same place; a sermon was preached, and the ceremony concluded with prayers. A commission was appointed to superintend the erection of the building, for which a large fund was assigned, and a Russian, named Vitberg, was the architect; but the work proceeded slowly, as thirty years were allowed for its construction; the money slipped through dishonest hands, and the original scheme was finally abandoned for a smaller edifice, still unfinished.

The two Empresses visited the neighbouring nobility, and the young Grand Duchess Alexandra attempted to keep up a lively Court in her own palace; but the Emperor lived a retired life, chiefly occupied with business and his religious duties, though it was nevertheless a gay winter in Moscow. He had the usual reception on his birthday; but early in December an entertainment was postponed, for the news of the death of the Princess Charlotte of England had been received with real sorrow by all the Imperial family. The Emperor gave an audience to an English missionary, Mr. Way, on his road to minister among the Tartars in the Crimea. He was accompanied by a Christian convert, Sultan Gherai, the son of the last Khan of the Crimea, on whom the

Emperor had settled a pension of 6000 roubles a year. Mr. Way said of his conversation with the Emperor, that it was not an Imperial audience, but the friendly intercourse of one Christian with another. To the Sultan, Alexander said as he wished him good bye, " You are now a young man, and if, in the course of a long life, and after hard labour among your poor deluded countrymen, you should be instrumental in leading only one sinner to Christ, you will still have reason to bless God and to rejoice at it through eternity." In October he went for a day or two to Czarco-Selo for the " Commemoration," as it would be called at Oxford, and the young student Pushkin read his ode on Infidelity before him, and was publicly saluted as a brother poet by the aged Derzharvin. The same month Alexander corresponded with Wellington and the allied Sovereigns on the subject of the indemnity still owed by France. The Duke wrote to the Emperor from Cambrai that he had reviewed the Russian corps; and Alexander informed the Duke (October 17th) that he had written to his brother Sovereigns to propose to them a diminution of the terms required, as it seemed impossible for France to pay them: she would therefore probably decline; while if they took the initiative, it would preserve the good faith of the treaty and give an example of moderation. Louis's Government was placed in great difficulties by the Republican agitation in France, which was connected with a secret society called the Carbonari, originally established in Naples to overturn the Bonaparte supremacy, but now extending its ramifications through Europe with the object of abolishing every reigning dynasty. The bills for damages sent in by all the nations of Europe, except England and Russia, far exceeded anything contemplated in 1815, and they also claimed back interest. Prussia was the most pressing and the most unwilling to lose an iota of her demands, and France showed no disposition to adhere strictly to her engagements. Alexander's remonstrance with Berlin, and the representations of his ambassador, Pozzo di Borgo, to the allied ministers succeeded in obtaining the desired reduction and a shortening of the term of occupation. He wrote again to the Duke from Warsaw to congratulate him on his escape, a man of the name of Cantillon having made an attempt on his life in Paris. The

French agents employed to investigate the matter tried to excite suspicion against Alexander or the Prince of Orange as having been concerned in it, and that was made the pretext for Cantillon's acquittal; the Emperor being still regarded as almost a Jacobin by the French Conservatives, and the Prince having unwisely lent some support to a radical faction who talked of displacing Louis in his favour. "I mentioned," writes the Duke, March 18th, 1818, "that I thought the great personage was brought forward to mislead us, and that they would name the Emperor of Russia, as it was hoped by all Jacobins, and therefore believed by them, that he was upon bad terms with England, and they could easily expect to get credit for his being concerned in a plot to assassinate me; or the Prince of Orange for another reason, that he was intimately connected with them. But I do not believe there is any great personage in the plot, and don't know who they would name. It is not impossible, however, that they might name the Duke of Kent; but the Prince of Orange is the most likely." Napoleon bequeathed a legacy to Cantillon as a reward for the attempt, which is a strong proof that it was instigated by the Bonapartists.

The Duke of Kent wrote to Alexander on the subject of Lancastrian schools, and several Russians were sent to London to be instructed in the system, with a view to its introduction for both boys and girls of the lower class. Schools, missions, and prison reform* occupied much of the Emperor's attention. At Moscow he built an exercising house, the largest room in the world without a pillar, constructed a public garden, now called after him, and erected a statue to "Citizen Minim and Prince Pojarsky" from "grateful Russia." In February he left for Moscow, where he arrived on the 13th of March, and opened the first Diet on the 27th. Constantine was elected as deputy for Praga by 103 votes against 6; but during its session was obliged to renounce his privilege as a senator, it being contrary to the Constitution for any member to have a

---

* It made a great advance in his reign. He was aided by Galitzin and some members of the English Bible Society. He ordered the leg-irons worn by the convicts to be always padded, a chapel to be attached to every prison, exercise to be permitted in fine weather, and the prisoner to receive religious instruction, to be employed in trade, and remunerated for his labour.

seat in both Houses at the same time. Alexander's speech on the occasion, which was delivered in the Polish language, gained much applause. He spoke strongly of the advantages of a constitutional government. "Your restoration," he added, "is decreed by solemn treaties; it is sanctioned by the constitutional charter. The inviolability of these exterior engagements and of this fundamental law secures to Poland an honourable rank among the nations of Europe, a privilege the more precious as she long sought it in vain in the midst of the most severe trials. . . . The organization in force in your country permitted the immediate establishment of those liberal institutions which have not ceased to be the object of my solicitude. With the assistance of God, I hope to extend their salutary influence to all the countries intrusted to my care, as soon as the elements of so important a work have obtained the necessary development there; and I trust you may prove to contemporary kings that the liberal institutions they pretend to confound with the disastrous doctrines in these days threatening the social system with a frightful catastrophe, are not a dangerous illusion, but that reduced in good faith to practice, and directed in a pure spirit towards conservative ends, and the good of humanity, they are perfectly allied to order, and the best security for the happiness of nations." He remained in Poland, laboriously occupied with the examination of State affairs, during the whole session, which extended to April 27th (the Russian Good Friday), and on the 30th left for Kiov and Odessa. There is little doubt that at this time the majority of the Poles were perfectly satisfied, though a few of the nobles, who aspired to the throne if Poland was a separate monarchy, still showed signs of discontent. Czartoriski lost no opportunity of pointing out to Alexander that even a Russian commissioner ought not to reside in Warsaw; that he ought to recall Constantine, and that Poland should be merely an allied Government; in short, that with the previous history of Poland in his recollection, Alexander should sever the only real tie which bound the Grand Duchy to Russia.

Alexander visited the colonies of Memnonites, Smolensko Refugees, and Dissenters, and was received with great enthusiasm at Odessa and in the Crimea, where he distributed money and orders and directed many improvements. At Kherson he left a sum of money for the erection of a monument over Howard's grave near that city. The inscription he selected for the philanthropist contained merely the date of his birth and death, and round a medallion displaying his portrait in bas-relief, the words, in Slavonic, "I was sick and ye visited Me, I was in prison and ye came unto Me." He also witnessed the launch of two men-of-war at Nicolaief. In the Crimea he gave strict orders for the preservation of the Greek remains of antiquity, and left 165,000 roubles for the restoration of the Palace of Batchi-Serai. The Tartars flocked from all parts to see him, and the confidence he showed in their loyalty, by travelling without any military escort, much impressed them. An English lady who visited the Crimea the same year, writes: "The mild and conciliating manners of this most powerful monarch won the hearts of the humblest of his subjects; few there are who do not boast of having seen the Emperor, and not a few who had the honour to converse with him." He seemed pleased with the attentions of this primitive people, and looking through his field-glass at a crowd round a house where he was going to pass the night, he said they were a fine and interesting race, and he would not on any consideration permit them to be disturbed. He minutely inspected Sevastopol and the places of interest on the southern coast, and then proceeded by way of Azov and Taganrog to Novo Cherkask, the capital of the Don Cossacks; but the old Hetman Platof had died the previous January, never having recovered the fatigues of the campaign of 1812-14.

From Novo Cherkask he went straight to Moscow, arriving June 13th, after traversing more than 2000 miles since he left Warsaw, minutely inspected every place of importance in Bessarabia, on the coasts of the Black Sea and the south of Azov, the Crimean peninsula, the country of the Don Cossacks, and also made some stay at the principal towns. At Kiov he received the news of the birth of his nephew (the present Emperor) on the Russian Easter Sunday, April 29th, at Moscow: and twelve days afterwards the Prince was baptized with his uncle's name. He was the first son born to the Imperial family since the Emperor's youngest brother in 1798.

Constantine met Alexander in Moscow, where the King of Prussia also arrived with his eldest son, having left Berlin directly he heard of his grandson's birth. He passed eleven days in exploring the city and its neighbourhood, and the wealthy Prince Youssoupof entertained him with the two Empresses at his palace at Archangelskoe, containing more curiosities, rare MSS., and works of art than all Berlin at that period. Alexander left for St. Petersburg on June 23rd, and was followed a few days later by the King and Imperial family; but they had hardly reached it when Nicholas and his wife fell ill with the measles, and the Crown Prince prolonged his visit two months to see them restored to health.

"It does not seem to me," wrote Lord Cathcart,[*] August 10th, "that the visit of the King of Prussia at this Court will produce any political effect. I believe the Emperor would not have been sorry if it had been postponed, as it interfered with many things he would have done between his return from the provinces and his departure for Germany. It would also have been pleasanter to have met after all discussions had been settled, than in the midst of discussions in which neither party was inclined to give way. Though the negotiation was removed to Berlin, still messengers arrived to each Sovereign with reports of warm and unsatisfactory discussions. The apartments formerly occupied by the late Empress Catherine, which had not been used or altered since long before her demise, were handsomely fitted up for this occasion. Though his Majesty frequently went to the ordinary parades and to the exercises at which the Emperor was present, he seemed desirous of giving as little time to see troops as possible, and all the great manœuvres expected here and at Moscow were countermanded. The King went to look at everything worth notice and attention, including all barracks, schools, hospitals, and manufactories, accompanied invariably by the Emperor, who is perfectly competent to show and explain everything to the minutest details and in the best manner.

"The squadron at Cronstadt was reinforced, and the Emperor carried the King one day to that fortress and on board the

[*] Despatches and Correspondence of the Duke of Wellington. Supplement.

admiral's ship in the roads. The illness of the Grand Duke (Nicholas), followed by that of the Grand Duchess, interrupted these arrangements (for various amusements), as the Empress's mother shut herself up in the Grand Duke's apartments great part of the time. The Emperor seems now to have resumed his usual habits and hours of business, and is making progress in getting through the accumulation of reports which await his decision. It is very generally believed that some changes will take place in the ministry before the Emperor's departure, and the age and infirmity of some of the ministers render it very necessary. . . . but the great change is reserved for his return, when it is believed all the governments of the empire are to be remodelled, and that the governors are to be military with very extensive powers, each to have under him a complete establishment of officers for which he is to be responsible to the Emperor, and is to report regularly on every point immediately to his Imperial Majesty. . . . I believe it is the only system by which order can be preserved, or any real progress in improvement and civilization expected, for here nothing succeeds, however wisely projected, but so long as it is under the eye of the Sovereign and while it continues a favoured pursuit. There are now above half a score of governors who have been suspected or arrested for malversation since 1815." This system was completed in 1823, and in practice made the Emperor if possible more thoroughly an autocrat than before, though it was projected in the hope of checking abuses. The ambassador says, the Emperor's speech in Poland, and the system of colonization, excited the most serious discontent, "and the language used is much more violent than could be expected in such a government as this." The harvest had again been most abundant, and the landowners complained that if the German and military colonies produced corn for exportation it would lower the price and damage their own fortunes. The Empress-Dowager had resolved to go abroad with the Emperor when he went to attend the Congress at Aix-la-Chapelle. Of this project, Lord Cathcart adds, "I am told that every endeavour was used to persuade the Empress-mother to relinquish her desire of travelling, to avoid the expense, but in vain; and this determination has forced the Empress Elizabeth also to go abroad. She cannot avoid reigning in the hearts of all the people, and that could not but become an object of jealousy. The nation is flattered by the part the Emperor takes in the politics of Europe, and is pleased with the interview on that account; but an outcry would be made if his Majesty were to remain absent for pleasure. Less has been said by the Emperor on the subject of the attention shown to the Grand Duke Michael (during a recent visit to England) than on that of the Grand Duke Nicholas, although the Empress-mother has said a great deal, and what was said by the Emperor appeared to be more studied and less in his usual open manner. Nothing can be more correct and irreproachable than the life the Emperor leads, as far as I can know of it; he is devout, and reads some chapters in the Bible every day. He is indefatigable in printing and publishing the sacred writings through his dominions in every language, and accompanied by the plainest and most useful tracts and guides for reading them he can find in our language. He protects the missionaries, and is easy of access on these subjects. He had two long conferences with Mr. Way, and approved much of him without, however, being equally sanguine in his expectations of converting the Jews. His Majesty respects the endeavour, and is disposed to support it and to make provision for converts. He is very attentive to every suggestion for improving prisons and forming penitentiaries, and for ameliorating the morals of the people. His language to me on subjects is firm and manly, as well as impressive, but I have seen no symptom of what might be termed Methodism. He gives great protection to the Moravians in his dominions."

When Alexander left Warsaw for his southern provinces in April he was accompanied by two Austrian officers, a Prince and Field Marshal, and his aide-de-camp, Count ———, who came to Warsaw to congratulate him on his arrival there, and to ask to inspect the fortifications in the Crimea. This was readily granted, and as the Emperor had known them both during the war with France, he allowed them to join his suite. They secretly drew up a memoir of their observations and presented it to Metternich, plainly showing the under-current of ill-feeling in Austria against Russia, between whom De Maistre was convinced there must soon be a war, and from the fact of the memoir being sent to the Duke of Wellington* it is evident that Austria looked upon England as her future ally. It is somewhat startling to see men in the position of the two Austrians take upon themselves the office of spies, and while receiving every attention and hospitality from their Imperial host, coolly devise the destruction of his empire. " His Majesty's condescension and favour," says the memoir, " increased from day to day. They were his uninterrupted companions, and enjoyed the double advantage of the consideration due to foreigners, and of the facilities which at the Emperor's express and reiterated commands were everywhere afforded to them for every research that they wished to make; nor was there one occasion during the whole journey where the knowledge of any circumstance appeared to be withheld. Their position enabled them to collect materials, and even to request information never before within the reach of a traveller. Prince ———— latterly never left the side of the Emperor, who found a relaxation in his society from the monotony of his own courtiers, and took pride and pleasure in exhibiting to strangers the great institutions and improvements extending over his large empire. The habits of daily intercourse, and the especial favour shown to them by the Emperor, enabled the ———— † to become gradually more intimate with the leading men who were their fellow travellers, and an attentive collation of their conversation with what fell from the Emperor, and with what came progressively under their personal observation, has combined to assure them of the statements contained in this memoir," to which was added a detailed picture of the Russian army.

The travellers had " ample opportunities for obtaining some insight into the Emperor's character and feelings. When travelling through the empire he is exposed to daily observation. In the course of his tour he reviewed the navy at Cherson, Nicolaief, St. Petersburg, Sevastopol, and Cronstadt." He seemed " well acquainted with the duties and details of a naval officer's occupation." They assert, appa-

---

* The memoir is given in the fourteenth chapter Supplementary Vol. of the Duke of Wellington's Despatches. Edited by his Son.
† The blank is in the memoir, but is evidently meant for Austrians.

rently with satisfaction, that in spite of the new constitution, "the ancient hatred of the Poles towards Russia will never under any circumstances be neutralized," and that an enemy might turn this to great advantage, but that it was Alexander's object to gain them. They think the Emperor must know he could not reign as a constitutional monarch over Russia. There "he can be nothing but autocrat; one half of his subjects would have to make sacrifices almost intolerable to them, and to the mass of the people the very word constitution would convey no definite idea." This memoir having been for years in the possession of the British Commander-in-chief, seems to have furnished the British Government with their scheme for invading Russia in the year 1854. The authors were of opinion that the empire was most vulnerable in the Crimea, particularly by means of Turkey, as the Moslem religion was professed by the Tartar inhabitants, and for this reason Alexander was advised to remove them to the interior of the empire. "If once taken, it would be easily held, and if the Turks managed their affairs well, it would always be a troublesome possession in time of war." The Austrian officers thought Sevastopol might be taken from the land side, and gave a minute description of that fortress, and of the whole peninsula. "The Emperor, as if aware that such ideas must present themselves to an attentive observer, spoke at Sevastopol (which is excellently protected towards the sea) of the possibility of taking that place 'à revers,' on which occasion he expatiated generally on the hazardous nature of all landings on an enemy's coast."

Alexander was advised to demolish Taganrog, Theodosia or Kaffa being more favourably situated for a commercial seaport; so he crossed the estuary of the Don, from Azov, to look at it; but seeing how flourishing it was, he refused to listen to such a proposal. "Aratchaief is his only confidant and immediate implement in whatever concerns the empire internally. Volkonski is his military deputy, and for his European connection Capo d'Istria; . . . but Volkonski's hold on the Emperor is rather through his personal attachment and the force of habit, in which respect he succeeded to the influence of Count Tolstoi. The Emperor esteems Yeromolof's capacity as a soldier beyond that of any other of his officers, but he hardly likes him personally. He, Vassilschief, Raiewsky, Voronzov, Diebitsch, Toll, Lambert, Witte, Menzikof,* Orlof, and Kupelon are the most distinguished at Court and among the generals." Alexander was believed to like Voronzov and Count Peter Pahlen.

"The Empress-mother is in the habit of exercising a certain degree of influence in public matters. The retired habits of the reigning Empress enables her to maintain an influential position, and she must ever be a person of some importance to any one who proposes playing a part at this Court. Her influence, however, extends in no shape or degree over the Emperor himself, who has long since withdrawn from the guardianship she would willingly have continued to wield. Among the Grand Dukes, Nicholas stands highest. He is heir to the throne, and has formed himself for his high destiny, whereas his two brothers are sheer corporals; not but that Nicholas also has a decided preference for military affairs. It is difficult to say what are the political opinions of a prince who systematically re-echoes what the Emperor says, but so much is certain, that both Nicholas and Constantine dislike Austria. The last, indeed, is often profuse of civilities to Austrian officers, but chiefly on account of his Imperial Highness's early recollection of the campaign of 1799, when he prides himself on the service he has seen, and respecting which he loves to display the powers of his extraordinary memory. Notwithstanding her good and amiable qualities, the Grand Duchess Nicholas is not popular, much owing to her aversion to the Greek religion. Should she have fortitude and cleverness enough to naturalize herself in Russia without the sacrifice of her German principles, she will certainly when on the throne become a person of great importance.

"Alexander is autocrat in the strictest sense of the word, and he knows well to what precise point he can be so. He loves his country, is proud of it, and jealous of its glory. His opinions concerning its spirit and the tendency of its character are clear and defined, while he considers himself destined to raise it to a high pitch of greatness; and the promotion of this design is the goal to which all his exertions are directed. The

* Celebrated in 1854.

reserved part it is the Emperor's option to act in foreign politics is the result of forethought and calculation, and not natural to him. Let us not be misled in our judgment on his real and secret opinions by his religious tendency, his proclaimed principles of political morality, or his Liberal doctrines. In the good he confers so largely on his empire the principle of aristocracy is ever uppermost, and in his relations with Europe engrossing influence is his first object : he is a despot towards his own subjects, and a conqueror towards Europe. .... Whoever has passed any length of time in his society, and closely watched the ebullitions of his natural temper (which, however, seldom break out, as he is almost ever master of himself), and also the effect which his presence, and still more, the slightest spark of anger, has on all those by whom he is surrounded—any such observer must see in the Emperor the essence of a despot; nor can he be misled as to his ambitious sentiments, whether in regard to Austria alone or generally to Europe. Such an observer discovers the primary object of the Emperor's plan of government is to place in its strongest light the subserviency of political Europe to Russia, and his own undeniable influence abroad, holding up these to his subjects as the fruits of the sacrifices and exertions made by them in the late troublesome and stormy times."

The author of this memoir seems willing to forget that continental Europe was reaping the fruits of its own narrow and selfish policy, when it had originally fallen so easily into the French snares. Its princes had not exerted themselves to recover their own independence till urged on by Russia, whom they only obeyed through fear; so that having permitted themselves to become vassals of Napoleon, and be dragged on by his armies when he chose to lead them into Russia, they were included in the Russian conquest of the French Empire, and had placed themselves in the position of vassals of the Czar. Alexander had neither robbed their towns, nor levied indemnities, but he had not the less conquered Europe; and when his people demanded some tangible result as the reward of the weary campaigns of 1813–14, it was not surprising that he satisfied them by representing the real and overwhelming influence acquired by their own government.

" It is impossible to be blind to his Imperial Majesty's great qualities. His extreme harshness and severity, even in trifles (the result oftentimes of his love for military discipline), his 'exigence' towards all around him, his taking his own will as his only rule of conduct, will not in Russia alienate the affections of his people. He understands his country and subjects, and possesses to an extraordinary degree the art of leading them on to the greatest personal devotion and sacrifices. A word of condescension at parade, an order conferred, or the slightest mark of Imperial favour, will sometimes suffice. He furnishes and deals out recompenses with systematic publicity, nor is the occasional kindness of his manner less remarkable and impressive than the ebullitions of passion. He raises men from the lowest classes by rapid degrees, while he never fears to humiliate a grandee. Under the mask of quiet uniformity of character there lies the power of adapting himself where and whenever he thinks it worth while, to the most varied positions, whether as towards men or circumstances. As his position is varied, he is no longer the same man; it requires the slightest provocation to rouse him to unbridled anger, especially if there should lurk under the fault committed a dereliction from his own principles, or a breach of that iron discipline with which he loves to conduct civil as well as military government. Nothing can be more meritorious than the energy, activity, and perseverance with which he follows up—even into the smallest details—every branch of the internal administration under his eye. The hospitals,* poor-houses, foundling hospitals, and houses for the reception of destitute women, are all on an efficient and, indeed, magnificent footing. Public education is a favourite object, and he is in regular official intercourse with Prince Galitzin, who is at the head of that department, and for whom he has a great regard. The prisons are established with much humanity, and little more than guarded barracks, as by law the culprit only remains there pending the trial. The punishment of

---

* The Quakers, Allen and Grellet, who spent two months in 1818 in St. Petersburg, call the largest hospital there "a perfect model. I have never seen it equalled anywhere." At the head of each bed the patient's name was neatly written in white chalk, and the name of the disease in Latin instead of Russian, at the Emperor's suggestion, who, going through it, observed it might have a depressing effect on some invalids to know the nature of their complaints.

death is abolished, and replaced by banishment to Siberia, to
the mines, or to the quarantines, and also by corporal punishment. Everywhere in Petersburg and in the rapid journey
through Russia, did the undersigned come upon the traces of
his Majesty's especial protection of trade. The sums and
benefits conferred on Odessa, the promising state of manufacture, of machinery, and especially of steam engines, which have
even found their way into Siberia. Europe has but an imperfect notion of the manufactures in Russia, for which the
Government attract artificers in great numbers from England
and Germany. The mint, the Imperial glass and plate-glass
manufactory, that for paper at Peterhof, the spinning establishment at Alexandrovsky, the war and marine arsenals, are
magnificent establishments. Remarkable likewise are the
Exchange, where business to the amount of 200,000,000 of
roubles is every year transacted, the various canals, the navigation on the Volga and the Neva, where several versts are
covered with shipping. Much of the good done is so far the
result of chance, that it is often the accidental consequence of
his Majesty's personal and rapid discrimination; thus it happens
that many trifling evils are corrected while greater abuses are
left untouched: every measure of this kind is carried into
quicker execution, as the severity with which the Emperor
exacts implicit obedience from those to whom he directly
issues his orders, is the measure of their conduct towards their
inferiors." Foreigners were astonished at the cleanly appearance of the towns of the interior. "On this subject his Majesty is severe in what he requires from the governors. Count
Aratchaief has introduced on his estates a plan for teaching
his peasants an improved style of building, less subject to
danger from fire," the scourge of ordinary Russian villages.
"The artillery is perfect, especially the horse artillery."
Four thousand cadets, many under five years old, and 46,000
soldiers' children were being educated in the Government
schools in 1818. The staff establishment under Prince
Volkonski for the scientific instruction of the soldier, "though
of very recent origin, has already arrived, through the determined will and profuse liberality of his Imperial Majesty, at a
wonderful degree of precision."

"Russia has made wonderful progress since 1812 in military

matters, mainly attributable to the iron severity of Aratchaief and the perseverance of the Emperor. The military hospitals, thanks to Aratchaief, are in perfect order. The origin of the faults committed in late campaigns is to be traced to the vitiated materials of which the higher classes of the army are composed"—(the Emperor had enlarged on the abuses, the want of order and discipline, the defective system of training, and the moral indolence among the officers formerly prevailing in the Russian army)—" and when the passionate tendency of the mind of the Emperor to military affairs is taken into consideration, as well as the number of intrigues to be found in a Russian head-quarters, ever ready to take some personal advantage of any reverse, it is to be expected that in the contingency of a war these causes will be again at work."

The Count gives a long description of the military colonies. "Formerly," as the Emperor expressed himself, "the recruits came from immense distances, tired and often too late for the service to which they were to have been applied; now the largest portion of the army will be derived from the same tract of country which will become their home, their property, and the scene of their vocation as soldiers and citizens. If allowed time for maturing his plan, there can be little doubt of its success, and he will bequeath the empire to his successor with double of its former military power." A colony was established at Vosnosensk with eight regiments of the Cossacks of the Ukraine, who sent their Hetman, Count Cantacuzene, to remonstrate with the Emperor; but he returned "infected with the plan." The inhabitants of the district who were Mahometans would not shave their beards, alter their costume, or receive Christians among them; and Count de Witt told the Austrians he was on thorns during the Emperor's visit, lest there should be some act of violence on the part of the men. "Neither Capo d'Istria nor his master are friendly towards England, its Sovereign, or Government; and this feeling is the more remarkable as it is the only unfriendly prejudice towards another State to which the minister now gives undisguised utterance. The prejudice in favour of everything Russian, till lately a leading feature of the King of Prussia's opinions, has sensibly decreased (Prussia had been forced against her will to yield to Russia on a mercantile point a fortnight before), and to this change may be traced the indifference that marks his conduct and observations at St. Petersburg, particularly at reviews and all military exhibitions; the Crown Prince has little short of a positive aversion for all military details, and both omit no opportunity of testifying in general conversation, in their manner towards Prince —— and Count ——, and indirectly through the general tone of their suite, how friendly are their sentiments towards —— (Austria), and Count —— has on several occasions remarked that this feeling has not been the less loudly expressed in the casual presence of Russian officers. The Crown Prince is eminently anti-Russian, and Colonel Schenck, his confidential aide-de-camp, as well as General Witzleben, often express their decided opinion that nothing short of a firm union with England can hereafter insure Austria and Prussia against a possible abuse of the colossal power of Russia." The Emperor dwelt on his unalterable personal attachment to the King and Crown Prince, who was not popular at St. Petersburg, but deprecated the King's diminished attention to military matters as prejudicial to the Prussian army, and blamed the Crown Prince's absolute indifference on those points.

"The commission for economy has absolute control over the expenses for all materials for war and equipment. If an employé is caught at a fraud the punishment is enlistment in the ranks, even if the offender was a general officer. The cavalry is excellent, the clothing of the whole army good, and the Emperor active and energetic in directing the many and various improvements carried on in the interior," &c.

In the year 1817, corn to the value of 125,000,000 silver roubles was exported, and both in that and the following summer the amount of paper money was reduced, and nearly 14,000,000 roubles paid off from the national debt. A loss was sustained in a huge wooden building on the Neva, fitted up with machinery and workshops for various branches of the navy, containing accommodation for 3000 sailors, which was burned in 1818. The same year a commercial treaty was formed between Russia and Sweden on behalf of Finland, and Great Britain invited Russia to enter into her league with Spain and Holland for the protection of trade against the Barbary corsairs. In July the States Assembly of Livonia was opened by the Governor Paulucci, who in a speech exhorted the nobility to follow the example set them by Courland and Esthonia, and emancipate their serfs. The marshal of the nobility, in the name of his order, replied they should feel happy to meet the wishes of his Imperial Majesty. The same message was delivered to Lithuania, but the nobles returned for answer, they would wait till the example was shown by their elder sister Russia. The descendants of those nobles now blame Alexander for not forcing them to carry out his wish, when they look at the industrious peasants of Livonia, who have had more than half a century to learn their duties as free men; but without the co-operation of the nobility, famine and insurrections must then have been the result of emancipation in Lithuania, not yet recovered from its sufferings in 1812. Alexander still hoped to place her under the same constitutional government as Poland, when convinced that the Poles would continue faithful to Russia; and to a foreign statesman he said that Russia was great enough to bear the sacrifice. But every year that elapsed since he had bestowed the constitution showed him more fully the impossibility of satisfying the Polish self-love, and the aspirations of the Polish nobles for their ancient oligarchy, consistently with justice to the Polish lower classes and his duties to his own empire. Already the Russians murmured loudly at the sums of money which passed from the Emperor's private purse and the public funds, besides Constantine's entire fortune, to the restoration of Poland, while not a farthing of her revenue came to Russia. They were discontented that he should spend a month of every year in Warsaw and Vilna, and a formidable conspiracy, silently gathering adherents throughout Russia, made this partiality one of its chief grounds of complaint against the Sovereign. And yet in 1830 the Polish Assembly could justify the insurrection against Russia, by asserting that Alexander was not sincere in his desire for their welfare, a charge styled as "the blackest ingratitude" by the Emperor Nicholas. The revival of every branch of industry, the creation of manufactures, good macadamized roads crossing the country on all sides, and rich crops ripening on a fertile soil where unhealthy marshes formerly stood; well-built villages in the place of wretched cabins, improved and embellished towns, paved streets, a bank formed from capital furnished by the Emperor for the development of trade, and flourishing finances in the place of an empty treasury without credit ; a magnificent army, vast arsenals, rivers made navigable, a native university, with the scientific chairs occupied by skilful foreign professors, primary schools, gymnasiums, schools for young girls, military colleges, theatres, charitable establishments and asylums, and an extensive foreign commerce ; these were the benefits which, in 1830, Alexander had bequeathed to Poland, and which enabled her for a year and a half to defy the whole power of Russia.*

* "The kingdom of Poland," writes Marmont (who had known it during Napoleon's ascendency) in 1826, "already bears the fruits of an enlightened administration. Fine roads in all parts. The army is the best paid in Europe. I came from Breitz to Warsaw on a magnificent high road, and a similar one existed as far as Kalisch." Compare his account with Wraxall, Coxe, Tweddell, and other writers on Poland in the last century.

CHAPTER VI.

1818—1822.

CONSPIRACIES AND REVOLUTIONS.

ÆTAT. 40-44.

THE Congress of Aix-la-Chapelle was summoned for September 20th, when a great concourse of strangers repaired to the ancient city: sovereigns, diplomatists, financiers, singers, artists, and even a female sibyl in Mdlle. Lenormand, formerly patronized by Napoleon and Josephine, but who now met with very little regard. Alexander paid rapid visits on his road to some of his western towns, and arrived in Berlin for the last time on September 9th, anxious to settle the conference as quickly as possible, and return to Russia. He was joined by the Empress on her road to Baden, and the Empress-mother at the same time undertook a journey to visit her three married daughters in Weimar, Stuttgart, and Brussels. At Berlin he assisted at the inauguration of the national monument on the Kreuzberg, remarkable for utterly ignoring the fact of Prussia's allies, or that the battles it commemorated were in some instances gained entirely by Russian soldiers, and he reached Aix-la-Chapelle on the 28th, having stayed at Frankfort on his road, and met the Emperor of Austria at Mayence. He received a letter from Las Cases, one of Napoleon's companions at St. Helena, urging him to rescue the ex-Emperor from British hands, but its exaggerated terms destroyed any effect it might otherwise have produced. The Count having returned to Europe, came to Frankfort to seek an interview with the Czar. "It was the surest means of accomplishing my object, everybody said," he writes, "and they considered it wrong not to attempt it," but on his arrival he was deterred by the fear that the interview might be useless—perhaps he was unable to obtain it—so contented himself with talking to Alexander's generals, though he had

much desired "the favour of approaching the first of the
monarchs, of conversing with him of whom Napoleon said
on his rock, 'If I die here, he is my heir in Europe.' "* It
was an unfavourable moment to suggest the release of any
political agitator, for France seemed already on the verge of a
revolution, and the attempt to assassinate the Duke of Wellington proved to be the first act in a plot for destroying
every Sovereign who took part in Napoleon's fall. It was
intended to seize Alexander, cutting the traces of his horses
when he arrived on the French frontier to visit his army of
occupation after the Congress, to compel him under pain of
instant death to sign a paper engaging to release Napoleon,
and establish his son as Emperor of France with Maria Louisa
for Regent, and also to send a courier to the Emperor of
Austria to obtain his signature. The conspirators were
variously stated to number 600, 1000, and 1600 men, and a
few went to Aix-la-Chapelle in the hope of a favourable opportunity for carrying out their design; but as this did not
occur, the borders of France were next proposed. The Duke
of Wellington, as commander of the allied army of occupation
(which terminated November 30th), superintended the reviews
held before the Royal and Imperial guests, and also represented
Great Britain at the Congress, with the aid of Castlereagh and
Canning. His correspondence shows the care he took to prevent any catastrophe during the various excursions which
Alexander made both in France and Belgium. He wrote to
the British and foreign generals under his command to be
ready for a review at Sedan, and to Sir Henry Fane that, as
the first critics in Europe were to be present, they must have
their regiments in the best order. The Emperor intended to
pass three days at Valenciennes in the middle of October.
" We must dine the two first days at four exactly, and have a
play in the evening on the three days immediately after the
review, and a ball at night."† To Baron Nagell, the minister
of the King of the Netherlands, he wrote on the subject of
the precautions to be taken when the Emperor went to Brussels to see his sister. "Whether the reported conspiracy is
true or false, a certain degree of ridicule attends the pre-

* Las Cases. Mémoires de Ste. Hélène.
† Wellington Correspondence.

cautions respecting which I wrote to you yesterday, and I know the Emperor will not be pleased if they are adopted, however necessary they may be. . . . I would advise the King to assemble as much cavalry and gendarmerie as he can with convenience near the high road from Liége to Brussels," &c. After receiving further information of the plot, the Duke writes two days later, that he had laid the details before Alexander, "who desired me to express his acknowledgment to the King and to your Excellency, and his confidence in whatever measures his Majesty may think proper to order." He adds that, as several of the leaders were arrested, and others fled, the scheme will probably never be carried into execution. "Under these circumstances, I recommend you not to place any troops on the road, more particularly as I know such a measure will be highly disagreeable to the Emperor. They might be drawn to the neighbourhood of the road, . . . and patrol it on Sunday and Monday, and early on Tuesday; but I am certain it is desirable in such cases as this not to show unnecessary precautions, and it is better with such miscreants as these with whom we have the misfortune to deal, to incur some risk rather than appear to be afraid of them. I am certain the Emperor will not like to see an assemblage of troops on the road, and will positively refuse to allow himself to be escorted." Three days later, when more discoveries were made, the Duke writes from Aix-la-Chapelle, that General Tripp having arrived, he told him his plan for disposing the troops "to guard the Emperor of Russia on his road to Bruxelles, and at the same time that his Imperial Majesty should have no knowledge of his being so guarded. He has the King's orders to offer the Emperor an escort, and, if the Emperor should decline, they will guard him as I have mentioned. It will be necessary that you should turn your attention to some measures of the same description during his Imperial Majesty's residence at Bruxelles. In general, he sends away his guard of honour, and keeps only two sentries; but General Tripp might arrange with Prince Volkonski, to whom I will talk upon the subject, that the proposed number of sentries might be placed round the house his Imperial Majesty will inhabit at night. He is in the habit of walking alone in the daytime, and I have no doubt will frequently cross the park from his own house to that of the Empress-Dowager and Princess of Orange, and it will be desirable to have a sort of surveillance in the Park to prevent crowds of improper people from collecting there. It will not be difficult to observe and guard the streets at night, as it will of course be known where he will pass every evening during his stay," &c. The Duke also wrote to General Tripp, to tell him to prepare a guard at Maestricht and Tongres round the houses where the Emperor would be lodged.

Alexander took Constantine and Michael with him to the Congress, while Nicholas and his wife, for the first time, presided over the Court in Russia. Ouvarof, Volkonski, Prince Menzikof, Colonel Danilevski, Boutourlin, and two more aides-de-camp, Wylie, the Emperor's valet, and a courier, formed the Imperial suite. General Paskievitch attended Michael, and Constantine brought two aides-de-camp and a secretary. Several of the same ministers were present on behalf of the great Powers as at Vienna, but instead of Talleyrand, the Duc de Richelieu represented France. He intended to quit the Cabinet, and the King, after vainly endeavouring to dissuade him, wrote to Wellington requesting him to ask Alexander to use his influence with the minister, and prevail on him to remain. "I hope," says the Duke, in answer, "that the Emperor's intervention will preserve to your Majesty the services of a minister whose loyal character has contributed so much to conciliate all the interests of Europe with those of France. I presented myself to the Emperor as soon as I could after his return from Spa, and his Majesty, after reading your letter, showed the most lively interest in it, and he assured me he will take the first occasion to speak with the Duc de Richelieu." At St. Helena, Napoleon said, that while Pozzo di Borgo was the Russian ambassador at Paris, he felt convinced Alexander knew Louis's throne to be in peril; but whenever he replaced that minister by a Russian, he should be sure Alexander knew Louis's position to be secure.* Napoleon was well aware that the Corsican continued his inveterate foe, and by diligently tracing out the plots of the Jacobins, who had formed a junction with the Bonapartists, once their deadliest enemies, he was at this time the King's

* O'Meara's Voice from St. Helena.

greatest support. When Louis gave his instructions to Richelieu, he mournfully impressed on him that, cost what it might, he must procure the complete evacuation of the French territory. "Tell my allies how difficult my government will be so long as it can be reproached with the misfortunes of the country; and yet it was not I, but Bonaparte, who brought the Allies upon us. Tell the Emperor Alexander that he has it in his power to render a greater service to my house than in 1814 or 1815; after having restored legitimacy, he *can* restore the national independence."

Richelieu's interview with Alexander was most satisfactory. The bankers, Hope, Baring, and Rothschild, were willing to advance the necessary loans to France, and the Czar had already agreed with his allies to withdraw their troops. "Your nation is brave and loyal," he said to Richelieu. "She supports her misfortunes with courage and resignation. Can you answer for her? Do you think that the Government is sufficiently established for the evacuation? I only ask your word. I do not fear the development of liberal principles in France. I am liberal myself, but I hate the Jacobins; take care not to throw yourself into their arms. Europe will have nothing more to do with them. An alliance founded on morality and religion is the only thing which can save the social order."

In the hope of giving Louis some moral support, the allied Powers signed a memorial in which they invited him to take part in all their present and future deliberations, and the mutual guarantee of the rights of nations, and thus publicly reinstated France in her position as one of the great Powers. Pozzo di Borgo drew up a memoir for his master to express his approval of the acts of the British Government during Napoleon's detention at St. Helena, which had lately been made a subject of discussion in the British Parliament, and on which Alexander had received various petitions from the Bonapartists. "I must render justice," writes Lord Castlereagh to Lord Bathurst, "to the Emperor and to his *faiseurs* in all this business, that they have been most handsomely anxious to court an irreparable breach with the Jacobins of all countries, and to uphold everything you have done. This piece will bring all the democratic fire of Europe upon the Emperor, and we must stand by him accordingly. This plot at Brussels is sufficient to prove that they begin to discover his Imperial Majesty is not disposed to enlist in their service."*

It was Napoleon's chief object to avoid being forgotten in Europe, and he kept up the popular interest in him by his innumerable complaints against the British officials. He was allowed every indulgence compatible with preventing his escape, the subject of constant machinations on the part of his attendants; and he told the Austrian Commissioner that he could easily effect it, but could not return to the world as only a private person; and his doctor, O'Meara, and Las Cases were dismissed from St. Helena on suspicion of lending aid to such a design. While only recently in receipt of 10,000 gold doubloons in addition to the handsome income allowed for his support, he pretended he was so poverty-stricken that he was forced to sell his silver plate to procure the ordinary necessaries of life; while every officer about him drank a bottle of claret daily (at 6l. per dozen without the duty), and he freely indulged himself both in this and champagne, he tried to make his poor, simple admirers in France believe that he was kept on actual prison rations. Though not intemperate, he was by no means the ascetic some have endeavoured to prove, and by his own account to Antommarchi always ate plentifully, though he preferred plain food, and after his principal meals drank several glasses of claret, less than an English pint, and one or two of champagne in addition when he wanted a stimulant. Before he abdicated he had adopted the habit of drinking strong green tea and brandy very frequently during the day to keep himself awake, but he seems to have discontinued it when he arrived in a tropical climate, though he still took quantities of snuff. After most undignified disputes with the much-enduring Governor of St. Helena, he refused to take any exercise, to avoid being inspected by an English officer, as there were express orders from the British Government that he should be seen every day; and this voluntary privation lasting four years soon told upon his health, which even Las Cases allows was excellent during his first six months' sojourn in the island, although a man who was suited by the snows of Russia might naturally feel some

* Castlereagh Correspondence.

inconvenience from the warmer regions of the south. Depending on his parole, which he readily gave, the governor extended his privileges; but finding he immediately broke it, he was reduced to a circuit of eight miles, beyond which he might have traversed the whole island if accompanied by an English officer, but he scorned to avail himself of either this companionship or the more limited promenade. Lord Holland, his admirer throughout his career, made an inquiry in the House of Lords into these complaints, but was answered by Lord Bathurst, who showed that eleven dozen bottles of champagne and claret, the most expensive that could be procured, were consumed by Napoleon and eight of his people weekly, and that his table was kept with proportionate liberality; that while he complained of not being allowed to have books, he had sent a list he required, and they had been forwarded to him at the Government expense, though they cost more than 1400*l.*, without the carriage. A new house was built for him at the cost of 60,000*l.*, because he did not like Longwood, and then he would not inhabit it; and far from preventing his correspondence with his family, only one member had written to him, and that was Joseph, whose letter was forwarded immediately. Alexander, with much justice, preferred to believe the statements of the British ministers to those of Napoleon's relations and followers, who did not cease to apply to him, comparing Napoleon's detention to that of Ferdinand of Spain at Bayonne, and to one of these he said, "we must not believe all the idle tales circulated by interested people." However, he spoke to the British plenipotentiaries on the advisability of allowing him to have a priest attached to his establishment, and also a physician chosen by his own family; and this advice was adopted, and Dr. Antommarchi, selected by the Bonapartes, was sent to reside at St. Helena.*

* The cause of Napoleon's death was quite a party question: his friends asserting that it was entirely due to the climate of St. Helena, and his enemies that it was hereditary disease probably coming on before he arrived in the island. A modification of both statements seems to be the truth. An English military doctor asserted that he had never seen any case of internal cancer similar, except with inveterate dram drinkers. It was a rapid species of the complaint, which would develop itself and destroy life very quickly in a hot climate; so that if it had come on in Europe he would probably have lingered longer, for, by his own account, he felt no pain from it till the spring of 1821, and only suspected its

Castlereagh was not mistaken about the democratic indignation at Alexander's supporting the British Government, and from this period those who cannot discern between the friends of constitutional government, the opponents of tyranny, the preservers of public order, and the revolutionists who would upset all authority and excite insurrections merely for the sake of becoming tyrants themselves, have accused him of departing from the liberal opinions of his youth; but, as Lamartine says, "he may have feared the excesses, but never the lights of liberty," and even Napoleon can be quoted as a witness to the need there was at that time for Alexander's influence in the maintenance of order on the Continent. "In ten years Europe will be Republican or Cossack," said the ex-Emperor, and considering the connection between the Bonapartists and republicans, few were more likely to know. It became Cossack in one sense, that its Cabinets were often guided by Alexander's counsel, and saved from attack by the knowledge that his enormous army could come forward at any moment to their support. It was the only condition of their existence, and without that influence the world might have seen once more the confusion and events of the years 1789 to 1814, instead of being allowed time to recover itself and increase in civilization and material prosperity. Was the social order to be overturned merely to gratify the poverty-stricken officers who, discharged from the French and Italian armies, now hoped to gain wealth and honours in the revolution which would entail the confiscation of the property of the rich, or to realize the fantastic dreams of the German students as they smoked pipe after pipe over their jugs of beer? Fear, selfish indifference, or base ingratitude could alone have quarrelled with that influence even if it chose to give itself the name of the Holy Alliance.

Probably the Jacobins only made use of Napoleon's name as a rallying point, otherwise, by keeping up a constant agitation in Europe, they were his most cruel enemies. He truly said (April, 1816), if Europe was wise and order re-established everywhere,

---

nature (though his father had died of it) about a month before his own decease. His habits, already described, so prejudicial to health, and the relaxing climate, doubtless weakened him, and predisposed his constitution to an attack.

he would not be worth the money and trouble he cost at St. Helena, and they would release him, though it might not be for four or five years. His object failed when he tried to sow distrust between the Allies, and excite a dread of Russia by telling the English commissioners Alexander was false and insincere; and as the bitter feeling against his rival which the Russian triumph had engendered began to wear away, he could speak of him with greater justice.* "Alexander is a generous man," he said to O'Meara; "he would have taken a pleasure in treating me well had I given myself up to him;" and later to his French attendants, that he knew no one so well fitted to be his successor. "A great heart, a noble soul, skilful as a Greek of the Lower Empire, proud and superb as an old Roman, he has often been my enemy, but I have always admired him. He is a true Cæsar. Alexander would be the only man capable of carrying out my work in Europe if, instead of being a Russian, he was a Frenchman."† Even at Fontainebleau, while smarting under his forced abdication, he admitted that if " he were not Napoleon, he should like to be Alexander."

The Congress of Aix-la-Chapelle was dull compared with that of Vienna, and Alexander spent his leisure moments in visiting the antiquities at Cologne, and other places of interest in the neighbourhood. The Duke of Kent, who had lately married Constantine's sister-in-law, the Princess Victoria of Saxe-Coburg, and was living in Germany, came to see the Emperor, and introduced to him the artist Dawe, who went to St. Petersburg to paint the principal Russian generals. Alexander had an hour's interview with Clarkson, October 10th, on

---

* Castlereagh wrote, October 4th, 1818, from Aix-la-Chapelle, "My belief is the Emperor of Russia is in the main in earnest in what he says. . . . I have reason to think he has been led to believe there are secret engagements existing between Great Britain and Austria; but with all these ideas working upon a jealous and haughty mind, he means to pursue a peace policy: he aims at sway, but has no desire to change his connections, or render the revolutionary spirit in Europe more active. I observe Prince Metternich's suspicions are much allayed, and now principally point against the Russian agents. He mentioned to me the Emperor's personal character as the only guarantee against the danger of Russian power. Upon the whole, it seems working as we could wish; and we have only to encourage the sentiments of attachment of which all the sovereigns are so prodigal towards each other, and which, I believe, are at this moment sincerely entertained," &c.

† Balleydier. Vie de Nicholas Ier.

the subject of the slave trade, and also saw Robert Owen, whose peace principles he said he entirely shared.

When the treaty for the immediate evacuation of France was signed, the Czar went for a single day to Paris to present it to the King, as he did not wish to review his armies on Louis's territories, and utterly ignore him. The attention was appreciated by the infirm old man, to whom a journey of nearly 400 miles, merely to make a morning visit, seemed a wonderful exertion, and in a confidential writing, dated December, 1818, he alludes to it* as one of "the happiest moments" of his life. "Without speaking of the extreme courtesy he showed in coming to see me, it was difficult not to be pleased with his conversation. He not only entered into all my thoughts, but he uttered them before I had time to express them. He highly approved of my system of government and line of conduct since September 5th, 1816," &c. "I have seen the Emperor pass," writes Madame Svetchine from Paris, on October 31st. "No one besides the King and Princesses can boast of more. The Princess Bagration is loud on his cruelty of not giving us even one night. As for me, I should have been satisfied with one day. He has been gracious. He is always handsome, and I thought him grown stouter."

After the reviews at Valenciennes, Alexander returned to Aix-la-Chapelle, where he arrived in the middle of the night, and the next morning called informally on the Duke of Wellington, at breakfast with his aides-de-camp, to thank him for his attention to the Russian troops while under his command, and to offer him the bâton of a field marshal of Russia. Early in November a review of the Russian troops was held in the neighbourhood of Sedan, which Lord Palmerston attended as a spectator, and has left rather a lively picture of a dinner-party at the Russian head-quarters. "When dinner was announced, the Emperor took Lady William Russell, the King of Prussia took Lady Worcester; Alexander beckoned for the King to go first; the King refused, the Emperor insisted, the King was obstinate, and the ladies looked foolish. The company expected a battle royal, when at last Alexander gave a vehement stamp with his foot, and the King, probably recollecting that his own

* Lamartine's Histoire de la Restauration.

cudgellers were at Sedan, a long day's journey off, consented to take the post of honour and go first. The second day the King said, that as he had given way before, he hoped Alexander would do him the favour to take his proper place, which was graciously assented to."* A critic† says of this story, "There were only four ladies present, Lady William Russell, Lady Worcester, Lady Francis Cole, and Lady Hervey. One of these, remarkable for quick perception and accurate memory, has retained a different impression of the scene. She says the dinner being at the Russian head-quarters, the Czar considered himself at home, and therefore requested the King to go first; that the contest was one of smiling courtesy on both sides, that there was no display of temper, no stamping of feet, and that the ladies did not look foolish, which most assuredly one of them never did."

Wellington took the opportunity of a solitary ride with Alexander (to a newly-invented pontoon bridge) to speak highly of Voronzov. Lord Palmerston says, "The whole Prussian system, dress, equipment, drill, &c., is copied from the Russian, and when a new regulation is issued at St. Petersburg, a copy is immediately sent to Berlin, that the King may have the benefit of it."‡

On leaving France Alexander's army sold some of its guns, horses, and war material, to avoid the expense of transport. The Russian soldiers returned to their native country by sea; but before the Congress was dissolved, on the earnest solicitation of the smaller States in Germany, the Allies signed an agreement in view of the strength of the French revolutionary party and the weakness of the Bourbons, that in case of an outbreak among the French threatening the peace of the Continent, the British army should assemble at Brussels to overawe the insurgents, the Prussians at Cologne, the Austrians at Stuttgart, and the Russians at Mayence, after the lapse of three months, on account of its great distance. A mere demonstration would, it was thought, be sufficient, without bloodshed. Alexander paid his visit to Brussels, where his mother had preceded him, astonishing the Belgians by her magnificence and liberality. She deposited 40,000*l.* sterling

* Diary in France, 1815-18.   † *Quarterly Review*, Jan. 1872.
‡ Diary in France, 1815-18.

in the bank to pay the expenses of her visit, and her son-in-law, the Prince of Orange, dressed in the Russian uniform, acted as her dutiful chamberlain the whole time she remained—no sinecure, as she preserved the activity of seventeen.

There is something insidiously captivating in republican opinions to the generous but inexperienced mind, who fancies it recognizes beneath their subtle exterior the patron of intellect and the friend of the poor; and as a youth entering upon life is apt to take as his model some long-established man of fashion, so the ardent youth of Russia, introduced for the first time to the feelings and opinions of Western Europe, were inclined to copy the old revolutionists, who still remained very numerous in France, and whose influence had in reality stirred the world far more than Napoleon's victories. The leaders of the republicans assiduously courted the officers attached to the Russian contingent, and the very novelty of their doctrines made them particularly attractive to men reared under a despotism. With the fickleness of the Muscovite character, they forgot the results of the French revolution, which spread blood and ashes through their own empire and well-nigh destroyed France.* Thrown among the Bonapartists, they imbibed their opinions, and began to conceive a profound admiration for the man who asserted that Russia's strength was incompatible with the safety of Europe, and to condemn their own gallant monarch for the part he took in their idol's fall. Alexander had paid for the education of many young Russians, the sons of aides-de-camp or officers in his service, at the most eminent schools and universities on the Continent, and introduced foreign tutors to supply the educational establishments he founded in Russia. Where a Russian appeared qualified to fill these posts he was always sure to be selected, but there were not enough educated men in Russia to take them; the French and German universities contained unpractical idealists, and the Russian students returned usually connected with some secret society, which soon adopted political reform as its aim. The foreign tutors also spread the same ideas among their pupils in Russia. The secret

* The papers which reached St. Helena January 18th, 1816, asserted that England had wished for the dismemberment of France, but that Russia had opposed it.

societies Catherine II. had attempted to suppress sprang up in all directions, endowed with new life, and their members could openly avow their connection with them without fear of punishment. It was the fashion for every young man to belong to an association of the kind. A Russian general who accompanied the contingent back to Russia in 1818, after its three years' sojourn in France, said that rather than let them go home, the Emperor would do better to drown them in the Baltic. As frequently happens with secret associations, these were joined by men for the sake of revenge, who had fancied personal grievances against the Emperor—some like Yakoubovitz, cashiered for taking part in fatal duels, always contrary to law in Russia, and others because they were poor. The more violent dragged on the rest by threats of exposure, and a movement which began with excellent motives ended in mere treason.

An English missionary heard complaints in 1816 of the prevalence of Freemasonry, and that it was spreading rapidly in Poland; the Roman Catholic Archbishop of Minsk, and many laymen, strongly suspected it had a dark political object. Alexander was warned on every side, and by numerous anonymous letters, that his Government was being gradually undermined, but he refused to take alarm. He remembered the days of his own youth, his predilection for republics, and his indignation at the abuses of Catherine's Government: he knew his empire had not yet reached perfection, and he hoped some day to find valuable assistants in these young reformers, whose suggestions he received in a gracious manner, even when he thought them utterly visionary. The press poured forth projects of legislation and plans of regeneration with an activity rarely seen even in England, and perhaps never before on the Continent. He thought this enthusiasm would exhaust itself, for there was hardly an officer in the army who did not carry about with him the plan of a constitution, or rather, of an oligarchy like ancient Poland and Venice. Some few desired an equal distribution of lands, as in Sparta, but hardly any wished for the emancipation of the serfs, which Alexander believed ought to precede everything. In vain his intimate friends told him that these societies were becoming conspiracies, and that even projects were beginning to be entertained against his life. He had heard of conspiracies constantly throughout his reign, and they had vanished without his interference, and he now would take no measures to suppress them. Some thought he was weary of existence, others that he was ashamed* to do it so long as he carried the bitter remembrance of having once been a conspirator.

On the dissolution of the Congress of Aix-la-Chapelle, Constantine and the King of Prussia went to Paris, where the last spent some time. The Grand Duke Michael was sent to make a tour in Italy, and Alexander returned home by Warsaw, as a slight disturbance had taken place in Poland. The Empress came back to Russia almost immediately afterwards, in deep dejection at the death of her brother, the Grand Duke of Baden, who expired December 8th, during her visit to Carlsruhe, at the age of thirty-three. As he left no son, her uncle Louis succeeded him. On the last day of the old year (January 12th) the Empress-Dowager returned to St. Petersburg, and the next day attended a public service with her son. Four days afterwards Alexander was obliged to break to her the news of the death of her daughter, Catherine of Würtemberg, whom she had lately visited, apparently in excellent health. She had taken cold from sitting up on several successive nights in severe weather with one of her children who had the measles, and was attacked with violent erysipelas, which affected her head, and terminated in apoplexy, carrying her off in a few days. She was only thirty, having survived her friend the Princess Charlotte scarcely fourteen months, and her death caused a most extraordinary sensation in Würtemberg, where she was much beloved, and had founded schools and hospitals from her private fortune.† Six hundred students from Tubingen and Stuttgart followed her coffin to the grave.

The Empress had overtaxed her strength in watching by her brother's death-bed, and the journey from Carlsruhe in the middle of the winter completed the wreck of her health. She was seized with nervous excitement on her return to St. Petersburg, and from this period to her death avoided all Court

---

* Wellington Correspondence. Supplementary vol. for 1826.
† Two Englishmen, who visited Stuttgart in 1818, have both described her in enthusiastic terms. She spoke of her visit to England as the happiest part of her life.

festivities, and lived in cloister-like retirement in her various palaces, only driving out when she thought she was likely to be least observed. An Englishwoman, Mrs. Pitt, and a lady-in-waiting, Mdlle. Waloueif, were almost her sole companions, with the exception of the historian Karamzin, who had rooms in the palace, and entertained her with his literary productions when she was able to hear them. In this unhappy situation Alexander was most attentive to her. When she was worse than usual he would sit up with her at night, after having been actively employed all day; and when she refused to take medicine, under the idea that she was being poisoned, he tasted it himself before offering it to her, to convince her it had not been tampered with. The Princess Mestchersky, who was intimate at the palace, said he treated his wife like a spoiled child.

Allen and Grellet visited St. Petersburg in the winter of 1818–19, and the reigning Empress having expressed a desire to see them, they were received in her private apartments. "There is much mildness in her countenance," writes Allen. "She received us very respectfully, and said that from what the Emperor had told her she wished to see some of our religious society. We had a good deal of conversation with her upon serious subjects, which was highly satisfactory. We feel much for her. After an interview of about three-quarters of an hour we withdrew." Alexander told them one reason "for keeping so large an army is, that the serfs who become soldiers after receiving their discharge are free men. He is discharging great numbers, and taking others in their place; and one great object of establishing schools in the army is to prepare these men for freedom." There was a library attached to the manufactory of Alexandrovsky for the use of the workpeople, and an Englishman writing in 1825 remarks on the extraordinary desire for education and books among the Russian soldiers; but the project was much opposed by many of the nobles, even "some valuable and pious persons," lest if the poor acquired the faculty of reading they might employ it for a bad purpose. "Independence of character and determination to see and judge for himself mark the mind of the Emperor."

Alexander paid a short visit to Finland, where he was always well received, in April, 1819. At Helsingfors he had given 1,600,000 roubles towards replacing the old wooden city burned down in the bombardment, with handsome streets of stone houses, and had bestowed these new dwellings as gifts on the former proprietors. In addition, he expended large sums on public buildings, as he intended to make it the seat of government. In May he went to Archangel, being the first Sovereign, except Peter the Great, who had visited this remote seaport. He travelled with his usual rapidity, and on the journey crossed two lakes in ordinary ferry boats, embarking on one occasion under a very stormy sky, instead of waiting for a finer day. There are frequently dangerous hurricanes on these inland Russian seas, and during the passage the gale increased till there was absolute danger, and the loyal steersman whose boat conveyed the Emperor was completely unnerved when he thought of his responsibility. Alexander reassured him, and at last quietly directed another sailor to take the helm. After many hours' delay they were brought safely to the shore, though all, including the Emperor, were soaked to the skin and nearly famished with hunger. He minutely inspected the hospitals and prisons at Archangel, and visited the ancient monastery of Kholmogri. At the end of June he joined the camp at Krasnoe-Celo (a short distance from Gateschina), where he had instituted the summer manœuvres still annually held by the Russian troops, and where the wide plain is dotted with canvas tents, the temporary abode of soldiers, officers, Grand Dukes, and Emperor.

Constantine came to St. Petersburg in the spring, and was driving one day with his brother when the Emperor alluded to his intention of abdicating, which he had revolved in his mind more or less since he was seventeen. "For a long time," he said, "you know I have wanted rest, and I only aspire to find it. After me the crown belongs to you. I warn you of my intention, that you may think of it and take your measures for the time when I shall effect my design." Constantine assured the Emperor he should not survive him, and would never consent to reign in his place. "Think seriously of it," said Alexander. "I must know to whose hands I shall transfer the burden, and if after reflecting on it you do not absolutely wish for the throne, write to me a letter that I can show to the Empress Mary, that I may confer with her, and provide for my successor." Constantine renewed his protestations. " How shall I write this letter ?" he said ; " you know how badly I write Russian." " Write it in French," Alexander replied. " I will translate it into Russian, and you can copy it,"* and this was what actually took place.

The Empress-mother generally took up her abode near Krasnoe-Celo with the Princesses during the manœuvres ; but in 1819 the Grand Duchess Nicholas often came to her husband's tent, where during several weeks he resided in the midst of his brigade. The troops were encamped, not *en masse*, as at present, but by turns, and the Emperor reviewed Nicholas's division of the Guards the day before it was replaced by another corps. He was more than usually kind to his brother, and praised his zeal and the order of his brigade, which was only intrusted to him the previous autumn. In the evening he dined alone with Nicholas and his wife; and after conversing in an agreeable manner on indifferent subjects, suddenly began rather drily on the succession to the throne. He said he saw with the greatest pleasure the conjugal and parental happiness of the young couple, for the education given both to himself and his brother Constantine was far from being directed in such a manner as to enable them to appreciate this kind of happiness, and moreover they had no children. A monarch sincerely desirous of conscientiously executing the constant and severe labours inseparable from the fulfilment of his duties, must feel the indispensable necessity —a necessity even more indispensable in our present century than it has ever been before, of possessing, in addition to other qualities, a large endowment of health and physical strength. These were gradually failing in himself, and he foresaw the certainty at no distant time of being unable to fulfil his duties in such a way as to satisfy his own conscience. He was resolved therefore to abdicate the throne on the first warning given by a perceptible diminution of his bodily or mental powers that the proper moment had arrived. " I have on more than one occasion," he said, " discussed the subject with Constantine ; but he being of nearly the same age as myself, and possessing

* Eynard. His authorities were Capo d'Istria and Alexander Tourgenef.

an aversion to the idea of reigning, has decidedly refused to succeed me. We are both the more confirmed in our respective determinations by seeing in you a proof of the particular blessing of Providence who has given you a son. You are therefore informed that you are destined at a future period to be invested with the Imperial dignity."[*]

Instead of being pleased, Nicholas and his wife were both so much distressed at it, even to tears, that the Emperor, " with that angelic kindness and delicacy which distinguished him," wrote his brother, " tried to encourage and tranquillize them." " The moment for the change which so alarms you," he said, " is not yet arrived; before it comes ten years perhaps will have passed over our heads, and my object in warning you is merely that you may accustom yourselves to the inevitable fate awaiting you." Nicholas vainly represented that he had never prepared himself for the Imperial dignity, and had not sufficient ability or strength of character; that he had no other wish or ambition than to serve the Emperor faithfully and with his whole powers in any sphere of duty which Alexander might point out to him. The Emperor said he was aware of it, and truly appreciated his loyalty; that at the period of his own accession he was equally unprepared; and besides, the Government was then in a most confused state owing to the absence of anything like fundamental principles of administration; for though during the last years of the Empress Catherine's life there was certainly a great want of order and system, nevertheless the mechanism of Government continued to go on, as it were, by its own *vis inertiæ*. From the accession of their father, however, from the adoption of the principle that the system hitherto followed was to be completely abandoned, even the small remains of order were annihilated without being replaced by any new system; and therefore his (Alexander's) position had been the more embarrassing, while now, after the reforms introduced in the course of his reign, Nicholas would find everything following a regular course and possessing a proper organization, so that his only task would be to maintain it.

[*] Baron Korff's narrative of the accession of Nicholas I. He gives this conversation, and the Grand Duke's feelings, &c., verbatim from Nicholas's own Memoir.

The conversation ended and the Emperor retired, but his auditors felt as if their prospect of a prolonged domestic peace was completely destroyed. Nicholas, as his own memoir asserts, " looked upon the dignity of Emperor with a feeling of awful veneration, particularly having before his eyes, in his brother, the living example of a Sovereign whose whole existence was an incessant sacrifice to duty, and who nevertheless had so seldom succeeded in securing even gratitude, at least from his contemporaries; and now all of a sudden, instead of the sphere of existence traced out for him beforehand by the natural order of succession, there opened before him a destiny so unexpected, that of having to bear an almost insupportable burden of tremendous responsibility to God and to his own conscience—the burden of ruling the most gigantic empire in the world."

Alexander afterwards mentioned this conversation to Prince William of Prussia, and frequently alluded to it again to Nicholas and his wife; but they always tried to avoid talking of it, having apparently a sincere wish to remain subjects rather than sovereigns; and when Prince William congratulated them, Nicholas assured him he never meant to accept the dignity, and hoped he would not refer to it any more. There had never been much cordiality between Nicholas and Constantine, the last having always shown a decided preference for Michael. Alexander was only forty-one, and Constantine just forty. They were both capable of enduring long journeys and fatigues far beyond the power of most ordinary men; many years of life probably lay before them in which they might change their minds, and perhaps Nicholas foresaw the trouble he had with Constantine, who, though submissive and respectful to an elder brother whom he admired and loved, was not equally so to one seventeen years younger than himself. Alexander's intention was not published, and no official act was drawn up for some little time, while Constantine jealously retained the title of Czarovitz, and was anxious to be regarded by the world as heir to the throne. Some think he only consented to renounce the succession by Alexander's advice and strong representation of the dangers* besetting the

* He told the Queen of Saxony his neck was not strong enough to reign.

throne, and the probability that sooner or later he would meet with a violent end. He was also anxious to form a marriage with a young Polish lady of neither royal nor noble birth. He made a last attempt in 1818 to procure a reconciliation with his wife; and his mother, desirous of preventing it and securing the succession to Nicholas, advised him to obtain a divorce. Marriage in the Orthodox Church can only be dissolved by the unlimited power of the autocrat; and after consulting the Holy Synod, Alexander published an act of divorce between his brother and the Princess of Saxe-Coburg,* who retained her Russian name and title as well as a handsome income. The same day, March 20th, 1820, he issued a manifesto declaring that a member of the Imperial family contracting a marriage with a person not of royal birth, could not transmit his right of inheritance to their children; and its object was explained on the following May 12th, by Constantine's marriage with Jeanne Grudzinska, the daughter of "a poor country gentleman," as he caused to be inserted in the marriage contract; and the Czar immediately created her Princess of Lowitz, and elevated her family to the rank of Counts of Poland. He also sent her some magnificent wedding presents, for she had been a maid of honour at the Court of Warsaw, and her character irreproachable. "I shall try," she said, "to render Monseigneur so happy that the Poles will benefit by it."

In the spring of 1819 Alexander acted as godfather by proxy to the newly-born daughter of the Duke of Kent; the Prince Regent standing in person as the other. The Duke insisted on the Emperor's name coming first, which prevented her from being also called Georgiana, as the Prince Regent said his own name ought to come second to none. She was therefore baptized "Alexandrina Victoria."†

The young poet, Alexander Pushkin, at this time filled a post in the ministry of foreign affairs. He had published a legendary romance, "Rustan and Ludmilla," when he made an essay in politics and brought out a poem called "Freedom,"

---

* She died in 1861.
† The Duke of York acted for the Emperor. The others were the Queen-Dowager of Würtemberg and the Duchess-Dowager of Saxe-Coburg.

which soon disappeared from circulation. The objectionable part was the conclusion, containing a violent denunciation of the Emperor Paul. " Crowned wretch, from my soul I abhor thee and thy whole race. The brightest day of my life would have been the morning which should have seen thy ruin and that of thy sons. Terror of the universe, shame of Nature, living anathema of our earth — adieu. When the moon has sunk down below the dark river, when all is asleep there is a point in the shade on which the poet casts a glance; it is on that black palace, where no fire is lighted, a threatening sepulchre buried in gloom, which appears to us sad as it floats in the mist, but sadder yet in memory's clouds."

The poem goes on to describe the "avenging band, a silent cortége of mysterious men, to whom the portal is opened by the unfaithful soldier, whose loud 'who goes there?' ought to have been heard. He lowers the bridge of the rugged citadel, delivering the royal owner who had confided in him. A passage is cleared by a hand bought by treachery, and in the sombre night, the lost soul flying, he cries, he falls, he dies, the crowned bandit." It ends with a caution to future Czars to take warning, " if they wished to save their fragile crowns." Not satisfied with merely its publication, Pushkin took an opportunity to waylay Alexander and offer it to him in the form of a petition.

There was not a Sovereign to whom such an insult could have been offered with impunity, and far from Alexander being reproached with Pushkin's exile, it was rather a proof of his extreme moderation, that he inflicted no more severe punishment than to send him to his father at Moscow. A short time afterwards he received a civil appointment at Odessa, where he became a frequent visitor at the Countess Voronzov's, and there seeing a picture of the Emperor, he made an impromptu verse, more complimentary to his Sovereign's personal appearance than to his brains. Perhaps the Countess thought he would get into further trouble, for by her advice he made a tour in the Caucasus, which inspired him with more than one beautiful ode. He was allowed to publish them, but was soon deeply involved in the conspiracy to overthrow the Government; and having resigned his post, it was owing to the accident of his being absent in Pskov at his father's country estate, at the time of the outbreak in St. Petersburg when Alexander died, that he was prevented from probably compromising himself for life. His genius also stood him in good stead; Alexander marked him out as "the future Racine of Russia" when his youthful follies should have evaporated; and Nicholas, instead of including him in the number of the proscribed, appointed him the historiographer of the empire.

In the spring of 1819 Alexander had received some complaints of the perversion of justice in Siberia, and appointed his old secretary, Speranski, to the supreme government, with directions to inquire particularly into the conduct of the local governors, and all cases of peculation and injustice. He received unlimited powers, and travelled from one end to the other of Russian Asia, penetrating into every prison or other receptacle for criminals. In one year he dismissed all the governors in the country except the commandant at Okhotzk, and several of these having undergone a trial in St. Petersburg, were condemned to serve in the ranks, or returned as convicts to their old quarters. Alexander heard Speranski's health was breaking down, and sent a physician, Dr. Burtzof, to him; but the governor believing that medical assistance was more required among the prisoners, dispensed with his services to enable him to devote his attention entirely to them. Cochrane met Speranski in Siberia in 1820, and writes, "I have never seen more true greatness of soul or goodness of heart." But he resigned his post at the end of seventeen months, when Eastern and Western Siberia were placed as before under separate governors-general, and the vice-governors of the principal towns made responsible only to the Imperial senate. In March, 1821, he returned to St. Petersburg after an absence of nine years. The Emperor received him very kindly, and desired him to resume his labours upon the "Digest of the Russian Law," and his seat in the Council of State.

In August, 1819, Alexander went to Riga, where a deputation presented him with the scheme for emancipation. "I am delighted," he said, "to see that the nobility of Livonia have accomplished my expectations. You have set an example that ought to be imitated; you have acted in the spirit of our age, and have felt that liberal principles alone can form the basis of the people's happiness." From Riga he came to Mittau, to attend the solemnity accompanying the final enfranchisement of the serfs of Courland, and on September 24th, heard the Te Deum sung in the cathedral to commemorate the event.

When a constitution was bestowed upon the Duchy of Warsaw, Lithuania and the Russo-Polish provinces had also received their old form of government, and the Lithuanian army was now placed under the command of the Polish General-in-Chief. A report was spread, and eagerly circulated by the secret societies, that Alexander meant to alienate these provinces, and even Kiov, which the Poles claimed, because in the days of Russia's humiliation under the Tartars, they had conquered and retained it for a short period, and that he intended to erect them into a separate kingdom. This made a great sensation in Russia, where the conspirators resolved to embrue their hands in the blood of their Sovereign rather than see him partition Russia. The indiscretions of the Polish press, and disturbances in the University which Alexander established at Warsaw, in place of their ancient one at Cracow, did not serve to bind the two nations; and on the one side Czartoriski continued to complain to Alexander of the proceedings of the local government at Warsaw. "When your orders are severe, their execution is prompt and vigorous; but when they are favourable to the constitution, there are always pretexts for delaying their development;" while on the other, Novossilzof wrote that Czartoriski's curatorship of the schools in the Russo-Polish provinces was entirely calculated to detach the students from Russia. "All that comes from your Majesty," writes Czartoriski, "only breathes goodness, greatness of soul, liberality of principles; the words and actions of his Imperial Highness are in quite an opposite sense. The lieutenant (General Zaionzek), on his side, incessantly repeats that the constitution is a code of anarchy, that it must be changed. Novossilzof alone does not contribute to unhinge and lower the public spirit." He also asserts that General Zaionzek has on essential points of legislation and administration, principles or prejudices quite contrary to those of the rest of the persons placed in the government; that having passed his life out of the country and in the military service, he understands very little of legislative matters. He is consequently often alone in his opinion, and attributes this result to a party spirit and a pretended enmity against him which does not exist. Unfortunately, the Grand Duke shares his opinion."

It was hardly likely that one of Napoleon's old generals, accustomed to military discipline and to his former master's mode of suppressing the Tribune and other popular assemblies, should possess the patience and long-suffering required to deal with a constitutional Poland. In the days of the Duchy of Warsaw under French protection, a row of cannon would quickly have ended such disputes in the Diet if they had ventured to appear. But his appointment was a concession to the Polish predilection for military renown, particularly when connected with France, and a proof of the extraordinary generosity of Alexander in bestowing it on one of his most constant enemies, and for that very reason, next to Kosciusko and the dead Poniatowski, the most popular man in Poland. He now merely did his best to remain faithful to his new Sovereign, and saw that the aim of the Diet was to cut their tie with Russia as soon as they had acquired the annexation of the Russo-Polish provinces. The Legislative Council proved the same stormy assembly as in ancient Poland. The right of appeal to the Sovereign was exercised on the most frivolous occasions, and to procure a perversion of justice rather than its execution, and against the ministerial decrees. Alexander sent a message to the effect that he was resolved to preserve the charter, but that on their side the Poles were bound to observe their duties rigorously, instead of delivering themselves over to chimerical dreams.

The Emperor's visit to Warsaw in September passed off quietly; but Czartoriski, who had lately married, went to Baden just before he arrived, on the score of his wife's health, and absented himself on the same occasion the following year. The Emperor called as usual on the old Countess of Tiesenhausen, the Princess Radzivil, and other Polish ladies of high rank, and asked the Princess Radzivil (a member of the Prussian royal family), when she was coming to St. Petersburg to see her niece, the Grand Duchess Nicholas.

He cut short all compliments rather impatiently—perhaps weary of profuse expressions of admiration not borne out—but otherwise seemed as popular as before; and Karamzin was stirred up to write a long letter to him, representing that if the report was true of his intended restoration of entire Poland, he would be acting most unjustly by his own people. He began by endeavouring to show that policy, not Christian forgiveness, ought to rule a State. It was only the strength of Russia which procured the obedience of Poland, but the Russians had acquired for the Emperor the glory of being the liberator of Europe. "You think of re-establishing the ancient kingdom of Poland. Is that compatible with the safety of Russia? Is it in conformity with your sacred obligations, to the love of your empire, to justice itself? Can you conscientiously deprive us of White Russia, Podolia, Lithuania, and Volhynia, the property of Russia long before your reign? Did not you swear to maintain the integrity of your empire? All these countries were Russian when the Metropolitan Plato handed you the crown of Monomachus, Peter, and Catherine; that Catherine whom yourself called the Great! If it was illegal for her to partition Poland, it would be still more illegal for you to repair Catherine's injustice by a partition of Russia itself. We conquered Poland by our sword—that is our right; it is to that right that all States owe their existence, for all were formed by conquest. Why not also re-establish the kingdom of Kazan and Astrakhan, the Republic of Novgorod, the Grand Duchy of Riazan, &c.? Moreover, White Russia, Volhynia, Podolia, and Galicia made at one time part of the constituent possessions of Russia. If you cede them they will demand of you the cession of Kiof, Tchernigof, Smolensko, for these towns for a long time belonged to hostile Lithuania. Would you, who love liberty, treat Russia like an inanimate thing? . . . . Sire, Russia is silent before you; but if ever (from which may God preserve us!) ancient Poland is re-established and produces an historian worthy of the name, that historian would condemn your magnanimity as fatal to your true country . . . . if in order to obtain the applause of the Poles you reduce the latter to despair. . . . I hear what the Russians say, 'We should lose not only our beautiful lands, but also our love for the Czar;

we should feel our patriotism grow cooler, seeing our country the toy of arbitrary caprice. . . . In one word, either the re-establishment of Poland will be the ruin of Russia, or our children will water the Polish soil with our blood, and will take Praga once more by assault.'"

He goes on to say that the only way of keeping Poland harmless is to keep her weak and powerless. The stronger she is made, the more she will desire to become independent, and her first step would be to separate from Russia. "In case of war those countries might all be against us." He enlarges on Russia's greatness : " You have already acquired the title of Great ; desire that of our Father. Let it live, let it flourish, the kingdom of Poland as it is now; but let Russia also live and prosper, as she is now, as she was left to you by Catherine. Catherine loved you tenderly, and loved our native country; her shade hovers here, I am silent.

" Czarco-Selo, October 17th, 1819."

When Karamzin sent this letter he told his wife to prepare to leave the rooms they occupied in the palace. The Russians were further irritated by the flight of a number of serfs into Poland, and Alexander, after consulting the ministers on their extradition, decided that Poland ought to enjoy the privileges of a separate kingdom in this respect, and they were allowed to remain. The same year he passed a law permitting serfs in every part of the empire to establish themselves as manufacturers or traders ; a privilege only enjoyed hitherto by free men, and all taking advantage of this law were relieved from the income-tax for four years. From Archangel he sent out the order for the first levy of recruits since the war, and took measures to colonize the portion of the army centred in Bessarabia, so as to complete a cordon from the Baltic to the Black Sea. This year Russia contracted a loan in Holland, to enable her to reduce her paper money, and as many assignats to the amount of 38,000,000 roubles were publicly burned. A law was passed directing that magazines of corn should be established in every district as a reserve against years of famine, and a commission was appointed under the presidency of the Emperor's uncle, the Prince of Würtemberg, charged with the maintenance of all the roads, bridges, and highways. In

1820 a macadamized road was begun between St. Petersburg and Moscow, a distance of 400 miles. It was completed early in the reign of Nicholas.

In 1819 a large colony of Prussian Dissenters received lands, and were allowed to settle in Russia on account of public opinion being strongly against them in their own country. Allen and Grellet met with six different kinds of Dissenting colonies during their tour in South Russia, all living in harmony, and all equally prosperous. At the end of this year Alexander paid a short visit to Moscow.

In 1820 an expedition was despatched to explore the northeast point of Asia, where it was reported a colony of shipwrecked Russian sailors had been found. The Czar also sent an exploring party into Central Asia, and an envoy to Bokhara, with which Russia had held communication long before. Great Britain possessed a foot of land in India. A mission was forwarded to China, and five Kalmuck chiefs who left Russia under Catherine II. now sent in the adhesion of their tribes to her rule. This year a steamer was launched on the Volga, and plied regularly between Kazan and Astrakhan.

The month of January, 1820, saw the close of the long reign of George III., who had begun it a contemporary of the Empress Elizabeth; but it caused no change in the English Cabinet, where the Conservatives under Lord Liverpool retained their seats. The King's fourth son, the Duke of Kent, died six days before his father, leaving one infant child, the present Queen.

The disputes long existing between Spain and her American colonies ended in 1820, by Mexico declaring herself independent, and the following year Brazil threw off her allegiance to Portugal. The agitations distracting the mother-country accelerated the division of the once formidable Spanish Empire, for since the restoration of Ferdinand VII. there was a continued struggle between the Royalists and clergy with the Liberals, who, like most continental Republicans, could not separate religion from despotism, and in Ferdinand they had to deal with the weakest and most superstitious of cruel despots. A rebellion broke out January 1st, which soon involved the peninsula in a civil war, and the mountainous nature of the country, and perhaps a want of energy in the royal troops, enabled the revolutionists, as at the present day, to protract it more than two years. The flame soon spread to Naples, already abounding in secret societies, for the King, with no reforming proclivities, had tied his hands by a secret article in his treaty with Austria in 1815, which bound him not to introduce into his Government any principles irreconcilable with those adopted by Francis in the north of Italy. In the course of the summer Sardinia and Naples were both in open revolt.

A melancholy catastrophe gave further evidence of the unpopularity of the Bourbons in France. The Duc de Berri, married for three years to a Princess of Naples, was stabbed at the door of the theatre in Paris, under the impression that with him the dynasty must become extinct (February 13th, 1820). His elder brother was childless, and his own infant daughter was precluded from the succession by the Salic law. But on September 20th the Duchesse de Berri gave birth to a son (the present Comte de Chambord), to the great satisfaction of the friends of order and legitimacy, threatened by the revolutionary pamphlets that for the last two years teemed from the press, openly advocating the assassination of princes, and exalting the leaders of insurrection. Alexander wrote a warm congratulatory letter to Louis on the birth of his heir; and another to the Duchesse de Berri, commending the exertions she made to obtain a pardon for two men who conspired against her life and that of her new-born child. He deplored to his own family the tragical death of the Duke, whose character he said had greatly improved, and offered in the future a guarantee of happiness to France, which seemed a permanent hearth of revolution. " What do the French wish? They enjoy a beautiful country, a happy climate, all the advantages of heaven and earth, as much liberty as they can reasonably desire." As had always been the case for a century, the French commotions found an echo in Poland. Her press advocated republics, and cried up the chiefs of insurrection. Her true friends would have counselled her to wait till the Russians had forgotten the ferocity with which the Polish contingent massacred unarmed men and women during the campaign of 1812. Eight years only had since elapsed, and the remembrance bringing forcibly to mind the horrors of a Polish insurrection, Alexander's Russian counsellors called loudly upon him to put some restraint upon their language and forestall such an event.

Two destructive fires took place the same night, in June, 1820, believed to be the work of political malcontents, as such ignorant and mischievous modes of vengeance have always been common in Russia. A wing of the palace of Czarco-Selo, including the Lyceum* founded by Alexander, and the Ismailov barracks in St. Petersburg were burned to the ground. The Emperor observed, that since two events of this kind were to happen, he was glad they should weigh on the Crown rather than on the richest of his subjects.

On March 25th, 1820, Alexander issued a ukaz abolishing the Order of Jesuits in Russia, and obliging them to leave the empire in two months' time. At Odessa they had publicly burned some Bibles lately translated into Russian, and committed other acts of intolerance. The decree stated that "The sacred duty of educating the youths of their confession was intrusted to the Jesuits, to enlighten the intellect with science and the heart with religion. While themselves enjoying ample tolerance, they have sown in weak minds the germs of a rude intolerance. They have attempted to overthrow the defence of the State, the attachment to the religion of their fathers, and so ruining the happiness of families by exciting painful differences of opinion. All the efforts of the Jesuits aim

* The first is described by Cochrane, who saw the catastrophe:—"As we proceeded, there suddenly rose to the south-east a tremendous blaze, the cause of which it seemed difficult to conjecture: immense masses of fire and sparks at intervals exploded and separated like a rocket. . . . It was the Emperor's favourite palace wrapped in an inextinguishable flame! It was midnight; parties of men surrounded the wasting pile. All was order and regularity; not a voice was heard amid the thousands of people employed. The Emperor was present, evidently impressed with extreme regret, but continued to give frequent directions with perfect coolness. Czarco-Selo was the palace where the Emperor and his brother Constantine were brought up, and passed their earliest years; here also the Emperor was accustomed to retire when the cares of State permitted him to lose amidst its beauties the anxiety of a throne and the toils of so great a government. He had greatly embellished it, and it was considered one of the most beautiful retreats in Europe. His Majesty gave a strong proof of steady collectedness. While the fire was raging from apartment to apartment, apparently mocking the resistance of man, he directed that the doors should be walled up with bricks. This was instantly done; and by such an expedient alone could the amber, the most valuable chamber, have been wrested from the general destruction."

at their own aggrandizement and extended power. They have already been warned; but the reports of the civil authorities state that they continue to draw into their communion pupils of the orthodox faith, placed in the college at Mohilef, at Saratov, and in Siberia. The Minister of Public Worship has constantly pointed out these transgressions to the Père Général of the Order since 1815, but without effect. By every means of seduction and conversion they continue to sow trouble in the Protestant colonies, and even to steal Jewish children from their parents." The landed property with which Paul formerly endowed them, was appropriated for the benefit of the Roman Catholic Church in Poland and Russia.

When Alexander was visiting the territory of the Don Cossacks in 1818, his carriage was violently overturned, and he was hurt in the leg. Wylie pressed him to take a week or two's rest in a recumbent position; but he was in the habit of fixing the exact date of his return from a journey irrevocably, and constantly on horseback or taking exercise on foot, he never gave it an opportunity of healing properly.*
He became subject to periodical attacks of erysipelas in the damaged limb, which obliged him to keep his sofa for weeks, and to walk lame for months. His general health was always affected, and he suffered from severe headaches when his usual long walks were checked; and this was the case in the spring of 1820, during which he nevertheless accomplished a tour of inspection among the military colonies, and visited Moscow. The usual military manœuvres took place at Krasnoe-Celo in the summer, when the alarming illness of the Grand Duchess Nicholas gave great anxiety to her family. Leaving her children in Russia, she was taken to Germany as soon as she could be removed, and remained there for the following ten months.

At the end of August Alexander went to Warsaw, which was much excited by the insurrections in Spain and Naples. Czartoriski preferred to plead the cause of the Poles by letter

---

* M. Dupré de St. Maure writes:—"The fall was serious, but he would have been quickly cured if, yielding to Dr. Wylie, he had taken rest. Fatigue and the want of precautions increased the malady, and periodically erysipelas has broken out in this suffering leg. At this moment (1821) the Emperor has kept his bed for several weeks. The doctors have been very uneasy, and I have met with more than one anxious face in public; but his journey in the autumn will take place nevertheless."

rather than in person to the Emperor, and had withdrawn from Warsaw for Genoa before he arrived; but he wrote to tell him it was "only the vigilant and paternal wisdom of his Majesty which could put an end to the confusion," and that the deficiency in the revenue might be arranged with good management. He concluded by saying it was reputed the coming Diet would be strongly agitated, but he did not believe it. However, this report turned out to be the truth.

On September 1st (o.s.) Alexander opened the Assembly as usual, dressed in the Polish uniform and wearing the white eagle. Warsaw was illuminated to receive him, and the ministerial reports spoke favourably of its material prosperity. A million had been added to the population since the war, and they had enjoyed good harvests; but a spirit of insubordination was evident, produced, it was said, by Polish youths returning from German universities. The Emperor declared in his speech that he would persevere in his intention of maintaining the charter, but the Poles held in their hands the fate of their country, dependent on their devotion to the throne, and their good disposition to second the efforts of the Government. To these warnings the Diet answered by refusing the projects of law proposed by the minister, particularly an amendment of the criminal code. The violent language used in the assembly exceeded anything ever heard in national debates in the present century, and Alexander would have been accused of great weakness if he had chosen to overlook it. In addition, the Diet refused to supply the payment of the taxes as agreed during the last five years, and caused a deficiency in the treasury by way of a defiance to the Government. Alexander raised the gauntlet. "Since Poland," he said, "cannot suffice to herself, and relieve her own necessities, we shall organize her differently. We have wished to extend the privileges already bestowed on you, but before the systematic hostility of the Diet, we are forced, in the interests of the general security, to modify the given charter." The restrictions were a censorship of the press, which had most decidedly abused its privileges; and as every species of literature except hostile political essays was still allowed free circulation, it was only those who wished to employ it for a bad purpose who had reason to complain. Also the public, who had added considerably to the confusion, were not in future admitted to the debates in the Diet, and the Diet itself was not called to sit again till 1825. When the Emperor closed the session, October 1st (o.s.), he severely and rather sarcastically reproached the members with delaying the development and strengthening of the national institutions. " Appeal to your consciences," he added, " and see whether in the course of your discussions you have rendered Poland all the service she expected from your wisdom; or if, on the contrary, drawn on by the too common seductions of the present day, and sacrificing a hope that more confidence and foresight would have realized, you have not checked in its progress the dawn of the restoration of your country. This grave responsibility will weigh on you. It is the necessary security of the independence of your votes. They are free, but a pure intention ought always to determine them. Mine are known to you. You have received good for evil, and Poland is restored to the position of a State. I shall persevere in my designs in this respect, whatever may be the opinion formed on the manner in which you have just exercised your prerogatives." " They compromise me with my own people," he said to one of the Polish nobles in Warsaw. After the closing of the Diet he stayed a few days longer with Constantine at the palace of Belvedere. He observed that his sister-in-law seemed rather saddened by her elevation, and was not long in discovering the cause. A woman who at one time had gained much power over Constantine remained in the neighbourhood. The Grand Duke said no one would turn even an old horse adrift; but Alexander paid her to retire into Germany. Constantine declared he was now as happy as was compatible with the lot of humanity. She consoled him, and sang to him in his hours of melancholy, and exercised a softening influence which soon showed itself towards his attendants. They went yearly to the German baths, spent their evenings together, and were often guests at the Court of Dresden. His marriage with a native of the country added to his popularity, and in 1825 he was more liked than Nicholas, who was supposed to have imbibed German sympathies.

Alexander gave a site for a statue of Poniatowski in Warsaw, and subscribed towards its erection, and on leaving Warsaw he visited the tomb of Kosciusko, who died in Switzerland in 1817, when his remains were transferred to Cracow at the Emperor's expense. He proceeded to Troppau in Silesia, where a Congress of Sovereigns had met at the Emperor of Austria's request, to consult on the affairs of Naples and Spain. Austria was greatly alarmed for her own possessions in Italy, and hoped to procure Alexander's consent to an active intervention by pointing out danger to his own throne, for Metternich ascertained there was a connection between a secret society in Milan and one in Russia. Before the Congress had sat many days the news arrived that the soldiers of the Simonovsky Guards had mutinied in St. Petersburg.

This event, almost unprecedented in the Russian military annals, is variously ascribed to the cruelty of a Courland officer, Colonel Schwartz, who had tried to reintroduce flogging in the regiment, and to the members of the secret societies, which comprised nearly all its officers, the sons of men for whom Alexander had a particular regard. It was his own regiment before he came to the throne, and on duty at the old St. Michael's Palace the night of Paul's murder. Having once been made the instrument of a revolution, the tradition still clung to it, and smoothed the difficulty in making it serve a political purpose now. Three nephews of Alexander's old tutor Muravief were among these officers. They were educated in France at Alexander's expense, and received much kindness from him, but were enthusiastic republicans; and as their father spent nearly all his life at foreign Courts, they were almost ignorant of their native land, and had belonged to secret societies abroad since 1816. Dr. Pinkerton declares that members of this conspiracy tried to raise opposition to the Bible Society, to call off the attention of the Government from their own traitorous designs, and they certainly made use of the Bibles served out to every soldier in the army who could read, to point out that the men would only be following the example set in Holy Scripture if they rose like the Israelites under Deborah and Barak against Schwartz, whom they compared to the foreign Sisera. It was suppressed by Miloradovitz, the Governor of St. Petersburg—a hero revered by the regiment. He persuaded them to lay down their arms, and enter the fortress quietly, where they were separately drafted off into distant battalions, and the older among them sent home. He sent an officer (Chadief) to carry his report to Alexander, and this man, himself a member of a secret association, loitered as long as he could on the road, so that a courier sent by the Austrian ambassador to Metternich brought the news first to Troppau. The Congress was sitting, and Metternich trying to convince the Sovereigns of the revolutionary state of all Europe, when Alexander replied, " I can answer for Russia's safety." " Sire !" exclaimed the Austrian, " you do not know what is going on in your own country ;" and he gave him an account of the revolt.

When Chadief at last arrived, Alexander reproached him very hotly for his delay, but the day afterwards repented of having spoken so strongly, when after all it might have been accidental, and offered him his promotion. But Chadief refused it, and only asked one favour—his dismissal—which Alexander gave him with regret. The officer remained abroad, serving his disaffected countrymen, but Alexander immediately returned to St. Petersburg, leaving Nesselrode to finish up the affairs of the Congress, which was soon adjourned; and this minister, always Austrian in sentiment, was now entirely swayed by Metternich, and agreed with him in declining to receive an emissary from the Neapolitan revolutionists.

As soon as the Emperor arrived at St. Petersburg, he ordered the insurgents to be treated with mercy, but cashiered the rebellious officers. He was engrossed with military matters till he returned to the Congress, removed to Laybach January 4th, and on December 2nd mournfully referred to its being the anniversary of " that unfortunate day," meaning Austerlitz, as he was transacting business with Miloradovitz. It was the coldest winter known for many years, and some starving wolves entered the streets of St. Petersburg. But he made the two long journeys in an open sledge, and arrived at Laybach on the 7th. At one of the earliest meetings he said : " The spirit of the age required liberal institutions, and a gradual admission of the people to power; but that they should proceed from the free will and well-weighed conviction of those whom God has rendered responsible for power, and not be forced upon them by their subjects; and therefore the Allies could hold no intercourse with the insurgents in Spain and Italy." He now gave the consent he withheld at Troppau, to an Austrian army being put at the disposal of the King of Naples, and maintained at the expense of the country. The meetings were held with closed doors, not even a secretary being present except Metternich. England and France gave no aid to the insurrection, but lent no opposition to its being suppressed; and Austria also took upon herself to put down the rebellion in Piedmont.

At Laybach Las Cases wrote again to Alexander, earnestly appealing to him to obtain Napoleon's release. "What would be your tardy, powerless regrets, which could not appease your heart, or restore to your memory a magnanimous generous act, the most enduring, the best kind of glory, the most dear to posterity, the best known perhaps with which you would be able to embellish your glorious life: I mean to say the forgetfulness of injuries, the disdain of vengeance, the remembrance of old friendship, and lastly, the respect due to Napoleon's majesty, to the anointed of the Lord." Napoleon had always persistently refused to see the Russian commissioner at St. Helena, and though never weary of complaining of the "heartlessness" of the allied Sovereigns, and that he never had a personal quarrel with Alexander, merely a political one, he only appealed to him indirectly through Las Cases; and having once set the counsels of his royal colleagues at defiance, and permitted Napoleon to live untrammelled in Elba, and seen the result, which had fallen the most heavily on France herself, Alexander would not again undertake to restore him to Europe at a moment when the French were prepared to receive with open arms any claimant to the throne in the place of Louis. He felt this extreme desire to return to public life might possibly be actuated by ambition, and who could say it was not, or that the ex-Emperor's first efforts to obtain an alliance would not establish a crusade against Russia? All his conversations at St. Helena tended in this direction. "She is the head of the Hydra, but where find the Hercules? We only dared to pretend to it, and we have attempted it awkwardly it must be confessed." Only one recorded observation shows he was beginning to see that a Sovereign is not placed over a great Power merely to indulge a love of conquest. If he were Emperor of Russia, he should march through Germany to Calais, and make himself arbiter of Europe; but he added, " And after all, to what good ?" A question Alexander had answered more than once in the same way. He had now all the power and dominion Napoleon had made it the work of his life to obtain, and Napoleon at St. Helena enjoyed the rest and retirement from the world, the means of philosophical and scientific study and reflection to which Alexander had looked forward during the last twenty-two years as the desirable haven he might some day attain. Neither of the two rivals secured the desire of his heart, but it was decidedly to the benefit of the world at large that their position was not reversed.

The Czar did however, in a private manner, through his ambassador, express his opinion that the British Government might hold out some hope to Napoleon of his ultimate release, and prevent him from falling into a state of despondency, and to the last fortnight of his life Napoleon's sanguine temperament buoyed him up with the expectation of being some day permitted to return. His death, May 5th, 1821, made little sensation, as all minds were engrossed with the Greek revolution, which followed closely on that of Naples and Spain, and its possible consequences to the so-called balance of power in Europe. Much as the Continent had been stirred by his supremacy, it in reality left no permanent effect but the ruin it brought on France, which has never since occupied the position she filled in the time of Louis XIV., and to the eve of the great revolution. Napoleon did not create his era, but was the creature of it, guided by no principle, but moulded by events, while Alexander inaugurated a new era for Russia, and introduced the reforms of the revolution to order and legitimacy in Europe, while he checked a new revolutionary spirit by peaceful methods without being compelled to restrain it through compromising the independence of other States.

Many of the generals and statesmen engaged in the long war had preceded Napoleon to the grave; among others the Prince de Condé, Prince Alexander Kurakin, Platof, Barclay de Tolly (created a Prince in 1815), and Vinzingerode, who all died in 1818; Blucher a year later, and Schwartzenberg, always a bon vivant, found peace more trying than a campaign, and died of apoplexy in 1820. In 1818 Benningsen, who was made a Count after Leipsic, also retired from the Russian service.

Alexander was detained by illness more than the pressure of public affairs at Laybach, for he was again attacked with erysipelas, and at the end of March received the news of an insurrection in Moldavia and Wallachia, headed by Ipsilanti, the grandson of that Hospodar beheaded at Constantinople in 1807, and himself an officer in the Russian service. He issued a proclamation indirectly holding out to the people the hope of Russian assistance, and at the same time wrote to Alexander to offer to drive out the Turks, and to deliver the Danubian Principalities into his hands. Russia had just closed a long diplomatic dispute with Turkey, and yielded a small strip of territory in exchange for the protectorate of the Christians in the Mahometan dominions; a treaty renewed by Nicholas, and the resistance offered to it by the Turks in 1853, brought on the Crimean war. The Czar at once disowned Ipsilanti's proceedings, and with Austria declared a strict neutrality. He struck his name from the Russian army list, and wrote to tell him that to assist revolted subjects or accept territory from them was entirely inconsistent with his principles. Low and debilitated from his illness, Metternich tried to persuade him that (whether true or false) this rising, and an insurrection which broke out almost simultaneously among the Greeks in the Morea, was but a link in the long chain of rebellion* which, extending through France, had reached Spain, Piedmont, and Naples, and finding sympathy in the German universities and Poland, had even fastened upon his favourite regiment which was often on guard in the interior of the Imperial palace, and was spreading its ramifications through Russia. But it was so unnatural that a Russian Emperor and the protector of his co-religionists should not sympathize with the Greeks in their gallant struggle for independence, that the Turkish Govern-

* Although the Duke of Wellington was never guided in his opinions by Metternich, whose "pitiful hypocrisy" he contrasts with the "honest straightforwardness" of the Emperor Nicholas, he still maintained this opinion, and believed that the insurrection in Greece was mainly promoted by the democrats, in the hope of embroiling Russia with Austria, and dissolving the Holy Alliance.—See Wellington Correspondence for 1826.

ment accused him of being in secret an accessory to the revolt, though as since proved nothing was more untrue. They accordingly violated the treaty as to Moldavia and Wallachia, seized two Greek vessels sailing under the Russian flag, and made a violent attack upon the residence of the Russian ambassador, Baron Strogonof, who had boldly remonstrated against their cruelty to the Christians and their insults to the Greek churches, and was now compelled to turn his palace into a fortress. His protests were disregarded: the angry Porte called on Russia to deny a refuge to the Greek population who were pouring into her territories, and was answered, that as long as the Turkish Empire lasted the Czar would grant an asylum to any Greek who demanded it; and an embargo was immediately laid upon Russian vessels passing through the Bosphorus.

While England, Austria, and France all united to prevent a war between Turkey and Russia, the struggle was carried on in Greece with the most savage cruelty on the side of the Turks. England, in her jealousy for her Mahometan protégé, had delivered up the town of Parga on the Albanian coast to the ferocious Ali Pacha in 1819, and the whole Christian population deserted it with the bones of their ancestors—a touching picture which caused great sympathy throughout Europe. The one idea of Great Britain was to keep Russia out of the Mediterranean, and no one was more aware of this than Alexander. She tried to smooth over every point of difference between Russia and Turkey. The Porte must be treated like a spoiled child for whom allowances should be made, and a *casus belli* with other nations ought not to be made a subject of difference with her. Young enthusiasts from all parts of Europe hastened to the scene of action to assist the Greeks, but were disavowed by their own Governments, who persisted in seeing nothing in the insurrection but secret societies and Muscovite intrigues. In Russia large sums were collected for the Greeks, and Alexander subscribed liberally to the fund for the exiles who arrived ragged and starving on his shores. The Greek Patriarch was hung at the door of his own church and thrown into the Bosphorus, whence his body, rescued by some Christian fishermen, was brought to Odessa and interred with all the honours befitting his rank. In the middle of July an ultimatum arrived from Russia to the Porte. Strogonof was to require an unconditional acceptance of its terms within eight days, or else leave Constantinople with his whole suite. The terms included no cession of territory or other personal advantage to Russia. The Emperor simply exercised the right to protect the Christians which his grandmother had bought by the restoration of Bessarabia and the Greek islands at the peace of Jassy in 1792, and which was confirmed to himself in 1812, when, contrary to the will of England, he insisted on the Servians being permitted to govern themselves constitutionally—a monument of his liberality at the present day. He now demanded the restoration of the Greek churches which the Turks had pillaged or destroyed, and of all property belonging to those churches; the protection of the Greeks from the barbarities of the Mahometan soldiery, and in the exercise of their religion; a proper distinction between the innocent and the guilty; reparation for the murder of the Patriarch, and the gross insults which followed it; and security for the future peace of the Greeks. In conclusion, if these demands were not complied with, he declared " Turkey would be placed in a position of open hostility with all the Christian world; that it would render the Greek defence lawful, as they would be merely fighting to resist inevitable ruin, and Russia would be compelled to offer the insurgents an asylum and protection, because she could not deliver her Christian brothers to the mercy of a blind fanaticism."

When this message was received by the Porte, it required the influence of all the foreign ambassadors to prevent Strogonof being imprisoned, like more than one of his predecessors, in the dungeons of the Seven Towers. He sailed for Odessa, August 9th, 1821, and met with a cordial greeting from his Sovereign, both at Vitepsk and St. Petersburg. As soon as he was gone, the Turks sent an answer to Alexander's ultimatum, and antedated it July 26th, the last day assigned for its reception. The Sultan tried to justify the murder of the Patriarch by the alleged discovery of letters implicating him in the disturbances in the Morea, but these letters were never produced; and also said it was the violence of the dregs of the people, exasperated by those disturbances which had caused the indiscriminate massacres, and the destruction of the churches. Orders were given to rebuild them, and if Alexander would deliver the Greek refugees (who amounted to four thousand at Odessa alone), all the treaties with St. Petersburg should be faithfully executed.

In the mean time Ipsilanti's band was defeated, and their leader fled to Transylvania, where he was quickly consigned to an Austrian dungeon, and it was only on Russia's remonstrance that he was at last released. By refusing to aid him, Alexander hoped to serve essentially the whole body of Christians in the Turkish Empire. He knew if Russia showed the least disposition to profit by the struggle, or even temporarily occupied Moldavia and Wallachia, Austria was prepared to help the Turks with an army in Epirus and Greece, and the insurrection would at once be set down as a Russian intrigue for the destruction of the Turkish Empire, and such, notwithstanding his cautious policy, it was very generally deemed. He hoped in this instance to bripg the grand principle of the Holy Alliance to bear upon the point of dispute, and by a united and energetic remonstrance on the part of all the Christian Powers to procure a semi-independent government for Greece without going to war. And everything might undoubtedly have been so arranged, if jealousy of Russia and her form of Christianity had not stifled all other feelings in the minds of the statesmen of Europe. Metternich worked to draw off the Russian army to put down the insurrection in Spain; and there is no doubt that a war with Turkey would have entailed a war with Austria (probably aided by France and England); for in 1828, Russia was only left unmolested to carry on hostilities with the Porte by the declaration of Charles X., that at the first shot fired by Austria on Russia, he would pour his army into Germany and Italy. But at this time Louis still occupied the throne of France, hating Russia all the more for his weight of obligation, and anxious to occupy his restless people with a popular war. Alexander remembered Pitt's assertion when the British Government remonstrated at the annexation of Georgia, "that the English people could not be induced to permit the destruction of the Turkish Power." They had a traditionary attachment to the

Porte. If he attacked Turkey single-handed, he would at once be opposed by all Europe, and he had not forgotten the secret treaty at Vienna; so that the forces intended to deliver the Greeks would be wasted in defending his own empire. Only nine years had passed since an invasion which Napoleon himself thought Russia could not recover for one hundred years, and his people were still paying the extra income-tax, levied to support that war, and not taken off till 1823. Time was essential to his finances before beginning another; and he was still carrying out reforms and improvements in his empire, for which money was his most urgent need. What adequate advantage had the costly wars for the deliverance of Germany and France, and the last war with Turkey, really brought to Russia? Might not another, though equally successful, have the same result? What had he not sacrificed to satisfy Poland's cry for independence? and she was already the vulnerable point in his empire where Austria could carry on intrigues in case of a dispute. To make use of Russia and then turn against her was the system invariably pursued by her allies. A tedious campaign might only end when Russia was exhausted, by the other nations of Europe closing in and wresting Turkey from her grasp; and as was the case in 1792, the Greeks might suffer all the more for the efforts Russia made in their behalf. There was a very small Russian fleet in the Black Sea, while the Turkish navy was well manned and strong. The Russian fleet in the Baltic, blocked in for half the year by ice, could only be serviceable to Greece in case of England's assistance, as she must pass Gibraltar, and have a port to refit in the Mediterranean Sea, and a fleet was essential to protect the Greek Islands and the Morea from the extremes of Turkish vengeance while Russia was advancing with her armies from the north.

Castlereagh addressed an elaborate letter (July 16th, 1821) to Alexander, to dissuade him from any interference in the affairs of Greece; and from that time till Alexander's death an active correspondence was kept up on the subject with the British Government, which after stating that it did not consider the disputed points justified a war between Russia and Turkey, at last definitely declined to join in any protest, or take any measure tending to release the Christian subjects of the Sultan from his control. Then Alexander, who had long been silently preparing his army, and collecting funds to enable him to support the war, single-handed if necessary, against all Europe, sent in his final ultimatum to the Turkish Government, when his death, and the ensuing troubles in Russia, postponed the war, and perhaps saved the Ottoman Empire.

A conflict between Turkey and Russia in 1821–2 must have been desperate, for the formidable guard of Janissaries still existed, and bands of Asiatic fanatics were being collected from all parts of Asia Minor to join in what was termed " a holy war of extermination against the Muscovites." But Russia possessed a more tried and enthusiastic army than in 1828. Alexander was himself an experienced general, perhaps the best in Russia, and would have led them with all the prestige obtained by previous victories. In the seven years' struggle the Greeks in the Peloponnesus were reduced to half their number, and their country turned into a desert. The Christian population in Roumelia could never have been much support, for they were without arms, but they were also decimated, so that in 1828 Russia had no other ally in the war.

In a memorandum (April, 1822) Wellington enumerates the four points, " the adoption of which by the Porte would induce his Imperial Majesty to resume the diplomatic relations of his Court with the Porte." They were those already stated, and also that the Porte should withdraw its troops from Moldavia and Wallachia, and name the Hospodar for the government of these provinces in conformity to the treaty with Russia. " The justice of these demands," he adds, " has been admitted by all the allied Courts, and they have been urged upon the Porte, who neither denies their justice nor declines to carry them into execution." However, in the delay which had elapsed before carrying them into execution Russia increased her demands on account of the ferocity the Turks displayed towards their Christian compatriots, and placed a proposal " under the consideration of the allied ministers at different Courts for the adoption of a plan for the amelioration of the condition of the Greeks under the rule of the Porte." The Turks, suspecting this, " had more than once called upon the allied ministers at Constantinople to guarantee them from ulterior demands of Russia." .... "It will be necessary to bring back the Russian demands to the exact state in which they were defined when first made, and then to convince the Porte that no more is in contemplation than expressed in the original demands." If a war breaks out between Russia and Turkey, the Duke entertains "no doubt as to the result. The Turkish Government in Europe will, in fact, be destroyed, which will probably be the smallest misfortune consequent on this state of things. This alone ought to induce us to adopt some strong measure to extricate the world from the existing difficulties. But when we consider that the serious operations in which the Emperor of Russia will be involved in the east of Europe must occupy his whole force; that the occupation chalked out for the Austrians in Italy, and which the events in the east of Europe will tend to render more onerous, will take up their whole force; and that there is nothing which can be trusted to check the tide of revolution from the Atlantic to the Austrian frontiers; that the first step taken by the Emperor of Russia in the course of this warfare will give rise to a most important question between him and the Emperor of Austria, the difficulty of solving which will be augmented by every subsequent step; and that these difficulties can end only by putting the two Imperial Courts in positive opposition to each other, and by the dissolution of the quintuple alliance, and probably a general war in Europe—I think it will be admitted that we should allow no trifling consideration, nor no speculation upon the advantage of having our ambassador at the Porte at a particular period, nor upon the difficulty of getting him back again, to prevent us from taking a step which may preserve peace and all its existing advantages. It must be observed that if it is right to adopt these measures" (recalling the English ambassador till the Emperor of Russia's first demands were complied with), "no time should be lost in adopting them. If the Principalities are not evacuated, I don't see how the Emperor can avoid marching early in June." But in spite of the massacre of Chios, and the proclamation of their national independence by the Greeks, the English Cabinet could not be brought to take even so strong a measure as the recall of her ambassador, Lord Strangford, who was supposed to have great influence over the Divan, and to be exerting it successfully to preserve peace and for the British interests. The British ministers hardly regarded those as Christians who adorned their churches with pictures and kept the days of saints; they rather preferred the "sublime simplicity" of the Mahometan worship; and to induce Alexander to shut his eyes to the slaughter of his co-religionists, they sent the Duke of Wellington to the Congress of the Allied Sovereigns, who met at Vienna and Verona in October, 1822. He went with instructions to advise non-interference, and if possible to maintain the grand alliance.

CHAPTER VII.

1821—1825.

THE LAST YEARS OF ALEXANDER'S REIGN.

ÆTAT. 43—47.

WHEN Alexander returned from Laybach he found all Russia greatly excited by the Greek Revolution, and the army eager to be led against the Turks, to gain laurels and decorations under the eye of their monarch. Count Capo d'Istria, the joint Minister for Foreign Affairs, a native of Corfu, was a member of a Greek society for the emancipation of his race from the Mahometan yoke; and he worked cautiously to instil his views into his colleagues, while Nesselrode, led by Metternich, acted according to the Austrian minister's advice. "Metternich," wrote Capo d'Istria, in 1825, "has decided to re-establish the Sultan's authority over this unfortunate people. During four years he paralyzed and deceived the noblest sentiments without respect to the delicate position of Russia, nor to her interests, abusing constantly the confidence accorded to him, and only making promises to break them." Metternich acted up to his professions as the patron of tyranny; but Great Britain, the friend of national independence, sternly repressed any sympathetic movement in the Ionian Isles, and only used her influence so far over the Sultan as to induce him to refrain from actually defying Russia, and giving her a personal grievance, regardless of the Greek heads posted on the gates of the seraglio and the sounds of mourning rising up from every part of Greece. Canning (who succeeded Castlereagh) wrote, "there was certain, sooner or later, to be a war between Russia and Turkey, but the longer the Allies could delay it the better;" and diplomatic negotiations were protracted till the best part of the Greek population had fallen victims to the violence of the Kurds and other wild tribes brought from Asia; and when Lord Strangford succeeded in persuading the Sultan to allow Russian vessels to enter the Bosphorus (the Turks were beginning to feel some inconvenience from the loss of Russian corn), the British diplomatists thought the Emperor had no longer a cause for complaint.

Capo d'Istria's complicity in the Greek secret society caused so much dissatisfaction to the Austrian Cabinet that he was obliged to leave the Russian service, and at first retired to Switzerland to watch the progress of events. Madame de Krudener, his warm personal friend, had not ceased to plead the cause of the Greeks in St. Petersburg from the moment the insurrection was announced; and she preached to as large an audience and with the same vehemence as formerly, when she exhorted her auditors in Paris to repentance. In her warmth she spared neither her Sovereign nor his ministers, and aided by the press and the Russian clergy, who were instilling the same enthusiasm into their flocks, she seemed likely to work up the whole country to a pitch of frenzy against the Turks such as it had felt in 1812, when invaded by the French. At last (in 1821) Alexander broke silence, and in a letter of eight pages told her he earnestly desired to fulfil the will of God, but could not yet, with consistency or with real advantage to the insurgents, mix himself in the affairs of Greece. He feared to favour revolutions which had already produced so many victims and so few happy men, and he had contracted obligations with his allies not to act in disunion with them, and could not at present take another part with honour. Then blaming the freedom with which she censured his Government, he told her, as a friend, that in adding to the embarrassments of his ministers and fomenting agitations round the throne, she failed in her duties as a subject and a Christian, and her presence could not be tolerated in the capital unless she was silent on conduct that he could not conform exactly to her wishes. He sent this letter by Alexander Tourguenef,* who was one of his household and her personal friend—a well-known enlightened patriot—with orders to read the letter† to her and bring it back to the Emperor. She listened with re-

---

* Tourguenef's brother was a conspirator.
† Vie de la Baronne de Krudener, par M. Eynard.

spect, but not being convinced, left St. Petersburg to join the Princess Galitzin, who had established a colony of Tartar converts in the Crimea. Her son-in-law and daughter accompanied her; and a French lady, said to be the once famous Comtesse de la Mothe, sentenced by French judges to be publicly flogged and branded in the reign of Louis XVI. The ladies preached in the open air to the wondering Mahometans in Southern Russia; and Madame de Krudener died there December 25th, 1824.

The revolutionary flame lighted throughout Europe inspired the opposite party with corresponding alarm, and this regarded Alexander* as the bulwark of vested interests and established law. At Laybach he induced the King of Naples to offer a constitution to his people—a promise afterwards withdrawn—and restored peace to Italy. In Russia the ministers were perplexed by the vague rumours of a conspiracy and the mutiny in the Guards, which seemed hardly explained, and those among them who had once supported liberal measures now became decided advocates of despotism. On their urgent solicitation a censorship was put upon the press, though it was a very mild one, for books were not admitted into Russia in the reign of Nicholas which were freely circulated in the time of Alexander; and although the Emperor could not be induced to re-establish the secret police, Aratchaief and Miloradovitz maintained spies to enable them to search out the disturbers of the peace in their respective departments. Prince Galitzin, the Minister of Education and Public Worship, and Admiral Shishkov, the Secretary of the Empire, both began to think that the education of the working classes was an error, and had been carried much too far; and the Archimandrite Photi launched the thunders of the Church against the English Bible Society, and those who advocated the translation of the Holy Scriptures; for several ignorant soldiers to whom they were distributed cut off their hands, put out an eye, and otherwise mutilated themselves, in obedience, as they supposed, to its precepts; others turned Jews, and a vast secession took place to the numerous fanatical dissenting sects in Russia. To add to the confusion, Magneski (Speranski's colleague), now Governor of Kazan, propagated freemasonry and German illuministic

* See Madame de Genlis, &c.

ideas into his province, so that Alexander is said to have regretted the banishment of such staunch Churchmen as the Jesuits. Photi's correspondence shows his bitter hostility to Galitzin and Tourguenef, as well as to all who had advocated the introduction of "the English heretics" into Russia: "Tourguenef, who disputes the authority of us, the heirs of the Apostles;" and as his religious influence over Alexander increased, he induced him to dismiss several foreign professors in the Russian universities whom he thought used their power to draw their pupils away from their fathers' faith. Still nothing could persuade Alexander to give up his annual subscription to the Bible Society, or to impede its work. Seraphim, the Archbishop of St. Petersburg, once its friend, followed the course of the stream, and Aratchaief, the disciple of Photi, was its deadly enemy. While Aratchaief worked assiduously to protect Alexander from assassins or revolutionists, he tried at the same time to undermine all who stood high in his regard. With extraordinary want of foresight, he lost no opportunity of showing his dislike to Alexander's younger brothers; and when the Emperor was away from the capital, and he was authorized to give out the daily orders to the aides-de-camp, he delighted to keep Nicholas and Michael waiting hours in his antechamber, transacting business with every other official before he gave either of them an audience. His loud voice was often the only one Alexander could hear, for his deafness had much increased since 1818, and being variable, important conversations with him were sometimes obliged to be written down. During his long absences from St. Petersburg, and when he was ill in 1824, Aratchaief was his chief substitute, and at other times seeing him daily, had more opportunities than any one else of imparting his own views. His influence has, however, been overrated, and was certainly on the wane when Alexander died.

Russia has never been a persecuting nation, but the spirit of her clergy was roused now by the barbarities inflicted on their fellow religionists in Greece and the British sympathy with Turkey during the contest. The English Evangelicals, such as supported the Bible Society in St. Petersburg, called the Greek form of worship idolatry; and to Photi this intolerance seemed to explain the British policy, which he thought was exercising such a fatal influence over the Russian Cabinet, and exasperated him to the borders of fanaticism in support of a martyr Church. A Russian who had destroyed the picture of the saint found in most houses of the lower class, was arrested on the strength of an old law of Peter the Great, condemning a man for such an offence to be imprisoned the first time for a week in a monastery, the second to receive eight blows with the knout, and the third to be discharged as incorrigible; but the Emperor, always inclined to mercy, practically dismissed the case by writing underneath the sentence, " Let our illustrious ancestor's penalty for the third offence be adopted." With Photi all penitence was as nothing without almost lifelong penances, and Galitzin's extravagant youth was brought forward by him as still existing sins, " because," said the stern monk, " he was not atoning for it by a sufficiently severe penance." One day they met in the chapel of the Countess Orlof, and Photi reproached him for his toleration of the Protestants, for the unexpiated follies of earlier days, and intimated that his visits to the houses of the members of the English Bible Society were actuated by less creditable motives than religious intercourse. Galitzin appealed to the Emperor for redress, but he refused to interfere. Galitzin was extremely mortified, and his retirement in 1824 is supposed to have been in consequence, although he still continued a constant guest at the Imperial Palace.

The Emperor himself only intended the repressive measures to be temporary, to tide over a disturbed epoch, like the suspension of the Habeas Corpus Act during an Irish riot; and the statements of the conspirators on their trial in 1825 show they were not instituted without a cause. Pestal, the most able of those implicated, was colonel of the Viatka regiment, and as early as 1817 organized a society called the Union of Salvation, or Worthy Sons of the Country, with the object of deposing the reigning family and establishing a republic; and the idea of a military insurrection occurred to them in 1821, after the example of Spain and Naples. A meeting was held in 1820 at St. Petersburg, in which the conspirators advocated a republic, except Colonel Glinka, who proposed to offer the crown to the Empress Elizabeth. At the next meeting all voted against a monarchy; even the British Constitution was not sufficiently liberal. "Half-measures are no good," said Pestal, advocating the extermination of the Imperial family; "we must make a clear house;" and one enthusiast offered to assassinate the Emperor with his own hand. Subsequently, when they formed a union with a secret Polish association, Pestal inquired if its leaders were prepared to treat Constantine as the Russians were prepared to treat his brothers; but was answered, "No Pole had ever imbrued his hands in the blood of his Sovereign." Many Russian members also objected to the murder of the Emperor, and Mouravief declared he would rather kill himself! Alexander's popularity was the greatest obstacle to their measures, and Pestal and his colleagues laboured assiduously to undermine it. They circulated a report that he meant to live in Warsaw and leave Russia to anarchy, which produced a great impression; and Alexander's character was privately slandered in every way; while he, utterly unconscious of the opportunity it gave his enemies to propagate their falsehoods, avoided society, and spent his leisure in strict retirement. Among the guards stationed about the palace more than one conspirator was at different times placed at his door to take his life, but at the last moment wanted resolution, for Alexander's apparent confidence and absence of all precautions proved a surer safeguard than his father's locked doors and moated fortress.

Alexander's favourite abode was Czarco-Selo, where he occupied two rooms; but the gardens and park were open to the public, whom he would not deprive of a favourite promenade. He was impatient if offered a petition, for there was a tacit understanding that he was not to be addressed during his walks by his subjects; a post-office a mile distant received every letter directed to him, and they were duly placed on his table the same day. As might be expected with 50,000,000 people, these letters and petitions were innumerable, often on very frivolous matters. Two secretaries assisted him to read them, and he spent more than two hours daily in this work alone. In his absence they accumulated, and on his return he redoubled his exertions in getting through the pile: some with a special address were forwarded to him wherever he might be; and except that he is said to have disregarded warnings of the conspiracy, and occasionally complaints against his ministers, there is no proof that he ever neglected giving them due attention; but if he had been liable to incessant importunities whenever he was met in the wide grounds at Czareo-Selo, he must have limited his exercise to the palace. He was not inexorable. If the petitioner persevered in spite of a few severe words, he generally obtained his end. A lawyer had a client who rented a wine cellar in some buildings sold to the Crown for the sake of being removed for the embellishment of the city. One of the clauses of the lease provided that, if sold, the wine merchant should receive from the purchaser 23,000 roubles as an indemnity for having to turn out. The lawyer thought the Government bound to pay this sum as it purchased the building, and his client refused to stir till it was paid. The works remained in suspense, and the wines were being forcibly removed. The lawyer set out for Czareo-Selo, but he did not find the Emperor. In a second attempt he met him, but Alexander simply bowed and went on, returning into the palace, and the same evening to St. Petersburg. A fortnight afterwards, hearing the Emperor was again at Czareo-Selo, he made a third and last effort. It was late in the autumn, and as a north-east wind was blowing violently through the park, it was deserted by everybody except the Emperor and the petitioner, who this time spoke. The Emperor said, rather sharply, "Sir, put on your hat; the air is too cold to remain bare-headed." The young man thought he ought not to obey. "Cover yourself, sir," Alexander added, more impatiently; and as the lawyer still hesitated, the Emperor took hold of the hat, and pressed it on his head himself. Then the lawyer rapidly made his request. Alexander listened, and said in a severe tone, "Take care, sir; do not deceive me; remember the money of Russia is not mine. On what do you found your claim?" "Sire," said the lawyer, "here is a petition." "I shall not take it, sir," he answered, "for to-morrow I shall be presented with a thousand. Look there," pointing out St. Sophia (a small town), "put that paper in the post-office. I shall receive it in an hour." "I will run there, Sire; but at least will your Majesty deign to cast your eyes over the clause of the lease?" and he held the contract open. The Emperor read it rapidly through, and walked away saying, "The claim appears to me to be just; to-morrow the money shall be paid." And it was.

A foreign lady, whose husband was condemned for forgery to the mines, waited in the park at Czarco-Selo with her six children, the youngest an infant in her arms, and threw herself on her knees at the Emperor's feet to ask for a pardon. He would not listen till she rose, and then he said, "Madam, I am extremely sorry for you and for these children, but I cannot interfere with the course of justice." "Ah, Sire," she replied, "does not the Bible say, 'Judge not, that ye be not judged,' and that those who refuse to forgive others must not expect their own sins to be forgiven?" "Madam," he said, "I have no personal enmity against your husband; he has broken the laws of the country, and as guardian of the law I am bound to protect it." Nevertheless, her husband received a considerable mitigation of his sentence.

An English lady was walking with some friends in the garden at Czarco-Selo, when two dogs running by the side of a gentleman at a little distance came towards her, and much frightened her. Their master called them away, and then came up, bowed, and apologized, and was going to walk on; when she, being a stranger, anxious to know the names of the various buildings in sight, detained him to ask him a few questions. He told her the history of the different monuments, and was again about to withdraw when she said, "But I want most of all to see the Emperor; where am I likely to do so?" "Oh, you are certain to see him soon enough, madam," he said; "he often walks here;" and bowing, he retired into a neighbouring wood. A little further on she met a Court official, and inquired who the officer was, describing his dogs, and that he was deaf. "That was the Emperor," he said; "I saw him myself a few minutes ago."

The park of Czarco-Selo, which was under the charge of military invalids, is dotted over with monuments of Catherine's wars and treaties: obelisks, pillars, and kiosks to the memory of Repnin, Romanzov, Orlof, Lanskoi, and Potemkin; it encloses hothouses producing quantities of rare fruits, which Alexander sent as presents to his officers and the people round, a farm containing the finest specimens of various breeds of cattle, lamas presented by the Mexican Viceroy, and flocks of merino sheep; for the Emperor was anxious to improve farming and agriculture throughout his empire. His rooms, as still shown, contained a small collection of books, among others the works of Fénelon, Moore, and Sir Walter Scott; several writing-tables, a strong eyeglass on each, and a hard narrow camp bed or sofa without curtains, blankets, or sheets, but a leather mattress and pillow stuffed with straw in a recess; an English shaving-case, and a shower-bath.

"I do not know if I deceive myself," writes M. Dupré de St. Maure,* " but I frequently observe in Alexander's features a sad and painfully preoccupied expression. If I meet him on the high road when alone in his carriage and he does not try to compose his face, I recognize that same expression. How many times I have said to my wife, 'I have just seen the Emperor. Ah! what shadows and uneasiness there were on his brow!' Nothing is more painful than to be forced to suspect a secret cause of bitterness in him whose glory and happiness is envied by all the world, or to perceive mental sufferings in the powerful being who gives no one else a cause for grief. The kind of life this prince has adopted for some years shows a deep-seated melancholy. In the prime of life he leads a sad and solitary existence. In all seasons he works from six till eight, then walks, and returns to breakfast. At twelve he drives with a servant to Paulovsky to see the Princesses (the Grand Duchess Nicholas and the Empress-Dowager), returning he dines alone or with the Empress, and walks some time. He comes home and is seen no more. He devotes to work or to dreamy walks the hours a Sovereign generally enjoys in friendly society; this is his country life. In the winter palace, except some slight changes, it is the same. At nine A.M. I see him punctually resort to the exercising hall to review his mounted guard. Towards noon he goes often on foot, and always without attendance, to see the Grand Duchesses; towards two he returns, dines, and all is ended as at Czarco-Selo. I have only seen him once at the public theatre. The representations of the Hermitage are quite given up; he very rarely calls on a private family to talk at his ease—formerly it was one of his chief pleasures. He is remarkable for an extreme simplicity and repugnance to the ceremonial of the throne—as if he wished to be the Emperor as little as possible. Except at the grand reviews, where he

* L'Hermite en Russie. He filled a post in the Imperial household.

is surrounded by a numerous suite, he always goes alone and without escort. He only assists at great solemnities when tradition requires his presence. Though writing and speaking very purely several languages, he is said to be indifferent to literature, except M. Karamzin, who sometimes talks with him."* Yet Dr. Lyall, writing in 1825, calls him "the patron of arts, science, literature, and information of every kind." He presented books and astronomical instruments to the Dorpat University, and 30,000 volumes after the fire of 1812 to the University of Moscow, besides an anatomical cabinet which he purchased for 10,000 roubles, and a museum of natural history. His efforts to extend education among all classes of his people, far exceeding those of any of his predecessors, have been described, as well as his early taste for music, painting, and reading; and it was to his credit that he did not indulge it when his whole energies were required by so many more important objects. "The diplomatic corps, so fêted in the time of Catherine, only see his Majesty, except in private audiences, three or four times a year, when he holds a grand Court. In the coldest weather he escapes from the city to go and pass three or four days at Czarco-Selo: he takes with him only the aide-de-camp on duty, yet often this officer never sees him, except when he crosses his apartment to go and walk in the gardens. In short, on the most elevated throne he leads almost the life of an anchorite. . . . . A minister cannot partake of the pleasures of his master who never tastes any. His love of order, and of an extreme cleanliness, shows itself in little things. All the tables and desks on which he writes are admirably neat; he will not put up with the least disorder nor the least trace of dust, nor the smallest morsel of paper not belonging to his work. On all his desks there is a handkerchief of folded cambric and ten pens newly mended; these pens are replaced if they have only served for a signature. Emancipation is one of his ruling ideas. A great part of the acts of his Government bear the impression of it. Under preceding reigns the Crown inherited from a proprietor who died without relations. Now such a one must

---

* At this very time Karamzin, Glinka, and Krusenstern were all publishing their works at his expense; and the poetess Anna Bunina had been sent at his cost to England for medical advice.

free his serfs, and then may dispose of his own wealth. The Government inherits only in case a seigneur has no heirs and dies intestate. The Sovereign's foresight opens many ways to serfs to make themselves heard, and everybody agrees these people are admirable in the expression of their grievances. He then orders a rigorous inquest, and if the complaint is true he punishes the oppressor with formidable severity. We have seen seigneurs degraded from their military rank, and women shut up in a convent. I have been a witness of several brilliant acts of Imperial justice. When Alexander is convinced of the cruel government of an estate he names a commission charged to receive the revenues, and from that moment the nobleman loses all the rights he abuses." Count Sergius Romanzov, brother to the Chancellor, gave entire liberty to his serfs.

"The Emperor sets out for Little Russia on the next 26th of August (1821). This journey will cover an extent of 7450 versts. He will return to the capital November 2nd (o.s.). Once fixed, his projects are immovable. We shudder to see this Sovereign incessantly traverse immense distances at a tremendous speed. He has met with accidents, leaving traces that medical science cannot efface, but his punctuality makes his doctors despair. These distant journeys are so much the more fatiguing, as he must arrive in such a place at such an hour for fear of keeping some regiment or some division waiting which he was to meet. After two or three days passed in a carriage the uncrowned traveller gives himself up to rest and refreshment, but the Emperor relaxes himself from one fatigue by another. A regiment is reviewed, Government officials received, military colonies visited, an establishment created, plans examined, &c. Sleep and food have great trouble to glide into the leisure of so busy a life." On one of these journeys (frequently over very bad tracks, and which another French writer* observes are scarcely credited in France), Volkonski accompanied him in the same carriage, and fell asleep; when ascending a steep hill the horses stopped, and the carriage began to recoil. Without awakening his aide-de-camp, Alexander immediately jumped out, and assisted in pushing the vehicle from behind, while the horses were

* Dumas.

dragged up; and the change of movement rousing Volkonski as the horses reached the summit, he saw the Emperor, covered with dust, taking his place again by his side. "Ah, Sire," he said, "why did you not awaken me?" "It is all right," answered the Emperor; "you were asleep, and sleep is too precious to be disturbed." And he added lower, as if speaking to himself, "It brings forgetfulness." Another of his aides-de-camp was driving with him, and also went to sleep, when his cloak, not being fastened properly, was blown open by the wind. His Sovereign buttoned it for him, lest he should take cold. A snow-storm once obliged him to shelter in a peasant's hut and remain there for several hours, when becoming faint for want of food, the peasant's wife produced some of her own humble fare, and the Emperor paid her* about a hundred times the worth of what he ate; but he took bottles of Neva water in his carriage, lest he should be unable to obtain good water on the road.

To one of his family who asked Alexander if more amusement would not be good for his health, he replied it was time his short leisure hours were spent in trying to expiate the faults of his reign. He told the Prussian Bishop Eylert, whom he met in Berlin in 1818, that he had formerly sought mental peace in diversion, but it was only since religion became the chief object of his life that he had found it,

---

* In 1824-5 a working man could buy more black bread in St. Petersburg than he could eat in a day for a sum equivalent to an English halfpenny; beef cost 2½d. per lb.; an entire quarter of a lamb, 1s.; a shoulder of mutton, 6d.; and other things in proportion. Much has been said about the small salaries of Russian officials being the cause of their dishonesty; but the judges and governors in Denmark had as small a salary, and were noted for their integrity, and the Russian officials were often lodged and their children educated at the Government expense. It was gambling and the extravagant tastes introduced by Catherine II. which kept the Russians poor, and peculation had been general since the days of Ivan the Great. Alexander said that the officials would steal his ships if they knew where to hide them, and would draw his very teeth if they could do it without awakening him; and the "severity" of which many complained in the latter part of his reign, was directed far more against robbery, extortion, and bribery than revolutionists. On one occasion he sent 300,000 roubles to a distressed province, and not a kopek ever reached it. But while the senators were glad to mark out the last for punishment, they were always ready to protect the first; and it is only since the higher education he introduced has borne its fruits in a second generation, that in this respect the Government has been able to effect any real improvement.

though it was not at once.* Even Dr. Lyall writes in 1824 that Alexander "has become an example for good principles and conduct to the potentates of Europe. He really seems to be a chosen vessel, and to have said in all sincerity, 'May I govern my passions with absolute sway, and grow wiser and better as life wears away.' Judging from the past we may prognosticate much happiness for Russia if it pleases Providence to prolong his years. The ardour and inexperience of youthful passion are replaced by coolness, vigour, and perseverance in a private and public course of virtue. The deeds of his life will entitle him to the gratitude of the living, and his memory will be venerated not only as the great but as the good Alexander."†

The father of Pestal succeeded Speranski in the government of Western Siberia, and was one of the most cruel viceroys Russia ever possessed. A citizen of Tobolsk was deputed by

* Eylert's account of the last years of Alexander contains most extraordinary inaccuracies. He was chaplain to Frederick William III. Peter the Great suffered so much from melancholy in the last years of his life that the burlesque of the election of a Patriarch, and ice mountains, now a popular amusement, were introduced in the hope of diverting his mind.

† Dr. Lyall, who lived many years in Russia, and is by no means partial, also says, "It cannot for a moment be contested, even by his enemies, that Alexander is not an excellent Sovereign for Russia . . . the greatest blessing and ornament of his country. . . . Few despots have swayed such a powerful sceptre with equal gentleness and mercy. His solicitude for the good of his country, and his humanity, deserve the highest encomiums. . . . When we candidly take into account the extremely corrupt Court at which he was educated, his early marriage, perhaps not with the object of his choice, the temptations by which so young a Sovereign was surrounded, and the extreme jealousy and rigid coolness of the Empress, we must think his failings greatly palliated, if not excused . . . perhaps not one in a thousand would have conducted himself so well as Alexander. As his years have increased, so has his wisdom, and I am assured he now shows his regret at the frolics of his youth by repentance and the kindest conduct to his Imperial consort, with whom he passes much of his spare time in the evenings. During the campaign he was an example to the whole army; his exemplary endurance of privations, cold, hunger, and fatigue animated his troops. His activity and solicitude were equally the theme of praise, while his affability and conciliatory manners gained him all hearts. His simplicity of manners and mode of life are very praiseworthy. He sleeps upon a hard mattress, whether in the palace or in the camp; he rises early, lives very moderately, employs much time in public affairs, and is indefatigable in his labours. He is extremely firm, and even obstinate in his own opinions. His chief amusement, if such it may be called, seems to be the organization and discipline of the army." Of Constantine, Dr. Lyall writes: "It is said he has begun a reformation, and it is to be sincerely hoped it may be completed before he ascends the throne of his country. But as the Emperor is not much older than he, enjoys good health, and lives most

his fellow-townsmen to carry a complaint to the Emperor, and to elude suspicion took a circuitous route, and delivered his petition into Alexander's hands at Czarco-Selo, entreating him to read it through. Alexander was shocked at the account he read, and talked with the citizen for some time, till convinced that his story was true. At last he sadly said to him, "Go home now, brother; the affair shall be examined." "Sire," replied the citizen, "I cannot go home; rather order me to go to prison. My conversation with your Majesty will not remain a secret. I shall be killed." The Emperor seemed startled, and sent for Miloradovitz, the Governor of St. Petersburg, telling him he must answer for the citizen's life. "Then allow me, Sire," said Miloradovitz, "to take him with me to my own house. I can only insure him there." And the citizen accordingly remained in it till the affair was ended. Pestal was dismissed by a ukaz dated February 2nd, 1822, on the ground of bribery and extortion, and two civil governors and 678 public functionaries in Siberia shared his punishment; but they had so many friends among the commissioners appointed to examine the matter, and also in the Senate, who helped them out of every difficulty, that their judges would inflict no heavier punishment, and though the Emperor sometimes availed himself of his prerogative on the side of mercy, he never overruled the decision of his law courts so far as to increase a penalty. Pestal was living in St. Petersburg in poverty at the insurrection of 1825.

temperately, the probability is that he will outlive Constantine, and who can say that the Emperor may not again become a legitimate father? . . . Truly the Russians have no just cause to be discontented with their Sovereign, who has ever shown the utmost wish to raise their character and to elevate them in the rank of nations." This testimony, written within a year of Alexander's death, besides many other authentic proofs, is of more value than the unsupported charges of those who tried to flatter his successor by depreciating his energy. It was to Nicholas's credit that he admired his brother's self-denying exertions in carrying on his duties, and was prepared to imitate them, and Russia may thank the conspirators of 1825 for turning him away from the liberal views of his youth to the most thorough despotism. All Russian Conservatives asserted that Alexander's mistaken liberality was the cause of the troubles which surrounded the throne in his last days, when the very men, like Pestal, who owed to him their position in the empire, conspired to depose him. Their crude ideas were enough to convince him that the *Tiers Etat* were not yet ripe for representation in Russia; and their conspiracy, and the measures thought necessary to repress it, prevented the reign of Nicholas being a progressive continuation of that of Alexander I.

The Grand Duke Michael was ill in the spring of 1821, and went to try the waters of Carlsbad. On his return he visited Warsaw, where Nicholas and his wife were shortly expected, after their long sojourn in Germany. Constantine referred to the increasing melancholy of the Emperor, and then for the first time told Michael he had waived his claim to the throne. "God grant we may not live to witness the greatest misfortune that can happen to Russia—the loss of the Emperor," he said;* "but if Fate decrees this blow should fall on us before my death, I have solemnly vowed in my own mind to renounce the Crown. I so love and honour my brother Alexander that I am filled with grief and horror at the idea of occupying his place; and my wife does not belong to any sovereign house, and is also a Pole; so the nation could not feel confidence in me, and our mutual relations would always be equivocal. In the mean time it must remain a secret between ourselves; but if ever Nicholas should speak to you on this subject, assure him for me that I shall be his faithful servant to the grave wherever he pleases to employ me; and if he should die in my lifetime, I will serve his son with the same zeal, perhaps even with more, because he bears the name of my benefactor."

The reserve maintained on so important a matter was due to the wish of Constantine himself, and also to his mother, whose early ambition to govern the empire revived at the prospect of her eldest son's premature decline. If Nicholas, whom she had brought up and still treated like a boy, was to succeed his brother, she imagined that she could reign under his name, and by finding him constant trivial occupation in addition to his military duties, she tried to prevent him from acquainting himself with public affairs; but "he, notwithstanding his religious respect for her, knew soon how to free himself from a dependence that his duty forbid him to support.† I was struck," writes Marmont in 1826, "with her imposing but theatrical manner. She sought to make effect by her discourse and striking words. Her active spirit renders her ambitious and greedy of power." Her majestic and hale appearance is described by another traveller in 1824, and that even at the age of sixty-four her waist was *très-serré*,

---

* Korff's Accession of Nicholas I.
† Marmont's Memoirs, book 23.

so as to colour her face; and she made a point of dressing precisely like one of her younger daughters. Both Marmont and Wellington, who visited Warsaw after Alexander's death, affirm that Constantine evidently regretted the throne, and that his abdication had cost him a great struggle. Wellington writes that, " Ever since the death of the Emperor Paul the whole family have been impressed with the apprehension of an attack which was to cut them all off. The Grand Duke Constantine, though respected on account of his talents and other qualities, is not very mild in his temper or manner, and it is supposed that it was a favourite object to set him aside, as the risk of the misfortune would be greater during his reign than if any of the other brothers should be upon the throne. His consciousness of the truth of these reasons induced him to make no objection;"* and this opinion is corroborated by the official correspondence between Alexander and Constantine in 1822, when the Emperor wrote it was " a new proof of Constantine's sincere attachment to the welfare of the empire, and of his care for its stability and happiness." He hoped, at the same time, that the Almighty would " bless the consequences of such generous and disinterested intentions." † It was a received opinion in the Imperial family, that though it had been to the interest of Russia that Alexander should accept the throne, however contrary to his own inclinations in 1801, it was equally to her interest that Constantine should decline it in 1822. Besides Nicholas and his wife the affair was only confided to the Empress-mother, the Grand Duchess Mary, who spent this winter at St. Petersburg, Aratchaief, Galitzin, and the Metropolitan Philarete; and the following year copies of Constantine's renunciation, and a paper by Alexander appointing Nicholas his successor, were deposited in the cathedral of Moscow and the archives of the Senate, not to be opened till the Emperor's death unless demanded back by himself. Alexander's manifesto concluded with a request, that "As it had ever been his highest earthly happiness to protect and foster the welfare of his people, they would now offer up their earnest prayers to our Lord and Saviour Jesus Christ, that in His unspeakable mercy He may receive our soul into His eternal kingdom."

The autumn of 1821 was passed by Alexander in his journey

* Wellington Correspondence. † See Korff.

to Little Russia, and an unusually cold winter set in, during which, owing to several coachmen being frozen to death, he passed a law prohibiting evening entertainments in St. Petersburg when there were seventeen degrees of frost. At the annual blessing of the waters, January 6th, he would not allow the usual escort of guards to be exposed to the weather, though he stood as usual bareheaded and without gloves on the ice during the prayers chanted by the Metropolitan, which lasted twenty-five minutes. Three of the Emperor's fingers were frost-bitten, and had to be rubbed with snow before he could venture into the palace, and one young courtier died from the effects of cold. In the spring he went to Moscow and Nijni Novgorod, where he had built bazaars for the annual fair in place of those burned in 1817 at Makarief, where it used to be held, and then set out for Vilna and Warsaw, on his way to a congress assembled at Vienna to regulate the affairs of Greece and Spain. The vigilance of the more loyal Polish officials detected a communication between the secret societies in the revolutionized parts of Europe and those of Poland, and on this discovery Alexander addressed orders to his Minister of the Interior, Count Kotchoubey, that in future no official should remain in the public service who would not bind himself to abandon any secret fraternity to which he might belong. "The existence in several countries," said the Emperor, "of secret societies, which, under the name of Freemasons, had no other than benevolent ends, but some of which have meddled with politics, has ended by disturbing public peace. The result has been disorders which several Governments have resolved to suppress. Personally I have paid minute attention to everything calculated to injure the empire, and I ought to be more than ever vigilant at a time when, unfortunately, the most insensate abstractions of modern philosophy have elsewhere produced the most deplorable consequences." Pestal, and many others of the conspirators continued, nevertheless, in the Government service. He had been a page in the Imperial palace, and after receiving a wound at Borodino had been nursed with the greatest care in the residence of the Empress-mother. Glinka owed his education and everything he possessed to the Emperor, but was led away by a desire to leave a name in history, and imitate the revolutionary leaders of other nations.

Alexander published a ukaz in September, 1821, announcing the exclusive right of fishing, and the annexation of American territory to the fifty-first degree of north latitude, where Russian settlements had existed since the last century, and which was first explored by Russian subjects. This produced much correspondence with Great Britain. Three years afterwards he relinquished his claim to some settlements further south, as it would have otherwise involved a war with the United States.

The disturbances in Spain still continuing, the merchants and other quietly disposed people in the country urged the allied Sovereigns for assistance. In September, 1822, a fresh insurrection broke out, and Spain and France both separately requested Alexander's aid. France, anxious to employ her dissatisfied troops, proposed to march an army to restore the King if Alexander would send an army into Piedmont to overawe the French republicans in its absence. He stipulated that the Spaniards should retain their constitution if the King was restored. England wished to leave the Spaniards to settle their own affairs, and objected to a constitution being imposed on the King; and Metternich advocated the same course in conversation with the English ministers, while he urged Russia to employ her armies in Western Europe, to draw them off from the direction of Turkey. Châteaubriand was sent as the French representative to the Congress, but carefully concealed the fact from the Emperor* that his Sovereign looked to the annexation of the Rhine provinces as a recompense for settling the affairs of Spain. Wellington attended the Congress for England in place of Lord Londonderry (formerly Lord Castlereagh), who the previous August died by his own hand. He arrived at Vienna September 29th, but finding it was removed to Verona, to accommodate the Italian princes, he wrote home for further instructions before he proceeded. Alexander came, September 27th, accompanied by six aides-de-camp and Nesselrode, and he was met at Verona by Prince Lieven and Pozzo di Borgo from London and Paris, and Tatischef from Vienna. When the Comte de Noailles, Louis's ambassador at St. Petersburg, was retiring, the King sent a list of French nobles to the Czar for him to select another envoy; Alexander chose M. de Ferronays, who came on this occasion to Verona, and

* Châteaubriand's Congrès de Vérone.

Count Caraman and the Duc de Montmorenci were sent to assist him. Lord Strangford, the British ambassador to the Porte, had also arrived, the King of Prussia, and a host of minor potentates, among others Napoleon's widow with her second husband.

William Allen came to Vienna to request Alexander's influence with Francis and the Kings of Sardinia and Naples, to relax their intolerant measures towards Bible societies, Protestants, and all schools for the poor. The Czar denied the story circulated in England, that he was closing his elementary schools. On the contrary, their numbers were increasing. They talked of the Greeks. "He seemed to feel deeply for them, and said their rebellion was organized by the revolutionary secret societies, who wished above all things for a general European war; but they were certainly a most oppressed people, though their resistance was premature, and they were now ten times worse off than before." To a lady in Warsaw who appealed to him on their behalf, he said the first movement of the Russians on the Danube would be the cause of a general massacre in the Peloponnesus unless the Greeks were at the same time protected by a fleet, for their position was so much exposed. He undertook to show Allen's pamphlet on the slave trade to Francis, and to ask him to let it be published in Austria.

Alexander was much annoyed by a statement in one of Lord Strangford's despatches, that Russian agents had stirred up the troubles in the Morea. In a note to Nesselrode, dated Vienna, Oct. 2nd. Wellington* regrets that the Emperor should have expressed his disapprobation through Nesselrode, and says: "Lord Strangford showed that the known conduct of his Imperial Majesty's Government, the events which had occurred, and every fact proved that it was impossible H.I.M.'s Government could have had any concern in producing the insurrection of the Greeks. If he did not proceed further to justify all the servants of the Russian Government who had been employed in the countries which were the seat of the insurrection, it was because his lordship had not in his possession the means of refuting the assertions of the Ottoman Minister. The undersigned regrets that when the précis of the conference of August 27th was laid before H.I.M., the despatch of September 3rd was not likewise brought to his knowledge. If his Imperial Majesty had

* Wellington Correspondence for 1822.

seen this despatch, the undersigned is convinced that those principles of justice which direct every act of H.I.M.'s glorious life would have induced him to refrain from passing a censure on a man to whom it is the greatest satisfaction that he has been the instrument in the hands of his own Sovereign to forward the views of H.I.M. in preserving the peace of Europe.—WELLINGTON."

The Duke wrote to Canning, October 4th, and described his audience with Alexander the day before. " I told his Imperial Majesty, if he had not commenced the subject I should have mentioned it, as I really thought he had not done justice to Lord Strangford, who had made such exertions to serve him and forward his views of peace. I had brought with me a copy of the despatch, taking out the names of the persons mentioned, which I offered for his perusal. He asked, 'Why strike out the names? why should I not be informed who is accused, and what are the proofs?' I answered, I could not make myself the informant against his servants, particularly having no proofs in my hands, and not being certain that the Ottoman Government possessed any. . . . His Majesty asked me very abruptly whether the person charged was M. Capo d'Istria. I answered No, and he then went into a long detail to prove, from the manner of doing business in Russia, no order could ever be sent by any minister, and no person to whom such order was sent was justified in obeying it unless H.I.M.'s approbation and signature were attached to it. The conversation ended very quietly, H.I.M. declaring that he did not intend to censure Lord Strangford, that he would receive him perfectly well (as he did afterwards); but he did not take from me the despatch." Wellington doubts if the Emperor has it in his power to remain at peace upon the terms of the original ultimatum (taking into consideration the state of his army, and its dissatisfaction with his continuing in peace with Turkey). " Since his ambassador withdrew from Constantinople, the Porte have issued orders prohibiting vessels navigating these seas from the use of flags differing from the nation to which they belong. The question is, whether it can be expected that the Emperor of Russia, having such good grounds of complaint against the Porte—having, as I have explained in another despatch, such cogent reasons for war, can sit down quietly in a worse situation than he was previous to the insurrection of the Greeks? . . . A great and powerful country like Russia cannot sit quiet and see the prosperity of its most important provinces checked, and even destroyed, by the capricious orders of its weaker neighbours; and I am anxious that Lord Strangford should be instructed to urge the Porte to give every facility to the negotiation of those Powers for permission to pass whose flags have not yet obtained it. The just rights of the Porte will be preserved, and as the Russian commerce will then be upon a better footing than before, . . . it may be hoped this advantage may enable the Emperor to preserve peace. It is very desirable everything should be done that is practicable to preserve the general tranquillity. Exclusive of the disadvantages which must be the result of engaging the Emperor of Russia in hostilities in the East, and of their probable success, they must bring in collision the two Imperial Courts, or these must agree in some partition of the advantages likely to result from the contest. France cannot remain quiet under such circumstances, and without reckoning upon revolutionary movements which may be fairly counted upon as the consequence of Russia being engaged in a contest in the East, we must expect that these hostilities will eventually involve all Europe.—WELLINGTON."

The Sovereigns and their councillors left Vienna for Verona, where they arrived October 16th ; and Metternich and Châteaubriand successively appealed to Alexander to aid in suppressing the Spanish revolutionists; but as soon as the first ascertained that, far from delivering the country to Ferdinand's vengeance, it was his intention to insist on its Constitution being restored, he altered his tactics, and also urged Châteaubriand to move Alexander in favour of peace. "Metternich," says Châteaubriand, "feigns to be a Russian while detesting Russia. He talked to me of the aberrations of the Emperor Alexander." Both the reports of Wellington and Châteaubriand agreed that Metternich made different statements to them and to Alexander ("whom," says Sir Charles Stewart, "he never really opposed"). Châteaubriand was equally displeased with Great Britain. "Russia alone has been perfectly frank, consistent, and noble-minded." He did not hide from Alexander that the real aim of France in sending an army into Spain, to restore order under the Duc d'Angoulême, was to assert once more the military prestige of the Bourbons. "Sire," he said, "I think that France should lose no time in regaining by her own exertions the rank which the treaties of Vienna caused her to forfeit. With recovered dignity she will become a more useful and honourable ally to your Majesty." Alexander thought it a bad principle to allow France to recommence her interference in other States. As she was resolved to go to war to recover her lost position, it was better to let her do it collectively with the approval of her allies, and as only a member of the Alliance, than to leave her to assert herself independently, and recommence the aggressive system which had made her a curse to Europe; but he restrained the King of Naples from adding to the complication and, at the instigation of Metternich, leaving his States at the mercy of Austria to claim the Regency of Spain, by recommending him to stay at home and take care of his own people. It was also decided that Austria should withdraw her troops from the Two Sicilies.

Châteaubriand had been introduced to Alexander in Paris, but at first avoided a personal interview at Verona, being afraid that his voice was not loud enough to make the Emperor hear. They passed each other daily in an early walk along the Adige, till one morning Alexander stopped to speak to him. In a subsequent conversation he said his aim was to prevent all selfish policy on the part of the great Powers, and to admit of only a general policy to act in common for the benefit of people and kings. He had carried out this principle with regard to Turkey, though nothing would have been more advantageous to Russia than a religious war on behalf of the Greeks, and every effort was made, including ridicule, to induce him to break with his allies. Providence had not placed 800,000 troops at his disposal for the gratification of his ambition, but for the defence of religion, morality, and justice, and to protect those principles of order on which human society depends. "Alexander was the only prince," said Châteaubriand, "for whom we ever entertained a sincere attachment. What are all the other Sovereigns of the earth? —mere necessities!" In their last meeting, an access of melancholy came over him, and he broke off, shook his companion by the hand, and walked away. Dr. Wylie afterwards stated that he was very nervous and much depressed all the time he was at Verona,* and the doctor advised him to divert

* Count Caraman told Dr. Lee in 1826, that at Verona he had often taken long walks with Alexander into the country round, "and that he

his mind by going to Rome, a city he had always desired to see; but he said if he went there an old report would be revived that he was about to become a Roman Catholic.

Wellington received instructions to preserve peace, especially between Russia and Turkey, and "not to discourage any measures the Allies might think necessary to curb the intriguing spirit and repress the dangerous designs attributed to this active and aspiring religious fraternity (the Jesuits), if their concerns were brought under the deliberation of the Congress."* The independence of the Spanish and Portuguese colonies was also acknowledged, and Wellington writes, that "the Emperor of Russia is as much interested as ever in the abolition of the slave-trade." . . . "We have had a stormy week. Metternich afraid lest the Emperor of Russia should return to his capital in a bad humour with the alliance." . . . "The terms of the ancient treaties between Turkey and Russia," he adds, "permit the Greeks to exercise the rites of their religion unmolested, to rebuild their churches, and to be free from persecution." . . . "I have seen the Emperor to-night, and this was the conversation: 'There are eight Sovereigns here, with their ministers, and they all concur in the absolute necessity of putting down this evil (the Spanish revolution). The Sovereigns of Italy are not safe so long as it lasts, nor is France nor Prussia, nor even I. The late Spanish minister in Russia laid out large sums of money to corrupt my officers and troops. I was obliged to send him away. I have a report which I will show, made by the Minister of War to the Cortes in a secret committee, showing the state of their army; nothing can be more miserable, or more destitute of resources than these people. I would attack them with the French army, and move mine and others to their support if wanted.'" Wellington pointed out the military difficulties which Spain presents. 'Well,' said the Emperor, 'I will call upon you some of these mornings, and we'll go to the bottom of the subject.'† From this conversation you see the idea of war is just as strong as ever.

was then afflicted with an unaccountable gloom and melancholy, and believed that he was destined to be miserable and unfortunate. He conceived that this feeling, with the horrible attack meditated on his life, reduced him to a state of utter despair, and rendered him anxious not to live, and induced him to refuse all help."—Lee's Last Days of Alexander.

* Wellington Correspondence for 1822. † Ibid.

However, I think if I can come to close quarters with him upon the operations I shall put them out of his mind altogether. He is too clear-sighted to go wrong if he cannot obtain his object, which is any operation if possible, if not a treaty."

"I really believe," he says again on the 28th, "the Emperor is anxious to settle this Turkish question if he can. I believe I told you it was my opinion, if he chose it, and we did not interfere with a fleet in the Black Sea to prevent him, the Emperor had it in his power to make the conquest of Constantinople in one campaign. It is impossible that he should not see the subject in this light; . . . but he knows he would lose a great proportion of his fine army in the operations against Constantinople; that the war would be one of peculiar hardship and difficulties, rather than of manœuvre and gallantry to those who should carry it on; that many would fall victims to the climate, &c. . . . The Emperor of Russia is in fact in his person the whole Russian Government, and every question into which he thinks proper to enter is decided according to his own personal sentiments and views. There is nobody better acquainted with the whole of the French conduct and intrigues in Spain; nobody has a worse opinion of their Government and of their army." But the Duke imagined that he wished to get out of the Turkish question, "and in order to effect this purpose, required the need of some affair in Spain." The event proved he was hardly just to Alexander, whose zeal in calming Spain was to enable the Allies to turn their whole attention to Greece, without fear of leaving Europe in a state of anarchy. This fear was the motive held out by the British Government and Austria for his non-interference in the affairs of Turkey; and Metternich intimated, if the revolutions could be quelled, Austria would join Russia in proposing some arrangement for the independence of Greece. Wellington adds, that Alexander was very much displeased with the Spaniards, and he believed with some reason, on account of the disrespect with which he had been treated personally in Spain, and the conduct of the Spanish minister at St. Petersburg. "It is not unnatural that a Sovereign at the head of a million of men in arms, among whom there have been some traces of a disposition to mutiny, should feel an inclination to destroy a system founded upon a mutiny which is the daily topic of exultation and boast in the country in which the system is established, and among the Jacobin party all over Europe."

Wellington again writes from Verona: " I waited upon the Emperor, who said he was not at all surprised at our course respecting Spain; he had always foreseen it, but he did not think we were more disposed than others to protect Jacobins and revolutionists; that, even upon our own principles, the conduct of these revolutionary fools was such as to require repression. I answered, there was one ally of which his Majesty had more than once availed himself, and that he appeared to me to have left entirely out of his calculations upon this occasion. He answered, 'Which is it?' I replied, 'Time.' Time will remedy many of the evils complained of as resulting from the Spanish and other revolutions; Time would strengthen France and place her in a situation to be more able to act her part in Europe, because in fact it was to France that we were all to look for the danger by which we were likely to be affected in consequence of the existence of revolutionary principles. I then observed, 'I could not see France go to war upon a revolutionary principle without feeling that the world was in danger, and I would rather trust to time for a remedy to the mischief to be apprehended from these revolutions than incur such a risk.' The Emperor replied, while we were waiting for the remedy of time much mischief would be done, and the *bons gens* would be lost. . . . He hoped I was satisfied with what he had done respecting Lord Strangford. I told him that I was much obliged to him, and was convinced that he had adopted the measures most likely to bring his affairs at Constantinople to a satisfactory termination."

Alexander thought the commonest feelings of humanity must at last bring his allies to aid the Greeks by diplomacy, if not by arms; and after his death, when it was known the Turks contemplated the entire extermination of the Greek population, and planting Egyptian colonies in their place, they began to see the affair from the Russian point of view, for the young untried man who then filled the throne of Russia was not the same object of jealousy as the Prince who had led her armies from Vilna to Paris. Tatischef told the British ministers at Verona that the good treatment of Greece was the *sine quá non* of his Majesty's reconciliation with the Porte; and Wellington wrote from St. Petersburg in 1826, "The success of the other Powers in obtaining justice for the demands of the Russians rather increases than diminishes their irritation, and many of them think the late Emperor (Alexander) was cajoled by the Allies to sacrifice the true interests of his empire in order to attend to their interests in other parts of the world."

The Servian ambassadors went to Constantinople by Alexander's advice in 1820, but were detained there contrary to the law of nations; the Morea was fast becoming a desert; and, as Wellington says, "The system of disrespect, and in some instances of insult, to Russia which the Turks have pursued, created a degree of irritation in St. Petersburg which it is impossible to describe." And yet Great Britain, France, Austria, and Prussia united in urging Alexander, for the sake of the peace of Europe, of which he had constituted himself the guardian, not to employ his forces in an absorbing war in the East; but when he proposed at once to secure the peace of Europe by suppressing the revolutionists, England and Austria endeavoured to hold him back. In this Spanish war he saw the means of restoring Greece, and showed his consistent liberality by wishing to give Spain a constitution. "It is certain," he said to Châteaubriand, "that Ferdinand must not be left to himself, as he will fall back on all the errors that so nearly ruined Europe. He will need a council, both as rein and bridle." But this policy was beyond the comprehension of his allies.

When Spain and Naples were both at peace he again sent a memoir on the state of Greece to England and the great Powers. "The deep and lively interest felt by his Majesty and his nation for the fate of their co-religionists," was urged as a reason for hastening the pacification. Yet so averse was the Tory Government to assist the Greeks, that their ambassador told Nicholas in 1826, that when he had presented a remonstrance, if the Turks did not attend to it the British Cabinet would not consider that as justifying war. At Verona, in 1822, the Allies undertook to obtain satisfaction for Russia in her demands on the Porte; and after a long and difficult negotiation Alexander sent M. de Miniacky as his chargé d'affaires to Constantinople, December 1st, 1824, at which time he had again urged the British Government to combine with him in a joint note to the Porte, or to send a representative to attend a conference at St. Petersburg. When both those requests were coldly refused, and "time" again invoked as an ally while the Turks sent an army of Asiatic fanatics to lay waste Wallachia, Alexander resolved to separate from the Alliance* and declare war himself on behalf of the Greeks and the Christian population of Roumania; and that of 1828-9, ending in the separation of Greece, was merely the result of this determination. In 1826 Nicholas told Wellington that he was his brother's heir by his will, and considered himself bound to carry out his last wishes and intentions as to the Greeks. "The late Emperor," his Majesty said, "imagined he had not been treated handsomely, and had determined that he would consult with no one. He should therefore follow his example, and should inform his allies of his determination after consulting with the English Government, who appeared better able and disposed to assist him."† All this time the Liberals hurled abuse on Alexander; for, ignorant of these diplomatic manœuvres and correspondence, they imagined he showed a

* "Austria," writes Canning to Wellington, February 10th, 1826, "never pretended to us to look for any other result from the conferences on the subject of Greece than to gain time, although to the Emperor Alexander Metternich held out expectations of an impression to be made on the Ottoman ministry, which would bring the Porte to reason and place the fate of Greece in the hands of the Alliance. So little pains indeed were taken by Prince Metternich to disguise the real meaning of all these promises in Paris last year, that the facility and almost dupery of the Emperor became matters of common talk, which being faithfully reported to H.I.M. by his ambassador Pozzo di Borgo contributed more perhaps than the subsequent failure of the steps taken by the several missions of the Allies at Constantinople to irritate the feelings of the Emperor Alexander, to destroy altogether his confidence in his allies, and to throw him back upon himself in that temper of gloomy abstraction in which it is now known, through Lord Strangford's despatch of the 17th of January, that he had resolved upon immediate war."—*Wellington Correspondence.*

† The Duke was sent to St. Petersburg to attend Alexander's funeral and obtain a promise of peace with Turkey from his successor, not, as an eminent historian says, to obtain Russia's joint co-operation in obtaining *good terms for Greece.* He did not share the common belief that Russia was actively plotting insurrections; and with respect to the Ionian Isles, "the Russian employés abroad think they have the same right that all his Majesty's subjects enjoy of plotting and contriving against and revolutionizing every country which they approach. I am not quite certain that some of our Liberal diplomatic servants have not an eye to revolution in some of the countries in which they are placed. Some of them I know have. But I believe the Russian Government have as little to say to such schemes at present as we have."

criminal indifference to the sufferings of the Christian subjects of the Porte.

The Emperor left Verona* December 22nd, passing through Bohemia, and staying for a few days at Warsaw. His note to the provisional government of Spain reminded it that he foretold the Spanish calamities in 1820, from the moment when perjured soldiers betrayed their Sovereign; that his fears had been justified, anarchy having marched in the train of revolution, and the colonies detached themselves from the mother-country; properties had been despoiled, blood has flowed in the palace of the King, the monarch and his family having been reduced to a state of captivity. "The Spanish revolutionists represent the revolution of Naples and Piedmont as their work, and announce that their plans of overthrow have no limit. They are stirring up strife in a neighbouring country, and attempt to gain accomplices in the most distant States. France is obliged to guard her own frontier. . . . This can only be the work of a party, for Spain's traditions are monarchical, and the loyalty of her people well known." The Russian ambassador was ordered to ask for his passports.

This note drew upon Alexander a torrent of invective from one of the Liberal orators in the House of Commons (Brougham), compared with which Napoleon's answer to his remonstrance on the murder of the Duc d'Enghien was mild. The speaker ended by reminding Francis of his debts to the English Government and his cruelties in Milan, Frederick William of his broken pledges to his people. "Even the Emperor Alexander, if the annals of Russian story may be trusted, however pure in himself, and however happy in always

---

* Before his departure he saw Allen at Verona, November 26th and 30th, for an hour or two in the evening, when, after some circumlocution, the Friend told him how afraid he was lest he should commit himself with others whose views and principles were not as pure as his own (alluding probably to Metternich, who, says Wellington, was Alexander's chief counsellor at Verona, "though, in order to keep this place, he is obliged to conform the government of Austria entirely to the Emperor's views"). Alexander took it very well, but told Allen he always weighed things in his own mind, and acted according to the best of his judgment. The Friend spoke of the advantage of mental prayer, even when discharging outward duties, and the Emperor said that it was his constant practice, and he did not know what he should do without it. "He pointed to a great pile of papers which, notwithstanding the interruptions he has here, must be got through."

having agents equally innocent, is nevertheless descended from an illustrious line of ancestors who have with exemplary uniformity, dethroned, imprisoned, and slaughtered husbands, brothers, and children, not that I can dream of imputing those enormities to the parents, or sisters, or consorts; but it does happen that these exalted and near relatives have never failed to reap the whole benefit of the atrocities, and have ever failed to bring the perpetrators to justice. In these circumstances, if I had had the honour of being in the confidence of his Majesty of all the Russias, I should have been the last person in the world to counsel my Imperial master to touch upon so tender a topic." He asked if blood had never flowed in a Russian palace, and went on for some time in much the same strain. On March 15th, Alexander, in a despatch to Count Lieven on the Spanish war, desired him to recall to the British Cabinet the fact that in similar circumstances the Opposition had met with eloquent adversaries in the members of the present ministry, and Lord Liverpool had been often of this number, and had more than once tried to strengthen the ties of the alliance, which he now seemed to despise. Lieven was desired to explain himself in this sense to Mr. Canning, and to observe to him that his Imperial Majesty was surprised to see England alarmed at the King of France expressing the principle she has implicitly admitted in all transactions which had France for an object, and that she now declared a cause to be just and unassailable in Spain, which she had sustained neither in Naples nor in Piedmont.*

The most unjust suspicion that Alexander had excited the revolution in Greece for the sake of crushing it, prevailed in consequence of such a line of conduct being adopted by France in Spain;† and there is little doubt that if Russia had

* Canning (Minister for Foreign Affairs) answered this speech by asking the Opposition to look back only for ten years and see that, if England had not been leagued with despots, if despots they could be called, "we should never have been able to override that Colossus of tyrants who, as it were, united all others in himself." He also observed that England had changed in the quality and elements of her society. England was now adopting the very policy of recognizing revolutionary Governments which Pitt had blamed in Paul, and which in 1801, 1806, and 1808 would have enabled her to make an advantageous peace with Napoleon.

† In a conversation with the French ambassador at St. Petersburg, September, 1823, Alexander said: "You complain of the mistrust shown

advanced to the aid of Greece in 1823, the few sparks of sympathy for the insurgents in Western Europe would at once have been extinguished, and three Powers at least been arrayed against her on behalf of Turkey, while Prussia, true to her favourite policy, would have been neutral. The applause with which Brougham's speech was received showed Alexander his own unpopularity in England. He alluded to the base motives attributed to him to an Englishman, who quoted Wilberforce's address to a missionary meeting to show there were others who did him justice: "I speak not of Alexander the Great, the destroyer of man, but of the Great Alexander, the friend of man." He seemed touched by it, and changed the subject, perhaps reflecting that for the thousands who had perished in the wars of his Greek namesake, his own military enterprises had cost Russia hundreds of thousands. His campaigns had already extended over twice the time and a much wider extent of country than the Macedonians, and yet they were perhaps not ended, for there was every probability of the dilatoriness of his allies forcing Russia into another war.

In 1822 died Prince Plato Zoubof, the last favourite of Catherine, one of the murderers of Paul, and twenty-six years

towards you by the Allies. You expect that without scrutinizing your intentions or right to advance, they will blindly subscribe to whatever you please, and that the Alliance should be but an auxiliary to act only as you shall direct. This is exacting too much. France has not yet given Europe such guarantees as should empower the lesser to control the greater. As you support both the risks and expense of this great undertaking, we ought to leave you entire liberty of action. I have opposed all measures that could constrain you. I have felt all that is due to your national pride, and have taken no offence at the silence in which the name of Alliance has been passed over." He then referred to the Prime Minister's (M. Villèle's) feeble support to the war in Spain. "Had he been as persuaded as M. de Châteaubriand that an entire victory was indispensable, and that the least reverse must be ruinous to France, he would have understood the advantage of her setting her army on foot and her navy afloat. Your troops achieve miracles, but their numbers are everywhere insufficient. Your blockades are ineffectual, and should you fail, those will not be able to console themselves who would not see that by multiplying resources and striking powerful blows they would diminish the dangers of the enterprise, while securing its success and doubling the glory of France. Since M. de Châteaubriand has been minister, he has displayed an energy and ability which gives him a right to our confidence and raises him to the first rank of a statesman, but he is not seconded. This explains and justifies the mistrust you deplore," &c.

Alexander wrote from Vosnesensk on the 28th of October (N.S.) to congratulate the King of France on the success of his arms.

previously the most powerful man in Russia. He was buried with great pomp at the Strelna monastery. The following year Rostopchine returned to Russia, after addressing a long letter to Alexander, in which he drew a striking picture of the state of France. He painted her uneasy at her lost influence in Europe, trying to regain it by means of revolution. "The Frenchman is most vain and ambitious, and believes himself a superior being, because his language is the most widely known. He is convinced, and tries to prove, that the French armies have never been beaten; that in 1812 the elements destroyed the heroes who conquered Russia; that in 1813 the battle of Leipsic would have been gained but for the desertion of the Saxons; that in 1814 it was the treachery of the marshals which delivered Paris to the Allies, and that the battle of Waterloo was only lost because Napoleon had lost his head." He describes the French inconsistency, shallowness, and love of effect. A ninth of the population of Paris was supported by charity, and 6000 proprietors lived in absolute idleness. "Paris is a world, a gulf, a hell for youth, an observatory for middle life, and the Elysian Fields of old age. There we can have everything about us, and lodged on the Boulevards see Europe in review. So every foreigner who has lived there becomes more or less its advocate, forgetting that it is a true Pandora's box from which springs every evil, and no Hope at the bottom. The Bourbons are not loved; opinion is against them. Good sense is contraband in France, . . . and notwithstanding all the disorders, the crimes, and the horrors that this infernal revolution has produced, there are still many who dream of a republic," &c.

Alexander's influence in the French Cabinet, and afterwards at Madrid, procured better conditions for the insurgents in Spain, and a more equitable government than they would otherwise have obtained. "The instructions of the Emperor of Russia, which I have seen and read," writes Châteaubriand, October 17th, 1823, "are extremely liberal in point of the necessity of giving new institutions to Spain. This fact will undeceive those who imagine that Pozzo arrived from St. Petersburg with the cap of the Inquisition in his pocket." The same month Alexander met the Emperor of Austria and the King of Prussia at Czernovitz. In 1823 Czartoriski finally quitted the public service, bequeathing disturbances in the university of Vilna to his successor, Novossilzof. These riots broke out May 15th, and the Prince declared them due to infection from the German universities. Consequently Alexander prohibited the Polish youth from entering those foreign universities supposed to be most in fault. Another attack of fever and erysipelas prevented him from making a projected journey to Tobolsk; but in the summer he passed a few days at Moscow, and in the autumn visited Warsaw and the line of military colonies to the borders of the Crimea: over-fatigue brought on a slight return of the malady, and was perhaps the means of saving his life. A review was arranged at Bobrouisk on the Beresina, where one of the colonels was a leading conspirator. He concerted a plan for seizing Nicholas, who was to accompany him and Diebitch, the chief of the staff; but as Alexander's illness prevented him from attending, the project was adjourned. Again, a similar attempt was prepared for the spring of 1824, when the Emperor was expected at a review at Belaia Tserkof, where he was to occupy a small house in the middle of the park of Alexandria belonging to the Countess Branicka. Some officers, disguised as soldiers, agreed to penetrate into his bedroom and strangle him in the night, when they would at once raise the camp and march on St. Petersburg and Moscow to excite an insurrection through the empire. But Alexander was again kept away by illness. He had gone for a few days to Czarco-Selo at the end of January, 1824, and taken his usual morning walk, often extended for two or three leagues in the park, when he was caught in a heavy shower of snow and rain, and received a thorough chill. On his return he retired to his room, where his dinner was brought to him, but he could not touch it, and in the course of the evening was attacked with fever and erysipelas, which appeared on his leg, and rapidly spread over his whole body to his head, so that his brain became affected and he was delirious. His attendants removed him in the night in a covered sledge to St. Petersburg, where he was attended by the principal doctors in the capital; and as symptoms of gangrene began to appear they were unanimous, with the exception of Wylie, in the opinion that it would be necessary to amputate his leg to save his life. This doctor, with Scotch caution, reflected that if he died under the operation the Russian nation would be more severe in their criticisms than if he perished from the disease, and he took the responsibility of preventing amputation upon himself. The doctors were threatened by the mob, and were provided with passports in case the illness ended fatally; for as soon as it was known, the most painful excitement prevailed throughout the city: the churches were crowded with the people offering up prayers for his life; and the arrival of Constantine, who came to attend Michael's wedding, February 20th, and also to confide some discoveries of the conspiracy to Alexander, did not tend to allay the universal alarm. At last the complaint yielded to cautery and the lancet, and, after the medical treatment of that day, issues were established in his leg, which began to heal. The first time he showed himself in public nothing could exceed the demonstrations of the popular joy; but he lived so low, in the hope of averting a recurrence of the complaint, keeping strictly to a vegetable diet, and almost entirely on fruit, that his constitutional vigour was not thoroughly re-established, and his nerves never recovered their tone.

This year was altogether one of calamity. His only child, the daughter of Madame Narishkine, had been educated in Paris and at Lausanne, consideration for the feelings of the Empress having prevented him from bringing her to Russia; but now, though only fifteen, she was betrothed to the young Count Shuvalov, an Imperial aide-de-camp, and when once a wife, perhaps the Emperor hoped he might occasionally enjoy her society, hitherto denied him. The young girl, who was particularly amiable and attractive, and the very image of her father, came to Russia for the wedding ceremony. Her health was delicate, and her physician told Madame Narishkine that it would never bear the climate of St. Petersburg; but her mother, anxious for the marriage, and hoping she would be publicly acknowledged by the Emperor, took no heed of this warning, and sent her, under the charge of a governess, to be received in Russia by the family of her betrothed. One day the Empress, walking with her lady-in-waiting in the gardens at Czarco-Selo, unexpectedly met her in company with the Shuvalovs. She stopped to speak to them, and keenly scrutinized her, never having seen her before, then giving her a kiss, she said: "I cannot help loving you for the likeness you bear; it is impossible to mistake it." Shortly afterwards the young girl broke a blood-vessel and very suddenly expired. This intelligence, totally unexpected, was carried to Alexander as he was engaged with a review. He grew extremely pale, and an expression of great pain passed over his face, while he said, loud enough for his aide-de-camp to hear, "This is indeed the punishment of my sins." He did not interrupt the manœuvres, but finished them as if nothing had happened, and made no allusion to the event to his wife till she expressed her deep sympathy with his sorrow. He thanked her affectionately, but never afterwards referred to the subject. The young Sophie Narishkine, as she was called, was buried near the Nevskoi monastery, and all the fashionable world of St. Petersburg followed her to the grave. Her trousseau, which had cost 200,000 roubles, arrived the morning of her death, and Alexander divided it among his sisters. Photi took this opportunity to try and work on the depressed and stricken Sovereign in the interests, as he imagined, of his Church; and he afterwards boasted he had moved him to tears. A ukaz for the colonization of the Jews of the Ukraine appears to have been the result. These people were accused of insulting the Christian worship on the great festivals, and living in "idleness, roguery, and dirt." Possibly their exemption from servitude and the conscription excited some jealousy among their neighbours. They were said to import the plague by their trade in rags; and on August 29th, 1824, the Emperor desired that all who were not physicians or established merchants should return to the occupation of their ancestors, and settle on lands assigned to them, where they were provided with cottages, seed, cattle, and agricultural implements, and relieved from all taxes for some years. They were allowed a year to decide on conforming to the will of his Majesty or quitting Poland and Russia.

In March, 1824, Alexander summoned a number of the provincial governors to St. Petersburg, to consult on an entire reform in the organization of the administration of the Russian empire, as he was of opinion that a system like that of the United States would be suitable to it. They held several meetings, in which these changes were discussed, and decided that they ought only to be introduced gradually; and though the Government of Orel was fixed upon in 1824 as the first in which an experiment should be tried, the matter was still under discussion when Alexander died.

The Emperor went to the military colonies in June, and to Warsaw early in August, and returned for a few weeks to Czarco-Selo before setting off through Moscow to Kazan, Ekaterinberg, and Orenburg in Russian Asia. During this interval some of the troops were encamped at Krasnoe-Celo, and he went almost daily to inspect them, and had sufficiently recovered from his illness to walk a league. The life at Czarco-Selo was described by a visitor as truly monastic. The Emperor still kept on a fruit diet, and took his meals alone. The Empress dined by herself, like her lady-in-waiting, Mdlle. Walouief, who daily accompanied her on foot or on a pony, but at hours and in parts of the park where they were not likely to meet the Emperor, for fear of wearying him. The Court was absolutely deserted. The ministers came by turns, each once a week, to see Alexander, and left immediately after their work. The Emperor retired to rest at ten in the evening, and a military band played under his window for the sake of producing sleep, but always melancholy airs of his own selection. He dreaded noise and light, so that the room in which he transacted his business was darkened by a mass of plants trained across the window, and a wax taper which burned all day in the apartment to seal his letters was carefully shaded. Only the servants, the aide-de-camp on duty, and the lady-in-waiting, besides the Sovereigns, occupied the Imperial residence; the other attendants and officials lived in the Chinese village, where any visitors who came from a distance and wished for an audience were also lodged, and their meals sent to them from the palace. One of these (Madame Choiseul-Gouffier), upon whom he called, asked him for the post of aide-de-camp for her son-in-law. He expressed his sorrow at having to refuse it, but told her to put herself in his place and judge if he could possibly pass over distinguished soldiers, colonels, Poles, who counted years of service—" and of what service?" he added; " constant war and frequent wounds, who looked upon such a post as a reward—in favour of a young man who had never been actively engaged." His refusals, said this petitioner, were always gentle, and as he left the house she followed him to say that she and her husband should ever entertain the most earnest wishes for his happiness. At this word he shook his head, and tears filled his eyes. He set out very early the following morning. It was a cold autumnal day, but the Empress took her usual walk, and remarked to Madame Gouffier, whom she met in the park, that she hoped this journey would do the Emperor good; he was always better after travelling. He made the distance to Moscow in forty hours, two less than had been achieved by Peter the Great, and received an enthusiastic reception at every point of his route. In the desert beyond the Volga he was entertained by a Kalmuck chief in his felt tent, and at Ekaterinberg descended into a Siberian mine and forged a bar of iron after the custom of the Mongul Khans, being the first Russian Emperor who crossed the Ural Mountains. Perm and Orenburg were the furthest points of his journey; but he held out hopes of visiting Tobolsk another year if his life was prolonged. "These wide distances," he observed, "are a real drawback to the prosperity of Russia." Whenever he set out on such an expedition he wound up all his affairs and put everything in order, so that, as he said, "If I die, like Potemkin, in a ditch on the road it need cause no confusion, and I should soon be remembered no more."

Only two days after Alexander's return to St. Petersburg a great misfortune overtook the city. There had been no serious inundations since the year of his birth, till on November 19th, a gale swept from the west, lining the British Channel with wrecks, tore off the roofs of many houses in St. Petersburg, and bringing up a wave from the Baltic, threatened to drown the whole city. As the Neva rose, guns were repeatedly fired from the fortress to warn the citizens of their danger, and on the 23rd it was ten feet above the level of the streets. Great exertions were made to rescue the prisoners and the patients from the hospitals; and the Imperial palace and other public buildings were opened by the Emperor's order to receive the fugitives in the rooms standing higher than the flood. A steamer was floated away, and landed in a field, and a ship of the line hurled into a public square at Cronstadt. Alexander left no steps untried to assist his subjects. He set the example of taking a boat, which was followed by many of the nobility, and rowed about throughout the day, to rescue sentinels and other drowning persons; though notwithstanding their efforts 480 people perished. The loss of property was estimated at 5,000,000*l*., and he headed a subscription list for the sufferers with 50,000*l*. The waters quickly subsided, and every day for weeks afterwards he crossed the Neva, to visit in person the wretched abodes of the ruined poor, distributing money, and with the kindest language soothing those who had lost their nearest relatives, particularly in the villages of Katerinof and Emelianof, where the drowned lay in heaps. The religious consolation he offered them was much tinged with self-reproach, for the morbid state of his mind was shown in the notion that the inundation had been sent as a judgment upon him for the faults of his youth.

At this time there seemed a favourable opportunity for opening a negotiation with Turkey on the subject of Greece, the Patriarch and Greek clergy in Constantinople having been permitted to resume their offices; but it was a temporary spark of conciliation, and backed, as they imagined, by British influence, the Turks were ready the following year to overrun the Principalities again with their savage mercenaries, and renew their defiant attitude towards Russia. Her chargé d'affaires was recalled in January, after only a month's residence at Constantinople, and Alexander again requested the British Government to send a deputy to join a conference assembled at St. Petersburg in March, 1825, on the subject of securing the permanent independence of the Morea. Austria and Prussia sent representatives, though merely to try and avert such a measure; but England refused to have anything to do with it, treating the insults to Russia (which Wellington allowed were most real) as a matter to be easily settled by the English envoy at the Porte. "I have very little doubt," writes Canning to Wellington, January 21st, 1825, "that the Emperor of Russia's anger will pass away; but I hear his Imperial Majesty's mind has received a considerable shock from the various successive misfortunes of the last few months, the death of his daughter, of a favourite aide-de-camp (Ouvarov), and the inundation, and that he is in a state of unusual irritation." "I think it unfortunate," the Duke answered, January

23rd, " that you had not taken your line before you should receive this Russian message, which is moderate enough in manner and expression, although the resolution itself is strong. Count Lieven would be disposed to soften it as much as possible, but I don't think he can, as the harsh part of the communication is the resolution that we shall have nothing to say to any questions between the Emperor and the Turks or the Greeks."*

Alexander was present at the fête of January 13th in St. Petersburg,† where it was reported an attempt was to be made to assassinate him, but he would permit no precautions to be taken, and looked more cheerful than usual, as was observed to be the case when his life was in danger. Twenty-five thousand tickets were distributed, and the people roamed at pleasure through the drawing-rooms of the Winter Palace, till even the Emperor was frequently so much crowded, that in protecting one of the Princesses whom he was conducting down the room, he trod on a merchant's foot. He expressed his regret, and added, " You see how we are pressed; you may do the same by me directly, but I shall not complain of it." " Sire," said the merchant, much pleased, " you have done me no wrong, *on the contrary*." Refreshments were served to all the guests; and in the supper-room, where 600 were seated, the Emperor walked up and down, talking to each of the ladies in turn in a lively manner; etiquette forbade them to rise, and the orchestra played the whole time.

The conference at St. Petersburg on the Greeks ended as unsatisfactorily as before. The note sent by Miniacky in December, 1824, demanding the release of the Servian deputies, and the evacuation of the Principalities, with the appointment of a Hospodar, according to treaties, had never

---

* Wellington Correspondence.

† " The first day of the year 1817 saw the return of the ordinary popular fête; an evening ball at the Winter Palace, and supper at the Hermitage. This assembly is unique in Europe. All classes are mingled in the palace of the Sovereign—the peasant elbows the Prince, and both approach their master. The people take an extreme pleasure in it, and any one must know little of the Emperor not to be sure that he takes pleasure in their pleasure. A Cashmere merchant and Czerny George (a Servian chief) were at the ball. He killed his father, killed his brother, and hung him with his own hands. The Mussulman stove produces these strange plants in Europe."—De Maistre.

been answered; and in October, 1825, he addressed an ultimatum from Taganrog, six weeks before his death, inquiring the reason of his last note having received no reply, and recapitulating his demands, to which were added those he mentioned at the treaty of Verona. He also addressed a private note to Prince Lieven and Pozzo di Borgo, in London and Paris, desiring them to ascertain if the Western Powers were likely to league against Russia in case of a war between Russia and the Porte. The answers did not arrive till after his death, and their opinion was, if he declared war it should be soon. He could have summoned nearly a million of men to his standard; the fleet was increased to seventy ships of the line and eighteen frigates. A commercial panic in 1821 had subsided, and the extraordinary taxes and loans for the French war had been paid off since 1822; the budget showed a considerable reduction on the side of expenditure, and in spite of his liberality, which according to Marmont approached prodigality,* he left a treasure of 4,000,000*l.* from his private revenues. Was this to be devoted to the emancipation of the serfs, or to fulfil the desire of his subjects in the conquest of Constantinople, and at the same time the deliverance of Greece? He fairly avowed to the French ambassador, that unless his Allies† came forward effectually, he must look to his own resources, and there is little doubt that he had resolved to march in the spring on Constantinople. "A crisis," writes Wellington, regarding it from the English point of view, "had arrived in this long pending question, even before Alexander's death, which crisis, if it was not precipitated, was at least not prevented by the system of conferences and joint interpositions. Nesselrode spoke in terms of bitterness and contempt of Metternich's worn-out policy. He declared further, that Alexander had never

---

* "The Emperor Alexander may be the object of various criticisms; but one quality, which no one disputes, is a boundless kindness of heart. His active benevolence, his desire to do good, showed itself every day and on every occasion. It was allied, perhaps, to an uneasy conscience, and to the desire of a tender soul to find some means of blessing. Generous habits resulted from it," &c. "There was not a family in St. Petersburg who were not under obligations to him."—Marmont, 1826.

† Wellington says : "Alexander complained with great reason ;" and no answer had as yet arrived when Nicholas ascended the throne. The Turkish army was a terror to the inhabitants of the Principalities.

relied on France for any honest or useful assistance. . . . The Turks are . . . . aware that the patience of the Emperor of Russia had been at length wearied out, and that the commencement of the war has only been intercepted by that event which has devolved his power and his projects into younger hands."

M. de la Ferronays wrote on March 26th, 1825, to Châteaubriand, that the Emperor perceived by degrees "all those circumstances develop which his penetration had foreseen. His natural enemies, England and Austria, commit errors, displaying weakness and want of skill. All parties have believed themselves able to attach this Prince to their respective interests. . . . The Bonapartists incessantly pester him in favour of young Napoleon, another party in favour of the Prince of Orange, or of Beauharnais, and another again in favour of the Grand Duke Nicholas."

This year Alexander sent surveyors and engineers to map out the districts of the Oxus and Ural, he founded a school for mechanics in Moscow, and might well look with satisfaction at the flourishing state of education and commerce in his empire. "The cares taken by Alexander for the education of youth can hardly be conceived," writes Marmont; and in 1824 he bought a palace from one of his nobles, to establish a college for the reception of cadets while they were waiting for commissions, to prevent them from wasting their time and getting into mischief. He caused several canals to be dug before the inundation, to drain St. Petersburg, and raised and planted the islands of Yelagin and Kameni Ostrov. In 1825 fresh efforts were made to raise the foundation of the city, and a commission was appointed to devise some means of preventing future floods. Its granite quays, its footpaths, the Admiralty, and many public buildings were due to him, and in 1824 he completed the new Michael Palace for his youngest brother. Early in 1825 he spent more time than usual in St. Petersburg, and took his daily walk, generally in plain clothes, along the quays, but in April he went to Warsaw for two months. On May 13th he opened the Polish Diet with a speech, and closed it again, after a most orderly session, in which all the laws proposed by the ministry were accepted. In Warsaw he received fresh information of the existence of the conspiracy, and even the names of some of the leaders, including Pestal. It has been reported, that in view of this crisis, and of this indisputable fact that in the army Constantine was more popular than Nicholas, also that Nicholas' wife seemed unable to bear the Russian climate, he pressed his brother to take the throne in case of its soon becoming vacant, and left him a copy of a constitution by which he was to govern the country. On June 25th he returned to St. Petersburg, and visited the hospitals at Cronstadt, where he ordered several improvements.* He then made a tour of inspection through the military colonies. Constantine and his wife went to Carlsbad, and Alexander's two sisters and their husbands came to Russia. He mentioned to the Prince of Orange, that as soon as he had a prospect of bequeathing to his successor a peaceable throne, he meant to resign it, and retire to some obscure corner of his dominions. The Prince, who was much attached to him, was distressed by such an idea. He tried to show, first in words, and afterwards in writing, that it would be a step fatal to Russia, and certainly misconstrued in Europe. Moreover, had he a right to throw off his responsibility? It would be attributed to a fear of assassination or a love of inglorious ease. Alexander listened courteously, but was not convinced. A higher Will than his own was to decide it.

As the following winter was expected to bring Russia and Turkey into collision, the Emperor planned a tour in the Crimea and to the fortifications on the Pruth for the autumn. The Empress's health became worse, and her physicians, attributing her disorder to water on the chest, which had carried off several members of her family, advised her to try the effect of a warmer climate. Her beauty had long completely disappeared, and her high colour showed the pressure on her lungs, which was afterwards ascertained to arise from disease of the heart. A vague uneasiness seemed to possess her with regard to her husband, and instead of going to Baden or Italy, she begged to be allowed to remain near him, and to accompany him to the south of Russia. He was

* This inspection was a proof of Alexander's careful supervision of the public institutions. An English work had lately appeared praising the management of the Russian hospitals with the exception of that of Cronstadt; and he immediately paid it an unexpected visit to ascertain the truth of this criticism, and adopt a remedy.

pleased by the request, and made inquiries to find the most salubrious spot for her residence. A malaria fever had prevailed during all the summer in Odessa and the Crimea, so Taganrog, which the Emperor had once visited, was preferred, and there he decided to establish their head-quarters, and make his journeys of inspection from it. The Empress talked of returning in January, but he did not as usual fix the day, or even the month. He saw one minister after another, and wound up everything as if for a prolonged absence, but that was his habit. Prince Galitzin was assisting him to arrange some of his papers in his private room, and after expressing a confident hope that he would return in perfect health, observed how inconvenient it would be if anything happened to him while the act of succession remained secret. Alexander seemed struck with the remark, but after a few minutes said the matter must be left in the hands of Providence. On his fête-day he attended a service at the monastery of St. Alexander; Nicholas accompanied him. "The Emperor was gloomy, but nevertheless particularly kind and affectionate to his brother," and among other things told him he meant to give him an estate near Peterhof. The same day they met for the last time at dinner, with their brother Michael. "It was here," to quote Nicholas's own words, "that he bade farewell to him for whom he ever cherished a sentiment of the deepest and most affectionate gratitude, and also to the Empress Elizabeth."*

Alexander ordered a service for the dead to be celebrated at the monastery of St. Alexander very early on the 13th, with directions that it should not be mentioned in the public papers, and he attended it at four A.M., when it was still dark, entirely alone. He visited the cell of a celebrated hermit monk, who had lately arrived there; and then rejoining his carriage, drove on to Czarco-Selo, where he was met by his suite, and wished his mother and sisters good-bye. His coachman afterwards said he stopped his carriage on a rising ground outside St. Petersburg, and took a long look in the direction of the citadel, and these circumstances, added to his parting from his family being unusually affectionate and gloomy, made many think he had a presentiment of his approaching end. He

* Accession of Nicholas I.

went on straight to Taganrog, where he arrived at ten P.M. on September 25th, having travelled 150 versts every day. He inspected several public establishments on his road, among others a lunatic asylum; for he always took particular interest in this form of human suffering, and paid annually 100,000 roubles towards the support of the "hospital for afflicted souls," as it is called, in St. Petersburg. He spoke to several of the patients, among others to a soldier, whose face he remembered as formerly in the ranks of his regiment. He asked the man if he recollected him, when the lunatic answered in a stentorian voice, "Is it likely that I should forget the Prince who had his own father murdered?" The Emperor turned deadly pale, but calmly walked on, and addressed a few words to each of the other patients. At Taganrog, the day after he arrived, he went over the Lazaretto and Government establishments, and selected the Empress's abode. On the 29th the Hetman of the Cossacks arrived, and dined with him; and the Empress, who had left St. Petersburg the day after her husband, but travelled slowly, appeared October 6th, the Emperor having met her at the last stage. Her health and spirits quickly improved in a genial climate, and she admired the town and the distant view of the Caucasus. She wrote to her own family that she had never in her life been so happy; but she was destined to enjoy her husband's companionship for only three weeks, exclusive of the days she passed by the side of his death-bed. In those three weeks he sent his ultimatum to Turkey, and gave orders for the provisioning of 100,000 men assembling on the shores of the Pruth. He found time to superintend the formation of a public garden, and walked out all weathers, though from the rain and the light soil he was often up to his ankles in mud, and proposed a plan for deepening the harbour by means of steam-power. Being unaccustomed to the neighbourhood of a Court, the inhabitants of Taganrog amused themselves with minute inquiries as to the habits of the Imperial pair. The Emperor rose very early, breakfasted on tea and a small piece of dry bread, dined at two, and drove out with the Empress in the afternoon. A Frenchman returning from the Caucasus frequently "met him in the streets, where he walked about in the exclusive company of the Empress. His face showed care and sorrow, but the remembrance of these walks, and the acts of benevolence resulting from them, is the most touching," he writes, " of my recollections in Russia. One morning the Emperor went to see an old bed-ridden widow, and after addressing to her some words of hope and comfort, took his leave and left on the table 500 roubles."* On October 23rd he drove to the capital of the Don Cossacks, and mounted on a splendid horse, attired in their picturesque uniform, made his entry into the town. He attended a ball, and danced a polonaise with the wives of the principal Cossacks. After visiting all the public establishments, and receiving the clergy and officials for miles round, he kept his mother's birthday by a service in the Cathedral, and returned through Azov to Taganrog on the 27th.

He had intended to visit Astrakhan, but was requested by Count Voronzov, who met him at Taganrog, to come first to the Crimea to attract the loyalty of his Mahometan subjects, in case of a war with Turkey.† He set off, November 1st, by Mariopol, Perekop, Sympheropol, Batchi-Serai, and Eupatoria, and arranged to traverse 900 miles in seventeen days. A thousand soldiers had been employed the last year in making a high road through the Crimea, and though they had suffered little from fever, it had since prevailed. Many thought it was the same which thirty-four years before decimated Potemkin's victorious armies, and that it had been revived by turning up the ground where their corpses were hurriedly laid. The Emperor seemed impatient to accomplish his journey. On the 5th he arrived at Sympheropol, and the next morning attended a service in the Cathedral, then rode on horseback thirty-five miles over a mountainous country to Yoursouf, where he arrived at four P.M. He was received by Count Voronzov, the Governor of South Russia, his aides-de-camp and others standing in a line while he dismounted. One of them (an English doctor) describes him as apparently in the prime and vigour of life. The Tartars crowded to see him on his road

---

* M. Fayot, Professor at Alexander Lyceum.

† Constantine, writing to La Harpe in 1828, says, " I own that, while pitying the Greeks, I do not think their cause just, and I cannot approve of the emancipation of a people for revolt against one's neighbour. Justice will always remain justice. It is immovable. The Greeks are a people conquered by the right of arms, and recognised as belonging to the Turks by treaties." His objection to the war is believed to have influenced Nicholas in delaying it after Alexander's death.

from Yoursouf to Aloupka, the following day; and he distributed money liberally to the poor. He visited some vineyards belonging to the Crown, and walked a great deal, going on foot to see the colony of the Princess Galitzin, though he was told fever prevailed in it; and also to look at Orianda, which he had just bought. There a Tartar woman appealed to him for redress, having been flogged and ill treated, contrary to his own law. The offending superintendent of police threw himself on his knees before the Emperor to implore pardon, but Alexander ordered him to be arrested, and severely told him it was an eternal disgrace to ill use a female, especially in her circumstances. The same evening he dined with Voronzov, Diebitch, his own doctor, Dr. Lee, and one or two officers. He made a frugal repast, and drank very little wine. He talked chiefly to Voronzov, who sat next to him, inquiring about the prosperity of the merchants at Theodosia, and other local topics. The conversation fell on natural history, and Dr. Wylie reminded the Emperor of a scorpion found in his bed at Verona. He seemed pleased with Orianda, and to the surprise of his auditors said, " When I send in my resignation I mean to establish myself there." He walked out after dinner, and a Mahometan effendi presented a petition to him. He retired early to rest in the Tartar cottage prepared for his reception; his aides-de-camp being lodged in cottages near. A courier arrived at midnight, and the Emperor rose to open his despatches, which were very important, as they gave all the particulars of the intended insurrection,* and the names of the leaders. He sent for Diebitch, who found him walking rapidly backwards and forwards in his room, evidently much disturbed. The general spent two hours with him, acting as his secretary, while he wrote himself to Constantine at Warsaw, and to Nicholas at St. Petersburg, and sent off these letters and other despatches by couriers in the course of the night. He came down early the next morning, apparently calm and in good humour, and talked for some little time in the garden with Voronzov's physician on the Empress's health. He walked about almost all the morning, and at noon set off in pouring rain, on horse-

* " It is indeed stated," says Wellington, " that the impression this made upon his mind was the cause of his death, ... and his nerves were so much affected that his medical attendants could not prevail upon him to take medicine, or to feel confident in any chance of recovery."

back, to Baidar, by a difficult pass over the mountains, between 3000 and 4000 feet high; after a hard ride of forty versts, he arrived greatly tired, and in a profuse perspiration, at his destination, and rather irritated at being provided with a very fidgety horse. Without tasting food he entered his carriage at Baidar, and proceeded to Balaklava; but mounted his horse again to review a regiment, and then rode, entirely alone, to the Monastery of St. George, across a ridge for several miles much exposed to the east wind. He stayed there two hours, it was believed to consult the Archimandrite on the propriety of allowing the Lutherans, who had petitioned for a chapel at Sympheropol, to restore a ruined Greek church for that purpose. He also granted a piece of land to the Roman Catholic inhabitants for a place of worship.

From the monastery, situated on a cliff overhanging the sea, the Emperor followed his suite to Sevastopol, arriving there at 8.30 P.M.; and went straight to a church for a short service; also reviewing the Marines by torchlight. Dinner was prepared at his quarters, but he ate nothing, and transacted business with Diebitch. The next morning (November 9th) he saw a ship launched from the same docks blown up by the English on quitting the Crimea in 1856, and visited the military hospital, about three versts from the town. On his return he held a levée, and then went in a boat to see a ship of war, and crossed the harbour to go through the Marine hospital and the barracks. He gave a State dinner in the evening to his generals, and afterwards worked later than usual with Diebitch; but he could not sleep all night, owing to the painful impression made on him by the wretched appearance of an officer under arrest, who threw himself at his feet in the barracks to ask for pardon. The following day he crossed the harbour again to examine the great fort of Constantine, where he watched some practice with red-hot shot, and the citadel; and afterwards set off in an open carriage to Batchi-Serai. On the way, contrary to his usual custom, he was observed to be asleep, though very uneasily, and was troubled with an obstinate cough. He spent the evening alone, and the next day rode to the Jewish fortress of Tchoufut Kalé, and visited several of the synagogues; and afterwards a Greek monastery, but the ascent to it was steep, and as he walked up to it he became so faint he was obliged to rest on the road. He returned to Batchi-Serai, where some of the Mahometan chiefs, including two muftis, dined with him; and in the evening he went incognito in the Tartar dress to a service in one of their mosques. He heard of the death of his wife's brother-in-law, the King of Bavaria, and sending for Wylie consulted him about the Empress, and regretted she should have received the sad news in his absence. He asked an official if he was acquainted with Colonel Pestal. "Sire," said the officer, "he is my near relation." The Emperor answered, he believed him to conceal treacherous designs under the garb of loyalty, and that he had kept his eye on him for a long time. From Batchi-Serai he went to Eupatoria, and visited the Quarantine and other public establishments. He talked for some time to the captain of a Turkish vessel who had not yet performed quarantine, though Wylie told him he was very imprudent. That night was passed near Perekop, where he visited the hospitals, and the following evening between the Isthmus and Orekof. Here his valet, who had been with him twenty-seven years, told Wylie he was sure the Emperor was ill, and asked if he had remarked his extreme pallor. Wylie had not observed it, but the next day he was driving with Diebitch to Mariopol, when he was attacked with violent shiverings and every symptom of ague, though as the place where they rested for the night offered miserable accommodation, the doctor treated him with merely a glass of hot punch, and advised they should push on as fast as possible to Taganrog. He was so chilly in his carriage that he mounted a horse and rode till he could no longer hold himself in the saddle. He had eaten scarcely anything for three days and nights, and slept very little, when on the evening of the 17th he reached his destination. In answer to Volkonski's inquiries, Alexander said he had felt a touch of the Crimean fever hanging about him ever since he left Batchi-Serai; and became worse while visiting the hospital at Perekop, but he thought it might mend his constitution. Volkonski answered, he ought to take more care than he did of his precious health, and not treat it with the same carelessness he had done at twenty years of age.

The next day (November 18th) the Emperor seemed worse, and wrote to his mother, telling her he had a feverish attack, which he thought would pass off. To his doctor he almost regretted the strength of his constitution, saying rather irritably, that however ill he was he always recovered, and supposed it would be ever the same. He took the medicines Wylie prescribed, and they relieved the paroxysms of fever and the pains he felt in his head and limbs; but he obstinately refused to take any more, and his attendants were convinced that he really did not wish to live. "Sleep, quiet, and cold water would do more for me than any medicine," he said; but after the mode of treating fevers then in vogue, Wylie objected to give him cold water, and he refused to drink anything else. It was afterwards found he had a much inflamed sore throat, which made swallowing difficult, but he did not mention this symptom. He transacted business the day after his arrival at Taganrog, and rose as usual, spending a few hours in the evening with the Empress, who on the 21st wrote to her sister-in-law, the wife of Michael, requesting her to inform the Empress-mother that Alexander was better, for she should not write herself lest she should think his disorder more serious than it was. More despatches arrived on the 19th, and the Emperor after reading them sent orders for the arrest of Pestal and the other leaders of the conspiracy at Moscow. It appeared they had resolved to begin a political movement on the following March 24th, when every member of the Imperial family was accustomed to attend a service in the chapel of the fortress of St. Petersburg for the repose of Paul's soul. They would surround the fortress and shut up the whole family in its prisons, then raise the population and deal with their Princes as circumstances pointed out. The ingratitude of Glinka and others like him, who had received their education and especial favour at the Emperor's hands, seemed to affect him painfully. "But what else could I expect? it is a just retribution," he exclaimed to himself.* "Almighty God, may thy

* He had long been in the habit of thinking aloud, from not hearing his own voice. This funeral service is described by Holman. At the door of the church the priests met the Imperial family, and formed a procession to Paul's tomb, followed by the Emperor between the two Empresses, the Grand Dukes and their wives in the rear. The Empress-Dowager every year threw herself on the ground before her husband's coffin, making every demonstration of the deepest affliction while the prayers were being chanted; and when she rose, each member of the

judgments fall on me alone, and not on my people." He had a restless night, and was very much worse the following day. His head was burning, and there was a marked change in his countenance. Wylie called in the Empress's physician, Dr. Stoffrogen, and both advised he should be bled; but he would not hear of it, saying bleeding always shook his nerves, and they were already in a most disordered state. "I have little faith in medical treatment," he said; "my malady is beyond your skill." He submitted to a large blister on his head and mustard plasters on his back, and on the 20th made an effort to write to Constantine. The next day he told Volkonski to write to his brother and to the Empress-Dowager, and inform them his illness was dangerous, though the doctors thought him slightly better. They complained he did everything to aggravate the disorder, rejecting even common comforts, getting up regularly in the morning till the 21st, receiving General de Witte who brought most disquieting news, and dictating despatches; and though from the 22nd he hardly spoke a word when he was sensible, he talked incessantly whenever he was delirious, which became frequent. Throughout his illness his pulse was seldom as low as 90, and often 125, but was always extremely small and feeble; and some were of opinion that under these circumstances his strength should have been sustained, and not treated with lowering remedies.

On the 22nd he had a long fainting fit, but on the next day seemed better, though when he tried to stand he fainted again. On the 24th he again revived, and the doctors pressed leeches upon him, but he would not hear of them; however, as he afterwards apologized for his impatience, and thanked his doctors for their attention: the advice was renewed the next day, and again rejected, though he allowed his doctors to use blisters, issues, and other external applications. He seemed when conscious to be pre-occupied with uneasy thoughts, and it was not without cause. A war with Turkey[*] was impending, probably also with Austria, and perhaps with

family in turn came forward and prostrated himself in prayer for a few moments before the coffin, all dressed in deep mourning.

[*] Count Bernstorff told Wellington Alexander would certainly have declared war in the spring.

the rest of Europe. His army, through which he had hoped gradually to educate and civilize the lower classes, was misguided by treacherous officers, and the intended tool for overturning the State. Other remembrances still more personally painful crowded upon him, to judge from his utterances when he was delirious, and the words Pahlen, Zoubof, and the Emperor mingled with Austerlitz, Moscow, Friedland; and words of command were constantly on his lips. "It was a horrible act," he said, fixing his eyes on Wylie; "he was not even permitted the prayer that the dying owes his Maker." And again, alluding to the conspiracy, he said he had ever laboured with no other object than to secure his people's glory and happiness. On the 26th erysipelas appeared on his leg, which seemed to relieve his head. He observed, without the slightest tone of regret, that he should die like his sister Catherine (of apoplexy brought on by the complaint being checked), and even sat up and shaved himself and wrote a short letter, but at twelve became worse, and Wylie told the Empress he was in great danger. Volkonski suggested a confessor ought to be summoned; on which the Empress asked Wylie to tell the Emperor of his condition, and inquire if he did not wish for the consolations of religion. Wylie did so. "Then you really think I am dying?" said the Emperor. The doctor replied, he refused to follow his prescriptions, and he must tell him now he had not a moment to lose. Alexander pressed his hand, and said it was the best news he had heard for many years; but he was in such a high fever that Wylie was afraid of exciting him too much, and advised the priest should be postponed to the next day. Later in the evening he had a long fainting fit, and was so ill in the night that the Empress was called up at four P.M., and a confessor, the Archimandrite Fedotof, was summoned to his bedside. The Emperor raised himself with difficulty, and asked to be left alone with the priest, whom he desired to sit down by him, and to treat him in all respects as the most ordinary individual. The interview was short, but the confessor said he had never seen more Christian humility, or a dying man more thoroughly prepared. The Empress was called to join in the Holy Communion, and then, instructed by the physician, the priest told the Emperor this service would be useless to him, for his death must be regarded by the Almighty as suicide if he persisted in refusing to try and avert it. He seemed struck by this,. and calling Wylie, told him to do what he pleased. He would object to nothing. To the Empress he said he had never felt greater happiness, and thanked her warmly for her care. The physician at once put thirty leeches* on his temples. They took two hours to bite, and he seemed much exhausted when they were taken off. He requested the Empress to go and take some rest, and then said to Wylie, "if I could but sleep; I feel as if sleep would do me good. Ah, my friend, I think you are deceived as to the nature of my illness; it is my nerves that need a cure." He seemed extremely agitated, and sensitive to sound, and very shortly became violently delirious, and did not even recognize his doctors when they approached his bed. Early in the morning he was seized with nervous convulsions, and continued alternately convulsed and unconscious throughout the day. During the night he was again delirious, trying to sit up, and as often fainting away, till his attendants thought every moment would be his last; but at six A.M. strong mustard plasters were applied, which restored his faculties. He thanked those about him for their services, and desired Volkonski not to quit the Empress after his death till he had brought her safely back to St. Petersburg, and he also spoke to her in a stronger voice. She wrote to his mother that "there was a very decided amendment in the state of the Emperor, who is an angel of goodness in the midst of his sufferings. He is however weak in the extreme. Dear mother, pray with us and 50,000,000 of men, that God may be pleased to grant his recovery." All hope however vanished when he was unable to swallow, and in the course of the day he was again seized with convulsions. On the morning of the 30th, he said, "Ah, le beau jour," as the sun began to stream in through the window, the curtains having been pushed aside. They were the last words he uttered, but shortly afterwards he seemed distressed with violent pain, and was again convulsed throughout the

* No English doctor would now prescribe bleeding for intermittent fever.

day. Towards evening he fell into a state of lethargy, though strong external applications restored him to apparent consciousness, and a blister relieved his breathing, which was much oppressed. On the morning of December 1st he opened his eyes and pressed the hand of his wife, who had hardly quitted the room for five minutes during the last thirty hours: he made a great effort, though ineffectually, to speak, and at 10.40 expired on a sofa in the presence of the Empress, Wylie, Volkonski, and Diebitch.

A post-mortem examination showed the appearances in the liver and spleen—the one congested, the other softened—common to those who have died of the intermittent bilious or gastric fever of the Crimea. Several ounces of water were found in the ventricles of the brain, where the veins and arteries were gorged with blood. There was an old adhesion arising from inflammation of the brain at some remote period, between the membranes called dura mater and pia mater; and both adhered to the skull at the back of the head, where Alexander had always felt pain when he had a headache. The heart and lungs were sound, but too vascular. The body was embalmed; but the face became so quickly discoloured that it was obliged to be covered when it lay in State. The Empress seemed inconsolable. She wrote to her mother-in-law, "Our angel has gone to Heaven, and I linger still on earth. Who would have thought that I, in my weak state of health, could ever have survived him? Do not abandon me, dear mother, for I am absolutely alone in this world of grief. Our dear deceased has resumed his look of benevolence; his smile proves to me he is happy, and that he gazes on brighter objects than exist here. My only consolation under this irreparable loss is that I shall not survive him. I hope soon to be reunited to him."

No one ever recollected such a profound and universal feeling of gloom as pervaded St. Petersburg when a courier brought the news that the Emperor was no more. It arrived while the Imperial family were attending a thanksgiving service for the favourable account previously received. It was changed into a requiem for the repose of his soul; and even one of the conspirators records the tears that rolled down the cheeks of the officers who proclaimed the accession of a new monarch. For three days the shops were all voluntarily closed ; and during that time not a single person was arrested for drunkenness or any other offence—an unprecedented circumstance in the annals of the city. Innumerable crowds filled the churches ; and not a face showed any expression but anxiety and mourning. The silence was also remarkable that prevailed in the streets. The newspapers, pulpits, and learned professors poured forth eulogiums to the memory of their beloved monarch. Many were so much affected by the intelligence as to be attacked by real illness : one merchant in Moscow, of eccentric and retired habits, who had been visited more than once by the Sovereign to thank him in person for his numerous charities, an hour after he received the news fell down dead.

The uncertainty as to the succession of Nicholas belongs to his history rather than to Alexander's. Aratchaief was not then in St. Petersburg. He had placed a female serf over his establishment, and she more than equalled her master in severity. One morning she was assassinated, and no one would bring forward the murderer. Aratchaief seems on this occasion to have been almost insane. For five days and nights he neither ate, slept, nor shaved, but sat staring with a blood-stained handkerchief, which had been tied over his housekeeper's face, bound round his head, and for several weeks seemed to forget everything else. This happened just after Alexander went to Taganrog, whence the Emperor wrote to Photi, telling him he had heard Aratchaief was a prey to despair, and that the Archimandrite alone could prevent the fatal consequences to be apprehended from it : " you whose words, full of holy unction, and whose unblemished life have recalled so many stray sheep to the fold." He ended by requesting Photi to summon Aratchaief to his side, to speak to him in the name of religion, and to strengthen his faith. " Exhort him to take care of himself for the sake of his country," &c. Photi accordingly brought Aratchaief away from his solitude to the monastery, where he stayed several weeks. But his desire for vengeance did not yield to religion ; and immediately he heard of Alexander's death, instead of coming forward to support the claims of Nicholas, he rushed off to his estate, anxious to satisfy his revenge during the interregnum, lest a general amnesty should be proclaimed and his victims escape. In Germany he had seen a criminal broken on the wheel, where it was still used; and he is said to have even employed this illegal punishment. A hasty trial was gone through, in which twenty-one serfs were convicted as accessories to the murder, and condemned to be flogged; among them, contrary to law, a woman who had an infant at the breast. In the mean time Nicholas ascended the throne; and though the trial was kept secret for several months, it was brought to his knowledge through the relatives of this woman; and, to the joy of all Russia, Aratchaief was deprived of his offices. From that time he lived quietly on his estates, where he died in 1834, and in his last years became a mild and benevolent landlord; seeking, he said, to prepare himself by religious exercises to join "the beloved object of his loyal devotion;" and in his dying moments he begged to be turned so that he might face a portrait of Alexander, which hung near his bed. He caused a clock to be constructed at great cost in Paris, which was the principal ornament in his room. It was surmounted by Alexander's bust, and struck only once a day—at the hour in which the Emperor died, when it played the beautiful air, "Peace amid the blessed." Paul's bust was also a prominent object in his apartment. Seldom indeed has any sovereign possessed a more devoted or unpopular servant. He bequeathed his entire fortune to various public institutions, with the exception of a sum of money left to accumulate in the charge of the Academy of St. Petersburg, to found a prize for the most complete biography of Alexander I.

Paul's other favourite, Rostopchine, displayed a very different feeling on the death of Paul's successor, whom he survived just two months. The Count was at Moscow, suffering from water on the chest, and too ill to leave his house to take the oath of allegiance to Nicholas. "By a singular coincidence," wrote the implacable old man, "Alexander has died at Taganrog—a town used in the last century as a place of exile for criminals; and it is certain that his corpse must have been embalmed by Wylie, his surgeon, the same who was one of Paul's assassins, and who cut his carotid artery after he was strangled."

Count Pahlen, the prime mover in that event, also died less than three months after Alexander. Panine and Benningsen followed the same year, and Zaieonzek, the Viceroy of Poland, died in June, 1826, when Constantine demanded the vacant office for himself, with the promise that he would resign it when he reached the age of fifty-seven. Romanzov and Karamzin, the literary ornaments of Alexander's Court, died in January and June, 1826, Alexander Narishkine in February, Count Gregory Orlof in June, Miloradovitz was shot in the insurrection of December 1825, and the Roman Catholic Primate closed the mortuary column for the same twelvemonth, which included a most unusual number of celebrated men.

Constantine concealed the fact of Alexander's dangerous illness in Warsaw even from Michael, who was staying with him, though it was observed that for several days he looked anxious and depressed, and the news of his death came like a thunderclap upon the whole city, who had seen him only the previous June in good health.

In Prussia, the King's natural sorrow at the death of a friend seven years his junior was mitigated by the elevation of his daughter to the throne. But a religious ceremony was performed in his presence, and a funeral panegyric pronounced. A few days later a second was put forth from the pulpits in Berlin: "What a brilliant example, but now hidden from the world, have we before us—a great and powerful Emperor, a well-tried and humble Christian, the faithful ally and beloved friend of our King, the friend of our nation, the benefactor of our country and of all Europe, known to each of us, revered, beloved, and now mourned by the whole world!" The Emperor Francis declared that he had lost his best friend. But the warmest eulogiums of the deceased prince were echoed by high and low amongst all shades of political opinion in France. The speech of Charles X. at the opening of the Legislative Chamber, January 31st, began with an allusion to the event: "Death has just struck down, in the middle of his career, one of our most magnanimous allies; this loss has profoundly afflicted my heart." The Duc de Montmorenci followed it up with a description of the benefits he had bestowed on France: "All the interests of humanity were dear and sacred to the generous heart of Alexander. He has given an example to monarchs in peace, to the world in generosity, in disinterestedness, in services to France. Poetry, eloquence, and history will render grateful and immortal praises to his memory." The old soldier of Napoleon, Marmont, writes, "The death of Alexander is a great event when we think of the manner in which Europe was accustomed to be guided by him. He made use of the magic of a moral power founded on his numerous armies, always ready to enter upon a campaign organized and furnished with everything as if they were to fight the next day; of the prestige which necessarily accompanies States so extensive and composed of the seventh part of the surface of the continents of the globe. To threaten often, to strike rarely, but with a sure blow, in a manner which made an impression and left remembrances—this is the policy Alexander has followed during the last years of his reign. In the ten years he has lived since the second Restoration, he has governed the world and settled the destinies of every people in Europe without engaging a single man, and by the sole power of his name." "The great reverses and great successes," writes Lamartine, " of his short existence had made him the hero of the North and the arbiter of Europe. He gave the example of brilliant virtues. Liberty owed to him a great remembrance in Europe. History will inscribe him among the few princes who reigned in presence of God and of their conscience, and who piously subordinated their own glory and their personal grandeur to the glory and to the greatness of humanity. The character of the reign of Alexander lies in its not being so much a Russian reign as a European reign. France and Europe, for a moment ungrateful, only rendered a tardy justice to his virtues."

"We must render homage," wrote the French press, " to the character of the Emperor Alexander. No one could make a more moderate use of a power which might have done anything." The French country pastors sounded his praises in their churches; the peasants in Champagne, who had seen him at the head of his armies, and profited by his bounty, offered up their humble prayers for the repose of his soul—a circumstance perhaps without a parallel when it came from the conquered for their conqueror. In England, where he was less known, one or two of the higher class of periodicals gave him his due; but he was loaded with abuse by the principal organs of the Liberal press. One eminent leader* of that party has, however, written that " for public and private virtues he must ever rank among the best of princes. Endowed with many accomplishments which would have distinguished an individual in common life, he was indefatigable in his attention to business. He was intrusted with power more vast in its extent and more uncontrolled than has fallen to the lot of any other man in modern times; and yet there never was any monarch by whom power was less abused." " He was wise, noble, and in all respects highly gifted," writes Count Munster. In Finland Professor Morgenstein delivered a discourse in his praise to the students at Abo; and this example was followed by Professor Wallensius, who spoke in Swedish at Dorpat. Funeral services were celebrated in his memory throughout all parts of his empire, not only among the established Christian sects, but by the Raskolniks, Fire-worshippers, Lamas, Mahometans, and Jews. At Astrakhan 4000 Tartars assembled in a wide plain and united their lamentations for his decease with a prayer for blessings on his successor.

In the mean while Alexander's coffin was on its road from Taganrog to its last resting-place in the citadel of St. Petersburg, a distance of more than 1000 miles. It lay in state in the Cathedral before its departure, delayed by a violent hurricane sweeping the steppes till January 9th; and the day it set forth several frozen corpses, found in the neighbourhood, were brought into Taganrog; the funeral procession being more than once stopped during the journey by furious gales and the extreme cold. The hearse was preceded by a detachment of Cossacks of the Don, each bearing a torch, who escorted it over boundless plains of snow, over rivers, through swamps, and the densest forests. The Emperor's coachman earnestly entreated to be allowed to drive it, but was refused on the

* Russell's Modern History of Europe.

score that he was not of sufficient rank. He pleaded that when the Imperial vehicle was once upset, his Majesty had said to him, that if he did not become more careful he would some day have to bring a shattered corpse back to St. Petersburg; but this reasoning was not admitted till he reached the capital, when Nicholas allowed him to take the reins once more. No orders were given, and the nobles and corporate bodies of every province received the august dead in the mode they thought most fit; and more honours were heaped upon his inanimate form than he would ever willingly receive in life. The order of march was invariably the same. At night, surrounded by wax lights, the coffin rested in a simple village church or a gorgeous cathedral, to which numbers resorted to pray for the dead man, while guards of honour relieved each other at intervals. In many places crowds collected, and took the horses out of the carriage to drag it along; at others the bishops and clergy met it at the entrance to their dioceses. In Tula the nobility caused services for his soul to be celebrated for six weeks, and during all that time distributed food to the poor. The corporation of citizens annulled debts to the extent of 30,000 francs, and at Kursk they defrayed the cost of a dinner to 1000 peasants. On February 2nd the corpse reached Moscow, and nearly the whole population, in spite of the cold, met it three miles outside the city, where it was transferred to a magnificent funeral car, surmounted with the crowns of Russia, Poland, Siberia, Georgia, Kazan, Astrakhan, and the Crimea, brought from the Treasury, and carried with it the rest of the way. In Moscow it was lodged in the Old Cathedral, and solemnly blessed by the Metropolitan; and the same at Novgorod. At Tver the nobility and citizens distributed alms to the poor. Two stages before it arrived at Czarco-Selo the procession was stopped by the Empress-mother and Nicholas. The coffin was opened in their presence, though the features were no longer to be recognized, and after resting in the chapel of the palace it arrived in St. Petersburg, March 18th. Every bell in the city was ringing, and guns were fired from the fortress as the hearse, drawn by eight black horses, and followed by two chargers which had carried the Emperor in France, slowly made its way to the Church of Our Lady of Kazan, and there a guard of honour kept watch day and night, and 1700 wax tapers flamed round the bier; while during a week, and twice every day, the clergy chanted the prayers for his soul.

Several foreign princes had arrived some weeks earlier in St. Petersburg, to be present at the funeral ceremony; Prince William (now Emperor) of Prussia, the Empress's uncle the Prince of Baden, the Archduke Ferdinand, the Princes of Mecklenburg-Schwerin, Saxe-Weimar, Orange, and Würtemberg, and the old soldiers Jomini, Wellington, and Marmont. The last solemnities took place on Saturday, March 25th, when the coffin was transferred by twenty-four general officers from the Kazan Cathedral to the Church of St. Peter and St. Paul, the 24th being purposely avoided as the day of Alexander's accession; and in spite of a heavy snow-storm and bitter wind, an immense concourse of people assembled in the streets, and exhibited much emotion, though four months had elapsed since the national loss. The Archimandrite Fedotof accompanied the coffin from Taganrog, and all the clergy in St. Petersburg preceded it to the fortress, stopping before the Roman Catholic church and every place of worship of all denominations to read a few prayers. Sixty pages carrying torches walked on each side. The Empress-mother and her daughter-in-law, with the young heir to the empire, followed the procession in a carriage, but the Princes went on foot at the head of an immense assembly of civil and military officers. Among the spectators were the ex-Queens of Georgia and Mingrelia. A tremendous discharge of artillery announced when the dead was deposited in its final abode, an act accompanied in the Russian service by the words, " For dust thou art and unto dust shalt thou return;" and at three o'clock the black flag was taken down which had floated nearly four months over the Winter Palace. Constantine could not be persuaded to come from Warsaw. He declared that neither his health nor his spirits would permit him to attend the ceremony. Alexander's coffin, inscribed with merely his name, was laid next to his father's in the Imperial vault; and by the end of three months that of the Empress Elizabeth was placed by its side, for she died at Belef, May 16th, on her way from Taganrog.

The forlorn widow, left alone to brood over her husband's last illness, never regained the strength she had lost during her close attendance by his dying bed. She grew rapidly worse, and her physicians, hoping a change of scene might revive her spirits, did not oppose her departure on May 8th, though she seemed scarcely fit to bear the journey. Oranienbaum was to be her future residence, and she intended to remain on Prince Volkonski's* estate at Kaluga till after the coronation in June. She asked the Empress-Dowager to meet her at Kaluga; " My only desire," she said, " is to see once more the mother of the angel who has preceded me." Some alarming symptoms appeared, Prince Volkonski wrote that she would be unable to proceed further than Belef, a small town in Toula, and thither the Empress-Dowager hastened; but although she reached Belef at six A.M. of May 16th, she found her daughter-in-law had quietly expired in her sleep two hours before, as the post-mortem examination showed, of a long-existing disease of the heart. " This mournful event," said the Imperial ukaz which announced it, " has taken place after a long sickness both of mind and body." Her corpse was conveyed to St. Petersburg, and entombed with great ceremony July 3rd.

Alexander's life was too active to enable him to add to the list of royal authors, even if he had been so inclined, but he bequeathed a commentary on the transactions of 1814 and 1815 to his successor, which, Nicholas told an English nobleman in 1836, contained his brother's opinions and instructions, and that he always religiously adhered to them. The papers found in his room at Taganrog after his death comprised a list of the names of the principal conspirators, which had been long in his possession, and other notes on their designs. His valet said he observed the Emperor always take a paper out of his pocket and transfer it to another when he changed his coat, and a search was made for it, believing it might be important, but it only contained references to the Holy Scriptures and prayers for special occasions. The Empress desired they should be buried with him. His official documents, State records, and private

* Volkonski died in 1852; Wylie in 1853.

accounts, most systematically arranged, were easily found in the palaces at St. Petersburg and Czarco-Selo, and Nicholas confirmed his ministers in their posts, with the exception of Aratchaief. The empire had increased more in extent, population, commerce, and prosperity in his reign of twenty-four years, than even in the much longer and much vaunted periods of Catherine II. and Peter the Great. It had changed in the same time from a thoroughly Asiatic to a civilized European Power. But the insurrection of December, 1825, when the insurgents resolved to plunder St. Petersburg, gave such alarm to the wealthy classes in Russia as in their eyes to cast a shade on the Government which had nurtured it, and converted even the Russian liberal party into decided reactionists. The prisons, they said, had been made too comfortable—people liked to be shut up in them; the criminal code was so mild it no longer presented any terrors to crime; whilst directing the thoughts of his people towards a constitutional monarchy, Alexander had turned them into republicans and revolutionists; even the censorship was so lenient that, under the guise of fables, traitors were permitted to slander the Sovereign himself. They said the privileges he had bestowed on the lower orders had made the serfs discontented; education enabled the soldiers to read the corrupt and revolutionary literature the conspirators had put into their hands; the translation of the Bible had induced many to desert the National Church; in fact, as an English traveller[*] observes, "the poor were impervious to the blessings Alexander would have conferred upon them, and the higher orders were too seriously interested in the continuation of existing abuse not to meet all his reforms with virulent hostility; but that he should have become himself the object of rancour and personal animosity is a stain which can never be effaced from the Russian name." The conspirators, however, formed but a small portion of the 55,000,000 who peopled Russia, though they comprised no inconsiderable number of youths of rank and talent; and it is not surprising that, pushed by these two extremes, the one for reaction, the other for the subversion of the throne, and his empire further threatened by the Polish revolt in 1830, that Nicholas should

[*] Raikes's Visit to Russia in 1827.

have rejected the path of reform which had proved so thorny to his predecessor, and preferred to retain the more easily sustained part of a despot in principle and deed.*

* Alexander is stated to have travelled more than any prince or general of ancient or modern times. His ministers, who were all older than himself, and to whom Nicholas succeeded, were, Nesselrode for Foreign Affairs, Lanskoi of the Interior, Cancrine of the Finances (he succeeded Gourief in 1823), Labanof Rostouski of Justice, Shishkov Education and Religion, Admiral Mollar of the Navy, and General Tatischef of War. Of the insurrection which inaugurated the new reign, Marmont speaks with much indignation, though himself educated in the midst of revolution. "Planned first against a Sovereign who has worthily borne the crown and raised so high the Russian name; against Alexander, the most philanthropical, the gentlest, the most benevolent of monarchs. And who are the chiefs of this horrible enterprise, of which the first consequence, in case of success, was the death of all the members of the Imperial family? They were men loaded beyond measure with benefits by the members of this august family. . . . I was at St. Petersburg during their trial. Never was inquiry made with more care, and never step was more regular; never were condemnations more just and better merited. The Emperor has commuted many penalties. . . . If Nicholas had, by an exaggeration of gentleness, pardoned all the culprits, it would have been thought a clemency influenced by fear. A reparation was necessary towards society, a public satisfaction was required," &c.—Marmont's Journey, 1826.

Five years after Alexander's death, not a nobleman in St. Petersburg would keep the anniversary otherwise than as a day of mourning.

THE END.

LONDON:
SAVILL, EDWARDS AND CO., PRINTERS, CHANDOS STREET,
COVENT GARDEN.

www.ingramcontent.com/pod-product-compliance
Lightning Source LLC
Chambersburg PA
CBHW030404230426
43664CB00007BB/748